GROUNDING SOCIALITY

NEURONS, MIND, AND CULTURE

EDITED BY

Gün R. Semin & Gerald Echterhoff

Routledge
Taylor & Francis Group
LONDON AND NEW YORK

First published 2011 by Taylor and Francis Group, LLC

2 Park Square, Milton Park, Abingdon, Oxon OX14 4RN
711 Third Avenue, New York, NY 10017, USA

Routledge is an imprint of the Taylor & Francis Group, an informa business

First issued in paperback 2016

Library of Congress Cataloging-in-Publication Data

Grounding sociality : neurons, mind, and culture / editors, Gün R. Semin, Gerald Echterhoff.
p. cm.
Includes bibliographical references and index.
ISBN 978-1-84872-899-8 (hbk. : alk. paper)
1. Social interaction--Psychological aspects. 2. Cognition and culture.
3. Evolutionary psychology. 4. Cognitive neuroscience. I. Semin, G. R. II. Echterhoff, Gerald.

HM1111.G76 2011
302--dc22 2010034543

ISBN 978-1-84872-899-8 (hbk)
ISBN: 978-1-138-99207-8 (pbk)

Contents

Acknowledgments

This volume was made possible by an expert symposium held in late 2007 funded by the European Social Cognition Network (ESCON) under the Research Networking Program of the European Science Foundation (ESF) and facilitated by grants from the Royal Netherlands Academy of Arts and Sciences (KNAW–ISK/4583/PAH) to the first editor and the German Research Foundation (DFG, grant EC 317/2) to the second editor.

Contributors

Louise Barrett
Department of Psychology
University of Lethbridge
Lethbridge, Canada

Boyka Bratanova
School of Behavioural Science
University of Melbourne
Melbourne, Australia

Adam Brown
The New School for Social Research
New York City, New York

Linnda R. Caporael
Department of Science & Technology Studies
Rensselaer Polytechnic Institute
Troy, New York

Gerald Echterhoff
Department of Psychology
University of Münster
Münster, Germany

Simon Garrod
Department of Psychology
University of Glasgow
Glasgow, United Kingdom

Markus Graf
Max Planck Institute for Human Cognitive and Brain Sciences
Leipzig, Germany

E. Tory Higgins
Department of Psychology
Columbia University
New York City, New York

William Hirst
The New School for Social Research
New York, New York

Marco Iacoboni
David Geffen School of Medicine
University of California, Los Angeles
Los Angeles, California

Yoshihisa Kashima
School of Behavioural Science
University of Melbourne
Melbourne, Australia

Kerry L. Marsh
Department of Psychology
University of Connecticut
Storrs, Connecticut

Martin J. Pickering
Department of Psychology
University of Edinburgh
Edinburgh, United Kingdom

Wolfgang Prinz
Max Planck Institute for Human Cognitive and Brain Sciences
Leipzig, Germany

Simone Schütz-Bosbach
Max Planck Institute for Human Cognitive and Brain Sciences
Leipzig, Germany

Gün R. Semin
Social and Behavioral Sciences
Utrecht University
Utrecht, The Netherlands

1

Introduction: *From Neurons to Shared Cognition and Culture*

GÜN R. SEMIN AND GERALD ECHTERHOFF

Human life as we know it is inconceivable without the social interdependence that makes it possible, and this is true despite the vast differences between hunter-gatherers or the current techno-postindustrial society, namely, for both the past human existence forms and the present state of our species. From the early origins via the rise of civilizations to contemporary societies, humans have relied on social bonds and collectives from small groups to larger entities like communities, tribes, nations, and (sub)cultures. The pronounced and multifaceted sociality of humans presumably has substantially contributed to their evolution and their remarkable success as a species (e.g., Dunbar, 1993) and pervades virtually all types of human activities around the world. Even today's Western societies, despite many claims of their individualistic orientation, rely on socially coordinated action. People's fates have become more and more dependent upon the actions of others, many of whom are anonymous and live in different parts of the globe.

Indeed, there is increasingly "hard" scientific evidence for a fundamental connectedness of people through social networks that accounts to a surprisingly large extent for their behaviors in various domains of life, such as health, altruism, violence, economic decisions, or voter turnout (see Christakis & Fowler, 2009). Even the most basic psychological functions, like one's subjective experience of reality, hinge on regular social contact and exchange. This is exemplified by the case of Richard Byrd (1938), who spent 6 months by himself, with no human contact, at an Antarctic weather station and soon suffered from severe depression, hallucinations, and surreal fantasies.

Although the pervasive role and benefits of sociality in various types of human life and activity are clear and undisputed, it is an ongoing challenge for research to identify the factors and processes that permit such sociality. Interest in the investigation of the roots and underlying mechanisms of sociality has surged in recent years. Questions about the grounding of sociality are of profound importance to all disciplines addressing social phenomena. How are individuals at all able to coordinate their actions; how do they share their innermost states like their thoughts and feelings; and how do they establish joint representations and relationships? How is sociality grounded? If one conceives of individual organisms as entities operating as autonomous and self-organized neural and cognitive systems, the very possibility of interindividual exchange might indeed appear like a wondrous feat.

What we refer to as the grounding of sociality has become an increasingly investigated topic in disciplines as far afield as ethology (e.g., Tomasello, 2008), cognition (Barsalou, Niedenthal, Barbey, & Ruppert, 2003; Hutchins, 1995; Prinz, 2002; Sebanz, Bekkering, & Knoblich, 2006), memory (Hirst & Manier, 2002; Weldon, 2001), social psychology (e.g., Echterhoff, Higgins, & Levine, 2009; Smith & Semin, 2004; Tindale & Kameda, 2000), developmental psychology (Meltzoff & Decety, 2003; Tomasello, 2000), neuroscience (e.g., Adolphs, 2003; Brass & Heyes, 2005; Gallese, Keysers, & Rizzolatti, 2004; Iacoboni, 2008), psycholinguistics (Liberman & Whalen, 2000; Pickering & Garrod, 2004), philosophy (Gordon, 2005; Metzinger & Gallese, 2003), evolutionary ecology (Barrett & Henzi, 2005; Caporael, 1997; Preston & de Waal, 2002; Richerson & Boyd, 2005), artificial intelligence and robotics (Anderson, 2003; Breazeal, 2002; Echterhoff, Bohner, & Siebler, 2006), and sociology (Christakis & Fowler, 2009; Thompson & Fine, 1999). Recent research has taken great strides in investigating the neural, behavioral, linguistic, cognitive, motivational, social-psychological, and cultural bases of sociality (see Enfield & Levinson, 2006). What is clear is that cognition and social interaction are functionally intertwined at a very basic level. For instance, burgeoning research on the mirror neuron system has started to illuminate the neural bases of imitation and interindividual synchronization of basic brain activities (e.g., Gallese et al., 2004; Rizzolatti & Craighero, 2004), suggesting direct links between sensory and motor representations (Brass & Heyes, 2005). An immediate connection between social perception and action further drives imitation by human infants (Meltzoff & Decety, 2003), human speech (Liberman & Whalen, 2000), conversations (Semin, 2007), and automatic social behavior (Dijksterhuis & Bargh, 2001). Other, sociocognitive processes that allow interpersonal coordination include joint action (Sebanz et al., 2006), physically co-present encoding or retrieval of information (Cuc, Koppel, & Hirst, 2007; Lindner, Echterhoff, Davidson, & Brand, in press), and the formation of socially shared reality (Echterhoff et al., 2009; Hardin & Higgins, 1996).

Despite these advances, important issues remain unresolved: First, what are the links between the processes that permit the grounding of sociality at different levels? For instance, what are the constraints that basic biological or neural mechanisms impose upon higher-order processes? To what extent are long-term cultural patterns of sociality insensitive to perturbation by short-term influences from individual-level processes? Second, how can theory and terminology developed in different traditions be coordinated and interfaced? Tackling these issues has been the driving force for putting together the current volume: The first goal is to examine different levels at which sociality can be grounded, with special attention to the interrelations between these levels. The second goal is to bridge disciplinary boundaries and lay the foundations for an integrated conceptualization of the bases of sociality.

This volume is the outcome of an expert symposium held in late 2007 and was designed to get the contributing authors to this volume together, so that they could present, and discuss their work thereby informing each other to make a more integrated contribution with clear links to the other chapters in the volume. Thus, the contributors to this volume have placed their own pertinent research within an integrated perspective on the grounding of sociality. The final product is divided into four general parts.

The first part presents four contributions on the foundations of sociality and communication. The first, a contribution by Marco Iacoboni, suggests that human sociality is driven by a biomarker of sociality shaped by evolutionary processes that have contributed to the formation of our neurobiological systems and that make us predisposed to social behavior. He argues that a neural system that is recruited during goal-oriented actions is also recruited when one observes somebody else performing the same actions. These cells, called mirror neurons, are likely to provide an immediate, automatic access to the mental states associated with the actions of other people. In elaborating on this point Iacoboni reviews evidence that the human mirror system is correlated with empathy in healthy volunteers and reduced activity in this system correlates with the social impairment of patients with autism, thus underlining his argument that this system is a biomarker of sociality.

The third chapter of the first part is by Markus Graf, Simone Schütz-Bosbach, and Wolfgang Prinz. They argue that the visual perception of human actions and manipulable objects activates not only visual but also motor representations. These in turn are used for action control. The function of such activation is a predictive one, namely, to predict how the behavior of a conspecific will unfold, or to predict potential motor interactions with an object. According to a common notion, action simulation involves a similarity relationship between the perceived and the represented action, whereas the motor involvement in object perception appears to be based on a complementarity relationship between object and potential actions. These authors discuss evidence in support of the view that complementarity applies to the action domain, too. Perceiving actions of conspecifics activates motor representations, which code complementary actions. In their view, the domain of complementary actions opens a new field of research, which is of tremendous functional importance for social interaction and communication. The coding of complementary actions requires scholars to extend the mirror metaphor, which guide current theories of action understanding.

The basic principles underlying sociality are further examined in the fourth chapter in this book, contributed by Kerry Marsh. She draws attention to the emergent, context-dependent self-organization of many instances of sociality, specifically interindividual coordination of actions not requiring strategic planning or premeditation. The aim of the chapter is to identify the processes that permit highly complex coordinated actions, like the evacuation of an airplane, which involve the spontaneous formation of a plural social "subject" of actions. According to the author, a key process is a dynamically unfolding interplay between the environment and integrated perception–action systems at the level of the individual. When individual capabilities are not sufficient to respond to the demands of the environment, the presence of other humans, particularly their movements and action repertoire, can signal additional opportunities for action—distinctly social "affordances" in the terms of ecological theory. Because individuals alone cannot perform many vital actions, humans are assumed to have evolved a special sensitivity to the affordances offered by conspecifics; they are pulled toward others and into spontaneously forming social units, which yield a "we-ness" emerging in the service of action coordination. Marsh illustrates this ecological account of sociality by presenting a rich body of empirical research, and concludes by discussing the uniqueness of human sociality vis-à-vis that of other species.

The fifth chapter in this book, by Gün Semin, focuses on a special case of sociality, that is, coordinated actions that follow particular timing patterns such as synchrony or rhythmic turn taking. His approach builds on the preceding chapters' conceptual assumptions and applies these to situations where two or more individuals engage in temporally coordinated actions like applauding in unison or the "wave" that is produced by thousands of individual sports fans in a stadium. The argument advanced in the chapter is that such unusual states give rise to dissolution of the boundaries between the self and the other. A model to explain such synchronized behavior is proposed in terms of the neural processes that are jointly recruited. One of the main implications suggested by this model is that taking part in or being part of a synchronized social interaction gives rise to a qualitative shift in subjective experience due to the difficulty of applying an individual-centered explanation to collectively produced spontaneous coaction.

The second part of the volume is concerned with research that introduces a social perspective on memory, a field that has been regarded exclusively as the prerogative of individual-centered processes in psychology. The first contribution in this part, by William Hirst and Adam Brown, reveals a hidden asset behind the assumed apparent weakness of the malleability and unreliability of memory, a general treasure trove of the literature examining individual memory processes. The authors argue that if individuals' initial disparate interpretations of an event were to form the basis of their long-lasting memories, then collective memories might rarely be formed. According to these authors, the strength of the malleability and unreliability of human memory grows out of its ability to allow distinctive individual memories to converge on a shared rendering of the past, and, in doing so, serving to create social bonds among individuals. They review relevant literature, including work on social contagion, socially shared retrieval-induced forgetting, and the saying-is-believing effect. In each case, these memory phenomena are argued to serve the promotion of collective memories and tie people together through their shared recollections.

Chapter 7, by Gerald Echterhoff and Tory Higgins, traces the formation of socially shared, converging memories to the domain of communication. The authors begin their quest with an issue that is at the heart of human sociality: the origins of culture, specifically of culturally relevant knowledge and beliefs. According to a common view in cultural social psychology, interpersonal communication is the principal arena for the emergence and perpetuation of cultural knowledge. Building on this insight, the authors describe research examining how communication shapes memory, specifically the saying-is-believing effect, to suggest an important qualification. They argue that communication shapes people's memory and knowledge to the extent that it is motivated by *the goal of creating a shared reality* with the communication partner (Echterhoff et al., 2009). The focus on memory is critical because for culture to be handed down cultural knowledge has to be retained over time. The authors conclude that the creation of shared reality through communication highlights a potentially important everyday mechanism underlying the construction of culturally shared memories and knowledge.

The third part of this volume pushes the discussion to a higher level with contributions that address sociality in terms of the foundations of sociality, dialogical practices, and cultural factors. Tory Higgins's chapter focuses on the motivational significance of the desire to share inner states, which is a uniquely human development. He argues that there are four fundamental developments of the human animal that together produce distinct human motives: (1) social consciousness or awareness that the outcomes or significance of a person's actions (self or other) depend upon how another person (self or other) reacts to it; (2) recognizing that people's inner states can mediate their outward behaviors; (3) relating the present to both the past and the future (mental time travel); and (4) sharing reality with other people. Higgins argues that *social consciousness* is critical to understanding what is distinctive about human motives. Such social consciousness involves an awareness that the outcomes of a person (self or other) are determined by the reactions of others to what that person does. Social consciousness could remain at the behavioral or action level. However, there is another fundamental human development that radically changes the nature of social consciousness—the recognition that *inner states*, such as beliefs, feelings, expectancies, and desires, *mediate human reactions to one another*. Children make this startling discovery between 3 and 6 years of age. This chapter describes the antecedents and the profound motivational consequences of this discovery. It then describes the development of shared inner states more generally and describes their significance for human self-regulation.

Chapter 9 in this part, by Martin J. Pickering and Simon Garrod, is about how people manage an extremely complex process, namely conversation, with such ease. To explain this, they argue that interlocutors construct equivalent representations during production and comprehension at many different linguistic levels. This, in their view, results from an apparently automatic process of *interactive alignment*. Additionally, they suggest that there is good evidence that comprehenders make predictions during comprehension by using the language production system. Such predictions are particularly useful in dialogue, both to construct aligned representations "ahead of time" and to allow management of aspects of the conversation such as turn taking. Moreover, according to their model, the regular switching between production and comprehension in dialogue specifically emphasizes production-based prediction. They interpret this account in terms of emulation and argue that it provides an example of how prediction supports social interaction.

Chapter 10, by Yoshihisa Kashima and Boyka Bratanova, examines open issues surrounding situated sociality and cultural dynamics. How can microlevel processes of individuals' interaction with other individuals in particular situations produce and reproduce macrolevel phenomena of global social and cultural patterns? How do the macrolevel phenomena in turn enable and constrain microlevel processes? The main purpose of this chapter is to sketch a preliminary social psychological account of how microsituated sociality can provide a basis for conceptualizing macrolevel dynamics about the formation, maintenance, and transformation of cultural ideas and practices. The authors motivate this discussion by first pointing out that people's robust intuition often dissociates the micro- and macrolevels of sociocultural processes despite social science's fairly uncontroversial recognition that they are interdependent. They then introduce a metatheoretical framework of cultural diffusionism, in which culture is conceptualized as the process of dissemination of ideas and practices. To this end, they provide a critical appraisal of pertinent contemporary theories, and then outline a model of microprocesses of cultural diffusion that takes situated sociality seriously. The aim is to use this model to provide a social psychological account of how the perceived dissociation of micro- and macrolevel dynamics may occur.

The final part of this volume, comprised of two contributions, is about evolution and sociality. In the first of these, Louise Barrett takes a constructively critical view on comparative research, which attempts to ground sociality from an evolutionary perspective. She argues that this standard view takes it for granted to turn to our closest living relative, the monkeys and apes, for clues about the origins and evolutionary significance of many of our own social behaviors and the cognitive mechanisms that underpin them. She argues that although this may seem perfectly sensible, it has, for the most part, resulted in the idea that social understanding involves highly developed cognitive strategies designed to track, monitor, cooperate with, and potentially outwit other individuals. According to her, this stems from an uncritical acceptance of a Cartesian, disembodied view of the mind and cognition, which often has very little to do with evolution at all. The result has been a view of primate social life that, while congenial to our own folk psychological understanding of ourselves, cannot actually tell us very much about the "folk psychology" by which monkeys and apes might understand each other. Barrett argues that we have taken our own rather erroneous views about human social cognition and projected them onto the other primates, thus compounding the error. After this critique of the standard comparative view, she argues for an embodied and distributed approach to primate cognitive evolution, which resists the temptation to put into the head of the monkey what evolution left to the world. Her approach presents us with the opportunity to explore primate social complexity in ways that allow the animals to speak with their own voice, and to ground our own sociality in a manner that seems much more likely to meet with Darwin's approval, if not Descartes's.

The concluding chapter to this part and the volume is by Linnda Caporael. She examines the fundamentally social nature of the human species—historically, developmentally, and in day-to-day life. As primates, she argues, humans are part of an order that has been group living for 40 million years. They have a long developmental period of dependency that enables the young to learn the salient features of their culture and also innovate new ones. Because humans are unable to reproduce and survive to reproductive age without a group, they are *obligately social*. This chapter is about an approach to evolution that goes beyond the usual focus on adaptive functions of traits. The proposed alternative is an evolutionary model of the face-to-face group as a nested structure of subgroups or "core configurations," based on considerations of task and subgroup size. In concluding, she discusses the epistemic implications of the model for the study of humans in modern societies.

We hope that the contributions, each by itself and taken together, manage to convey the main message of this volume: that the study of the grounding of sociality can greatly profit from an integrative multilevel approach. Such an integrated understanding of how sociality is grounded, which genuinely requires perspectives from different fields and disciplines, may have great practical relevance. It could reveal new ways of improving social coordination in different social spheres, including interpersonal relations, organizations, and society at large. For instance, once the neurobiology of social interaction is sufficiently understood, it may be possible to develop or refine medical treatments for social interaction problems such as autism. Likewise, understanding the grounding of social interaction may help researchers to improve the design of socially skilled robots or of digital immersive environments that allow people to practice social interaction skills. From both an applied and a basic-research perspective, the approach advocated in this volume has the potential to provide new insights into the basis of human living and the forces that keep individuals connected and "in tune" with each other.

REFERENCES

Adolphs, R. (2003). Cognitive neuroscience of human social behavior. *Nature Reviews Neuroscience, 4*, 165–178.

Anderson, M. L. (2003). Embodied cognition: A field guide. *Artificial Intelligence, 149*, 91–130.

Barrett, L., & Henzi, P. (2005). The social nature of primate cognition. *Proceedings of the Royal Society London, B 272*, 1865–1875.

Barsalou, L. W., Niedenthal, P. M., Barbey, A., & Ruppert, J. (2003). Social embodiment. In B. Ross (Ed.), *The psychology of learning and motivation* (Vol. 43, pp. 43–92). San Diego: Academic Press.

Brass, M. & Heyes, C. (2005). Imitation: Is cognitive neuroscience solving the correspondence problem? *Trends in Cognitive Sciences, 9*, 489–495.

Breazeal, C. (2002). *Designing sociable robots*. Cambridge, MA: MIT Press.

Byrd, R. E. (1938). *Alone*. New York: Putnam.

Caporael, L. R. (1997). The evolution of truly social cognition: The core configurations model. *Personality and Social Psychology Review, 1*, 276–298.

Christakis, N. A. & Fowler, J. H. (2009). *Connected: The surprising power of our social networks and how they shape our lives*. New York: Little, Brown and Company.

Cuc, A., Koppel, J. & Hirst, W. (2007). Silence is not golden: A case for socially-shared retrieval-induced forgetting. *Psychological Science, 18*, 727–733.

Dijksterhuis, A. & Bargh, J. A. (2001). The perception-behavior expressway: Automatic effects of social perception on social behavior. *Advances in Experimental Social Psychology, 33*, 1–40.

Dunbar, R. I. M. (1993). Co-evolution of neocortex size, group size and language in humans. *Behavioral and Brain Sciences*, 16, 681–735.

Echterhoff, G., Bohner, G., & Siebler, F. (2006). Social Robotics und Mensch-Maschine Interaktion: Aktuelle Forschung und Relevanz für die Sozialpsychologie [Social robotics and human–machine interaction: Current research and perspectives for social psychology]. *Zeitschrift für Sozialpsychologie, 37*, 219–231.

Echterhoff, G., Higgins, E. T., & Levine, J. M. (2009). Shared reality: Experiencing commonality with others' inner states about the world. *Perspectives on Psychological Science, 4*, 496–521.

Enfield, N. J. & Levinson, S. C. (Eds.). (2006). *Roots of human sociality: Culture, cognition and interaction*. Oxford, UK: Berg.

Gallese, V., Keysers, C., & Rizzolatti, G. (2004). A unifying view of the basis of social cognition. *Trends in Cognitive Sciences, 8*, 396–403.

Gordon, R. M. (2005). Intentional agents like myself. In S. Hurley & N. Chater (Eds.), *Perspectives on imitation: From neuroscience to social science* (Vol. 2). Cambridge, MA: MIT Press.

Hardin, C. D. & Higgins, E. T. (1996). Shared reality: How social verification makes the subjective objective. In R. M. Sorrentino & E. T. Higgins (Eds.), *Handbook of motivation and cognition: The interpersonal context* (Vol. 3, pp. 28–84). New York: Guilford Press.

Hirst, W. & Manier, D. (2002). The diverse forms of collective memory. In G. Echterhoff & M. Saar (Eds.), *Kontexte und Kulturen des Erinnerns* [*Contexts and cultures of remembering*] (pp. 37–58). Constance, Germany: UVK.

Hutchins, E. (1995). *Cognition in the wild*. Cambridge, MA: MIT Press.

Iacoboni, M. (2008). *Mirroring people: The new science of how we connect with others*. New York: Farrar, Straus, and Giroux.

Liberman, A. M. & Whalen, D. H. (2000). On the relation of speech to language. *Trends in Cognitive Sciences, 4*, 187–196.

Lindner, I., Echterhoff, G., Davidson, P. S. R., & Brand, M. (in press). Observation inflation: Your actions become mine. *Psychological Science*.

Meltzoff, A. N. & Decety, J. (2003). What imitation tells us about social cognition: A rapprochement between developmental psychology and cognitive neuroscience. *Philosophical Transactions of the Royal Society London, B 358*, 491–500.

Metzinger, T. & Gallese, V. (2003). The emergence of a shared action ontology: Building blocks for a theory. *Consciousness and Cognition, 12*, 549–571.

Pickering, M. J. & Garrod, S. (2004). Toward a mechanistic psychology of dialogue. *Behavioral and Brain Sciences, 27*, 169–225.

Preston, S. D. & de Waal, F. B. M. (2002). Empathy: Its ultimate and proximate bases. *Behavioral and Brain Sciences, 25*, 1–72.

Prinz, W. (2002). Experimental approaches to imitation. In A. N. Meltzoff & W. Prinz (Eds.), *The imitative mind: Development, evolution, and brain bases* (pp. 143–162). New York: Cambridge University Press.

Richerson, P. J. & Boyd, R. (2005). *Not by genes alone: How culture transformed human evolution*. Chicago: University of Chicago Press.
Rizzolatti, G. & Craighero, L. (2004). The mirror-neuron system. *Annual Review of Neuroscience, 27*, 169–192.
Sebanz, N., Bekkering, H., & Knoblich, G. (2006). Joint action: Bodies and minds moving together. *Trends in Cognitive Sciences, 10*, 70–76.
Semin, G. R. (2007). Grounding communication: Synchrony. In A. W. Kruglanski & E. T. Higgins (Eds.), *Social psychology: Handbook of basic principles* (2nd ed., pp. 630–649). New York: Guilford Press.
Smith, E. R. & Semin, G. R. (2004). Socially situated cognition: Cognition in its social context. *Advances in Experimental Social Psychology, 36*, 53–117.
Thompson, L. & Fine, G. A. (1999). Socially shared cognition, affect, and behavior: A review and integration. *Personality and Social Psychology Review, 3*, 278–302.
Tindale, R. S. & Kameda, T. (2000). "Social sharedness" as a unifying theme for information processing in groups. *Group Processes & Intergroup Relations, 3*, 123–140.
Tomasello, M. (2000). Culture and cognitive development. *Current Directions in Psychological Science, 9*, 37–40.
Tomasello, M. (2008). *Origins of human communication*. Cambridge, MA: MIT Press.
Weldon, M. S. (2001). Remembering as a social process. In D. L. Medin (Ed.), *The psychology of learning and motivation: Advances in research and theory* (Vol. 40, pp. 67–120). San Diego: Academic Press.

Section I

Foundations of Sociality

2

Mirroring as a Key Neural Mechanism of Sociality

MARCO IACOBONI

INTRODUCTION

The study of the neural basis of social behavior is fairly recent. There are probably two major factors that have biased previous neuroscience research toward the study of human behavior that is not intrinsically social. The first one is obviously that social behavior is perceived as very complex, and its complexity very difficult to reduce to the point that the phenomenon is experimentally tractable with neuroscience methods. The second one is more insidious. I think that a latent, hidden dualism has favored the view that biological determinism may be at the basis of self-serving individualism, whereas prosocial behavior may be explained by assuming that our intellect makes us rise above our neurobiological makeup. In this chapter I will argue, in contrast, that recent neuroscience findings suggest that the evolutionary process has shaped neurobiological systems that make us predisposed to social behavior and that in principle could even account for a secular morality.

To build my argument, I will first review findings obtained with single-unit recordings in monkeys that suggest neural mechanisms at the single-cell level that seem perfectly tailored for social behavior. I will then describe and discuss the common neuroscience practice of using data from single unit recordings in monkeys to frame the interpretation of brain imaging data in humans. I will subsequently discuss brain-imaging data in humans that suggest that human areas likely containing mirror neurons may be considered biomarkers of sociality. I will conclude with a discussion of the implications of these new neuroscience data for a better understanding of the nature of our sociality and of the relationships between neuroscience and society.

MIRROR NEURONS IN THE MACAQUE BRAIN

In an area of the ventral premotor cortex of the macaque brain, called F5, there are neurons that fire during goal-oriented actions such as grasping, holding, manipulating, tearing, and so on (Rizzolatti et al., 1987). The discharge of these neurons co-occurs with specific actions, rather than with specific muscle contractions. For instance, a ventral premotor neuron may discharge during grasping but not while the monkey is scratching its head, even though there is a large overlap between body parts (fingers, hands, forearms) and muscles involved in both actions. In some cases the discharge of the cell seems to suggest that the aspect of the actions that it is coded for is its goal. For instance, the same neuron may discharge when the monkey uses the right hand, the left hand, and also the mouth to grab food (Rizzolatti et al., 1987). Interestingly, however, different types of grasps are coded by different neurons. For instance, a ventral premotor neuron in area F5 that discharges during precision grip (a type of grasp performed with two fingers to grab a tiny object like a raisin) will not fire during whole-hand prehension (a type of grasp performed with all fingers and palm to grasp a bigger objects like an apple or a banana; Rizzolatti et al., 1988).

The motor properties of neurons in area F5 are fascinating. Subsets of these cells, however, also have sensory properties, because the cells also fire when the monkey is completely still and is simply processing sensory stimulation. The sensory properties of area F5 neurons are even more fascinating than their motor properties. Among the F5 neurons with sensory properties, there is a class of neurons that is called mirror neurons. These cells fire when the monkey is observing another individual performing actions (di Pellegrino, Fadiga, Fogassi, Gallese, & Rizzolatti, 1992; Gallese, Fadiga, Fogassi, & Rizzolatti, 1996). There are two major types of mirror neurons: strictly congruent and broadly congruent. Strictly congruent mirror neurons are cells that fire at the sight of the same action that they code from a motor standpoint. For instance, a strictly congruent mirror neuron that fires during the execution of a precision grip will also fire during the observation of a precision grip performed by somebody else, but not during the observation of a whole-hand prehension performed by somebody else. Broadly congruent mirror neurons instead fire also for actions that are not exactly identical to the action that they code from a motor standpoint. The observed action that triggers the discharge of broadly congruent mirror neurons tends to achieve the same goal or to be logically related to the executed action (di Pellegrino et al., 1992; Gallese et al., 1996; Rizzolatti & Craighero, 2004).

It is important to emphasize that the majority of mirror neurons belong to the latter category. Indeed, two thirds of mirror neurons are broadly congruent and a third are strictly congruent. These neuronal properties seem very useful for flexible social interaction. While mirroring is essential for social interaction—as I will argue later on—one cannot simply mirror what others do. Broadly congruent mirror neurons may be very important to predict the intentions of others and to facilitate cooperative, coordinated behavior (more on this later).

The properties of mirror neurons suggest that these cells implement some sort of inner imitation (or simulation) of the actions of other people. This neuronal system may support a simple, parsimonious, but highly efficient form of empathy and "mindreading." Obviously, actions take many forms. After the initial observations, a series of experiments attempted to better describe the responses of mirror neurons. For instance, actions may sometime be partially hidden. This does not preclude us from understanding the actions of others. What do mirror neurons do in the case of partially occluded actions? Approximately 50% of mirror neurons discharge even when the completion of the action cannot be observed (Umiltà et al., 2001). In this experiment, the monkey observed a graspable object on a table. At some point during the trial a screen would occlude the sight of the graspable object. When one of the experimenters reached behind the screen, 50% of mirror neurons fired. In a control condition, the monkey saw that there was no graspable object on the table. Again, the screen occluded the sight of the table and the experimenter reached behind the screen. Note that at this point this control condition is visually identical to the previous one that triggered the firing of approximately 50% of mirror neurons. The only difference between the two conditions is the prior knowledge about the presence or absence of a graspable object behind the screen. In this control condition, none of the mirror neurons fired. Thus, mirror neurons are able to code for observed but partially occluded actions and can use prior information to discriminate between a true grasping action and a simple reach without grasping (Umiltà et al., 2001).

A later study demonstrated that mirror neurons also fire at the sound of an action, even when the action is not observed (Kohler et al., 2002). For instance, a mirror neuron that would fire at the execution and the observation of breaking a peanut would also fire while the monkey was simply listening to the sound of somebody breaking a peanut (Kohler et al., 2002). Thus, the properties of these cells seem to provide a fairly abstract coding of the actions of others. How abstract is this coding? Can mirror neurons also differentiate the same action associated with different intentions? To address this question, neuronal responses in area PF/PFG, in the anterior sector of the inferior parietal lobule were recorded. Indeed, this parietal sector is anatomically connected with area F5 of the ventral premotor cortex and also contains mirror neurons. In this experiment, it was first observed that grasping neurons in the parietal mirror neuron area may differently code the same grasping action performed to achieve different intentions (Fogassi et al., 2005). Neuronal responses were recorded while the monkeys were grasping food to eat or to place it in a container (after placing the food in the container, the monkeys were rewarded with food, such that the amount of reward was similar for both execution conditions). Among neurons that discharged at the time of grasping, approximately three quarters discharged differently for grasping-to-eat and grasping-to-place. Not surprisingly, the majority of these cells preferred grasping-to-eat, although almost a third preferred grasping-to-place.

Subsequently, the animals were tested while observing an experimenter grasping food. Here, the presence of a container signaled the intention of the experimenter. When the container was present, the experimenter placed the grasped food in the container. When the container was absent, the experimenter brought the food to the mouth and ate it. Mirror neurons in the parietal mirror neuron area obviously fired at the time of grasp, well before seeing the completion of the action. However, as in the execution conditions, approximately three quarters of mirror neurons discharged differently for observed grasping-to-eat and observed grasping-to-place. As in the execution conditions, grasping-to-eat was preferred by approximately two thirds of mirror neurons coding differently the grasping action, whereas the remaining third preferred grasping-to-place (Fogassi et al., 2005). These data clearly suggest that a large number of mirror neurons code not only the observed action, but also the intention associated with it.

So far, I have described mostly neuronal responses associated with hand actions. However, there are mirror neurons that code mouth actions, both ingestive (like biting a banana) and communicative (like lip-smacking, a facial gesture of positive valence involving lip protrusion; Ferrari, Gallese, Rizzolatti, & Fogassi, 2003). This is important, because with our faces we often communicate our emotions. The existence of mirror neurons for mouth actions suggests that this neuronal system may also be critical for empathy and emotional contagion.

FROM SINGLE-UNIT RECORDINGS IN MONKEYS TO BRAIN-IMAGING DATA IN HUMANS

A common practice in neuroscience is to use data from single-unit recordings in monkeys to interpret brain-imaging data in humans. There are two main reasons why this practice is widespread in the neuroscience community. First, single-unit recordings in humans are too invasive and can only be performed as a form of "opportunistic" science when medical procedures require the surgical implantation of depth electrodes in neurological and psychiatric patients. Because of its invasiveness, depth electrode implantation—both location of the electrode and duration of the implantation—is dictated exclusively by medical reasons. Even under these clinical constraints, data from depth electrodes in humans are obviously extremely valuable but they are also extremely rare. Brain imaging, on the other hand, is readily available. The most widely used brain imaging technique, functional magnetic resonance imaging (fMRI), is also extremely safe (although some precautions are necessary) and subjects can be repeatedly studied with it. Obviously, brain-imaging techniques—which in most cases measure neural activity indirectly, by measuring blood flow or blood flow oxygenation as in the case of fMRI—cannot achieve the exquisite spatial and temporal resolution that can be obtained with single unit recordings in macaques. How do we reconcile brain-imaging data in humans and single-unit recordings in macaques? One way of reconciling these data is by framing both types of data within the evolutionary framework, which is the second reason why this common neuroscience practice is quite solid. It makes sense to infer that human areas studied with brain imaging contain neurons described by monkey neurophysiologists, provided that the imaging data show a pattern of activity compatible with the single-unit recordings and that these human brain areas are anatomically homologous to the macaque brain areas from which the single-unit recordings were obtained.

There are many examples of this practice in systems neuroscience. For instance, brain-imaging data on reward processing in the ventral striatum (Montague, King-Casas, & Cohen, 2006) are commonly interpreted as suggesting that the human ventral striatum contains reward-processing neurons described by monkey neurophysiologists (Schultz & Dickinson, 2000). Another example is provided by the dorsal premotor cortex and conditional motor learning. Conditional motor learning tasks study the ability to associate a motor response to an arbitrary sensory stimulus (for instance, when we brake at a red traffic light). Both lesion studies and single-unit recordings have demonstrated that the dorsal premotor cortex is essential for conditional motor learning (Passingham, 1993; Wise, 1985). Brain imaging studies in humans are consistent with the monkey data and they are typically interpreted as suggesting that the human dorsal premotor cortex contains neuronal mechanisms similar to the ones described in the monkey dorsal premotor cortex (Passingham, 1993). The same logic is also applied to many other systems, for instance, higher-order visual areas processing motion, color, and so on.

Obviously, after the discovery of mirror neurons in macaques, it made sense to use brain-imaging techniques to investigate the mirroring properties of the human brain, using the same logic adopted for all the other neural systems. The next section of the chapter will review some of the brain-imaging data.

THE HUMAN MIRROR NEURON SYSTEM

The first attempts to demonstrate the existence of a mirror neuron system in humans were performed using experimental tasks very similar to the ones used in macaques, that is, grasping observation and execution. The very first human study that provided evidence for neural mirroring was not a brain-imaging study, but rather a transcranial magnetic stimulation (TMS) experiment (Fadiga, Fogassi, Pavesi, & Rizzolatti, 1995). TMS painlessly and noninvasively stimulates the brain by placing a copper coil over the head of experimental subjects. The coil is encased in plastic. Electric pulses are sent through the coil such that they generate a magnetic field, which in turn induces an electric current in the brain tissue underneath the coil. With the use of different stimulation parameters applied to different "states" of brain activity, TMS can induce both excitation and inhibition in the stimulated neural system.

The first study to investigate human neural mirroring used TMS to measure the level of excitability of the motor system while subjects were watching grasping actions or some control visual stimuli (Fadiga et al., 1995). The rationale behind the study was the following: When the TMS pulse is delivered over the motor cortex of resting subjects, it induces an involuntary muscle twitch. The amplitude of the muscle twitch is an index of the excitability of the motor system. Given that mirror neurons are located in the premotor cortex, only one synapse away from the primary motor cortex, an excitation of mirror neurons should also spread to the primary motor cortex. Such spreading of excitation should increase the excitability of the motor cortex. This reasoning leads to a straightforward prediction: If there are mirror neurons in the human premotor cortex, there should be higher motor excitability while watching other people performing grasping actions than watching control visual stimuli not involving actions. Indeed, this was the case (Fadiga et al., 1995). This phenomenon suggests that mirror neurons induce some sort of motor resonance between people. While watching you use your body in some actions, my motor system "resonates" with yours. In fact, there are many behavioral studies that have also described such motor resonance (Hatfield, Cacioppo, & Rapson, 1994).

Two early brain-imaging studies used positron emission tomography (PET) and grasping execution/observation/imagination tasks (Grafton, Arbib, Fadiga, & Rizzolatti, 1996; Rizzolatti et al., 1996). PET is a brain-imaging technique based on radioactive material that binds with certain molecules and allows various forms of measurements of brain activity. The PET technique used in these early studies was somewhat limited and while both studies provided evidence compatible with the notion of an existing and functioning mirror neuron system in humans, the evidence was not fully conclusive.

Given the properties of mirror neurons, however, it also made sense to expand the experimental tasks to investigate the existence and the behavioral relevance of the mirror neuron system in the human brain. In my lab, we decided to use imitation tasks to study the human mirror neuron system. Imitation is a pervasive, ubiquitous, and important human behavior that is studied in many disciplines, from psychology to sociology, and from economics to philosophy, just to name a few (Hurley & Chater, 2005). We reasoned that mirror neurons have physiological properties that seem ideal for imitation and designed a series of experimental tasks to investigate the links between imitation and human brain areas that may contain mirror neurons. Our starting point was the observation that the discharge of mirror neurons in macaques is approximately twice as strong during action execution than during action observation. Thus, we expected that putative mirror neuron areas in the human brain would also have a response twice as strong during action execution than during action observation. Furthermore, given that during imitation subjects were both watching and executing the action, we assumed an additive response, such that the response of putative mirror neuron areas in the human brain during imitation was approximately the sum of the responses measured during action execution and action observation. To test these predictions, we used fMRI and a series of tasks comprising observation, execution, and imitation of finger movements. We found two areas in the human brain that displayed the pattern of activity predicted on the basis of the discharges measured in individual mirror neurons in macaques. These two areas were located in the inferior frontal cortex and in the anterior part of the posterior parietal cortex (Iacoboni et al., 1999), that is, two areas anatomically compatible with the areas in the macaque brain that were already known to contain mirror neurons. The mirror neuron area in the inferior frontal cortex overlapped with the posterior part of Broca's area, a major language area in the human brain. This was theoretically important, because it supported evolutionary theories that propose a critical role of mirror neurons in language evolution (Rizzolatti & Arbib, 1998).

The activation of a language area during a nonlanguage task, however, is a double-edged sword. Indeed, the activation may in principle represent covert verbalization during the task. This is one of the limitations of the fMRI technique.

It gives you only correlational, not causal information. Admittedly, in our study the putative mirror neuron area in the inferior frontal cortex overlapping with Broca's area had a pattern of activity (some activation during action observation, approximately twice as much activation for action execution, and approximately the sum of the previous activations for imitation) that was difficult to explain with covert verbalization. However, we decided to test the causal links between activity in Broca's area and imitation with repetitive TMS (Heiser, Iacoboni, Maeda, Marcus, & Mazziotta, 2003). This TMS technique is known to interfere with the underlying brain activity, thus producing some sort of "transient lesion" in the brain of the experimental subjects. In this study, we applied trains of pulses at high frequency. Subjects performed an imitation task and a control visuomotor task while we applied TMS over the posterior part of Broca's area and a control brain area. The data demonstrated a selective impairment during imitation only when Broca's area was stimulated (Heiser et al., 2003), thus revealing causal links between activity in the inferior frontal mirror neuron area and imitation. These data also demonstrated that Broca's area is a brain area not exclusively dedicated to language. These findings have theoretical relevance, because they are not consistent with some theories of language that propose that the language function is encapsulated and requires dedicated neural machinery.

Further studies investigated the relations between mirror neuron areas in the human brain and imitation (Koski, Iacoboni, Dubeau, Woods, & Mazziotta, 2003; Koski et al., 2002). The picture that emerged from these studies is that while the inferior frontal mirror neuron area seems to be more concerned with the goal of the action to be imitated, the parietal mirror neuron area seems more concerned with the motor details of the action to be imitated (Iacoboni, 2005).

In another fMRI study our group investigated the role of human mirror neuron areas in coding the intention associated with observed actions (Iacoboni et al., 2005). The experimental design of this study (which has been called the "tea party experiment") is somewhat similar to the design of the monkey experiment on intention described earlier. Indeed, this imaging study preceded the monkey study and partly inspired it. The starting point of this experiment was the fact that the same action can be associated with different intentions. We reasoned that the context in which the action occurs can give the observer a clue regarding the intention of the agent. In our experiment, subjects observed three types of clips. One type, which we call CONTEXT, shows a scene with various objects: a teapot, a cup, cookies, napkins, and so on. There are two kinds of scenes. In one, everything is neatly organized, suggesting that somebody is going to have tea. The other scene is messy: There are cookie crumbs, a dirty napkin, and so on. This scene suggests that somebody already had tea. The second type of clip, which we call ACTION, shows only a hand grasping a cup, with no context surrounding the grasping action. Finally, the third type of clip, which we call INTENTION, shows a hand grasping a cup surrounded by a context. There are two kinds of context, the neat one and the messy one shown in the CONTEXT clips. Obviously, the neat context suggests the intention to drink associated with the grasping action, whereas the messy context suggests the intention to clean up. With this experimental design, the predictions are relatively straightforward: If mirror neuron areas code only the action, they should activate similarly for both ACTION and INTENTION clips. If they code also the intention associated with the action, they should activate more for the INTENTION clips, and possibly should activate differently between the two intentions, drinking and cleaning. Indeed, the results revealed that the right inferior frontal mirror neuron area had higher activity for the INTENTION clips compared to the ACTION clips, and it had higher activity for the drinking intention than the cleaning intention (Iacoboni et al., 2005).

These results clearly support the hypothesis that mirror neuron areas implement a simulation-based form of understanding the intentions of other people. Mirror neurons, which are after all only a special type of motor neurons, most likely implement an implicit form of understanding the intentions of other people. This implicit understanding, however, may be the basis for more explicit forms of understanding other people's mental states, what is typically called mindreading. How does the implicit process of understanding others' minds translate into the explicit process of mindreading? One possibility is that to understand other people's mental states explicitly, we need to embody what they do, or at least we need to simulate such embodiment process, which is what mirror neurons seem designed to do. Thus, the implicit understanding of other people's minds may represent the foundational aspect of explicit mindreading.

This is consistent with behavioral data that have suggested that we understand and empathize with others through the body and its actions. Social psychology studies have indeed revealed that the more we tend to imitate others, the more we tend to empathize with them (Chartrand & Bargh, 1999). These behavioral data suggest a functional link between imitation and empathy that suggests functional links between neural systems important for imitation and neural systems important for emotion processing. Thus, mirror neuron areas involved in imitation may interact with limbic areas, specialized in emotion processing, to support a simulation-based form of empathy. In an fMRI study of imitation and observation of facial emotional expressions, we described a large-scale functional network composed by mirror neuron areas, the insula, and the limbic system, and proposed that mirror neurons recognize the facial expression and send signals to the limbic system via the insula. The activity in limbic areas would make us feel what others feel (Carr, Iacoboni, Dubeau, Mazziotta, & Lenzi, 2003).

To further test this model, we have recently studied children using the same paradigm of imitation and observation of facial emotional expressions (Pfeifer, Iacoboni, Mazziotta, & Dapretto, 2008). In this study, the children were also assessed regarding their ability to empathize and their interpersonal competence. Both empathy scores and interpersonal competence scores correlated with activity in all areas belonging to the network, although mirror neuron areas had the highest correlations. These data indicate that mirror neuron areas are a biomarker of sociality. Correlations between empathy scores and activity in mirror neuron areas during action observation (Kaplan & Iacoboni, 2006) and while listening to speech sounds (Gazzola, Aziz-Zadeh, & Keysers, 2006) have also been observed in adults.

If the mirror neuron system is a biomarker of sociality, its activity should be reduced in subjects that find social interaction difficult. The mirror neuron hypothesis of autism assumes that the reduced functioning of the mirror neuron system is a core deficit in autism. To test this hypothesis we studied children with autism spectrum disorder (ASD) and typically developing (TD) children with fMRI (Dapretto et al., 2006). The activation task was the same of our previous studies: imitation and observation of facial emotional expressions. As predicted by the mirror neuron hypothesis of autism, ASD children had reduced activity in mirror neuron areas, compared to TD children. The activity in mirror neuron areas in ASD children was also correlated with the severity of the disease. The more impaired the child, the more reduced the activity in mirror neuron areas. These results obviously reinforce the hypothesis that the mirror neuron system is a biomarker of sociality. The properties of these cells, and their role in human social behavior, have far-reaching implications. The next section of this chapter will discuss them.

IMPLICATIONS FOR SOCIALITY

What are the theoretical implications of the discovery of mirror neurons for our understanding of the basis of human sociality? I believe there are many implications. A good place to start is the so-called problem of other minds. In philosophy of mind, the problem of other minds can be formulated (in a simple form) as follows: If I have access only to my own mind, how can I possibly understand the minds of other people? The basic assumption of the problem of other minds is the view of the mind as solitary, detached, irreparably separated from the outside world; a rather Cartesian view. Mirror neurons reveal that evolution has devised an ingeniously simple mechanism to overcome the difficulties posited by the Cartesian view of the mind. We are interconnected with one another through powerful, automatic, but also flexible mechanisms of neural mirroring.

These considerations have implications for our concept of the self. Indeed, mirror neurons suggest an intimacy between self and other that we typically find difficult to accept. With mirror neurons, the other becomes "another self" (Gallese, 2006). The self and the other are two sides of the same coin, and mirror neurons are the metal this coin is made of (Iacoboni, 2008). If this is true, one would predict high activity in mirror neuron areas in tasks that require self-recognition. Indeed, a series of studies using a variety of experimental approaches had demonstrated an important role of inferior frontal and posterior parietal areas in self-recognition (Keenan, Gallup, & Falk, 2003). The areas implicated in previous studies seemed quite similar to mirror neuron areas. In my lab, we have recently investigated this issue in more detail. We have first performed an fMRI study on self-recognition using morphed faces (the morphs were a mixture of the face of the subject and of a close friend). Indeed, we noticed high activity in a posterior parietal area of the right cerebral hemisphere that most likely contains mirror neurons during self-recognition (when the morph was mostly composed of self; Uddin, Kaplan, Molnar-Szakacs, Zaidel, & Iacoboni, 2005). We subsequently performed a repetitive TMS study in which we stimulated the parietal mirror neuron area, to test whether the activity in this area is essential to the self-recognition task. In this study, we used a low-frequency repetitive stimulation protocol. This protocol too, as the high-frequency repetitive TMS protocol used in our previous study on Broca's area and imitation described earlier

(Heiser et al., 2003), interferes with brain activity underneath the coil. Indeed, the stimulation of the right parietal mirror neuron areas induced a selective deficit in self-recognition (Uddin, Iacoboni, Lange, & Keenan, 2007; Uddin, Molnar-Szakacs, Zaidel, & Iacoboni, 2006), thus demonstrating a causal link between activity in this area and the ability to self-recognize.

But if self and other are two sides of the same coin, and mirroring is a powerful way of connecting and communicating between individuals during social interaction, what happens to our long-cherished notion of free will? Our sociality is probably our highest achievement, and still during social interaction the powerful influence mediated by mirror neurons may limit our free will. This is an unsettling idea. Given its possible wide implications even in policy (for instance, the links between media violence and imitative violence or the role of imitation in drug addiction relapses), we should consider it seriously, even though it unsettles us. Obviously, when I argue that mirroring limits our free will I do not imply that we are forced to make decisions *against* our free will. The important point to keep in mind, here, is that we make many decisions in our everyday life by-passing a careful and elaborate deliberation process. The emotional state we are in (that we may have "caught" from others through mirroring), and the state of being primed to perform certain kinds of actions that mirroring instantiates, may be powerful influences in the common, less deliberate decision making we execute most of the time.

Another important implication of the discovery of mirror neurons is related to the role of neuroscience in our society. The research on mirror neurons is telling us—in contrast with the traditional idea that our biology is all about self-preservation and individualism—that evolution has made us wired for empathy. This is a major revision of longstanding beliefs. Traditionally, evolutionary models put the individual front and center. Obviously, a corollary of the emphasis of these models on the individual is that competition is a critical factor in evolution. Alternative models that emphasize cooperation, rather than competition, better fit the evolutionary picture that is suggested by the discovery of mirror neurons and their role in social behavior. Furthermore, until now we were not fully aware of our capacity for mirroring. Mirroring operates at an implicit level, not at an explicit one. Societies, in contrast, are built on explicit discourse. This explicit discourse, based on political and religious beliefs, has divided us. With the discovery of mirror neurons we are now finally aware that we are wired for empathy, that our biology may be the basis of a secular morality, as opposed to a morality that is traditionally based on religious beliefs. This awareness may be injected in our public discourse and hopefully change it for the better, to create a more empathic and caring society.

CONCLUSION AND FUTURE DIRECTIONS

We are at the very beginning of a research project on mirror neurons and sociality that promises to be exciting and transforming. Indeed, the transformations on our thinking on how the brain works, the neural basis of sociality, the relations between self and other, and the many other issues briefly touched here are so radical that we should probably talk about a revolution, the mirror neuron revolution. A critical aspect of this revolution is the shift of the focus of attention of the scientific discourse from individuals to groups, from competition to cooperation, from organisms to societies. This is a major change, a change that may be resisted by many scholars who still prefer the old paradigm focusing on the individual. The mounting evidence, however, will eventually weaken such resistance and the new paradigm will flourish.

Scientific practices may also change because of the research on mirror neurons and sociality. More interdisciplinary work will emerge, creating a common language between scientists and humanists interested in the broad implications of the research on mirroring for us humans. Furthermore, the interest raised by mirror neurons in the general audience will force important changes in how scientific discoveries and scientific thinking are communicated to the public. Science tends to be too isolated and almost trapped in its ivory tower, often relying on jargon incomprehensible for nonspecialists. The side effects of such isolation are disastrous, with the flourishing of irrational thinking in our societies. The interest raised in the general public by the discovery of mirror neurons is a wonderful opportunity to create a more effective bridge between science and society. In the future, it will be important to be able to communicate in an effective way the progress on this research to the society at large. The integration of scientific progress and societal awareness of such progress will be essential to make it possible that the science on sociality will have a transforming beneficial impact on our society.

ACKNOWLEDGMENTS

For generous support I thank the Brain Mapping Medical Research Organization, Brain Mapping Support Foundation, Pierson-Lovelace Foundation, The Ahmanson Foundation, William M. and Linda R. Dietel Philanthropic Fund at the Northern Piedmont Community Foundation, Tamkin Foundation, Jennifer Jones-Simon Foundation, Capital Group Companies Charitable Foundation, Robson Family, and Northstar Fund.

REFERENCES

Carr, L., Iacoboni, M., Dubeau, M. C., Mazziotta, J. C., & Lenzi, G. L. (2003). Neural mechanisms of empathy in humans: A relay from neural systems for imitation to limbic areas. *Proc Natl Acad Sci USA*, 100(9), 5497–5502.

Chartrand, T. L. & Bargh, J. A. (1999). The chameleon effect: The perception–behavior link and social interaction. *J Personality Soc Psych*, 76(6), 893–910.

Dapretto, M., Davies, M. S., Pfeifer, J. H., Scott, A. A., Sigman, M., Bookheimer, S. Y., et al. (2006). Understanding emotions in others: Mirror neuron dysfunction in children with autism spectrum disorders. *Nat Neurosci*, 9(1), 28–30.

Di Pellegrino, G., Fadiga, L., Fogassi, L., Gallese, V., & Rizzolatti, G. (1992). Understanding motor events: A neurophysiological study. *Exp Brain Res*, 91(1), 176–180.

Fadiga, L., Fogassi, L., Pavesi, G., & Rizzolatti, G. (1995). Motor facilitation during action observation: A magnetic stimulation study. *J Neurophysiol*, 73(6), 2608–2611.

Ferrari, P. F., Gallese, V., Rizzolatti, G., & Fogassi, L. (2003). Mirror neurons responding to the observation of ingestive and communicative mouth actions in the monkey ventral premotor cortex. *Eur J Neurosci*, 17(8), 1703–1714.

Fogassi, L., Ferrari, P. F., Gesierich, B., Rozzi, S., Chersi, F., & Rizzolatti, G. (2005). Parietal lobe: From action organization to intention understanding. *Science*, 308(5722), 662–667.

Gallese, V. (2006). Intentional attunement: A neurophysiological perspective on social cognition and its disruption in autism. *Brain Res*, 1079(1), 15–24.

Gallese, V., Fadiga, L., Fogassi, L., & Rizzolatti, G. (1996). Action recognition in the premotor cortex. *Brain*, 119(Pt 2), 593–609.

Gazzola, V., Aziz-Zadeh, L., & Keysers, C. (2006). Empathy and the somatotopic auditory mirror system in humans. *Curr Biol*, 16(18), 1824–1829.

Grafton, S. T., Arbib, M. A., Fadiga, L., & Rizzolatti, G. (1996). Localization of grasp representations in humans by positron emission tomography. 2. Observation compared with imagination. *Exp Brain Res*, 112(1), 103–111.

Hatfield, E., Cacioppo, J. T., & Rapson, R. L. (1994). *Emotional contagion*. Paris: Cambridge University Press.

Heiser, M., Iacoboni, M., Maeda, F., Marcus, J., & Mazziotta, J. C. (2003). The essential role of Broca's area in imitation. *Eur J Neurosci*, 17(5), 1123–1128.

Hurley, S. & Chater, N. (2005). *Perspective on imitation: From neuroscience to social science*. Cambridge, MA: MIT Press.

Iacoboni, M. (2005). Neural mechanisms of imitation. *Curr Opin Neurobiol*, 15(6), 632–637.

Iacoboni, M. (2008). *Mirroring people*. New York: Farrar, Straus & Giroux.

Iacoboni, M., Molnar-Szakacs, I., Gallese, V., Buccino, G., Mazziotta, J. C., & Rizzolatti, G. (2005). Grasping the intentions of others with one's own mirror neuron system. *PLoS Biol*, 3(3), e79.

Iacoboni, M., Woods, R. P., Brass, M., Bekkering, H., Mazziotta, J. C., & Rizzolatti, G. (1999). Cortical mechanisms of human imitation. *Science*, 286(5449), 2526–2528.

Kaplan, J. T. & Iacoboni, M. (2006). Getting a grip on other minds: Mirror neurons, intention understanding and cognitive empathy. *Soc Neurosci*, 1(3), 175–183.

Keenan, J. P., Gallup, G. G., & Falk, D. (2003). *The face in the mirror. The search for the origins of consciousness*. New York: Ecco.

Kiefer, M., Sim, E. J., Helbig, H. B., & Graf, M. (in press). Tracking the time course of action priming on object recognition: Evidence for fast and slow influences of action on perception. *Journal of Cognitive Neuroscience*.

Kohler, E., Keysers, C., Umiltà, M. A., Fogassi, L., Gallese, V., & Rizzolatti, G. (2002). Hearing sounds, understanding actions: Action representation in mirror neurons. *Science*, 297(5582), 846–848.

Koski, L., Iacoboni, M., Dubeau, M. C., Woods, R. P., & Mazziotta, J. C. (2003). Modulation of cortical activity during different imitative behaviors. *J Neurophysiol*, 89(1), 460–471.

Koski, L., Wohlschläger, A., Bekkering, H., Woods, R. P., Dubeau, M. C., Mazziotta, J. C., et al. (2002). Modulation of motor and premotor activity during imitation of target-directed actions. *Cereb Cortex*, 12(8), 847–855.

Montague, P. R., King-Casas, B., & Cohen, J. D. (2006). Imaging valuation models in human choice. *Annu Rev Neurosci*, 29, 417–448.

Mukamel, R., Ekstrom, A. D., Kaplan, J., Iacoboni, M., & Fried, I. (2010). Single-neuron responses in humans during execution and observation of actions. *Current Biology*, 20, 750–756.

Passingham, R. E. (1993). *The frontal lobes and voluntary action*. New York: Oxford University Press.

Pfeifer, J. H., Iacoboni, M., Mazziotta, J. C., & Dapretto, M. (2008). Mirroring others' emotions relates to empathy and interpersonal competence in children. *Neuroimage*, 39(4), 2076–2085.

Preston, S. D. & de Waal, F. B. M. (2002). Empathy: Its ultimate and proximate bases. *Behavioral and Brain Sciences*, 25, 1–72.

Prinz, W. (2008). Mirrors for embodied communication. In I. Wachsmuth, M. Lenzen, & G. Knoblich (Eds.), *Embodied communication in humans and machines* (pp. 111–128). Oxford: Oxford University Press.

Rizzolatti, G. & Arbib, M. A. (1998). Language within our grasp. *Trends Neurosci*, 21(5), 188–194.

Rizzolatti, G., Camarda, R., Fogassi, L., Gentilucci, M., Luppino, G., & Matelli, M. (1988). Functional organization of inferior area 6 in the macaque monkey. II. Area F5 and the control of distal movements. *Exp Brain Res*, 71(3), 491–507.

Rizzolatti, G. & Craighero, L. (2004). The mirror-neuron system. *Annu Rev Neurosci*, 27, 169–192.

Rizzolatti, G., Fadiga, L., Matelli, M., Bettinardi, V., Paulesu, E., Perani, D., et al. (1996). Localization of grasp representations in humans by PET: 1. Observation versus execution. *Exp Brain Res*, 111(2), 246–252.

Rizzolatti, G., Gentilucci, M., Fogassi, L., Luppino, G., Matelli, M., & Ponzoni-Maggi, S. (1987). Neurons related to goal-directed motor acts in inferior area 6 of the macaque monkey. *Exp Brain Res*, 67(1), 220–224.

Schultz, W. & Dickinson, A. (2000). Neuronal coding of prediction errors. *Annu Rev Neurosci*, 23, 473–500.

Uddin, L. Q., Iacoboni, M., Lange, C., & Keenan, J. P. (2007). The self and social cognition: The role of cortical midline structures and mirror neurons. *Trends Cogn Sci*, 11(4), 153–157.

Uddin, L. Q., Kaplan, J. T., Molnar-Szakacs, I., Zaidel, E., & Iacoboni, M. (2005). Self-face recognition activates a frontoparietal "mirror" network in the right hemisphere: An event-related fMRI study. *Neuroimage*, 25(3), 926–935.

Uddin, L. Q., Molnar-Szakacs, I., Zaidel, E., & Iacoboni, M. (2006). RTMS to the right inferior parietal lobule disrupts self-other discrimination. *Soc Cogn Affect Neurosci*, 1(1), 65–71.

Umiltà, M. A., Kohler, E., Gallese, V., Fogassi, L., Fadiga, L., Keysers, C., et al. (2001). I know what you are doing. A neurophysiological study. *Neuron*, 31(1), 155–165.

Wise, S. P. (1985). The primate premotor cortex: Past, present, and preparatory. *Annu Rev Neurosci*, 8, 1–19.

3

Motor Involvement in Action and Object Perception: *Similarity and Complementarity*

MARKUS GRAF, SIMONE SCHÜTZ-BOSBACH, AND WOLFGANG PRINZ

ABSTRACT

Visually perceiving both human actions and manipulable objects engages not only visual representations but also motor representations—representations that are normally used for action control. We propose that motor representations are activated to internally simulate actions on the basis of one's own motor repertoire. Action simulation may help to predict the future behavior of conspecifics and may facilitate potential motor interactions with an object. While action simulation is usually understood to involve a similarity relationship between perceived and performed, or to-be-performed, action, motor involvement in object perception is based on a complementarity relationship between the object and the potential actions it affords. Here, we shall discuss evidence in support of the view that complementarity also applies to the action domain. Perceiving actions of others may activate motor representations that code for one's own complementary actions. The domain of complementary actions opens a new field of research which is of tremendous functional importance for social interaction and communication. We conclude that the mirror and resonance metaphors, which dominate current discussions on motor involvement in action understanding, need to be extended since they cannot account for the coding of complementary actions.
Keywords: action perception, object perception, affordances, simulation theory, prediction, complementary actions, mirror system, motor involvement.

INTRODUCTION

When we perceive human actions or even objects, processing is not confined to the visual areas in the brain, but also involves specific cortical networks, which are normally used for motor control (e.g., Chao & Martin, 2000; Gallese, 2003; Jeannerod, 2001; Rizzolatti & Craighero, 2004). The activation of motor representations through perception implies a strong linkage between perception and action. This notion can be traced back to William James, who claimed that "every representation of a movement awakens in some degree the actual movement which is its object" (James, 1890, p. 1134). Later Greenwald (1970) made a similar proposal by stating that an action can automatically be induced not only by internally representing an action (goal) but also by perceiving it in the external world. Meanwhile, there is plenty of evidence that perceptual processing and action planning are intrinsically linked, and coded in a common representational medium (e.g., Hommel, Müsseler, Aschersleben, & Prinz, 2001; Prinz, 1990, 1997).

Research in this field was boosted by the discovery of mirror neurons in the monkey premotor cortex (area F5). These neurons respond not only when the monkey performs a certain action, but also when it just observes an experimenter performing a similar action (e.g., di Pellegrino, Fadiga, Fogassi, Gallese, & Rizzolatti, 1992; Gallese, Fadiga, Fogassi, & Rizzolatti, 1996). In recent years studies using neuroscientific methods, such as functional imaging techniques or transcranial magnetic stimulation (TMS), have provided evidence for the existence of a "mirror system" also in humans (for an overview see Mukamel et al., 2010; Rizzolatti & Craighero, 2004).[1] The discovery of mirror neurons in the frontal lobes of macaques and their implications for human brain evolution has been considered to be one of the most important findings in neuroscience in the last decade (Ramachandran, 2000). An assessment like this is meant to acknowledge the computational power of mirror neurons for mediating between perception and action in individuals. Yet, at the same time it is also meant to acknowledge the enormous potential that mirror neurons in the brain and mirror systems in the mind have for supporting action perception and action understanding across individuals, that is, functions that are crucial to social life (e.g., Oberman, Pineda, & Ramachandran, 2007). Some have even claimed that this social component is the proper function for which mirror systems have evolved (e.g., Gallese & Goldman, 1998; Rizzolatti & Sinigalia, 2007). Accordingly, mirror systems can be considered as dedicated systems for social interaction and communication. This claim is grounded in those systems' inherent capacity for social mirroring. The notion of social mirroring refers to individuals' capacity for resonating with others through direct matching of perception to action (i.e., perception of others' action to production of corresponding own action; cf. Prinz, 2008).

Importantly, area F5 in the monkey premotor cortex does not only contain mirror neurons, but also so-called canonical neurons. Canonical neurons respond when the monkey performs an action, or when it perceives an object that affords a congruent action. For instance, a specific canonical neuron responds not only when the monkey performs a power grip but also when it simply perceives a bar (Murata et al., 1997; Murata, Gallese, Luppino, Kaseda, & Sakata, 2000). Perceiving manipulable objects, such as tools, induces motor activations in humans (e.g., Chao & Martin, 2000; Grèzes, Armony, Rowe, & Passingham, 2003; Grèzes, Tucker, Armony, Ellis, & Passingham, 2003; Martin, Wiggs, Ungerleider, & Haxby, 1996). Motor representations also seem to contribute to the recognition of manipulable objects (Helbig, Graf, & Kiefer, 2006), and to the activation of concepts (for reviews, see Barsalou, 1999; Barsalou, Simmons, Barbey, & Wilson, 2003; Borghi, 2005; Gallese & Lakoff, 2005). The involvement of motor representations in object perception is reminiscent of Gibson's (1950, 1986) notion of "affordances," suggesting that we perceive how we can interact with objects in our environment.

In this chapter we focus on the role of the motor system in action perception as well as in object perception. Our goal is twofold. First, we want to outline basic principles underlying the perception of actions and objects. We will argue that both the perception of actions and the perception of manipulable objects involve internal simulation processes for predictive purposes. This predictive function was originally developed for motor control purposes (based on forward models), and has been exploited for perception (e.g., Grush, 2004; Prinz, 2006; Wilson & Knoblich, 2005). This motor involvement is believed to be based on a similarity relationship, because the underlying motor representations are similar to the observed action sequences (see section "Motor Involvement in Action Perception: Similarity").

In contrast, motor representations in the perception of manipulable objects involve a complementarity relation between the object and the action it affords. A grasping action, for example, is complementary to the shape of the object that is being grasped. Seeing an object can activate representations for complementary actions that specify potential interactions with this particular object (see section "Motor Involvement in Object Perception: Complementarity").

Our second goal is to direct attention to the domain of complementary actions. As perception ultimately aims at enabling us to act in the world, we argue that the main purpose of this predictive function is to facilitate action planning. However, when interacting with others we are usually not just imitating (mirroring) them, but tend to respond to their actions in a complementary way. For instance, when someone attacks us we typically generate an evasive maneuver, for instance, we sidestep or block the punch. Consequently, the predictive function of simulation is only truly functional if it can also be used to plan actions that are complementary to the observed action. In the section "Motor Involvement in Action Perception: Complementarity" we will review existing evidence for the coding of complementary actions.

Though a rich experimental literature on motor involvement in perception has emerged in recent years, there is so far no generally accepted terminology, neither at the level of empirical observations nor at the level of theoretical constructs. In this chapter we use the term *motor involvement* as an umbrella term referring to a broad variety of experimental observations that either imply or suggest that the perception of objects, actions, and events may engage functional mechanisms and/or brain structures that are normally involved in action production. Likewise, we use the term *simulation* (or *motor simulation*) as an umbrella term to refer to a variety of putative mental operations and/or brain processes assumed to underlie such motor involvement in perception.

Perhaps our use of that latter term requires some clarifications. The notion of simulation is widespread in the literature on perception of movements, actions, and mental states. In that literature this term is applied to such diverse contexts like imitation of movements (e.g., Brass, Bekkering, & Prinz, 2001; Brass, Bekkering, Wohlschläger, & Prinz, 2000; Kilner, Paulignan, & Blakemore, 2003), perception of manipulable objects (Barsalou, 1999; Gallese, 2003; Gallese & Lakoff, 2005) or understanding of others' mental states (Gallese & Goldman, 1998). In this chapter we speak of (motor) simulation to refer to any kind of: (i) covert activity in functional systems for action production (i.e., activity that is not related to executing or controlling overt behavior); (ii) which is induced by the perception of objects and events in the perceiver's environment; and (iii) is related to these objects and events in a meaningful way.

This definition captures two interrelated defining features that appear to be crucial and indispensable to any use of the concept of simulation: representation and correspondence. First, a simulation of something is not the real thing itself but rather some kind of representation of it. This criterion is fulfilled by the covert nature of the motor activity. Second, a representation needs to exhibit, in important respects, structural correspondences with the real thing itself. This criterion is fulfilled through the fact that the covert motor activity has the capacity to trigger and control corresponding overt activity. It thereby provides an internal simulation of the external action to which it could give rise.

Note that this definition does not directly capture one particular feature that it is often thought to be crucial to simulation of actions and mental states: the feature of similarity between the inducing environmental events and the induced motor activity. Instead, our definition offers a broader criterion: that of a meaningful relationship between inducing events and induced activity. For instance, when the concept of simulation is applied to the domain of object perception (Barsalou et al., 2003; Borghi, 2005; Gallese, 2003; Gallese & Lakoff, 2005) the notion is not that the action simulates the object but rather that the covert motor activity simulates overt actions that would be appropriate for dealing with that object. Notably, the criterion of a meaningful relationship does include similarity-based relationships as one particularly important class of such meaningful relationships, but it allows for inclusion of other kinds of such relationships as well. In fact, one of the central issues of this chapter is to argue that motor simulation may not only be based on similarity but also on complementarity between inducing events and induced motor activity.

MOTOR INVOLVEMENT IN ACTION PERCEPTION: SIMILARITY

A large number of findings suggest that watching or imagining an action leads to an involvement of the observer's motor system, that is, excites motor programs that are normally used to execute this particular action (for reviews, e.g., Gallese, 2003; Jeannerod, 2001; Sommerville & Decety, 2006). In this section we will review evidence suggesting that these motor activations are simulation processes that mirror or "covertly imitate" the observed actions in order to predict what the observed actor will most likely do next (for an overview, see Wilson & Knoblich, 2005). The perceptual-induced motor representations are similar to the observed actions.

Basic Evidence

Evidence for motor involvement in action perception comes from different fields of research. For instance, behavioral experiments demonstrated that people show an unconscious tendency to mimic others' behavior, which is known as the "chameleon effect" (e.g., Chartrand & Bargh, 1999). Beyond this behavioral imitation, there is also a tendency to unconsciously adopt the emotional state of others, called "emotional contagion" (e.g., Hatfield, Cacioppo, & Rapson, 1994). This kind of behavioral imitation seems to be a fast and automatic response tendency rather than controlled behavior (see Prinz, 2002, 2005 for reviews; but see Heyes, Bird, Johnson, & Haggard, 2005). Further evidence for motor influences on perception has been provided by studies showing interference effects between observed and simultaneously performed actions (Brass et al., 2000, 2001; Hamilton, Wolpert, & Frith, 2004; Kilner, Hamilton, & Blakemore, 2007; Kilner et al., 2003; Stürmer, Aschersleben, & Prinz, 2000; for review see Schütz-Bosbach & Prinz, 2007). For instance, Kilner and colleagues (2003) asked participants to perform a sinusoidal arm movement while they observed similar movements performed by another person that were either congruent or incongruent with their own movements. Strong interference effects resulted, that is, participants' movements tended to become more variable when the observed movements were incongruent to the movements concurrently produced by the participant.

Evidence for motor involvement has also been provided by neurophysiological studies. The most prominent examples are mirror neurons, found in monkey premotor and parietal cortices. These neurons respond when the monkey performs an object-directed action and when the monkey perceives the same action performed by someone else (e.g., di Pellegrino et al., 1992; Gallese, Fadiga, Fogassi, & Rizzolatti, 2002; Nelissen, Luppino, Vanduffel, Rizzolatti, & Orban, 2005; Umiltà et al., 2001). Thus, mirror neurons code the execution of actions and the perception of similar actions—even when the monkey does not execute overt behavior.

There is converging evidence for a mirror system also in humans. When humans observe actions of others, neural activity increases in a cortical network that is normally used for motor control. This mirror network includes parietal and premotor brain areas (e.g., Buccino et al., 2001, 2004; Grèzes & Decety, 2001) as well as the cerebellum (Calvo-Merino, Glaser, Grèzes, Passingham, & Haggard, 2005; Calvo-Merino, Grèzes, Glaser, Passingham, & Haggard, 2006).[2] Whereas mirror neurons in monkeys mainly respond to object-directed (transitive) but not to intransitive actions (for an exception see Ferrari, Gallese, Rizzolatti, & Fogassi, 2003), motor activations in humans are less strictly bound to transitive actions. Motor activations also occur when complex, intransitive whole-body movements, such as dancing, are observed. The activation is greater for subjects who are motor experts for the movements they observe (Calvo-Merino et al., 2005, 2006; Casile & Giese, 2006; Cross, Hamilton, & Grafton, 2006), indicating that mental simulation of action involves the observer's own motor repertoire. In other words, we apparently use our motor memories to run a simulation of the observed movement. Finally, patients with frontal lobe lesions sometimes show an automatic and uncontrollable tendency to overtly imitate actions they observe (Brass, Derrfuss, Matthes-von Cramon, & von Cramon, 2003; De Renzi, Cavalleri, & Facchini, 1996).

Possible Functions

Why does the motor system of the observer internally simulate the actions performed by others? Several possible functions of these simulation processes have been suggested. Action simulation can facilitate overt imitation, and thus, may provide the basis for imitation learning (Iacoboni et al., 1999; for reviews, see Brass & Heyes, 2005; Prinz, 2002, 2005). Simulation may help us to understand the actions of others (Rizzolatti, Fogassi, & Gallese, 2001), even in terms of their underlying intentions (Blakemore & Decety, 2001; Fogassi et al., 2005; Iacoboni et al., 2005). Furthermore, the mirror system may subserve working memory functions (Wilson, 2001) and may play a role in the evolutionary development of language (Arbib, 2005). The most important function of action simulation, however, seems to lie in the *prediction* of others' actions (Blakemore & Frith, 2005; Csibra, 2007; Prinz, 2006; Sommerville & Decety, 2006; Wilson & Knoblich, 2005; Wolpert & Flanagan, 2001; see also de Vignemont & Singer, 2006; Pickering & Garrod, 2007; for an extension to the prediction of events, see Schubotz, 2007). Several studies point to a predictive function of the motor system in action perception. For instance, when subjects observe an actor performing a block stacking task, the coordination between the observer's gaze and the actor's hand is predictive, rather than reactive (Flanagan & Johansson, 2003). That is, observers showed a proactive gaze behavior, which was highly similar to the gaze–hand coordination when they performed the task themselves. Motor-related areas in the observer's brain are activated even before the action of the actor is initiated, provided that the onset of the action can reliably be predicted (Haueisen & Knösche, 2001; Kilner, Vargas, Duval, Blakemore, & Sirigu, 2004). Moreover, a subset of mirror neurons respond even when the final part of an observed action is hidden by an occluder and can therefore only be inferred (Umiltà et al., 2001).

Why should the motor system be involved in predictive tasks? For accurate visuomotor control it is fundamental to know the current state of one's body. However, sensory signals that convey information about body states are delayed due to receptor transduction, neural conduction, and central processing. Therefore, if one would rely solely on sensory information to estimate the current state of the body, behavioral errors could occur, especially in situations in which rapid motor responses are required. Alternatively, the present state of the body could be estimated by using predictive algorithms based on efference copies of motor commands. The estimate can then be made ahead of the movement, which solves the time delay problem. In order to fulfill this function, predictive (forward) models need to operate time locked to ongoing real events. In other words, forward models need to proceed in real-time to predict the sensory consequences of actions correctly (e.g., Wolpert & Flanagan, 2001). Several researchers have proposed that those real-time forward models, which normally control motor behavior, may also be involved in perceptual tasks, such as predicting the actions of others (Blakemore & Frith, 2005; Grush, 2004; Prinz, 2006; Wolpert, Doya, & Kawato, 2003; Wolpert & Flanagan, 2001).

Recent evidence supports the assumption of real-time simulation in action prediction (Graf et al., 2007). In this study, participants observed brief videos of point-light actions, followed by an occluder and a subsequent static test posture of the point-light figure. Both the duration of the occluder and the movement gap (i.e., the time between the endpoint of the action and the test posture) were varied. Prediction performance was best when occluder time and movement gap corresponded, that is, when the test posture was a continuation of the movement sequence that matched the occluder duration. These findings suggest that perceptual action prediction involves a simulation process that operates in real time.

Internal simulation is not only relevant for the prediction of actions, but also for the recognition of intentions implied by actions of others. Studies have demonstrated motor contributions to inferences of action-related intentions of other persons (Fogassi et al., 2005; Iacoboni et al., 2005). The processing of others' intentions seems to be based also on a mental simulation of the action that expresses a certain intention of the actor (for review, see Blakemore & Decety, 2001). It has been proposed that the associations between our own intentions and corresponding motor acts can be used to infer the intentions of others. Again, these simulation processes appear to involve prediction. Understanding of others' intentions is, by definition, a predictive endeavor, because intentions point to the future, and thus involve a predictive component.

Similarity

The evidence discussed so far strongly relies on the concept of similarity. If observers mentally simulate observed actions by mirroring them in their motor system, then the underlying motor representations need to code for the same or similar actions. In other words, the coding is based on a similarity relationship between actions observed in others and performed by oneself (e.g., Grèzes, Frith, & Passingham, 2004; Knoblich & Flach, 2003; Kornblum, Hassbroucq, & Osman, 1990).

MOTOR INVOLVEMENT IN OBJECT PERCEPTION: COMPLEMENTARITY

Most work related to the role of motor aspects in perception has focused on the domain of action observation. However, some studies have investigated the involvement of motor representations in the perception of manipulable objects, that is, objects with which we interact. We will argue that the perception of manipulable objects is based on a complementary relationship between the shape of the object and the actions it affords. For instance, a power grip is complementary to the shape and the orientation of a bar that the hand encompasses.

Perception Primes Action

One important line of evidence for a strong link between object perception and action comes from neurophysiology. So-called canonical neurons in area F5 in monkey premotor cortex respond to specific object shapes (even when the monkey is not required to act on that object) and to types of motor actions corresponding with these shapes (Murata et al., 1997). Neurons that are tuned to both shapes and actions have been found not only in premotor areas but also in parietal cortex in the anterior intraparietal area (AIP; Murata et al., 2000). Thus, a neural network is activated that is similar to the mirror system, involving (pre)motor and parietal areas (Murata et al., 1997; see also Rizzolatti, Fogassi, & Gallese, 2002).

In accordance with these findings, imaging studies in (right-handed) humans show that the perception of man-made manipulable objects, such as tools, activates not only object-related areas in the ventral visual stream, but also the left premotor cortex and the left parietal lobe (Chao & Martin, 2000; Grèzes & Decety, 2002; Grèzes, Tucker et al., 2003; Martin et al., 1996). This has been demonstrated for a variety of tasks, like passive viewing, categorizing, and silent naming of objects. Activation of motor areas in object categorization tasks have also been found in EEG studies looking at event-related potentials (e.g., Kiefer, 2001, 2005). Interestingly, the motor-related areas involved in tool naming are very similar to those areas that are activated when participants name actions associated with certain objects (Martin et al., 1995), process action verbs (Hauk, Johnsrude, & Pulvermüller, 2004; Hauk & Pulvermüller, 2004), draw upon information about object manipulation (Boronat et al., 2005), or imagine interacting with objects (Decety et al., 1994). These observations are consistent with the view that action-related information is particularly important for representing manipulable objects (Farah & McClelland, 1991; Kiefer & Spitzer, 2001; Warrington & Shallice, 1984).

Like action perception, the processing of object affordances seems to depend on experience and expertise. Viewing photos of cigarettes, for example, induced an increased activation in motor-related areas in the brains of smokers (Smolka et al., 2006). The extent of motor activation was correlated with severity of nicotine dependence, as measured by self-report, suggesting that perceiving cigarettes may have facilitated grasping actions in smokers.

The impact of action affordances has also been investigated in visuomotor priming tasks (e.g., Craighero, Fadiga, Rizzolatti, & Umilta, 1999; Grèzes, Tucker, et al., 2003; Pavese & Buxbaum, 2002; Phillips & Ward, 2002; Tucker & Ellis, 1998, 2001, 2004). These studies show that viewing manipulable objects more or less automatically activates representations of actions that are associated with the typical use of the object, or which are afforded by visual object properties. In one of their experimental studies on visuomotor priming Tucker and Ellis (2001) required participants to categorize objects as biological or artificial (man-made) by responding with either a power grip or a precision grip. Critically, the type of response was either compatible or incompatible to the size of the object. Although the size of the object was irrelevant to the task, participants showed a better performance when response type and object size were compatible. That is, reaction times (RTs) were faster when subjects had to respond to a large object with a power grip rather then with a precision grip.[3] In general, visual priming is reminiscent of so-called utilization behavior (Lhermitte, 1983, 1986) that is sometimes observed in patients with frontal lobe damage. These patients have difficulties in resisting the impulse to "utilize" objects that are located within their visual field and within their reaching space.

Action Primes Perception

Although these studies suggest that perceiving manipulable objects is accompanied by motor activations, they do not allow the stronger conclusion that object recognition can be facilitated by motor activations. Functional MRI has a low temporal resolution, and therefore the activations in the motor system may have occurred after the recognition, and thus, may not be functionally or causally involved in the process of object recognition itself. Similarly, visuomotor priming effects may simply be a consequence of visual object recognition. Action-related effects on object recognition were tested directly with an action priming paradigm that used highly familiar objects with overlearned action associations (Helbig et al., 2006). Two briefly displayed masked objects were presented sequentially, either affording congruent or incongruent motor actions. Naming accuracy was superior for object pairs with congruent as compared to incongruent motor interactions (Experiment 1). Thus, the recognition of the second object was facilitated when the first object afforded a similar motor interaction. The effect was absent when the prime stimulus was presented as a word (Experiment 2), suggesting that visuomotor action representations rather than semantic action knowledge underlie the action priming effect. Together, the results provide first evidence that action representations are functionally involved in the recognition of manipulable objects. Note that the action priming effect has been observed although subjects were not instructed to interact with the objects, but simply had to name them. The action priming effect in object recognition was confirmed in a study that investigated event-related potentials (ERPs) using the same stimuli and a similar task. An effect of action congruency on ERPs started at about 100 ms after the onset of the target object at fronto-central electrodes close to the motor cortex. This early congruency effect was absent when the first stimulus was a word rather than an object (Kiefer, Sim, Helbig, & Graf, 2008). Moreover, a further behavioral study demonstrated that simply observing an action can prime object recognition (Helbig, Steinwender, Graf, & Kiefer, in press). Participants viewed a short video clip showing hands performing an action, and subsequently had to perform a picture–word matching task. Recognition accuracy was higher when the target object afforded motor interactions that were similar (congruent condition) to the prime action, as compared to actions that were dissimilar (incongruent condition). This action priming effect appeared although the objects had been deleted from the video clips and were not visible, and even though the objects used in the recognition task were different from the objects used in the action sequences in the video clips (Helbig et al., 2010).

It should be noted, however, that a previous study failed to obtain clear evidence for an involvement of action knowledge in object recognition (Bub,

Masson, & Bukach, 2003). In this study, participants were required to learn gesture–color associations in a training phase. In a subsequent test phase objects were presented and participants had to perform either a gesture in response to the object's color or identity, or they just had to name the object. The gesture associated with a certain color was either congruent or incongruent with the gesture that is typically performed when using the object. Congruency effects on response latencies were found in action-related tasks (gesture-to-color and gesture-to-object tasks), whereas no such effect was found in the object recognition (naming) task. The absence of a congruency effect in the recognition task may be due to fact that the associations between colors and actions were arbitrary and not extensively trained, and thus may have influenced perception and action tasks differently.

Related Processing Principles

Given these strong interrelations between object perception and action it seems surprising that almost all current models of object recognition neglect motor aspects for recognition and rely on purely perceptual processes (Biederman, 1987; Edelman, 1998, 1999; Hummel & Biederman, 1992; Hummel & Stankiewicz, 1998; Perrett, Oram, & Ashbridge, 1998; Riesenhuber & Poggio, 1999, 2002; Wallis & Bülthoff, 1999; but see Graf, 2006). Along similar lines, functionally and neuroanatomically separate visual streams have been proposed that operate on the basis of fundamentally different processing principles (Goodale & Milner, 1992; Milner & Goodale, 1995). The studies reviewed here, however, suggest that the visual system and the motor system operate in close interaction (see also Creem & Proffitt, 2001; Goodale & Haffenden, 2003). Furthermore, in contrast to the notion of strictly separate streams, the processing principles underlying object recognition and visuomotor control seem to be similar, both relying on coordinate transformations based on neural gain (amplitude) modulation (Graf, 2006). Orientation and size congruency effects in object recognition suggest that recognition involves the adjustment of a perceptual coordinate system. For instance, an object that is misoriented in the picture plane is recognized more easily when it is preceded by a different object shown in the same orientation (e.g., Gauthier & Tarr, 1997; Graf, Kaping, & Bülthoff, 2005; Jolicoeur, 1990, 1992; Tarr & Gauthier, 1998). Such congruency effects were found even for dissimilar objects, suggesting that the effects are not shape specific, but due to transformations of a coordinate system. In a similar vein, visuomotor control requires coordinate transformations, because sensor surfaces and effectors are coded in different coordinate systems, which constantly move relative to each other. Evidence for coordinate transformations as a processing principle both in object recognition and motor control has been found in behavioral and neurophysiological studies (for review, see Graf, 2006), and has been confirmed by neurocomputational modeling (Pouget & Sejnowski, 1997, 2001; Salinas & Abbott, 1997, 2001; Salinas & Sejnowski, 2001). The close interaction between object recognition and action, which is suggested by the studies reviewed in this section, is easier to account for when both systems rely on similar processing principles.

Complementarity

Similar to action perception, the motor activations involved in the perception of manipulable objects seem to rely on simulation processes (Gallese, 2003; Gallese & Lakoff, 2005; Tipper, Paul, & Hayes, 2006). Participants process action affordances of an object by running internal simulations of potential motor interactions with the particular object. Thus, the motor involvement also has a predictive function in object recognition as it helps to anticipate potential (or likely) motor interactions. In accordance with this predictive function of the motor system in perception it has been demonstrated that the premotor cortex is involved in serial prediction tasks, even for purely perceptual stimuli that cannot be mapped onto the human body (Schubotz & von Cramon, 2002, 2003, 2004; for review see Schubotz, 2007). These anticipations of potential motor interactions seem to feed back into the visual object recognition system (Helbig et al., 2006; Schubotz, 2007). It is important to note that motor interactions with an object are complementary to the shape of the object. Consequently, simulation processes in object perception rely on motor representations that are complementary to object shape.

MOTOR INVOLVEMENT IN ACTION PERCEPTION: COMPLEMENTARITY

After having reviewed motor aspects of object perception, based on the principle of complementarity, let us return to the domain of actions. In the first section we looked at action perception, focusing on the principle of similarity. We will now investigate whether the principle of complementarity is also fruitful for the domain of actions. Perceiving actions and manipulable objects both seem to involve simulation processes for prediction.[4] Prediction of upcoming events is clearly indispensable for action planning, as it helps to rapidly select an appropriate response. However, appropriate responses are in most cases not just imitative, but are often complementary to an observed action, especially in social interactions (see Csibra, 2005, 2007; Jacob & Jeannerod, 2005). Although we often unconsciously mimic (or mirror) others' behavior (for reviews see, e.g., Prinz, 2002, 2005; Sommerville & Decety, 2006; Wilson & Knoblich, 2005), human interaction typically means to respond to someone else's action in a complementary way. Thus, the predictive function of simulation is truly functional if it includes the planning of actions that are complementary to observed actions.

Kata and kumite, the two basic training forms in karate training, are an example of similarity and complementarity relations, respectively. Whereas kata is the imitation of a sequence of karate movements, kumite means to respond to the opponent's movements, and thus act in a complementary way, for instance, by blocking the opponent's attack. Basic forms of human interaction, such as turn-taking, require complementary behavior. In general, behavior in communicative situations is not only imitative, but involves responsive reactions and thus complementary actions (see Csibra, 2005, 2007; Jacob & Jeannerod, 2005). In joint-action situations, actions need to be coordinated, and responses are required that are complementary to the actions of others (Newman-Norlund, van Schie, van Zuijlen, & Bekkering, 2007; Sebanz, Bekkering, & Knoblich, 2006; van Schie, van Waterschoot, & Bekkering, 2008; for review see Newman-Norlund, Noordzij, Meulenbroek, & Bekkering, 2007). Therefore, complementary actions have a tremendous functional importance for human interaction.

Evidence

Recent studies provide first evidence that the human mirror neuron system is involved in coding complementary actions. In an fMRI experiment participants were required to prepare imitative or complementary actions in a joint action situation (Newman-Norlund, van Schie, et al., 2007). Participants repeatedly viewed an actor grasping a manipulandum using either a power or a precision grip. Subjects were required to respond either by imitating the action or by performing a complementary action. Remarkably, the authors found stronger cortical activity in the mirror system (i.e., right inferior frontal gyrus and bilateral inferior parietal lobes) when participants were preparing for a complementary as opposed to an imitative action. This stronger activation for complementary actions is consistent with the higher number of broadly congruent (2/3) as compared to strictly congruent (1/3) mirror neurons (Newman-Norlund, Noordzij, et al., 2007; Rizzolatti & Craighero, 2004). Related to this, a further fMRI study examined brain activation in a single action versus joint action situation (Newman-Norlund, Meulerbroek, & Bekkering, 2008). In this study, participants were asked to lift and balance a virtual bar either alone or cooperatively with another person. Although there were no differences between the single and joint condition with respect to accuracy, differences in brain activations were found in the mirror system. Specifically, the joint-action condition engaged right inferior parietal and inferior frontal gyri to a greater extent than the solo action condition. Together both studies suggest that the mirror system is not only involved in coding imitative actions, but generally couples action observation with action execution, and thus also codes complementary actions.

Brain activity during the recognition of cooperative actions between two persons was also studied by using near-infrared spectroscopy (Shibata, Suzuki, & Gyoba, 2007). Video clips were shown in which a person passed an object to another person and participants were requested to rate the appropriateness of the hand-motion pattern of the receiver. The relative oxyhemoglobin concentrations in regions belonging to the mirror system (i.e., the inferior frontal and precentral areas) were measured by near-infrared spectroscopy. Oxyhemoglobin concentrations increased to a greater extent during the observation of appropriate as compared to inappropriate receiving actions. This result again suggests that the mirror system is involved in the comprehension of cooperative, that is, complementary, actions.

Supporting evidence comes from single-cell studies. In one of the first papers on mirror neurons, di Pelligrino et al. (1992) reported that about 38% of all mirror neurons in area F5 were "broadly tuned" or "logically related." That is, they respond when the monkey sees someone else performing a certain action, and they also fire when the monkey performs a different action that could logically follow the observed one, and thus is potentially complementary to the observed action. For instance, the effective observed action was placing an object on the table, while the effective executed action was bringing food to the mouth or grasping the object (di Pellegrino et al., 1992, p. 179; Fogassi & Gallese, 2002, p. 19; see also Csibra, 2005, 2007). Further studies suggest that about 60% of mirror neurons are broadly congruent or logically related (for review, see Rizzolatti & Craighero, 2004; for related findings, see Fogassi et al., 2005; Iacoboni et al., 2005).

Evidence for the representation of complementary actions has also been found in behavioral studies. Complementary actions were, for example, investigated in a joint-action setting (van Schie et al., 2008). The rationale of this study was as follows: When someone passes you a cup while holding it at its handle (with a precision grip), it is obvious to select a complementary action such as grasping the cup at its body (using a power grip). The authors investigated whether such complementary stimulus–response associations can outpace imitative response tendencies. They instructed participants to grasp a response device at its top or bottom. The device consisted of a small cylinder (to be grasped with a precision grip) that was mounted on top of a big cylinder (to be grasped with a power grip). At the beginning of each trial participants observed a virtual coactor displayed on a computer screen who either grasped the large or the small cylinder. In the imitation condition participants had to imitate the grasping behavior of the virtual coactor, whereas in the complementary action condition participants had to perform the action that was opposite to the coactor's action. As expected from previous studies (e.g., Brass et al., 2000, 2001), clear reaction time advantages were found for the imitation condition. More important, in 40% of the trials participants were required to perform a predefined action independent of the coactor's action, that is, either a precision or power grip in response to a color cue. Critically, the action of the participant was either the same or complementary (opposite) to the posture of the model. The authors now found a clear reaction time advantage when subjects prepared for an action that was complementary to the model's action. This indicates that action observation does not necessarily introduce an automatic imitative bias, but can also prime complementary actions (see also Catmur, Walsh, & Heyes, 2007).

Further support for the representation of complementary actions has been found in a visual detection task (Neri, Luu, & Levi, 2006). Sequences of two interacting actors were presented as masked point-light displays. The point-light displays showed both actors either acting in synchrony or in asynchrony with respect to the timing. Participants saw two intervals containing either one or two actors and were asked to select the interval in which two actors were present. Visual detection performance was better in the synchronous condition, even though there was no formal need to consider the temporal matching of the two displays. These effects were found for antagonistic actions (e.g., fighting) and cooperative actions (e.g., dancing). Control experiments ruled out explanations in terms of low-level motion information, or interagent occlusion. The synchronized and desynchronized stimuli were matched in all respects apart from interagent relationships. Moreover, there was a negative correlation between the ratio of the synchrony/asynchrony thresholds and explicit judgments about the meaningfulness of the actions.

Neri et al. (2006) concluded that the synchronicity effect is a consequence of human implicit knowledge about how actions of interacting agents are related.

The representation of complementary actions influences one's own actions even when there is no need to take the other agent into account (Sebanz, Knoblich, & Prinz, 2003). Sebanz et al. (2003) distributed a spatial compatibility task between two people so that each participant took care of one of two responses. The participants' task was to respond to a color change of a ring on a finger on the screen that pointed either to the left or right. Critically, one participant was required to respond to a green ring and the confederate was asked to respond to a red ring. Interestingly, a spatial compatibility effect occurred in this situation. That is, the participant who, for example, attended to the red ring responded faster when the finger was pointing in his direction. This effect did not occur when the identical task was performed by one of the participants alone. Moreover, the Simon-like effect only emerged when participants coacted with a biological agent, but not with a wooden hand (Tsai & Brass, 2007). These results suggest that one's own and others' actions are represented in a functionally equivalent way and that complementary responses are represented in a shared task.

Further evidence for the coding of complementary actions can be derived from experiments investigating ideomotor movements in cooperative and competitive task settings (Häberle, Schütz-Bosbach, Laboissière, & Prinz, 2008). Ideomotor movements are bodily movements that can automatically arise in observers while they watch other people's actions (e.g., pressing phantom brakes when a driver approaches a traffic light too quickly). In the competitive settings, observers were instructed such that their intentions were opposite to the intentions of the observed agents. The results indicate that, although observers understood the intentions of others, their ideomotor movements were guided by their own intentions, and not by the intentions of the observed agents. Thus, the observers did not simply imitate the observed agents, but the observers' ideomotor movements were complementary to the observed actions (and intentions).

Evidence for the coding of similar but also complementary actions comes also from social psychology. In line with the similarity account, it has been found that priming with a social category can lead individuals to behave in a similar way as members of this category (Dijksterhuis & Bargh, 2001). The activation of the social category "elderly," for instance, led to a slower walking speed in young participants (Bargh, Chen, & Burrows, 1996). More important here, social categories can also prime complementary behavioral responses toward members of this social group (Jonas & Sassenberg, 2006). In a lexical decision task participants were first primed with a social category and then had to decide whether a target word was either a predicate or an object. Recognition of predicates that described a complementary response behavior was facilitated for matching as compared to mismatching social category primes. In other words, when a sick individual goes to see a doctor for treatment in a foreign town, he or she still knows how to properly react toward this member of the social category of "doctors." Accordingly, the word "doctor" primed the processing of words describing complementary actions toward doctors.

Mechanisms

Together, a growing body of evidence suggests the importance of coding complementary actions, but how are complementary actions represented in our mind and brains? There are at least two ways in which complementary actions can be coded (see Figure 3.1). First, the observation of an action leads to an internal simulation which mirrors that particular action in order to predict how it will continue. In a subsequent step (or maybe concurrently), complementary actions are primed or activated in response to the observed (or predicted) action (see Fogassi et al., 2005; Iacoboni et al., 2005; Figure 3.1a). This indirect coding scheme is flexible and allows the coding of a variety of potential responses to an observed action. Although the coding is indirect, it may still be relatively fast due to the real-time aspect of action prediction.

Second, we propose that there may also be a more direct route for the coding of complementary actions. The observation of an action may directly activate a complementary action representation (Figure 3.1b). Thus, with respect to its motor aspects, the visually perceived action is represented by its complementary response. In other words, the motor system supports the visual system by internally simulating behavior that is complementary to the observed behavior. In a karate master, for example, the observation of an opponent's punch may lead directly to the activation of a complementary (blocking) action. As there is *no intermediate* mirror (or "covert imitation") process interposed, the response can occur faster. So far

Figure 3.1 Indirect and direct route for coding of complementary actions. The fighter on the right-hand side attacks. The thought bubbles represent the internal simulation in the motor system of the attacked fighter (on the left-hand side). (a) In the indirect route, the attacked fighter first internally simulates the aggressor's punch by mirroring (or "covertly imitating") it, and then, in a next step, prepares to block the attack as a complementary response. (b) In the direct route, the attacked fighter directly simulates the block as a complementary response to the opponent's punch.

there is no evidence that would allow one to decide between these two alternative processing routes. Note that they are not mutually exclusive. It rather seems reasonable that with growing expertise an individual switches from an indirect to a more direct encoding of complementary actions. Both coding schemes raise the interesting question of whether one's own complementary actions are planned in the same representational medium in which the external (observed) actions are represented. This would require that the mirror network in premotor and parietal areas (1) can simultaneously represent several actions, and (2) keep these actions apart by elaborate binding mechanisms (see Newman-Norlund, Noordzij, et al., 2007). Both the aggressor attacking me needs to be internally simulated, and at the same time my complementary response has to be planned in the same representational medium—maybe even based on the same simulation. This necessity for the representation of multiple actions seems to be a general challenge in joint-action situations (Newman-Norlund, Noordzij, et al., 2007), not only when complementary but also when similar (mirror) actions need to be performed (e.g., in action synchronization).

A complementary relationship between an observed and to-be-executed action relies on interactive experiences and learned associations. These learning-based relations are in contrast to a proposed innate direct imitative mapping of one's own and others' actions on the basis of similarity (Meltzoff & Moore, 1977, 1989). And indeed, a recent study elegantly showed activations in the mirror system not only when observed and performed actions were similar, but also when they were arbitrarily connected by associative learning (Catmur et al., 2007). The authors used TMS to induce motor evoked potentials (MEPs) in the abductor muscles of participants' hands. They replicated the typical mirror findings: The MEP amplitudes recorded from the subject's index finger muscle were greater when they watched a video of a hand moving the index finger, and the MEP amplitudes recorded from the subject's little finger muscle were greater when the video showed movement of the little finger (cf. e.g., Fadiga, Fogassi, Pavesi, & Rizzolatti, 1995). Most important, participants were then trained to perform movements that were incongruent to the hand movements they saw in the video. That is, they were asked to move the little finger in response to index finger movements on screen and vice versa. Remarkably, after this training procedure, the MEP modulation followed this newly learned association; the MEP amplitudes were now greater in the little finger muscle during the observation of index finger movements and vice versa. These newly acquired associations between an observed and to-be-executed movement turned the mirror system in a way into a "countermirror system" that operated against the natural tendency to mirror or imitate an observed action.

Conclusion and Open Questions

The representation of complementary actions can fulfill at least two important functions. First, it allows initiation of fast responses in competitive situations (e.g., fighting) and in action coordination between individuals (e.g., dancing; Csibra, 2007; Newman-Norlund, Noordzij, et al., 2007). In this sense the representation of complementary actions is similar to the perception of manipulable objects; in both cases the motor system needs to predict or anticipate upcoming interactions with the environment. Second, the representation of complementary actions may support the observation and prediction of interacting agents, and thus the understanding of social situations. For instance, when two agents interact in a complementary way, then the actions of one agent can provide implicit temporal cues that can be used to predict the expected trajectory of the other agent with higher precision (Neri et al., 2006). In both cases, the coding of complementary actions involves a predictive component. Both functions are directed into the future by connecting perceived behavior with a reactive response of the observer, either for response preparation or observation. In this way the coding of complementary actions allows fast processing (due to learned associative links; e.g., Brass & Heyes, 2005) and supports action planning processes.

Given its importance for social interaction, the domain of complementary actions and its underlying neurocognitive mechanisms need to be further addressed. An important question is, for instance, whether the coding of complementary actions is modulated by expertise. Alternatively, TMS might be useful to investigate whether the mirror system is causally involved in the coding of complementary actions. If complementary actions are "automatically" encoded, there may be clinical examples of automatic activation of actions complementary to those performed by others, analogous to frontal lobe patients showing an uncontrollable tendency to imitate (Brass et al., 2003; De Renzi et al., 1996) or utilization behavior as a result of seeing objects (Lhermitte, 1983, 1986). To our knowledge, an automatic activation of complementary actions has not yet been tested in patients, presumably because complementary actions have only recently gained scientific interest.

OUTLOOK

Internal simulation processes are not limited to the motor system, but researchers have extended similar ideas to the domain of emotions, suggesting a kind of emotional mirror system. Brain imaging studies have shown that observing emotions in others, for instance disgust, can lead to activations of cortical networks that are normally involved in the observer's experience of the same emotion (for reviews, see Decety & Jackson, 2004, 2006; de Vignemont & Singer, 2006). Mirror properties have been found also for sensations, like pain (Hutchison, Davis, Lozano, Tasker, & Dostrovsky, 1999; Singer et al., 2004). Interestingly, the predictive aspect seems important also for emotions. It has been proposed that empathy provides a more precise and direct estimate of other people's future actions because shared emotional networks elicit the activation of associated motivation and action systems. By sharing the emotional states of others, we also share their motivational significance, which allows better prediction. Following the same logic, one can also apply the principles of similarity and complementary to the emotional system. Prediction accuracy depends on the similarity between the emphasizer's and the target's emotional repertoires (Decety & Jackson, 2004). Furthermore, similarity modulates empathy; we tend to be more empathic with people that are similar to ourselves (e.g., Batson, Lishner, Cook, & Sawyer, 2005; Cialdini, Brown, Lewis, Luce, & Neuberg, 1997; Preston & de Waal, 2002). The notion of complementarity of emotions is reflected in the literature on behavioral complementarity in interpersonal relationships, charting responses within a circumplex ordering on complementary dimensions such as friendly–hostile or dominant–submissive (e.g., Carson, 1969; Kiesler, 1983, 1996; Leary, 1957). This notion has also found resonance in psychotherapy and clinical research (e.g., Benjamin, 1993; OPD Task Force, 2008). In accordance, complementarity has an important role in emotional processing. For instance, psychoanalytic theory suggests the existence of both concordant and complementary countertransference. In concordant countertransference the therapist identifies with the patient (or with some aspects of the patient's self-image) and shares her or his emotions (a similarity relationship). In contrast, complementary countertransference means that the therapist identifies with an (internalized) "attachment figure" of the patient, and thus adopts an emotional position that is complementary to the patient (Racker, 1968). For example, a fearful patient who has been severely punished and suppressed as a child may evoke sadistic impulses and anger in the therapist.

Finally, the coding of complementary actions and its importance for social interaction requires modification or extension of the metaphors that guide research in the field of action understanding. The resonance metaphor, which has often been used in this context (e.g., Gallese et al., 2004; Rizzolatti & Craighero, 2004; Rizzolatti, Fogassi, & Gallese, 2001; for a critical account, cf. Jacob, 2009), does not fully encompass the role of motor representations in action and object perception. In physics, resonance is the tendency of a system (e.g., a tuning fork) to oscillate at maximum amplitude when its eigenfrequency matches the excitation frequency of another object. Resonance has two basic features. First, it is an automatically arising response to the excitation frequency. Second, it relies on similarity between excitation frequency and eigenfrequency: It increases with increasing match between the two. Clearly, the idea of complementarity is not covered by this metaphor.

The same applies to the mirror metaphor. This metaphor also implies, or at least suggests, an automatic relationship between perception and action that is based on similarity (or even identity) between perceived and produced action, and it has no way to encompass a complementarity relationship between the two. Neither do the resonance and mirror metaphors account for motor processes in the perception of manipulable objects, which also rely on a complementarity relation. Therefore we propose to use the term *motor simulation* as the most general term indicating the involvement of motor representations in perception.

ACKNOWLEDGMENTS

Markus Graf is funded by a scholarship from the Max Planck Society.

NOTES

1. In addition to these motor-related areas, there is also activation in areas of the ventral visual stream, such as the superior temporal sulcus, which is involved in conscious perception or recognition (e.g., Buccino et al., 2001, 2004; Grèzes & Decety, 2001; for review, see Rizzolatti & Craighero, 2004).
2. These affordance effects do not occur completely automatically but are mediated by attention. Only those properties of the visual stimulus can trigger certain actions that are actively attended by the observer (Tipper, Paul, & Hayes, 2006). For example,

when participants were asked to discriminate the shape of an object (which is an action-relevant feature), clear action affordance effects were observed. In contrast, when participants were required to discriminate the color of an object (which was not relevant for action), no affordance effects occurred.

3. Despite the similarities between action perception and object perception, there are also important differences. Actions have more pronounced temporal dynamics as compared to objects, because they typically involve systematic changes over time and are usually directed to a specific goal.

REFERENCES

Arbib, M. A. (2005). From monkey-like action recognition to human language: An evolutionary framework for neurolinguistics. *Behavioral and Brain Sciences, 28*, 105–124.

Bargh, J. A., Chen, M., & Burrows, L. (1996). Automaticity of social behavior: Direct effects of trait construct and stereotype activation on action. *Journal of Personality and Social Psychology, 71*, 230–244.

Barsalou, L. W. (1999). Perceptual symbol systems. *Behavioral and Brain Sciences, 22*, 577–609.

Barsalou, L. W., Simmons, W. K., Barbey, A., & Wilson, C. D. (2003). Grounding conceptual knowledge in modality-specific systems. *Trends in Cognitive Sciences, 7*, 84–91.

Batson, C. D., Lishner, D. A., Cook, J., & Sawyer, S. (2005). Similarity and nurturance: Two possible sources of empathy for strangers. *Basic and Applied Social Psychology, 27*, 15–25.

Benjamin, L. S. (1993). *Interpersonal diagnosis and treatment of personality disorders*. New York: Guilford.

Biederman, I. (1987). Recognition-by-components: A theory of human image understanding. *Psychological Review, 94*, 115–147.

Blakemore, S. J. & Decety, J. (2001). From the perception of action to the understanding of intention. *Nature Reviews Neuroscience, 2*, 561–567.

Blakemore, S. J. & Frith, C. (2005). The role of motor contagion in the prediction of action. *Neuropsychologia, 43*, 260–267.

Borghi, A. (2005). Object concepts and action. In D. Pecher & R. A. Zwaan (Eds.), *Grounding cognition: The role of perception and action in memory, language and thinking* (pp. 8–34). Cambridge, UK: Cambridge University Press.

Boronat, C. B., Buxbaum, L. J., Coslett, H. B., Tang, K., Saffran, E. M., Kimberg, D. Y., et al., (2005). Distinctions between manipulation and function knowledge of objects: Evidence from functional magnetic resonance imaging. *Brain Research: Cognitive Brain Research, 23*, 361–373.

Brass, M., Bekkering, H., & Prinz, W. (2001). Movement observation affects movement execution in a simple response task. *Acta Psychologica, 106*, 3–22.

Brass, M., Bekkering, H., Wohlschläger, A., & Prinz, W. (2000). Compatibility between observed and executed finger movements: Comparing symbolic, spatial, and imitative cues. *Brain and Cognition, 44*, 124–143.

Brass, M., Derrfuss, J., Matthes-von Cramon, G., & von Cramon, D. Y. (2003). Imitative response tendencies in patients with frontal brain lesions. *Neuropsychology, 17*, 265–271.

Brass, M. & Heyes, C. (2005). Imitation: Is cognitive neuroscience solving the correspondence problem? *Trends in Cognitive Sciences, 9*, 489–495.

Bub, D. N., Masson, M. E., & Bukach, C. M. (2003). Gesturing and naming: The use of functional knowledge in object identification. *Psychological Science, 14*, 467–472.

Buccino, G., Binkofski, F., Fink, G. R., Fadiga, L., Fogassi, L., Gallese, V., et al., Seitz, R. J., (2001). Action observation activates premotor and parietal areas in a somatotopic manner: An fMRI study. *European Journal of Neuroscience, 13*, 400–404.

Buccino, G., Vogt, S., Ritz, A., Fink, G. R., Zilles, K., Freund, H. J., et al., (2004). Neural circuits underlying imitation learning of hand actions: An event-related fMRI study. *Neuron, 42*, 323–334.

Calvo-Merino, B., Glaser, D. E., Grèzes, J., Passingham, R. E., & Haggard, P. (2005). Action observation and acquired motor skills: An fMRI study with expert dancers. *Cerebral Cortex, 15*, 1243–1249.

Calvo-Merino, B., Grèzes, J., Glaser, D. E., Passingham, R. E., & Haggard, P. (2006). Seeing or doing? Influence of visual and motor familiarity in action observation. *Current Biology, 16*, 1905–1910.

Carson, R. C. (1969). *Interaction concepts of personality*. Chicago: Aldine.

Casile, A. & Giese, M. A. (2006). Nonvisual motor training influences biological motion perception. *Current Biology, 16*, 69–74.

Catmur, C., Walsh, V., & Heyes, C. M. (2007). Sensorimotor learning configures the human mirror system. *Current Biology, 17*, 1527–1531.

Chao, L. L. & Martin, A. (2000). Representation of manipulable man-made objects in the dorsal stream. *NeuroImage, 12*, 478–484.

Chartrand, T. L. & Bargh, J. A. (1999). The chameleon effect: The perception–behavior link and social interaction. *Journal of Personality and Social Psychology, 76*, 893–910.

Cialdini, R., Brown, S., Lewis, B., Luce, C., & Neuberg, S. (1997). Reinterpreting the empathy–altruism relationship: When one into one equals oneness. *Journal of Personality and Social Psychology, 73*, 481–494.

Craighero, L., Fadiga, L., Rizzolatti, G., & Umilta, C. (1999). Action for perception: A motor-visual attentional effect. *Journal of Experimental Psychology: Human Perception and Performance, 25*, 1673–1692.

Creem, S. H. & Proffitt, D. R. (2001). Grasping objects by their handles: A necessary interaction between cognition and action. *Journal of Experimental Psychology: Human Perception and Performance, 27*, 218–228.

Cross, E. S., Hamilton, A. F., & Grafton, S. T. (2006). Building a motor simulation de novo: Observation of dance by dancers. *NeuroImage, 31*, 1257–1267.

Csibra, G. (2005). Mirror neurons and action observation. Is simulation involved? http://www.interdisciplines.org/mirror/papers/4

Csibra, G. (2007). Action mirroring and action understanding: An alternative account. In P. Haggard, Y. Rossetti, & M. Kawato (Eds.), *Sensorimotor foundations of higher cognition: Attention and performance XXII* (pp. 435–459). Oxford, UK: Oxford University Press.

Decety, J. & Jackson, P. L. (2004). The functional architecture of human empathy. *Behavioral and Cognitive Neuroscience Reviews, 3*, 71–100.

Decety, J. & Jackson, P. L. (2006). A social–neuroscience perspective on empathy. *Current Directions in Psychological Science, 15*, 54–58.

Decety, J., Perani, D., Jeannerod, M., Bettinardi, V., Tadary, B., Woods, R., et al., (1994). Mapping motor representations with positron emission tomography. *Nature, 371*, 600–602.

De Renzi, E., Cavalleri, F., & Facchini, S. (1996). Imitation and utilization behavior. *Journal of Neurology, Neurosurgery & Psychiatry, 61*, 396–400.

De Vignemont, F. & Singer, T. (2006). The empathic brain: How, when and why? *Trends in Cognitive Sciences, 10*, 435–441.

Dijksterhuis, A. & Bargh, J. A. (2001). The perception–behavior expressway: Automatic effects of social perception and social behavior. In M. P. Zanna (Ed.), *Advances in experimental social psychology* (Vol. 33, pp. 1–40). San Diego, CA: Academic Press.

Di Pellegrino, G., Fadiga, L., Fogassi, L., Gallese, V., & Rizzolatti, G. (1992). Understanding motor events: A neurophysiological study. *Experimental Brain Research, 91*, 176–180.

Edelman, S. (1998). Representation is representation of similarities. *Behavioral and Brain Sciences, 21*, 449–498.

Edelman, S. (1999). *Representation and recognition in vision*. Cambridge, MA: MIT Press.

Fadiga, L., Fogassi, L., Pavesi, G., & Rizzolatti, G. (1995). Motor facilitation during action observation: A magnetic stimulation study. *Journal of Neurophysiology, 73*, 2608–2611.

Farah, M. J. & McClelland, J. L. (1991). A computational model of semantic memory impairment: Modality specificity and emergent category specificity. *Journal of Experimental Psychology: General, 120*, 339–357.

Ferrari, P. F., Gallese, V., Rizzolatti, G., & Fogassi L. (2003). Mirror neurons responding to the observation of ingestive and communicative mouth actions in the monkey ventral premotor cortex. *European Journal of Neuroscience, 17*, 1703–1714.

Flanagan, J. R. & Johansson, R. S. (2003). Action plans used in action observation. *Nature, 424*, 769–771.

Fogassi, L., Ferrari, P. F., Gesierich, B., Rozzi, S., Chersi, F., & Rizzolatti, G. (2005). Parietal lobe: From action organization to intention understanding. *Science, 308*, 662–667.

Fogassi, L. & Gallese, V. (2002). The neural correlates of action understanding in non-human primates. In M. I. Stamenov & V. Gallese (Eds.), *Mirror neurons and the evolution of brain and language* (pp. 13–35). Amsterdam: John Benjamins.

Gallese, V. (2003). The manifold nature of interpersonal relations: The quest for a common mechanism. *Philosophical Transactions of the Royal Society B, 358*, 517–528.

Gallese, V., Fadiga, L., Fogassi, L., & Rizzolatti, G. (1996). Action recognition in the premotor cortex. *Brain, 119*, 593–609.

Gallese, V., Fadiga, L., Fogassi, L., & Rizzolatti, G. (2002). Action representation and the inferior parietal lobule. In W. Prinz & B. Hommel (Eds.), *Common mechanisms in perception and action: Attention and performance* (Vol. XIX, pp. 247–266). Oxford, UK: Oxford University Press.

Gallese, V. & Goldman, A. (1998). Mirror neurons and the simulation theory of mindreading. *Trends in Cognitive Sciences, 2*, 493–501.

Gallese, V. & Lakoff, G. (2005). The brain's concepts: The role of the sensory-motor system in conceptual knowledge. *Cognitive Neuropsychology, 22*, 455–479.

Gauthier, I. & Tarr, M. J. (1997). Orientation priming of novel shapes in the context of viewpoint-dependent recognition. *Perception, 26*, 51–73.

Gibson, J. J. (1950). *The perception of the visual world*. Boston: Houghton Mifflin.

Gibson, J. J. (1986). *The ecological approach to visual perception*. Hillsdale, NJ: Lawrence Erlbaum.

Goodale, M. A. & Haffenden, A. M. (2003). Interactions between the dorsal and ventral streams of visual processing. *Advances in Neurology, 93*, 249–267.

Goodale, M. A. & Milner, A. D. (1992). Separate visual pathways for perception and action. *Trends in Neurosciences, 15*, 20–25.

Graf, M. (2006). Coordinate transformations in object recognition. *Psychological Bulletin, 132*, 920–945.

Graf, M., Kaping, D., & Bülthoff, H. H. (2005). Orientation congruency effects for familiar objects: Coordinate transformations in object recognition. *Psychological Science, 16*, 214–221.

Graf, M., Reitzner, B., Corves, C., Casile, A., Giese, M., & Prinz, W. (2007). Predicting point-light actions in real-time. *NeuroImage, 36*, T22–T32.

Greenwald, A. G. (1970). Sensory feedback mechanisms in performance control: With special reference to the ideo-motor mechanism. *Psychological Review, 77*, 73–99.

Grèzes, J., Armony, J. L., Rowe, J., & Passingham, R. E. (2003). Activations related to "mirror" and "canonical" neurones in the human brain: An fMRI study. *NeuroImage, 18*, 928–937.

Grèzes, J. & Decety, J. (2001). Functional anatomy of execution, mental simulation, observation, and verb generation of actions: A meta-analysis. *Human Brain Mapping, 12*, 1–19.

Grèzes, J. & Decety, J. (2002). Does visual perception of object afford action? Evidence from a neuroimaging study. *Neuropsychologia, 40*, 212–222.

Grèzes, J., Frith, C. D., & Passingham, R. E. (2004). Inferring false beliefs from the actions of oneself and others: An fMRI study. *NeuroImage, 21*, 744–750.

Grèzes, J., Tucker, M., Armony, J., Ellis, R., & Passingham, R. E. (2003). Objects automatically potentiate action: An fMRI study of implicit processing. *European Journal of Neuroscience, 17*, 2735–2740.

Grush, R. (2004). The emulation theory of representation: Motor control, imagery, and perception. *Behavioral and Brain Sciences, 27*, 377–442.

Häberle, A., Schütz-Bosbach, S., Laboissière, R., & Prinz, W. (2008). Ideomotor action in cooperative and competitive settings. *Social Neuroscience, 3*, 26–36.

Hamilton, A., Wolpert, D., & Frith, U. (2004). Your own action influences how you perceive another person's action. *Current Biology, 14*, 493–498.

Hatfield, E., Cacioppo, J. T., & Rapson, R. L. (1994). *Emotional contagion*. New York: Cambridge University Press.

Haueisen, J. & Knösche, T. R. (2001). Involuntary motor activity in pianists evoked by music perception. *Journal of Cognitive Neuroscience, 13*, 786–792.

Hauk, O., Johnsrude, I., & Pulvermüller, F. (2004). Somatotopic representation of action words in human motor and premotor cortex. *Neuron, 41*, 301–307.

Hauk, O. & Pulvermüller, F. (2004). Neurophysiological distinction of action words in the fronto-central cortex. *Human Brain Mapping, 21*, 191–201.

Helbig, H. B., Graf, M., & Kiefer, M. (2006). The role of action representations in visual object recognition. *Experimental Brain Research, 174*, 221–228.

Helbig, H. B., Steinwender, J., Graf, M., & Kiefer, M. (2010). Action observation can prime visual object recognition. *Experimental Brain Research, 200*, 251–258.

Heyes, C. M., Bird, G., Johnson, H., & Haggard, P. (2005). Experience modulates automatic imitation. *Cognitive Brain Research*, 22, 233–240.

Hommel, B., Müsseler, J., Aschersleben, G., & Prinz, W. (2001). The theory of event coding (TEC): A framework for perception and action planning. *Behavioral and Brain Sciences, 24*, 849–937.

Hummel, J. E., & Biederman, I. (1992). Dynamic binding in a neural network for shape recognition. *Psychological Review, 99*, 480–517.

Hummel, J. E. & Stankiewicz, B. J. (1998). Two roles for attention in shape perception: A structural description model of visual scrutiny. *Visual Cognition, 5*, 49–79.

Hutchison, W. D., Davis, K. D., Lozano, A. M., Tasker, R. R., & Dostrovsky, J. O. (1999). Pain-related neurons in the human cingulate cortex. *Nature Neuroscience, 2*, 403–405.

Iacoboni, M., Molnar-Szakacs, I., Gallese, V., Buccino, G., Mazziotta, J. C., & Rizzolatti, G. (2005). Grasping the intentions of others with one's own mirror neuron system. *PLoS Biology, 3, e79*, 0529–0535.

Iacoboni, M., Woods, R. P., Brass, M., Bekkering, H., Mazziotta, J. C., & Rizzolatti, G. (1999). Cortical mechanisms of human imitation. *Science, 286*, 2526–2528.

Jacob, P. (2009). The tuning-fork model of human social cognition: A critique. *Consciousness and Cognition, 18*, 229–243.

Jacob, P. & Jeannerod, M. (2005). The motor theory of social cognition: A critique. *Trends in Cognitive Sciences, 9*, 21–25.

James, W. (1890). *The principles of psychology*. New York: MaxMillan.

Jeannerod, M. (2001). Neural simulation of action: A unifying mechanism for motor cognition. *NeuroImage, 14*, S103–S109.

Jolicoeur, P. (1990). Orientation congruency effects on the identification of disoriented shapes. *Journal of Experimental Psychology: Human Perception and Performance, 16*, 351–364.

Jolicoeur, P. (1992). Orientation congruency effects in visual search. *Canadian Journal of Psychology, 46*, 280–305.

Jonas, K. J. & Sassenberg, K. (2006). Knowing how to react: Automatic response priming from social categories. *Journal of Personality and Social Psychology, 90*, 709–721.

Kiefer, M. (2001). Perceptual and semantic sources of category-specific effects: Event-related potentials during picture and word categorization. *Memory & Cognition, 29*, 100–116.

Kiefer, M. (2005). Repetition priming modulates category-related effects on event-related potentials: Further evidence for multiple cortical semantic systems. *Journal of Cognitive Neuroscience, 17*, 199–211.

Kiefer, M., Sim, E.-J., Helbig, H. B., & Graf, M. (in press). Tracking the time course of action, printing on object recognition: Evidence for fast and slow influences of action on perception. *Journal of cognitive Neuroscience.*

Kiefer, M. & Spitzer, M. (2001). The limits of a distributed account of conceptual knowledge. *Trends in Cognitive Sciences, 5*, 469–471.

Kiesler, D. J. (1983). The 1982 interpersonal circle: A taxonomy of complementarity in human transactions. *Psychological Review, 90*, 185–214.

Kiesler, D. J. (1996). *Contemporary interpersonal theory and research: Personality, psychopathology, and psychotherapy*. New York: Wiley.

Kilner, J. M., Hamilton, A. F., & Blakemore, S. J. (2007). Interference effect of observed human movement on action is due to velocity profile of biological motion. *Social Neuroscience, 2*, 158–166.

Kilner, J. M., Paulignan, Y., & Blakemore, S. J. (2003). An interference effect of observed biological movement on action. *Current Biology, 13*, 522–525.

Kilner J. M., Vargas, C., Duval, S., Blakemore, S. J., and Sirigu, A. (2004). Motor activation prior to observation of a predicted movement. *Nature Neuroscience, 7*, 1299–1301.

Knoblich, G. & Flach, R. (2003). Action identity: Evidence from self-recognition, prediction, and coordination. *Consciousness & Cognition, 12*, 620–632.

Kornblum, S., Hassbroucq, T., & Osman, A. (1990). Dimensional overlap: Cognitive bases for stimulus-response compatibility—a model and taxonomy. *Psychological Review, 97*, 253–270.

Leary, T. (1957). *Interpersonal diagnosis of personality*. New York: Ronald.

Lhermitte, F. (1983). "Utilisation behaviour" and its relation to lesions of the frontal lobes. *Brain, 106*, 237–255.

Lhermitte, F. (1986). Human autonomy and the frontal lobes. Part II: Patient behavior in complex and social situations: The "environmental dependency syndrome." *Annals of Neurology, 19*, 335–343.

Martin, A., Haxby, J. V., Lalonde, F. M., Wiggs, C. L., & Ungerleider, L. G. (1995). Discrete cortical regions associated with knowledge of color and knowledge of action. *Science, 270*, 102–105.

Martin, A., Wiggs, C. L., Ungerleider, L. G., & Haxby, J. V. (1996). Neural correlates of category-specific knowledge. *Nature, 379*, 649–652.

Meltzoff, A. N. & Moore, M. K. (1977). Imitation of facial and manual gestures by human neonates. *Science, 198*, 75–78.

Meltzoff, A. N. & Moore, M. K. (1989). Imitation in newborn infants: Exploring the range of gestures imitated and the underlying mechanisms. *Developmental Psychology, 25*, 954–962.

Milner, A. D. & Goodale, M. A. (1995). *The visual brain in action*. Oxford, UK: Oxford University Press.

Mukamel, R., Ekstrom, A. D., Kaplan, J., Iacoboni, M., & Fried, I. (2010). Single-neuron responses in humans during execution and observation of actions. *Current Biology*, 20, 750–756.

Murata, A., Fadiga, L., Fogassi, L., Gallese, V., Raos, V., & Rizzolatti, G. (1997). Object representation in the ventral premotor cortex (area F5) of the monkey. *Journal of Neurophysiology, 78*, 2226–2230.

Murata, A., Gallese, V., Luppino, G., Kaseda, M., & Sakata, H. (2000). Selectivity for the shape, size, and orientation of objects for grasping in neurons of monkey parietal area AIP. *Journal of Neurophysiology, 83*, 2580–2601.

Nelissen, K., Luppino, G., Vanduffel, W., Rizzolatti, G., & Orban, G. A. (2005). Observing others: Multiple action representation in the frontal lobe. *Science, 310*, 332–336.

Neri, P., Luu, J. Y., & Levi, D. M. (2006). Meaningful interactions can enhance visual discrimination of human agents. *Nature Neuroscience, 9*, 1186–1192.

Newman-Norlund, R. D., Meulenbroek, R. G., & Bekkering, H. (2008). Anatomical substrates of cooperative joint action: A continuous balancing task. *Neuroimage*, 41, 169–177.

Newman-Norlund, R. D., Noordzij, M. L., Meulenbroek, R. G. J., & Bekkering, H. (2007). Exploring the brain basis of joint action: Co-ordination of actions, goals and intentions. *Social Neuroscience, 2*, 48–65.

Newman-Norlund, R. D., van Schie, H. T., van Zuijlen, A. M. J., & Bekkering, H. (2007). The mirror neuron system is more active during complementary compared with imitative action. *Nature Neuroscience, 10*, 817–818.

Oberman, L. M., Pineda, J. A., & Ramachandran, V. S. (2007). The human mirror neuron system: A link between action observation and social skills. *Social Cognitive and Affective Neuroscience, 2*, 62–66.

OPD Task Force (Ed.). (2008). *Operationalized psychodynamic diagnosis OPD-2. Manual of diagnosis and treatment planning*. Göttingen, Germany: Hogrefe.

Pavese, A. & Buxbaum, L. J. (2002). Action matters: The role of action plans and object affordances in selection for action. *Visual Cognition, 9*, 559–590.

Perrett, D. I., Oram, W. M., & Ashbridge, E. (1998). Evidence accumulation in cell populations responsive to faces: An account of generalization of recognition without mental transformations. *Cognition, 67*, 111–145.

Phillips, J. C. & Ward, R. (2002). S-R correspondence effects of irrelevant visual affordance: Time course and specificity of response activation. *Visual Cognition, 9*, 540–558.

Pickering, M. J. & Garrod, S. (2007). Do people use language production to make predictions during comprehension? *Trends in Cognitive Sciences, 11*, 105–110.

Pouget, A. & Sejnowski, T. J. (1997). Spatial transformations in the parietal cortex using basis functions. *The Journal of Cognitive Neuroscience, 9*, 222–237.

Pouget, A. & Sejnowski, T. J. (2001). Simulating a lesion in a basis function model of spatial representations: Comparison with hemineglect. *Psychological Review, 108*, 653–673.

Preston, S. D. & de Waal, F. B. M. (2002). Empathy: Its ultimate and proximate bases. *Behavioral and Brain sciences*, 25, 1–72.

Prinz, W. (1990). A common coding approach to perception and action. In O. Neumann & W. Prinz (Eds.), *Relationships between perception and action: Current approaches* (pp. 167–201). Berlin: Springer-Verlag.

Prinz, W. (1997). Perception and action planning. *European Journal of Cognitive Psychology*, 9, 129–154.

Prinz, W. (2002). Experimental approaches to imitation. In A. N. Meltzoff & W. Prinz (Eds.), *The imitative mind: Development, evolution, and brain bases* (pp. 143–162). New York: Cambridge University Press.

Prinz, W. (2005). An ideomotor approach to imitation. In S. Hurley & N. Chater (Eds), *Perspectives on imitation. From neuroscience to social science—Volume 1: Mechanisms of imitation and imitation in animals* (pp. 141–156). Cambridge, MA: MIT Press.

Prinz, W. (2006). What re-enactment earns us. *Cortex, 42*, 515–517.

Prinz, W. (2008). Mirrors for embodied communication. In I. Wachsmuth, M. Lenzen, & G. Knoblich (Eds.), *Embodied communication in humans and machines*. Oxford, UK: Oxford University Press.

Racker, H. (1968). *Transference and countertransference*. New York: International Universities Press.

Ramachandran, V. S. (2000). Mirror neurons and imitation learning as the driving force behind "the great leap forward" in human evolution. *Edge*. http://www.edge.org/3rd_culture/ramachandran/ramachandran_p1.html

Riesenhuber, M. & Poggio, T. (1999). Hierarchical models of object recognition in cortex. *Nature Neuroscience, 2*, 1019–1025.

Riesenhuber, M. & Poggio, T. (2002). Neural mechanisms of object recognition. *Current Opinion in Neurobiology, 12*, 162–168.

Rizzolatti, G. & Craighero, L. (2004). The mirror-neuron system. *Annual Review of Neuroscience, 27*, 169–192.

Rizzolatti, G., Fogassi, L., & Gallese, V. (2001). Neurophysiological mechanisms underlying the understanding and imitation of action. *Nature Reviews Neuroscience, 2*, 661–670.

Rizzolatti, G., Fogassi, L., & Gallese, V. (2002). Motor and cognitive functions of the ventral premotor cortex. *Current Opinion in Neurobiology, 12*, 149–154.

Rizzolatti, G. & Sinigalia, C. (2007). *Mirrors in the brain: How our minds share actions and emotions*. New York: Oxford University Press.

Salinas, E. & Abbott, L. F. (1997). Invariant visual responses from attentional gain fields. *Journal of Neurophysiology, 77*, 3267–3272.

Salinas, E. & Abbott, L. F. (2001). Coordinate transformations in the visual system: How to generate gain fields and what to compute with them. In M. A. L. Nicolelis (Ed.), *Advances in neural population coding. Progress in brain research* (Vol. 130, pp. 175–190). Amsterdam: Elsevier.

Salinas, E. & Sejnowski, T. J. (2001). Gain modulation in the central nervous system: Where behavior, neurophysiology, and computation meet. *The Neuroscientist, 7*, 430–440.

Schubotz, R. I. (2007). Prediction of external events with our motor system: Towards a new framework. *Trends in Cognitive Sciences*, 11, 211–218.

Schubotz, R. I. & von Cramon, D. Y. (2002). Predicting perceptual events activates corresponding motor schemes in lateral premotor cortex: An fMRI study. *NeuroImage, 15*, 787–796.

Schubotz, R. I. & von Cramon, D. Y. (2003). Functional-anatomical concepts on human premotor cortex: Evidence from fMRI and PET studies. *NeuroImage, 20*, 120–131.

Schubotz, R. I. & von Cramon, D. Y. (2004). Sequences of abstract non-biological stimuli share ventral premotor cortex with action observation and imagery. *The Journal of Neuroscience, 24*, 5467–5474.

Schütz-Bosbach, S. & Prinz, W. (2007). Perceptual resonance: Action-induced modulation of perception. *Trends in Cognitive Sciences, 11*, 349–355.

Sebanz, N., Bekkering, H., & Knoblich, G. (2006). Joint action: Bodies and minds moving together. *Trends in Cognitive Sciences, 10*, 70–76.

Sebanz, N., Knoblich, G., & Prinz, W. (2003). Representing others' actions: Just like one's own? *Cognition, 88*, B11-B21.

Shibata, H., Suzuki, M., & Gyoba, J. (2007). Cortical activity during the recognition of cooperative actions. *Neuroreport, 18*, 697–701.

Singer, T., Seymour, B., O'Doherty, J., Kaube, H., Dolan, R. J., & Frith, C. D. (2004). Empathy for pain involves the affective but not sensory components of pain. *Science, 303*, 1157–1162.

Smolka, M. N., Bühler, M., Klein, S., Zimmermann, U., Mann, K., Heinz, A., et al., (2006). Severity of nicotine dependence modulates cue-induced brain activity in regions involved in motor preparation and imagery. *Psychopharmacology, 184*, 577–588.

Sommerville, J. A. & Decety, J. (2006). Weaving the fabric of social interaction: Articulating developmental psychology and cognitive neuroscience in the domain of motor cognition. *Psychonomic Bulletin & Review, 13*, 179–200.

Stürmer, B., Aschersleben, G., & Prinz, W. (2000). Correspondence effects with manual gestures and postures: A study of imitation. *Journal of Experimental Psychology: Human Perception and Performance, 26*, 1746–1759.

Tarr, M. J. & Gauthier, I. (1998). Do viewpoint-dependent mechanisms generalize across members of a class? *Cognition, 67*, 73–110.

Tipper, S. P., Paul, M. A., & Hayes, A. E. (2006). Vision-for-action: The effects of object property discrimination and action state on affordance compatibility effects. *Psychonomic Bulletin & Review, 13*, 493–498.

Tsai, J. & Brass, M. (2007). Does the human motor system simulate Pinocchio's actions? Co-acting with a human hand versus a wooden hand model in a dyadic interaction. *Psychological Science, 18*, 1058–1062.

Tucker, M. & Ellis, R. (1998). On the relations between seen objects and components of potential actions. *Journal of Experimental Psychology: Human Perception and Performance, 24*, 830–846.

Tucker, M. & Ellis, R. (2001). The potentiation of grasp types during visual object categorization. *Visual Cognition, 8*, 769–800.

Tucker, M. & Ellis, R. (2004). Action priming by briefly presented objects. *Acta Psychologica, 116*, 185–203.

Umiltà, M. A., Kohler, E., Gallese, V., Fogassi, L., Fadiga, L., Keysers, C., et al., (2001). I know what you are doing. A neurophysiological study. *Neuron, 31*, 155–165.

Van Schie, H. T., van Waterschoot, B. M., & Bekkering, H. (2008). Understanding action beyond imitation: Reversed compatibility effects of action observation in imitation and joint action. *Journal of Experimental Psychology: Human Perception and Performance, 34*, 1493–1500.

Wallis, G. & Bülthoff, H. (1999). Learning to recognize objects. *Trends in Cognitive Sciences, 3*, 22–31.

Warrington, E. K. & Shallice, T. (1984). Category specific semantic impairments. *Brain, 107*, 829–854.

Wilson, M. (2001). The case for sensorimotor coding in working memory. *Psychonomic Bulletin & Review, 8*, 44–57.

Wilson, M. & Knoblich, G. (2005). The case for motor involvement in perceiving conspecifics. *Psychological Bulletin, 131*, 460–473.

Wolpert, D. M., Doya, K., & Kawato, M. (2003). A unifying computational framework for motor control and social interaction. *Philosophical Transactions of the Royal Society of London B, 358*, 593–602.

Wolpert, D. M. & Flanagan, J. R. (2001). Motor prediction. *Current Biology, 11*, R729–R732.

4

Sociality, From an Ecological, Dynamical Perspective

KERRY L. MARSH

In a fiery plane crash in early August 2005, people evacuated the burning plane in about two minutes and as a result no lives were lost. In an editorial in the *New York Times*, one researcher wrote in an op-ed piece (Fischhoff, 2005),

> The Air France evacuation required an extraordinary degree of social coordination, which emerged among a group of strangers with virtually no time to prepare. Once out of the wreckage, they were aided by other strangers who, on the spur of the moment and with no expertise in emergency situations, had pulled off a nearby highway and calmly charged into the scene. … Indeed, the critical first responders in almost any crisis are ordinary citizens whom fate has brought together. As Kathleen Tierney, head of the University of Colorado's Natural Hazards Center, has noted, "The vast majority of live rescues are carried out by community residents who are at the scene of disasters, not by official response agencies or outside search and rescue teams."

As this example illustrates, coordinated action among strangers can emerge on-line, spontaneously, in response to demands of the situation, with no planning and little ability to strategize. Fundamental to this chapter is an understanding how such action is possible, and how we might best understand how individuals spontaneously form a cooperative unit to complete an action. That we are pulled to help others even when it may put ourselves at some risk implies that a pull toward others is rather fundamental to our social nature. Less obvious aspects of this example, however, are also informative about "sociality," or the pull toward connectedness with others. In particular, the example illustrates how much of our cooperation and coordination is "self-organized," that is, emerges out of basic ongoing dynamical processes rather than mediated by top-down, strategic processes. For goal-oriented tasks, even one as simple as taking a walk together, becoming a "plural subject" of action involves a simultaneous binding of wills (Gilbert, 1996). Some research discussed in this chapter, however, implies that the fundamental pull toward others can also be manifested in more mundane ways that are not goal driven. That is, individuals' tendency to coordinate even incidental movements with those around them—to move one's rocking chair in sync with another's, for instance—may well speak to the nature of sociality (see Marsh, Richardson, & Schmidt, 2009). In escaping a burning plane, although the situation urgently presses upon the victims the goal of escaping an enclosed, increasingly dangerous space safely, the swift accomplishment of this involves important perception and action processes neglected in social psychology. Individuals must automatically attend to the movements of those around them, and respond on-line in a synchronous or complementary fashion. Crucially, the perception of unfolding events and other's movements jointly determine and, conversely, are determined by, the perceiver's actions. This kind of view rather notably emphasizes overt behavior (e.g., embodied cooperation; Richardson, Marsh, & Baron, 2007) but, as well, body motion that may seemingly have only biological, not social, significance (Baumeister, Vohs, & Funder, 2007; Fowler, Richardson, Marsh, & Shockley, 2008; Schmidt & Richardson, 2008).

The perspective presented in this chapter is a new look at how ecological perception theory (Gibson, 1966; Gibson, 1979; Michaels & Carello, 1981; Richardson, Shockley, Fajen, Riley, & Turvey, 2008) can be instantiated in social psychological processes (Baron, 1980, 2007, 2009; Marsh, Johnston, Richardson, & Schmidt, 2009; Marsh, Richardson, Baron, & Schmidt, 2006; McArthur & Baron, 1983; Newtson, 1980, 1990, 1998), and it draws from tenets of dynamical systems approaches as well (Fuchs & Jirsa, 2008; Kelso, 1995; Nowak & Vallacher, 1998; Nowak, Vallacher, & Zochowski, 2005; Thelen & Smith, 1994; Vallacher & Nowak, 1994; Vallacher, Read, & Nowak, 2002; Warren, 2006).

This perspective yields the conclusion that a coordinated social unit, a temporary "we," is often an emergent phenomena rather than an intentional, cognitively mediated choice. In this chapter dynamical principles are first discussed, as they provide the means via which a social unit can come into being. Next are discussions of basic perception and action processes, conceptualized from an ecological perspective. Crucial to understanding self-organization is an understanding of how tightly intertwined, and inseparable, perception is from action. Inferential processes likely play a role in a plane rescue, as not all information will be available for rescuers to fully see what is happening; inferences about the situation may be required. But more important is to understand that cognitive processes emerged *in service* of action (van Dijk, Kerkhofs, van Rooij, & Haselager, 2008); action does not require mediation by some internal representational or simulation process (Marsh, Richardson, & Schmidt, 2009). Nor is perception mediated by inferences; perceptions precede inferences and strategic decisions. A great deal of information is available for an active perceiver—the victims' pain and fear, the difficulty of simultaneously exiting an enclosed space, the urgency of the situation. As one acts, perception is further transformed; one moves closer and sees new information; one's actions change the situation. As a rescuer removes an obstacle, what she sees is changed by her actions, and new perceptions and actions follow in turn.

Next in the chapter I discuss how a social unit emerges at crucial points where there are limits in individual abilities, when considered against environmental constraints. An ecological dynamical approach is fundamentally a functionally oriented account, one with similarity to Jamesian pragmatism (Heft, 2001). It is because of the situational demands, the presses the environment makes upon the individual, that individuals shift from solo to cooperative action. Rather critically, an ecological account predicts that it is quantifiable aspects of the environment *taken with respect* to the individual's capabilities that determine this shift. At crucial points when individual capabilities provide a poor fit to the demands of the environment, the presence of others nearby provides new possibilities for action, that is, new "affordances." A "we" can do things that solo "mes" cannot. A victim who was previously too heavy to carry alone can now be carried out of harm's way by a pair of rescuers. Qualitatively new ways of escaping a plane might be possible with multiple cooperating individuals than were not possible for a solitary individual. Two individuals could hold the end of a broken escape chute down while another pulls someone over a barrier at the top of the chute.

Finally in the chapter, recent research is discussed that illustrates how an ecological, dynamical account of sociality might proceed.

DYNAMICAL PRINCIPLES OF EMERGENCE

A simple claim of this perspective on sociality is that social units emerge spontaneously through self-organized processes. With the emergence of this social unit of being entirely new qualities, new modes of action are possible. The rich flexibility and adaptability of multiple minds and bodies acting in concert is in stark contrast to the chaos and turbulence we would imagine should result on an international flight where individuals may differ in age and thus abilities, may come from diverse countries and cultures, and likely have differing dispositions. There is a surprisingly easy unity with which we automatically fall into step with another, or navigate an unfamiliar task with others who are there to help.

Despite the incredible richness of new possibilities from being a "we," the unexpected ease with which this can occur, as in the plane escape, is telling. In particular it suggests that the processes by which a social synergy emerges, whether it be a temporary social bond, a brief positive or aversive interaction, or a lifetime connection, might not be different in kind from other dynamic structures that come into being spontaneously and flexibly as any organism interacts with its environment. Being able to rapidly become a functioning social unit may be as fundamental to our survival and as integral a part of our capabilities as it is for us to learn to walk and drum—to develop the skill to harness huge numbers of diverse within-body systems to complete a simple action. Universal principles of dynamics suggest that there are certain dynamical principles by which new states (e.g., coordination of one's arms and legs in walking, or a cooperative state between individuals) come into being that hold true *regardless* of the individual components that comprise the system. Although it may seem far-fetched to think, evidence supports the claim that the effortless coordination of innumerable muscles, joints, and tendons into a few coordinated states (e.g., when drumming) informs us how people, with no mechanical links between them, only informational linkages, coordinate (Schmidt & Richardson, 2008). Within the body, innumerable complexities and thus possibilities, or potential "degrees of freedom" (numbers of muscles, connections, and motor neurons) are pulled together, harnessed effortlessly, adaptively collapsing down to a temporary, unified structure that is elegantly describable by a few "collective" variables. A dynamical perspective suggests (and provides evidence) that the same logic holds true for social "collective" states—not merely in a metaphoric sense, but in a real sense, in terms of similar coordinated dynamics of movement.

A mystery of *action* has been how, given the nearly infinite possibilities for the way joints could theoretically move in combination, systems of the body work together so rapidly and coherently, and in some very constrained ways. It would seriously tax cognitive resources to rely on motor programs that could possibly provide the required flexibility (Warren, 2006). As for *perception*, the challenge for vision, for instance, was how we extract a coherent single object when each two-dimensional "snapshot" of what appears on the retina is incomplete. The classical answer has been to conceive of perception as a constructive process, but a quite taxing one indeed. If we allow that the perceiver might also be in motion and have an action task, perception as a constructive task seems even more insurmountable. From such a perspective, the incredible elegance of an outfielder catching a ball is a huge challenge—calculating where in space the ball is, where one's body is, and where one needs to run to catch the ball is a calculation nightmare.

The solution to these problems turns out to be the same one that essentially underlies an explanation for what it means for a social unit to spontaneously come into being. It requires (a) understanding of the issue that embodied, distributed social cognition has been tentatively approaching: how to truly *embed* humans in some context, and (b) understanding self-organization as well.

The first part of this issue, understanding what it means to be embedded in an environment, requires an understanding of basic ecological perception principles of perceiving and acting, discussed next. The second issue of emergence through dynamical principles is then discussed.

PERCEPTION

Many core misconceptions about perception reside in the assumption that the information for perceiving stimuli is impoverished. Our phenomenological experience is that when we catch a glimpse of a man walking down an aisle in a plane, partially obscured by a row of seats and then enter our aisle and sit down, we see the man as a coherent entity at all times. We also seem to readily separate what part of what we are seeing is man and non-man, and we automatically see that the chair's edges are partially occluding the man. Our phenomenological experience, however, is at odds with the fact that at each moment in time the two-dimensional image on the retina portrays different parts of the person and chairs. The traditional view of perception that predates Darwin (Heft, 2010) is that our phenomenology is wrong. Because each "snapshot" on the retina is different from one another, and all are incomplete, the mind must fill in the gaps, somehow sort out which patches of color are man and which are seats, and somehow piece together the images to produce coherent wholes.

This traditional, and still dominant, view is challenged by a well-validated theory about the richness of information available to an active perceiver in that environment. Ambient light, for instance, is a critical medium for information about the world for many creatures on our earth. We evolved in a world that is filled much of the time with an endless array of light bouncing off of every surface. Optical patterns created as light bounces off surfaces and edges of objects, and the transformations that occur, for instance, as the chair occludes part of the man, and then parts of the man come back into view, accurately specify that the seats are in front of the passenger, and that the seats and passenger are separate entities. Invariants in the optical patterns created as the passenger moves specify the unchanging part of that environment: the sameness of the passenger throughout the event. In the end, theorizing about the information available to be picked up by vision (and in other perceptual systems as well) required the radical recognition that there is a one-to-one correspondence between objects in the world and the structures in and transformations of a dynamic, changing array of light rays bouncing off objects. So long as the perceiver is allowed to be in motion,[1] there are invariants, structural persistence in the optic array over time, that specify properties of the world to the perceiver.

The development of James Gibson's ideas about extracting invariant patterns from the world for a dynamic perceiver was influenced by his attempt to address important applied problems near the middle of the 20th century, such as trying to figure out what information pilots needed to be able to land a plane (Gibson, 1947). It became clear that a constructivist view of how we see the world was not of practical significance in determining what information people normally use to see where they were heading and where they were in space; the approach was of no help in trying to decide how visual displays should be constructed for pilots. In many ways, the strongest evidence for the ecological view of perceiving has always been its utility—in figuring out what information a pilot needs to land a plane, or in figuring out how a robot can be built to move around an environment and pick up objects, or, for human factors researchers after the first World Trade Center bombing, figuring out how to redesign the WTC stairwells to provide better information for egress during fires (Fahy & Proulx, 1995). In sum, the information for perceiving is adequate. The crucial issue is that it requires dynamics to be able to pick up such invariants—the information mathematically specifies that a coherent object is present, but only as an event across time. Optical patterns relevant to vision exist over time, not as isolated snapshots in time, which then require reconstruction.

Another principle of an ecological, direct perception approach is that it demands that the scientist demonstrate that individuals are in fact *sensitive* to the specifying information. Thirty years of experiments systematically determining what the invariants are in vision or audition has been able to meet this demand—showing that people's perceptions (and actions) are quite sensitive to the invariants (Richardson, Shockley, et al., 2008).

Research has not been limited to examining nonsocial properties of the world but has also explored crucial features of individuals, especially those associated with broad and important categories of individuals. Such features include sex and age of face, and features critical to survival. Thus, negative versus positive emotional states of an individual, identity, sexual availability and state of fertility, and dispositional social tendencies (e.g., extroversion) are all variables that have been demonstrated to be specified in some visual or auditory information that observers are highly sensitive to and pick up accurately (see Marsh et al., 2006 for a review). Participants are even sensitive to subtle differences such as smiles that convey enjoyment versus staged smiles (Miles, 2009; Miles & Johnston, 2007).

To recap, the first two well-established principles of perception (Gibson, 1979; Michaels & Carello, 1981; Richardson, Shockley, et al., 2008) indicate that we do not have to reconstruct the world in our head in order to know it. Specifically, modern, evolution-informed views of perception recognize that (a) information is sufficiently rich to provide an adequate basis for perception and (b) we evolved sensory and action systems (ability to move our eyes, our heads, and our bodies to get the information flowing as is crucial for any invariants to be detectable) that allow accuracy in information pick-up. Reconstruction of the world in our head is not needed: We have the equipment to see the world, and the medium of ambient light (among other sources of information—such as auditory, haptic) is adequate for conveying of information.

Moreover, since other individuals are the most important aspects of our environment, we should presumably be particularly sensitive to invariants that specify properties of other people. Namely, we should be sensitive to invariants that specify stable attributes of people (the dominant focus of previous social ecological research; Marsh et al., 2006), but equally so to their current transient state, and the meaning and tenor of their current activities and motions. Even when we intentionally try to ignore the movements of others, we are unable to do so (Issartel, Marin, & Cadopi, 2007). How this sensitivity to changing features of others (their actions and their movement) links to the pull to connect with others, however, requires some unpacking.

First, note that this view is a deeply relational perspective: The abilities and needs of a person can only be understood *with reference to* the environment in which they are embedded (Järvilehto, 1998). Understanding that we see some aspects of the world directly is less difficult if we grasp that evolution carved *animal–environment systems*, or "niches," out of places. As a consequence creatures have sensory systems, the ability to move, and other abilities that reflect the exigencies and offerings of their niche. Therefore, humans' wants and yearnings tell us something not merely about their current deficient state, but inform us as well about the longer-term possibilities in their niche (but which happen to be immediately absent). Such states point to what their environment can normally provide, just as features of the environment such as opportunities for energy and shelter point to the existence of animals that will utilize these features.

Second, assume that the most critical features of the animal–environment system for humans are other humans, that for humans the niche is an animal–*animal*–environment system, a *social* niche (Marsh et al., 2006). Creatures with unmet biological needs must have sufficient drive or motives that impel them to act to seek in their environment for the nonsocial resources they need as well as the capabilities to detect invariants that specify such resources, and ability to act to obtain them. The logic surely holds true for social features of our niche: We must have highly evolved sensitivity to actions and movements of others, and the pull to attend to others. Moreover, if the hypothesis is correct that there are substantially new possibilities for action unique to the social unit, that some actions and needs can only be completed at this level, then it suggests that there should be a tendency for individuals to be pulled into a social unit of some kind. Such a bond might be a lasting one or only a temporary state of connection with others, a "social eddy" in which the motions of the individuals that compose the unit flow as a coherent whole.

Positing new possibilities for action at the level of the social unit follows a third principle of perception, from the theory of affordances (Gibson, 1977, 1979). Not only does information directly support detection of objects and surfaces, and relatedness of objects and surfaces (where things are relative to each other—what is behind, in front, a part of, and separate from), but information is sufficient to directly convey a host of what objects and surfaces *are good for*, what we personally can do with them, or what is termed "affordances" (Fajen, Riley, & Turvey, 2008; Gibson, 1977; Michaels & Carello, 1981). Thus, standing at a gaping hole in a burning plane we perceive not only that it affords escape, but that its edge, if far above the ground, is also fall-off-able. Empirical research verifies that researchers can determine what specifies affordances, such as whether risers can be walked up (Warren, 1984) or the usefulness of various tools, and confirms that humans and other animals are sensitive to this information. Information when quantified in terms of properties of an object/environment calculated *with reference to* an organism veridically specifies what can be done with that object (e.g., how good it is for precisely wedging open an exit that is jammed versus forcefully smashing a barrier).

Socially, research has demonstrated not only that interactions that are cooperative or competitive are specifiable to an observer (Kean, 2000; Newtson, Hairfield, Bloomingdale, & Cutino, 1987) but that observers are sensitive to functional features of solo actors, such as muggability (Gunns, Johnston, & Hudson, 2002; Johnston, Hudson, Richardson, Gunns, & Garner, 2004) or cyclical variation in sexual fertility (Johnston, Miles, Carter, & Macrae, 2005; Johnston, Miles, & Macrae, 2008; Pipitone, Gallup, & Gordon, 2008). Children's different intent (reluctance to play) when approaching a (not depicted) child with physical disabilities (relative to approaching a child without disabilities) is also detectable by observers (Van Acker & Valenti, 1989).

Humans, however, dramatically push the limits of direct perception in that the most uniquely human abilities, advanced cognitive and communicative capabilities, allow for new forms of information transmittal that are not bound by natural law. Although words (or nonverbal communications) are transmitted via visual or auditory medium, as symbols that re-present other things, they are an informational medium of their own. They can provide a rapid means of conveying complex information about what one affords to other perceivers, information that might otherwise take a perceiver extensive time and immense amounts of perceptual experience to acquire. Words can thus be a rapid catalyst for calling others into connection and can rapidly put individuals on equal footing in terms of a shared understanding of the world. But the cognitive capabilities to be able to imagine desirable action possibilities if one but conveys the right information also allow humans to intentionally convey incorrect information, to mislead.

Mostly words have an embodied grounding (Semin, 2007). They occur in an interaction context where pragmatics and shared assumptions about communication as well as more embodied processes (e.g., movement) ensure individuals have a shared sense of truth and meaning, and can coregulate communication and behavior (Clark, 1996; Grice, 1975; Semin & Cacioppo, 2008). But words stripped out of context, or used to carefully construct an artificial reality, operate much like vision does in an Ames room[2] or when perceiving a point of light in the severely constrained environment of a darkened lab room. Contextless, without a perceiver's ability to actively inspect the grounding of the words, the recipient of an utterance is like one whose head position is rigidly fixed to make sure that the visual illusions of the Ames room works. Words isolated from an embedding context are not bound by physics; their structure is not induced by the optics of light rays bouncing off them. Rather, words' structural nature is constrained only by the physics of articulation and auditory detection (e.g., Galantucci, Fowler, & Turvey, 2006). Unlike visual information, information conveyed by words is not compelled by physical laws to display a one-to-one correspondence to things in the world. The information words convey may be lies.

As a consequence, social knowing can often require substantial inferential processes that go well beyond mere picking up of information. With inferences involved, there is much more latitude for incorrect judgments regarding social affordances than there is, for instance, for an adult to misunderstand the meaning of a cliff. Of course, a focus on the inferential aspects of social knowing has been the dominant focus throughout social psychology's history. Like the classic theory of perception (based in pre-Darwinian logic), however, traditional perspectives on social knowing assume that we know the world only through constructive processes. Psychology's perspective has typically had a thought-centric focus (Richardson, Marsh, & Schmidt, 2008), viewing all contact with properties of the social world as mediated through cognition. In contrast, an ecological perspective views social interaction not only as a meeting of chatty minds, but as minds grounded in bodies with other capabilities, and embedded in an environment with certain constraints (Richardson, Marsh, & Schmidt, 2008). The suggestion here is not a new one (e.g., Baron, 1980; McArthur & Baron, 1983): that much more attention be given to the aspects of social knowing that involve basic perception and action. In particular, more emphasis should be given to the nature of a social unit as emergent from basic dynamical, perception–action processes.

ACTION

From an ecological perspective, perception and action are different sides of the same coin, or better, different "sides" of a Mobius strip, not the distinctly separable processes traditional psychology imagines them to be. That action is seen as a wholly different problem for much of psychology is reflected in scientists' surprise that perceiving *others*' actions leads to stimulation of parts of the brain that are associated with our own carrying out of those same actions (i.e., mirror neurons;

Rizzolatti & Arbib, 1998; Rizzolatti & Craighero, 2004). What unifies those tasks is perception, particularly perception of meaningful actions and enactment of affordances. Ripping a piece of paper, seeing someone else ripping a paper, and hearing the paper being ripped behind the other's back (Kohler et al., 2002) all have to do with the detection of enactment of affordances. That certain regions of the brain show activation when we perceive (visually or auditorally) the enactment of affordances is strong evidence for the third principle of ecological perception discussed earlier—that affordances are directly perceived. More generally it appears that it is human (rather than, e.g., robotic) movement of personal significance that activates such processes, and that object manipulation or achievement of a concrete end state is not required (e.g., Calvo-Merino, Glaser, Grèzes, Passingham, & Haggard, 2005; Kilner, Hamilton, & Blakemore, 2007).

But if the "impoverished image on the retina" is the core mystery for nonecological accounts of perception, the mystery of how we can understand another person's actions (even though we have the exact same action in our repertoire) is the core mystery with regard to action. For traditional views, explaining how individuals can rapidly and dynamically coordinate their actions with another is a major computational challenge. It involves not only recognizing another individual's actions, but somehow managing to calculate what the other's body position in the near future is likely to be, and then planning to move oneself to the correct future location. For most researchers, the solution to the problems involves common neural coding of one's actions and others' actions, or internal mental simulation of what the person is doing. In this way the other person's actions can in some way be mapped on to, or re-presented to oneself, the actions that one can also do oneself.

For traditional views, coordinating our movements with another person is particularly dubious because great gulfs are seen between merely what it means for one individual to perceive and to act, not to mention between seeing action *as* the actor versus watching it as a passive observer. For an ecological perspective, the comparability of these is much like the comparability of seeing the same object from two very different perspectives. The invariants present specify the same object (or the same meaning of the event) to a perceiver regardless. Ecological perspectives undermine the false dichotomy between perceiving the world and acting, and thus illustrate how coordination of movement with others can be a less mind-centric and more emergent process.

What is physical action and how does it differ from mere perceptual acts? Ecological and dynamical accounts of action draw substantially from writings of the Russian physiologist Bernstein for guidance in identifying the problems that a psychology of action would need to solve (see Turvey, 1990, 2007). Understanding movement involves a variety of problems unique to the challenge of harnessing vast numbers of muscles, tendons, and neurons to produce constrained actions (Rosenbaum, 1991). Such issues are beyond the scope of this chapter. We need only understand more basic issues to grasp how we move with others to form a coordinative unit of action with them, and how we can see and understand another's movement to do so.

Action is tightly coupled to perception. Just as people's perceptual judgments alone of the affordances of a tool are very precisely predicted by features of the tool (length, center of mass, weight) *taken with respect* to quantifiable features of the individual (their own strength, arm length, skill), so too are their actions. What tools people use and how they use them, and when their actions switch from one mode to another (e.g., grasping an object with one hand rather than two, when people can climb risers normally rather than requiring using their hands to help them climb up a vertical rise) are very precisely predicted by a body-to-environment relational metric. So too is people's cooperative action with others precisely predicted by relational metrics (Richardson, Marsh, & Baron, 2007). Action follows tightly as a result of what information about affordances is detected via perception; perception guides action continually during action, and with views changing continually, action adjusts accordingly continually. "So we must perceive in order to move, but we must also move in order to perceive" (Gibson, 1979, p. 223).

An excellent illustration of the interplay between perceiving and acting in a social synergy comes from Asch (1952), in his writing about two boys moving a log together:

> The boys are fitting their actions to each other and to the object and are involved in a give-and-take requiring considerable sensitiveness. The two do not apply force in succession, or in opposite directions; they bring a common force to bear simultaneously. If one moves somewhat faster or swerves slightly, the other adapts his movement correspondingly. There is an immediate, direct communication between them through the object. The amount of movement, timing, pace, and direction are regulated and continuously checked by the corresponding action of the partner. Here is a unity of action that embraces the participants and the common object. The performance is a new product, strictly unlike the sum of their separate exertions. … Neither boy would act in just the same way in the absence of the other; what each contributes is a function of his relation to the other in the task. (pp. 173–174)

Understood in this context, it is clear that responding to another's action is not a mental, computational task, but a dynamic, embodied process of perceiving and acting. Responding to the actions of another person follows naturally from detecting visual invariants in the optical and haptic patterns of our experiences. Throughout the flow of movement, we are informed, in a more immersive and multimodal way (via vision, and hearing the other speak, and via pressure and inertial processes of haptic perception), about the current state of the situation.

Unique Properties of Action

Some features that our intuitions suggest to us are special to action, not true of perception, turn out to be inaccurate when we understand how active perception is. Action may seem more intentional, more guided by anticipation of what will follow, and more involving of the flow of something (motion), but each of these is substantially true of perception as well. For instance, without motion (at minimum, eye saccades) we cannot perceive. Action does uniquely involve the physics of forces, gravity, and the challenge of hauling weight around. Although these are highly relevant to perceivers, who pick up such kinematics via vision, for instance

(Runeson & Frykholm, 1981, 1983), kinematics do not in the same way affect the "doing" of seeing and hearing and smelling at the scale of our ecological niche—gravity can be ignored without peril.

But the most crucial aspects of physical action are (a) the richness of perception, because of its potential multimodality, its (b) direct contact of body with the world, and (c) how dramatically it changes perceptions and states of the world.

There is not some mysterious difference between what is carried by perception and what is carried by action, but there can be more information of the world conveyed when we contact it in some way ourselves through action. There is a sense of separateness of self from other, of action at a distance, in vision, in contrast to the potential for a more direct touching of the world with movement. Action involves additional systems of the body, more extensive and often more intentional movement of broader systems of the body, and more extensive cross-modal experiencing of the world, and more continued, extended contact of the world with self. The implications of these features of action are very important for social connectedness, in that it grounds those coparticipating in the action more thoroughly than mere joint attention can. There is more shared immersion.

Actions also more radically change perceptions. As we move an object, or engage in some action, what we perceive is changed, and our perceptions are continually retuned in a more continual and perfect way than if we only make perceptual judgments about the world, without acting on them. Action is a continual change in information, as our actions actively transform the situation, as the log gives way to our exertions. As soon as we act on the action possibilities provided by the world, our perceptions become continually updated online. As we get closer to a log, to grab it for instance, and as we start to lift it and maybe feel the slipperiness of the log, and start our lift, then we perhaps realize it is heavier than anticipated. Järvilehto believes that all perception is anticipation. If that is correct, then we can understand action as continual checking of our anticipation with more information than we get from perception alone. Thus, action "reorganizes the organism-environment system" (Järvilehto, 1998), that is, it changes how we stand with respect to the environment, and it gives us better information about the world.

Another aspect of action's reorganization effect is that there may be goal-relevant consequences of some actions. Action is often about getting goals achieved; participation in such a process has particular implications for social connection. In Asch's example, if two people merely engaged in joint attention by watching the log-moving event unfold, there is a less sense of connection than if the two people participate in the act of moving the log. Greater feeling of connection follows from the mutual responsiveness involved in interaction (Insko & Wilson, 1977) as well as the shared experience of goal achievement. For the researcher Järvilehto, the *result* of behavior is a key crucial principle of action: the consequent reorganization of the organism–environment system if a behavior is successful, or otherwise, a disorganization with negative consequences (e.g., Järvilehto, 1998, 2001). When a social synergy is created to move a log, successful organization and synergy creation occurs in the situation where the obstacle is moved. With disorder or breakdown in the organization, the log might be dropped. The boys' actions might be at cross-purposes so that the log slips out of one of the boy's hands.

For nongoal-oriented movement, we also can demonstrate a pull to the movement of another (and show activation of relevant brain areas) even when movement is not goal relevant. The stakes are lower for slipping in or out of socially synchronous states than the stakes are, for instance, when coordinating with others in rescuing plane crash victims. Thus it seems likely that mundane coparticipation in shared movement, and low-level joint action of mere shared perception, as well as the more extensive potential payoffs (positive and negative) of goal-oriented coordination, could all play important roles in connecting socially.

In sum, action is maximally embedded perception. It is maximal immersion of self within one's environment, rather than observing it with only a few sensory systems. It is also maximally embedded in that its effects can exert a change in the organization of an animal–environment synergy, it can even become an entirely new thing as a result of our exertions. This should be true as well when a social synergy emerges through action. Becoming a coherent unit with another person by being pulled into their movement orbit means more maximal social embedding.

Perceiving Others' Actions

Importantly, perceiving others' actions is not in some way mysteriously different than other instances of directly perceiving events. Invariants detectable in their dynamical movement—those aspects of the structure that remain constant across the transformations—can specify intent and meaning. Just as we have the sensory systems to be able to detect nonsocial information and pick up nonsocial affordances, so too can we perceive coherent actions and others' enactment of affordances. If we see subtle movements that do not have meaning for us, there may be limits in our ability to detect their meaning—as in the case of observing the motions of an unfamiliar animal with a very different body structure from us. Still some things would be specified. Even if we did not know that some creatures could fly we could tell that a new flying creature was locomoting, moving under its own power. But we have special access to other humans' movements. Since the outcome of actions are a function of attributes of a creature considered with reference to an environment, having live access to the creature side of the equation allows for much more understanding of their activities. If we see an animal struggling to locomote up some unfamiliar, somewhat deformable surface, an animal that differs substantially from us, we may grasp from its velocity, size, and other properties the degree to which its difficulty may be due to the creature's capabilities. The way the surface gives way or resists deformation as the creature climbs will also inform us about the difficulty. But if the creature is another human, from merely watching them climb the surface we know what the affordance properties are of the surface in a more precise way. Our capabilities are their capabilities, and we more readily know from the style of their movement what the experience of them walking up that sand dune is, even if we never knew that such surfaces existed.

EMERGENT CONSEQUENCES OF PERCEPTION AND ACTION

Thus, from an ecological account of perception we see that action is fundamental for perception, and how rich the information is that specifies features of the world, particularly action-relevant functional properties appropriate to our own social niche. The challenge for ecological social psychology is that determining what part of a judgment is lawful—based on veridical perception—and what part is based on fallible inference is unanswerable for attributes that are more difficult to assess than sex, age, facial expression, and the like. This challenge emerges from an individual-oriented, rather than more relational, view of ecological social psychology (see Marsh et al., 2006). Considering the same problems from a perspective that preserves perceptions' interconnectedness to action, that is, by focusing more explicitly on affordances, is somewhat more fruitful, many have argued (e.g., Marsh et al., 2006; McArthur & Baron, 1983). In the most recent reinvigoration of an ecological perspective, however, it is the developments in dynamics (Baron, 2002; Baron, Amazeen, & Beek, 1994; Nowak & Vallacher, 1998; Vallacher et al., 2002) that have led to the logical conclusion that methods should not primarily involve what an individual can perceive of another isolated individual, but rather should focus more seriously *on* the social unit, an integrated social perceiving-acting system, a "we" of some kind (e.g., Baron, 2002, 2007).

The second feature of a reinvigorated ecological perspective on social psychology is a new look at mere movement and collective behavior with an eye to how it serves the emergence of this social synergy of perceiving and acting (Marsh et al., 2006). The notion that the causal origins of meaning in the world can lie outside of our heads, literally residing in the self-organizing processes that result from the perception and action processes of individuals highly embedded in a social world, is fundamentally at odds with the way we mostly think about causality in social and cognitive psychology (Richardson, Marsh, & Schmidt, 2008). A few examples to illustrate what self-organization, spontaneous emergence of new structure means may be helpful.

For social psychology, Asch's example of the two boys moving a log together, or the coordination of victims (or rescuers) in the plane crash, illustrates spontaneous emergence of a new coordinative social structure. Skeptics might doubt that such processes follow from self-organization processes, however, given humans' highly advanced mental and verbal capabilities as well as the extensive social learning opportunities adults have had. For the emergence of a social synergy, it may be difficult to entirely rule out inferential, top-down strategic and social learning processes despite the computational difficulties entailed. It is easier to illustrate emergence in species without the same cognitive capabilities—creatures we can view more objectively.

Seeing complicated patterns in intentional creatures usually suggests to most psychologists either the existence of some preexisting pattern (e.g., genetic endowment) or else complex cognitive processes required to do the calculation, planning, and imagination to create such patterns. Patterns might be something as simple as noting the evenly spaced distribution of birds on a line, or the incredible coordination of a group of birds' flight. Or patterns might be as complex as social termites' construction of impressively elaborate nests. We may be amazed in these cases by the smartness of evolution to have eventually yielded animals with these programs coded in their genes.

But not all patterns are products of cognitive construction or mere genes. An ecological dynamical account would instead ask what the properties of birds' movement are, how much space does an animal need to take off, how far do their wings extend when perched, and how far can the protection of hearing other birds' warning cries extend given birds' hearing capabilities. Perhaps sophisticated termite nest construction is a different matter though, given that its apparently cooperative, collective action is directed toward creating a structure so complex it even has arches. Termites individually drop material, which also gives off pheromones, which attract other termites' droppings, and eventually results in a pillar. Pheromone gradients turn these pillars into arches. These structures, ecological psychologists have demonstrated, do not reflect a plan that termites have programmed in their head, but rather are emergent consequences of each individual termite flying around initially randomly but whose trajectory and behavior obey two simple motivational principles (Kugler & Turvey, 1987). Termites are "preprogrammed" only to fly toward regions with the strongest pheromone concentration and to deposit building materials at the strongest point of pheromone concentration. The physics of pheromone dispersion and the physics of droppings deposited do the rest of the work in ensuring the nest becomes structured as it is.

How a new social structure comes into existence, a coordinated dyad moving a log, or a coordinated plane evacuation may also follow simple individual perceptions of action possibilities, and simple pull in one's movement toward the movement of another. What is most crucial to the notion of emergence is interaction among elements, attraction, and repulsion of one atom or neighbor to another, change in one neighbor as a consequence of other nearby neighbors, and connectedness of things in time as well. There must be a nonindependence of the present with regard to its past or future states; being at a critical juncture in time can mean something different for the future depending on the path by which one got there. Thus two couples at the same current state in the landscape of attraction may be heading for disaster or ecstasy depending on the immediate path by which they reached that state (Tesser, 1980; Tesser & Achee, 1994).

Also fundamental to emergence is the connectedness with regard to a surrounding. Embedding of an individual within an environment changes everything in a way that is hard for us to understand the consequences of unless we see action unfold. Because we are not machines, isolation of the part from the whole means that the properties of the part may be changed by unembedding it. As individuals, our environment, our social niche, constrains us in key ways, but they are context-sensitive dependencies. A machine part is dependent on other parts of the machine (it may need input of energy or matter to function) but it is not a context-sensitive dependency. But parts of biological systems, studied in isolation, may seem to have a very different manner than they do when studied in context. The field of proteonomics, in studying how the functions of a protein are affected by their folding (as in the case of mad cow disease), illustrates how the properties of something understood in isolation from its normal embedding context can be totally different from the characteristics it has *within* its normal context. Researchers found that their previous simulations of how proteins in the body function were completely wrong in some cases because the surrounding molecules in which the proteins are normally embedded (i.e., water molecules) were not in the simulations. When embedded in the body (i.e., water) proteins' structures are changed: They fold differently, and thus their functions are entirely changed by embedding (Gerstein & Levitt, 1998). The lesson is that the surround is not a mere backdrop for biological systems, but an integral, inextricable *part* of that which is being studied (Järvilehto, 1998). This is no less true of humans than it is of our body's proteins. Animals isolated from their normal environmental surround, raised in social isolation, are fundamentally lacking in some of the basic characteristics that normally describe their species (Harlow, 1958; Shattuck, 1980).

RESEARCH ON THE DYNAMICS OF MOVEMENT AND THE EMERGENCE OF A SOCIAL UNIT

One signature of self-organizing, dynamical systems is their adherence to universal dynamical principles. If a dynamical approach to the emergence of a social synergy is correct, then the conditions under which participants can and cannot be pulled to become a coherent unit of perceiving and acting—and yet one that has a unity and reality of its own—should obey what is known about how dynamical systems operate. Research indicates that we are spontaneously pulled to attend to the movements of others, and as a consequence our own movement is often tethered to that of others nearby even when we are in the most minimal of interactions with them.

Early social psychological research used coding of videotapes and subjective judgments about whether body postures were similar to one another, or ratings of perceived interpersonal coordination to assess individuals' tendencies to mirror the movements of others (LaFrance, 1982; LaFrance & Broadbent, 1976) or coordinate their movement with others (Bernieri, Reznick, & Rosenthal, 1988; Bernieri & Rosenthal, 1991). More recent research has used movement sensors to objectively track movement continually in space and time. In this research, the pull to coordinate rhythmic movement via vision was studied by having individuals do an easy rhythmic movement that they can sustain easily and automatically. Paradigms used include swinging about one's wrist a hand-held pendulum-like stick with a weight at the end (Amazeen, Schmidt, & Turvey, 1995; Schmidt, Bienvenu, Fitzpatrick, & Amazeen, 1998; Schmidt & Turvey, 1994), swinging legs while sitting (Schmidt, Carello, & Turvey, 1990), walking (van Ulzen, Lamoth, Daffertshofer, Semin, & Beek, 2008), and moving in a rocking chair (Richardson, Marsh, Isenhower, Goodman, & Schmidt, 2007). Research has also examined how less overt movement of one individual, one's postural sway during standing, is influenced by others' sways during conversation. This research demonstrates that auditory information provides a medium in which the tendency to coordinate one's movement with another is realized in conversation via speaking similar words as a co-present interactant (Shockley, Baker, Richardson, & Fowler, 2007; Shockley, Santana, & Fowler, 2003).

Extensive social psychological research on mimicry has examined the link between social bonds and being influenced by others' gestures (e.g., foot swinging and nose scratching). Mimicry in an interaction reflects coparticipation in a social unit, a shared perspective, or other-directedness, being in some way unified with the other. For instance, individuals higher in empathy show more mimicry (Sonnby-Borgström, Jönsson, & Svensson, 2003). Mimicking another increases liking (Lakin & Chartrand, 2003), provided the context is viewed as a relational context (Sanchez Burks, 2002). Moreover, those who are liked are more likely to be mimicked (Chartrand & Bargh, 1999; Chartrand & Jefferis, 2003; Dijksterhuis & Bargh, 2001). In addition, being mimicked can lead to more expression of interdependent self-construals, higher inclusion of self in the other, more prosocial behavior, and closer proximity to an interactant (Ashton-James, van Baaren, Chartrand, Decety, & Karremans, 2007).

Dynamic measures should offer a particular window into the emergence of a basic connectedness with others, in that they should allow us to assess how and when a unit comes into being, and explore the conditions that make such formation of a transient social bond difficult. An ecological perspective also provides a parsimonious explanation for how we can coordinate with others. Assuming that coordination is cognitively mediated would require the positing of untenable assumptions about cognitive resources. An ecological perspective allows for an explanation that has a simple elegance, much like it describes how an outfielder catches a ball in baseball (e.g., Michaels & Oudejans, 1992). As it turns out, an informational variable that reflects the change in the size of the image of the ball on the retina can be capitalized on. If an outfielder is in perfect position, then this informational variable, the vertical optical velocity, will remain constant. All an outfielder needs to do is continually advance and retreat so as to continually zero out optical acceleration; if the outfielder does so he will reach the ball. No calculations are necessary, sensitivity to a simple informational variable that specifies relations and the ability to move to explore how to get that variable to a desired summary value is all that is essential.

The ability to spontaneously coordinate with others is likely a comparable process of being automatically aware of information that specifies the *relation* between where one is in space and time and where the other is. No calculation of "where" that is exact is necessary, only sensitivity to a difference and a pull to reduce this difference is necessary. In the process of being pulled into the eddy of another's movement, others help keep us in a real sense "moored" in space and time and can pull us toward states that we may have been unlikely to otherwise have the ability to experience. Research demonstrates, however, that we can only be moored by others within a certain range of values that are possible behaviors for ourselves. Research indicates that when our own rhythms differ naturally from another's rhythms (e.g., because the weighting of our rocking chairs differ), the less likely that our movement will be spontaneously captured by the other's movements (e.g., Richardson, Marsh, Isenhower, et al., 2007). Coupling of movements requires some overlap in one's natural movement patterns. Moreover, spontaneous coordination between individuals reflects only relative coordination rather than lockstep motion.

Being pulled to regularize our movement with others is essential for tasks that explicitly require coordination or competition with others. Using frame-by-frame Eschol coding of videotapes (to assess amount of total movement change across all body segments), Newtson and colleagues (1998) demonstrated that coordinating individuals showed patterned "waves" of amount of movement (regular patterns of increase in amount of movement, and decrease in movement) that were linked in reliable ways to the behavior waves of each other. A clip of a competing dyad (two people playing basketball) also showed displayed coordination, but there were lead–lag relationships in the waves, with the person who was dominating in the game showing a lead in the behavior wave.

Using sensors that detect movement allows for less onerous and more continual quantification of coordination. For instance, even when apparently standing still we have postural sway. Although complicated, multidimensional space is required to describe postural sway; it can be summarized using a technique called phase-space reconstruction. CRQA (cross-recurrent quantification analysis) can be used to examine the similarity of one person's trajectory thru phase space relative to another, and lead–lag relationships as well (Richardson, Schmidt, & Kay, 2007; Shockley et al., 2003).

A simpler way to quantify coordination is available for any continuous rhythmic movement that can be described by a simple sine wave of motion forward and back. Synchrony here is assessed by whether people are at the maximum point forward in their trajectory when the other is as well (i.e., in-phase behavior) or when the other is at the maximum point backward in their trajectory (i.e., anti-phase behavior). Crucially, a measure of how much an individual's movement is coupled with another (whether in sway, using CRQA, or in rocking or walking and using relative phase) is a *relational* measure.

As mentioned before, a fundamental tenet is the universality of natural law processes across different systems. Thus if a social unit can be said to be a true and coherent system, the patterning and emergence of this unit should obey dynamical principles, just as the emergence of coordinated states within an individual (e.g., coordinating swinging of right and left arms) does. Research on interpersonal coordination of rhythmic movement, conducted over 20 years by Schmidt and his colleagues, establish that interpersonal coordination is in fact a dynamical system (for a review, see Schmidt & Richardson, 2008). In sum, individuals can coordinate only certain patterns of movement (in-phase and anti-phase) and not others. In-phase is a stronger attractor than anti-phase behavior, such that when individuals unintentionally coordinate their movement, in-phase occurs somewhat more than anti-phase (e.g., Richardson, Marsh, & Schmidt, 2005). Moreover, when there is increased press on the system (e.g., by forcing individuals to move more rapidly), individuals spontaneously, abruptly, and unintentionally switch to in-phase behavior if they are in anti-phase behavior. The opposite—a shift from in-phase to anti-phase—does not spontaneously occur; this asymmetry in trajectory of behavior is referred to as hysteresis.

Recent research (see Marsh, Johnston, et al., 2009, for details) indicates that being pulled into the orbit of another's body may be a fundamental, body-based way for instantiating a socioemotional connection with another. In an experiment using the pendulum paradigm we required individuals to attempt to coordinate their movement with another individual, under either difficult or easy coordination conditions. As hypothesized, under the easy coordination conditions, participants had more positive feelings about the interaction (e.g., perceived harmoniousness). A second experiment used the rocking chair paradigm to examine unintentional coordination. Strength of informational coupling was manipulated using a method that has been demonstrated to somewhat reduce unintentional coupling, but not reduce intentional coupling: having individuals either focus only peripherally on the others' movement or provide them focal visual information. We found that the manipulation was successful at affecting degree of coordination, and when individuals showed more coordination, they also afterward expressed stronger feelings of teamness with the other individual on upcoming tasks. Finally, we examined the possibility that groups of individuals who show significant deficits in social connection with others, namely, children diagnosed with autistic spectrum disorder, ASD, might display less spontaneous coordination with their parent who heard through earphones an auditory signal to rock at a set pace (a frequency appropriate to the size of the child's chair). As predicted, we found that during periods of rocking, children of typical development (intellectually age-matched to the ASD sample) had significantly greater incidence of periods of in-phase behavior with their parents than did children with ASD.

Our research has explored the most minimal conditions for the emergence of a social connection with others. In natural settings, there are likely to be many other, more overt ways by which we are rapidly pulled to be a "social eddy" with others. Verbal, proxemics, and haptics—speaking a word to someone else while looking toward them, or saying their name, or approaching close to them or touching them—would be among the most effective means of rapidly pulling another into joint action with us. But a mere gesture toward another or simply gazing toward another person until the gaze is returned are also likely to be ways of creating a temporary social bond with another. Perhaps the most important reason for inducing a social unit to be temporarily created is to engage the involvement of another to get their help in completing some task.

RESEARCH ON THE AFFORDANCES OF SOCIAL UNITS

An ecological dynamical approach argues for a more embodied and embedded means of studying phenomena such as cooperation that have traditionally been studied as if products of individual, unembodied minds, operating strategically via cognitive processes alone. Typically, cooperation is studied using game theoretic approaches in which an individual has to weigh the costs and benefits of cooperating, with the contrast choices being competitive action. Such a perspective on cooperation differs substantially from the example of boys moving a log in which they become a singular "unity of action" as they continually adjust their movements in response to the movements of another (Asch, 1952). If cooperation can be studied from an ecological perspective using embodied methods that do justice to Asch's example, several things should be true. First, the appearance of cooperation versus autonomous action should obey principles of animal–environment fit.

Second, the shifts in behavior should display dynamical properties that signify a dynamical system.

Using a simple task of moving planks of wood of a wide range of length, we found support for both principles (Richardson, Marsh, & Baron, 2007). Pairs of individuals participated in an experiment in which they were to move planks of wood that were presented on a conveyor belt in a random sequence of sizes, as well as in a sequence in which they were presented in ascending order and descending order. Participants were told to imagine the planks had wet paint on their middles and that they could thus only move them by touching the ends (e.g., by one person touching both ends, or by two people touching only one of the ends, moving them together). Some were of such length that they could be comfortably moved with two hands, whereas some required that they be moved by cooperating. Analogous experiments were also conducted using individual participants, examining one to two hand shifts in behavior, and one-hand to one hand plus claw-tool lifting. Experiments were also conducted examining perceptual judgments alone. Consistent with ecological research on how solo individuals shift between action modes (and our own experiments on solo grasping), we found that shifts between solo action and cooperative action modes were predicted precisely by a relational measure (called a "pi number") of fit between arm length and plank length (Isenhower, Carello, Richardson, Baron, & Marsh, 2010; Richardson, Marsh, & Baron, 2007).

In addition, both perception processes and action processes displayed the important dynamical feature of multistability. Multistability means that there are ranges of values for the pi number where multiple states are possible—where two individuals or one individual could readily carry wood. In such regions, the past trajectory of action (hysteresis) or the future states of the system that are anticipated (enhanced contrast) should influence which state the system is in, if it is a dynamical system.

Interestingly, in experiments examining perception alone, where no action was present to reset the system, enhanced contrast occurred. Individuals, looking forward in time, shifted to making "two person" judgments at smaller planks of wood when the sequence was increasing in size (relative to how the plank was judged in the descending condition). Individuals shifted to making "two hand" judgments at the earliest edge of two-hand movability in the descending sequence. In contrast, when perception was integrated with action, allowing for perpetual retuning of the system, there was persistence in the past sequence of action. That is, hysteresis occurred (a process comparable to "assimilation" in priming studies), where the past states of the system persist longer into the future. In particular, in the descending condition, people persisted in cooperative action longer such that they continued picking up smaller pieces of wood together, whereas these same pieces, in the ascending condition, were picked up alone.

The significance of these experiments is that they support the universality of basic dynamical principles; the pi number was very close across multiple systems, whether solo perception–action systems (solo actors shifting between one- and two-hand grasping), an individual perception–action system that involved a tool, or a joint perception–action system. The patterns shown in perceptual judgments of enhanced contrast were also comparable across the systems, as was true for the pattern of hysteresis across systems for action. The experiments provide compelling evidence that embodied cooperation processes, as described by Asch 50 years ago, can be pursued using the methods of ecological science by having two individuals co-present, allowing for emergence of a cooperative unit of perceiving and acting. It also provides a beginning avenue to exploring social meanings—the action possibilities of social units of acting and perceiving. Individuals extend our "grasp" in simple quantitative ways as in the case of moving planks of wood, but there are more interesting qualitative ways in which new possibilities for action are possible for social units. Examining the abilities of pairs of individuals to move planks of wood involves a simple initial task that can lead to exploration of affordances that are more extensive and are of other interest social psychologically. The experiments can also provide a way to understand the link between experience and expectations, and how these attune individuals to cooperative action. It also is an avenue for understanding how an individual's dispositional states can set different "initial conditions" that dictate where a pair is likely to be on the dynamical space (i.e., nearness to a cooperative attractor). For instance, extroversion and agreeableness appear to be dispositional characteristics that have relevance to the strength of the cooperation attractor (see Marsh, Richardson et al., 2009).

PROPERTY ASSUMPTIONS IN EMERGENCE OF SOCIAL UNITS

One relatively unexplored area of research is determining what structural properties of humans and of environments provide the distinct architectures that ground sociality. For termite nest construction for instance, an intrinsic marker of producing regularities is pheromone marking, and a necessary feature of termites is their response to such pheromones. The physics of the building materials (pheromone diffusion and properties of the droppings) are no less important in determining the nature of the final structure. The sociobiological and environmental parallels in the pull toward a social synergy is a substantially neglected area of study, but existing research suggests some possible directions.

According to the evolution-informed, functional perspective of ecological psychology, it is likely that all levels of organism and environment will have structures that are all jointly necessary for emergence of a social synergy. The dominant tendency in psychology is to privilege the neurophysiological level. Given what we know in psychology thus far, however, it seems likely that all of the following are essential substrates in the emergence of a social bond: increased arousal in the presence of others (Zajonc, 1965), the hormone oxytocin (Kosfeld, Heirinchs, Zak, Fischbacher, & Fehr, 2005), mirror neuron regions of the brain (Rizzolatti & Craighero, 2004), as well as crucial dynamical attention and motoric abilities. Whereas for species such as termites a specific medium of response (detection of pheromones) is the crucial avenue for creating a coordinative structure, for humans the avenue is more broadly an informational medium rather than tied specifically to only one chemical detection mechanism. Such information can be carried by vision, audition, touch, and language. Catalysts (low energy, rapid switching mechanisms; Iberall & Soodak, 1987) for rapidly calling a connection into being are likely to be, in order of decreasing immediacy: touch, physical proximity (e.g., violation of personal space boundaries; Sommer, 1969), spoken language, and evidence of perceptual contact (e.g., eye contact, Argyle & Cook, 1976). To be able to respond to the information detected, it is also essential that someone have the ability to accurately see (or otherwise detect) motion in the correct ecological time scale. Moreover, motoric deficits (e.g., timing problems) will also make social bond creation difficult. Intriguingly each of these features mentioned, from arousal to motor timing difficulties, are implicated in disorders involving major social disconnection, namely, autistic spectrum disorder (Grossberg & Seidman, 2006).

Environmental features are no less important although it does not appear that any particular physical structure is causally necessary for bond creation. Certain environmental structures, those that increase proximity and access, should affect social bond creation (Festinger, Schacter, & Back, 1950). Research from older eras of environmental psychology and more recent work describing behavior settings could also guide directions for future research. These include features such as arrangement of furniture, shape of tables in rooms, and density (inhabitants-to-room size) as well as more ecologically relevant "behavior setting" features (e.g., Barker & Wright, 1951; Bell, Fisher, & Loomis, 1978; Heft 1988, 2001; Heft & Kyttä, 2006; Sommer, 1969; Whyte, 1980). Substantial work in this area needs to be done, particularly as it is in large part the properties of the *social* environment that compel (but more often, constrain) the creation of social bonds (e.g., social norms and societal structuring in terms of power and affiliation relations). Even though such features are not necessarily bound by biological or physical laws (but consider, e.g., incest taboos), ecological approaches imply there may be information in physical settings that specifies such social constraints to perceivers (Heft, 2007).

UNIQUENESS OF THE SOCIAL SYNERGY

Is the social unit of perceiving and acting a special coordinative structure? Anecdotally, a commentator reacting to an ecological account of social perceiving and acting once said that it made it seem like humans were no different from rocks or snakes. Are humans, embedded in a social niche, any different than the rocks are within their niche—a useful vessel for fostering and spreading bacteria and viruses in the former case, and a useful home under which insects can nest in the latter? Answering this question is a more obviously simple one but the snake challenge deserves further attention.

Animals trump rocks (and even plants) because of energy conservation principles. Being a creature that must seek out energy sources rather than having it in ready abundance necessitates that it have motion. Motion requires the need to attend to potential sources of energy, which requires sensory and movement systems that allow for the intake of information and energy, and as a consequence of action, creates transformation of their surround. Animals have stronger footprints on their surround than rocks do, more like rivers than rocks because of dynamics, that is, they move. But because they are energy dependent they are more vulnerable to the environment as well. Animals die and die in a more irreversible way than does a dried-up riverbed, for instance. And because of the special problems that such movement–perception–energy generation systems entail, even the longest-lived (whales) cannot manage to live as long as some nonlocomoting living things can (giant sequoia trees).

The emphasis of the ecological perspective is that humans are not special, if by special we mean endowing them with particular powers not allowed to other animals, of having a man who replays what is going on in the world in his head and reconstructs the world so that we then (indirectly) "know" it. Ecological psychologists therefore view most traditional views of cognitive processing as entailing bad science. The emphasis from ecological processes of perceiving and acting is strongly postevolutionary in emphasis. It emphasizes the wholeness of the animal–environment niche and understanding how natural law impacts humans no less than any other animal that exists in its own niche.

Certainly humans are not unique in merely having sociality. Many other creatures have at least superficially social natures—their way of being is changed by what other creatures are around them, and they interact with others of their species in patterned and yet adaptive ways (e.g., bees). And many creatures have sociality in clearly nonsuperficial ways—bonobo apes (de Waal, 1997), elephants, and of course our pets. Humans are not the only species that are biophilial as well as sociopetal, experiencing a pull to at least be around *some* kind of living animal, as humans know from their relationships with cats and dogs and horses. We cannot even say that humans are unique in the peculiar combination of sociality paired with self-awareness, since we know that dolphins, apes, and elephants can pass the body-marking mirror test (Marino, Reiss, & Gallup, 1994; Plotnik, de Waal, & Reiss, 2006). Although we are rather aware of how limited our sensory capabilities are—cats, dogs, and birds can see, smell, or localize sound better than we can—we do have special body capabilities that are crucial in our uniqueness. Although some animals show incredible sophistication in their coordination of movement in hunting prey, humans not only have opposable thumbs to aid in wielding tools but, importantly, they have the better ability to utilize the throwing dynamics of objects. The other apes that can throw have a very restricted range; humans can throw an order of magnitude further, which it has been argued is intertwined with the development of sophisticated cooperation abilities in humans (Calvin, 1983).

But humans' most important capabilities involve our abilities to see affordances further into the future, to be able to extend our perceptions of what is possible further into the future than other animals, and to be able to share our far-off imaginations of the world better than other animals via more sophisticated verbalizations (Penn, Holyoak, & Povinelli, 2008). As a consequence of the ability to see affordances extended much further in space and time (and collaborate with others in such acts of imagination), we not only have a qualitatively deeper potential to understand the world, to flexibly adapt to a world, and to change the world, but we also have the ability to formulate more sophisticated intentions than other animals. We can harbor intentions grounded not in a relatively limited space and time, and tied more exclusively to our own body's capabilities, but have a much more sophisticated ability to capitalize and shape our environment to create tools for further actions and create our own niches (Heft, 2007). Because we have the cognitive capabilities to see a more extended piece of time when attending to affordances and because of language, we can therefore in a real sense hold onto awareness of potential affordances further in time and distribute across individuals our knowledge of what can be done, and to finally result in final completion of action far into the future. Thus it is that an animal with only a medium-long lifetime—only midway between the 2 weeks of worms and 200 years of whales—can, as a set of overlapping social synergies, construct a world in which individuals are entirely dependent on some aspect of the socially constructed world for nearly all aspects of our functioning.

It is as a result of these special capabilities, presumably, that humans have the biggest and strangest footprints of all on the world. "Biggest" is obvious—the ability to bring the world to the brink of cataclysm or indeed to leave the world behind to find new ones. "Strangest" is the ability to construct creations whose affordances seem very far removed from the more obvious requirements of living and procreating universal to animals: purely aesthetical creations. Such things are created for the pleasure they create, or as a way to articulate desires and fears that otherwise are difficult to express via mere practical actions. Being able to be captivated by such creations, to find pleasure in the play of art, is far removed from the pleasure-inducing social play that so many animals, at some developmental stages, engage in.[3] The effectance motivation (White, 1959) that drives such apparently purposeless play—chasing imaginary prey, and play fighting—results in the development of skills essential for adult survival. In contrast, humans have the biological capabilities for extended affordance perception, the ability to share such knowledge via language and thus to distribute perceptions and intentions across individuals and extended time. These mean not only the ability to construct tools and reshape environments to more efficiently have basic animal needs met (Heft, 2007), but to also be able to create works that do not seem to have any purpose apart from their own aesthetic experience and sharing in aesthetic and emotional experiences with others.

ACKNOWLEDGMENTS

Research reported in this chapter was supported by National Science Foundation grants BSC-0342802 and BSC-0240277, a grant from Cure Autism Now Foundation, and grants from the University of Connecticut Research Foundation. Thanks to Claire Michaels for commenting on portions of an earlier version of this chapter, and to Bill Mace for suggesting the example that opens this chapter.

NOTES

1. One must always be in motion in order to perceive. Even when we feel our gaze is fixed, our eyes show rapid saccades. Even when "standing still" we sway, which also means that there is continual flow in visual information.
2. An Ames room is a classic demonstration of perceptual illusions. In the constructed room, information that normally conveys size and distance is staged such that, for instance, a near object in the room is made unusually small (relative to a nearby normal-sized object) to give the appearance of being far off. The perceiver must peek at the room through a small aperture because the illusion of an Ames room completely evaporates if the perceiver is allowed to move her head and visually explore the scene.
3. For photos that illustrate biophilia and play in animals (a polar bear and husky dog at play), see http://nifplay.org/polar-husky.html.

REFERENCES

Amazeen, P. G., Schmidt, R. C., & Turvey, M. T. (1995). Frequency detuning of the phase entrainment dynamics of visually coupled rhythmic movements. *Biological Cybernetics, 72*, 511–518.

Argyle, M. & Cook, M. (1976). *Gaze and mutual gaze*. London: Cambridge University Press.

Asch, S. (1952). *Social psychology*. New York: Prentice-Hall.

Ashton-James, C., van Baaren, R. B., Chartrand, T. L., Decety, J., & Karremans, J. (2007). Mimicry and me: The impact of mimicry on self-construal. *Social Cognition, 25*, 518–535.

Barker, R. G. & Wright, H. F. (1951). *One boy's day: A specimen record of behavior*. New York: Harper.

Baron, R. M. (1980). Contrasting approaches to social knowing: An ecological perspective. *Personality and Social Psychology Bulletin, 6*, 591–600.

Baron, R. M. (2002). Exchange and development: A dynamical, complex systems perspective. In B. Laursen & W. G. Graziano (Eds.), *Social exchange in development. New directions for child and adolescent development* (pp. 53–71). San Francisco, CA: Jossey-Bass/Pfeiffer.

Baron, R. M. (2007). Situating coordination and cooperation between ecological and social psychology. *Ecological Psychology, 19*, 179–199.

Baron, R. M., Amazeen, P. G., & Beek, P. J. (1994). Local and global dynamics of social relations. In R. R. Vallacher & A. Nowak (Eds.), *Dynamical systems in social psychology* (pp. 111–138). San Diego, CA: Academic Press.

Baumeister, R. F., Vohs, K. D., & Funder, D. C. (2007). Psychology as the science of self-reports and finger movements: Whatever happened to actual behavior? *Perspectives on Psychological Science, 2*, 396–403.

Bell, P. A., Fisher, J. D., & Loomis, R. J. (1978). *Environmental psychology*. Philadelphia: Saunders.

Bernieri, F. J., Reznick, J. S., & Rosenthal, R. (1988). Synchrony, pseudosynchrony, and dissynchrony: Measuring the entrainment process in mother–infant interactions. *Journal of Personality and Social Psychology, 54*, 243–253.

Bernieri, F. J. & Rosenthal, R. (1991). Interpersonal coordination: Behavior matching and interactional synchrony. In R. S. Feldman & B. Rime (Eds.), *Fundamentals of nonverbal behavior* (pp. 401–432). Cambridge, UK: Cambridge University Press.

Calvin, W. H. (1983). A stone's throw and its launch window: Timing precision and its implications of language and hominid brains. *Journal of Theoretical Biology, 104*, 121–135.

Calvo-Merino, B., Glaser, D. E., Grèzes, J., Passingham, R. E., & Haggard, P. (2005). Action observation and acquired motor skills: An fMRI study with expert dancers. *Cerebral Cortex, 15*, 1243–1249.

Chartrand, T. L. & Bargh, J. A. (1999). The chameleon effect: The perception–behavior link and social interaction. *Journal of Personality and Social Psychology, 76*, 893–910.

Chartrand, T. L. & Jefferis, V. E. (2003). Consequences of automatic goal pursuit and the case of nonconscious mimicry. In J. P. Forgas, K. D. Williams & W. Ven Hippel (Eds.), *Social judgments: Implicit and explicit processes* (pp. 290–305). New York: Cambridge University Press.

Clark, H. H. (1996). *Using language*. New York: Cambridge University Press.

De Waal, F. B. M. (1997). *Bonobo: The forgotten ape*. Berkeley: University of California Press.

Dijksterhuis, A. & Bargh, J. A. (2001). The perception-behavior expressway: Automatic effects of social perception on social behavior. In M. P. Zanna (Ed.), *Advances in experimental social psychology* (Vol. 33, pp. 1–40). San Diego, CA: Academic Press.

Fahy, R. F. & Proulx, G. (1995, March/April). Collective common sense: A study of human behavior during the World Trade Center evacuation. *NFPA Journal*, 59–67.
Fajen, B. R., Riley, M. A., & Turvey, M. T. (2008). Information, affordances, and the control of action in sport. *International Journal of Sports Psychology, 40*, 79–107.
Festinger, L., Schacter, S., Back, K. (1950). *Social pressures in informal groups: A study of human factors in housing*. Stanford, CA: Stanford University Press.
Fischhoff, B. (2005, August 7). A hero in every aisle seat. *New York Times*. Retrieved from http://www.nytimes.com/2005/2008/2007/opinion/2007fischhoff.html?_r=2001&scp=2002&sq=fischhoff&st=cse&oref=slogin
Fowler, C. A., Richardson, M. J., Marsh, K. L., & Shockley, K. D. (2008). Language use, coordination, and the emergence of cooperative action. In A. Fuchs & V. K. Jirsa (Eds.), *Coordination: Neural, behavioral and social dynamics* (pp. 261–279). Berlin: Springer-Verlag.
Fuchs, A. & Jirsa, V. K. (Eds.). (2008). *Coordination: Neural, behavioral and social dynamics*. Berlin: Springer-Verlag.
Galantucci, B., Fowler, C. A., Turvey, M. T. (2006).The motor theory of speech perception reviewed. *Psychonomic Bulletin & Review, 13*, 361–377.
Gerstein, M. & Levitt, M. (1998). Simulating water and the molecules of life. *Scientific American, 279*, 100–105.
Gibson, J. J. (1947). Chapter 9: Perception and judgment of aerial space and distance as potential factors in pilot selection and training. *Motion picture testing and research. Aviation Research Reports, No. 7* (pp. 179–195). Washington: U.S. Government Printing Office. (Reprinted in E. Reed & R. Jones (Eds.), *Reasons for realism: Selected essays of James J. Gibson*. Hillsdale, NJ: Erlbaum, 1982.)
Gibson, J. J. (1966). *The senses considered as perceptual systems*. Boston: Houghton Mifflin.
Gibson, J. J. (1977). The theory of affordances. In R. Shaw & J. Bransford (Eds.), *Perceiving, acting, and knowing: Toward an ecological psychology* (pp. 67–82). Hillsdale, NJ: Erlbaum.
Gibson, J. J. (1979). *The ecological approach to visual perception*. Boston: Houghton Mifflin.
Gilbert, M. (1996). *Living together: Rationality, sociality, and obligation*. Lanham, MD: Rowman & Littlefield.
Grice, H. P. (1975). Logic and conversation. In A. P. Martinich (Ed.), *Philosophy of language* (pp. 165–175). New York: Oxford University Press.
Grossberg, S. & Seidman, D. (2006). Neural dynamics of autistic behaviors: Cognitive, emotional, and timing substrates. *Psychological Review, 113*, 483–525.
Gunns, R. E., Johnston, L., & Hudson, S. M. (2002). Victim selection and kinematics: A point-light investigation of vulnerability to attack. *Journal of Nonverbal Behavior, 26*, 129–158.
Harlow, H. (1958). The nature of love. *American Psychologist, 13*, 673–685.
Heft, H. (1988). Affordances of children's environments: A functional approach to environmental description. *Children's Environments Quarterly, 5*, 29–37.
Heft, H. (2001). *Ecological psychology in context: James Gibson, Roger Barker, and the legacy of William James's radical empiricism*. Mahwah, NJ: Erlbaum.
Heft, H. (2007). The social constitution of perceiver–environment reciprocity. *Ecological Psychology, 19*, 85–105.
Heft, H. (in press). Affordances and the perception of landscape: An inquiry into environmental perception and aesthetics. In C. W. Thompson, P. Aspinall, & S. Bell (Eds.), *Innovative approaches to researching landscape and health; Open space: People space 2* (pp. 9–32). New York: Routledge.
Heft, H. & Kyttä, M. (2006). A psychologically meaningful description of environments requires a relational approach. *Housing, Theory and Society, 23*, 210–213.

Iberall, A. S. & Soodak, H. (1987). A physics for complex systems. In F. E. Yates (Ed.), *Self-organizing systems: The emergence of order* (pp. 499–520). New York: Plenum.

Insko, C. A. & Wilson, M. (1977). Interpersonal attraction as a function of social interaction. *Journal of Personality and Social Psychology, 35*(12), 903–911.

Isenhower, R. W., Richardson, M. J. Carello, C., Baron, R. M., & Marsh, K. L. (2010). Affording cooperation: Dynamics and action-scaled invariance of joint lifting. *Psychonomic Bulletin & Review, 17*, 342–347.

Issartel, J., Marin, L., & Cadopi, M. (2007). Unintentional interpersonal co-ordination: "Can we march to the beat of our own drum?" *Neuroscience Letters, 411*, 174–179.

Järvilehto, T. (1998). The theory of the organism-environment system: I. Description of the theory. *Integrative Physiological & Behavioral Science, 33*, 321–334.

Järvilehto, T. (2001). Feeling as knowing–part II: Emotion, consciousness, and brain activity. *Consciousness & Emotion, 2*(1), 75–102.

Johnston, L., Hudson, S. M., Richardson, M. J., Gunns, R. E., & Garner, M. (2004). Changing kinematics as a means of reducing vulnerability to attack. *Journal of Applied Social Psychology, 34*, 514–537.

Johnston, L., Miles, L., Carter, C., & Macrae, C. N. (2005). Menstrual influences on person perception: Male sensitivity to fluctuating female fertility. *Social Cognition, 23*, 279–290.

Johnston, L., Miles, L., & Macrae, C. N. (2008). *Male or female? An investigation of factors that modulate the sex-categorization of strangers*. Unpublished manuscript.

Kean, K. J. (2000). An investigation into the interpersonal kinematics of cooperation and competition. *Dissertation Abstracts International: Section B: The Sciences and Engineering, 60*, 4965.

Kelso, J. A. S. (1995). *Dynamic patterns*. Cambridge, MA: MIT Press.

Kilner, J., Hamilton, A. F., & Blakemore, S. (2007). Interference effect of observed human movement on action is due to velocity profile of biological motion. *Social Neuroscience, 2*, 158–166.

Kohler, E., Keysers, C., Umilta, M. A., Fogassi, L., Gallese, V., & Rizzolatti, G. (2002). Hearing sounds, understanding actions: Action representation in mirror neurons. *Science, 297*, 846–848.

Kosfeld, M., Heirinchs, M., Zak, P. J., Fischbacher, U., & Fehr, E. (2005). Oxytocin increases trust in humans. *Nature, 435*, 673–676.

Kugler, P. N. & Turvey, M. T. (1987). *Information, natural law, and the self-assembly of rhythmic movement*. Hillsdale, NJ: Lawrence Erlbaum Associates Inc.

LaFrance, M. (1982). Posture mirroring and rapport. In M. Davis (Ed.), *Interaction rhythm: Periodicity in communicative behavior* (pp. 279–298). New York: Human Sciences Press.

LaFrance, M. & Broadbent, M. (1976). Group rapport: Posture sharing as a nonverbal indicator. *Group and Organization Studies, 1*, 328–333.

Lakin, J. L. & Chartrand, T. L. (2003). Using nonconscious behavioral mimicry to create affiliation and rapport. *Psychological Science, 14*, 334–339.

Marino, L., Reiss, D., & Gallup, G. G. J. (1994). Mirror self-recognition in bottlenose dolphins: Implications for comparative investigations of highly dissimilar species. In S. T. Parker & R. W. Mitchell & M. L. Boccia (Eds.), *Self-awareness in animals and humans: Developmental perspectives* (pp. 380–391). New York: Cambridge University Press.

Marsh, K. L., Johnston, L., Richardson, M. J., & Schmidt, R. C. (2009). Toward a radically embodied, embedded social psychology. *European Journal of Social Psychology, 39*, 1217–1225.

Marsh, K. L., Richardson, M. J., Baron, R. M., & Schmidt, R. C. (2006). Contrasting approaches to perceiving and acting with others. *Ecological Psychology, 18*, 1–38.

Marsh, K. L., Richardson, M. J., & Schmidt, R. C. (2009). Social connection through joint action and interpersonal coordination. *Topics in Cognitive Science, 1*, 320–339.
McArthur, L. Z. & Baron, R. M. (1983). Toward an ecological theory of social perception. *Psychological Review, 90*, 215–238.
Michaels, C. F. & Carello, C. (1981). *Direct perception*. Englewood Cliffs, NJ: Prentice-Hall.
Michaels, C. F. & Oudejans, R. R. (1992). The optics and actions of catching fly balls: Zeroing out optical acceleration. *Ecological Psychology, 4*, 199–222.
Miles, L. & Johnston, L. (2007). Detecting happiness: Perceiver sensitivity to enjoyment and non-enjoyment smiles. *Journal of Nonverbal Behavior, 31*, 259–275.
Miles, L. K. (2009). Who is approachable? *Journal of Experimental Social Psychology, 45*, 262–266. doi: 10.1016/j.jesp.2008.08.010.
Newtson, D. (1980). An interactionist perspective on social knowing. *Personality and Social Psychology Bulletin, 6*, 520–531.
Newtson, D. (1990). Alternatives to representation or alternative representations: Comments on the ecological approach. *Contemporary Social Psychology, 14*, 163–174.
Newtson, D. (1998). Dynamical systems and the structure of behavior. In K. M. Newell & P. C. M. Molenaal (Eds.), *Applications of nonlinear dynamics to developmental process modeling* (pp. 199–220). Mahwah, NJ: Lawrence Erlbaum Associates.
Newtson, D., Hairfield, J., Bloomingdale, J., & Cutino, S. (1987). The structure of action and interaction. *Social Cognition, 5*, 191–237.
Nowak, A. & Vallacher, R. R. (1998). *Dynamical social psychology*. New York: The Guilford Press.
Nowak, A., Vallacher, R. R., & Zochowski, M. (2005). The emergence of personality: Dynamic foundations of individual variation. *Developmental Review, 25*, 351–385.
Penn, D. C., Holyoak, K. J., & Povinelli, D. J. (2008). Darwin's mistake: Explaining the discontinuity between human and nonhuman minds. *Behavioral and Brain Sciences, 31*, 109–130.
Pipitone, R. N. & Gallup, G. G. (2008). Women's voice attractiveness varies across the menstrual cycle. *Evolution and Human Behavior, 29*, 268–274.
Plotnik, J. M., de Waal, F. B. M., & Reiss, D. (2006). Self-recognition in an Asian elephant. *PNAS Proceedings of the National Academy of Sciences of the United States of America, 103*, 17053–17057.
Richardson, M. J., Marsh, K. L., & Baron, R. M. (2007). Judging and actualizing intrapersonal and interpersonal affordances. *Journal of Experimental Psychology: Human Perception & Performance, 33*, 845–859.
Richardson, M. J., Marsh, K. L., Isenhower, R. W., Goodman, J. R. L., & Schmidt, R. C. (2007). Rocking together: Dynamics of unintentional and intentional interpersonal coordination. *Human Movement Science, 26*, 867–891.
Richardson, M. J., Marsh, K. L., & Schmidt, R. C. (2005). Effects of visual and verbal interaction on unintentional interpersonal coordination. *Journal of Experimental Psychology: Human Perception & Performance, 31*, 62–79.
Richardson, M. J., Marsh, K. L., & Schmidt, R. C. (2008). Challenging the egocentric view of coordinated perceiving, acting and knowing. In L. F. Barrett, B. Mesquita, & E. R. Smith (Eds.), *The mind in context* (pp. 137–154). New York: Guilford Press.
Richardson, M. J., Schmidt, R. C., & Kay, B. A. (2007). Distinguishing the noise and attractor strength of coordinated limb movements using recurrence analysis. *Biological Cybernetics, 96*, 59–78.
Richardson, M. J., Shockley, K., Fajen, B. R., Riley, M. A., & Turvey, M. T. (2008). Ecological psychology: Six principles for an embodied-embedded approach to behavior. In P. Calvo & T. Gomila (Eds.), *Elsevier handbook of new directions in cognitive science* (pp. 161–187). Amsterdam: Elsevier.

Rizzolatti, G. & Arbib, M. A. (1998). Language within our grasp. *Trends in Neurosciences, 21*, 188–194.

Rizzolatti, G. & Craighero, L. (2004). The mirror-neuron system. *Annual Review of Neuroscience, 27*, 169–192.

Runeson, S. & Frykholm, G. (1981). Visual perception of lifted weight. *Journal of Experimental Psychology: Human Perception and Performance, 7*, 733–740.

Runeson, S. & Frykholm, G. (1983). Kinematic specification of dynamics as an informational basis for person-and-action perception: Expectation, gender recognition, and deceptive intention. *Journal of Experimental Psychology: General, 112*, 585–615.

Rosenbaum, D. A. (1991). *Human motor control*. San Diego: Academic Press.

Sanchez Burks, J. (2002). Protestant relational ideology and (in)attention to relational cues in work settings. *Journal of Personality and Social Psychology, 83*, 919–929.

Schmidt, R. C., Bienvenu, M., Fitzpatrick, P. A., & Amazeen, P. G. (1998). A comparison of intra- and interpersonal interlimb coordination: Coordination breakdowns and coupling strength. *Journal of Experimental Psychology: Human Perception & Performance, 24*, 884–900.

Schmidt, R. C., Carello, C., & Turvey, M. T. (1990). Phase transitions and critical fluctuations in the visual coordination of rhythmic movements between people. *Journal of Experimental Psychology: Human Perception & Performance, 16*, 227–247.

Schmidt, R. C. & Richardson, M. J. (2008). Dynamics of interpersonal coordination. In A. Fuchs & V. K. Jirsa (Eds.), *Coordination: Neural, behavioral and social dynamics* (pp. 281–307). Berlin: Springer-Verlag.

Schmidt, R. C. & Turvey, M. T. (1994). Phase-entrainment dynamics of visually coupled rhythmic movements. *Biological Cybernetics, 70*, 369–376.

Semin, G. R. (2007). Grounding communication: Synchrony. In A. W. Kruglanski & E. T. Higgins (Eds.), *Social psychology: Handbook of basic principles* (2nd ed., pp. 630–649). New York: Guilford.

Semin, G. R., & Cacioppo, J. T. (2008). Grounding social cognition: Synchronization, coordination, and co-regulation. In G. R. Semin & E. R. Smith (Eds.), *Embodied grounding: Social, cognitive, affective, and neuroscientific approaches* (pp. 119–147). New York: Cambridge University Press.

Shattuck, R. (1980). *The forbidden experiment: The story of the Wild Boy of Aveyron*. New York: Farrar Straus Giroux.

Shockley, K., Baker, A. A., Richardson, M. J., & Fowler, C. A. (2007). Articulatory constraints on interpersonal postural coordination. *Journal of Experimental Psychology: Human Perception & Performance, 33*, 201–208.

Shockley, K., Santana, M. V., & Fowler, C. A. (2003). Mutual interpersonal postural constraints are involved in cooperative conversation. *Journal of Experimental Psychology: Human Perception and Performance, 29*, 326–332.

Sommer, R. (1969). *Personal space: The behavioral basis of design*. Englewood Cliffs, NJ: Prentice-Hall.

Sonnby-Borgström, M., Jönsson, P., & Svensson, O. (2003). Emotional empathy as related to mimicry reactions at different levels of information processing. *Journal of Nonverbal Behavior, 27*, 3–23.

Tesser, A. (1980). When individual dispositions and social pressure conflict: A catastrophe. *Human Relations, 33*, 393–407.

Tesser, A. & Achee, J. (1994). Aggression, love, conformity, and other social psychological catastrophes. In R. P. Vallacher & A. Nowak (Eds.), *Dynamical systems in social psychology* (pp. 95–109). San Diego, CA: Academic Press.

Thelen, E. & Smith, L. B. (1994). *A dynamic systems approach to the development of cognition and action*. Cambridge, MA: MIT Press.

Turvey, M. T. (1990). Coordination. *American Psychologist, 45*, 938–953.

Turvey, M. T. (2007). Action and perception at the level of synergies. *Human Movement Science, 26*, 657–697.

Vallacher, R. R. & Nowak, A. (1994). *Dynamical systems in social psychology*. San Diego: Academic Press.

Vallacher, R. R., Read, S. J., & Nowak, A. (2002). The dynamical perspective in personality and social psychology. *Personality and Social Psychology Review, 6*, 264–273.

Van Acker, R. & Valenti, S. S. (1989). Perception of social affordances by children with mild handicapping conditions: Implications for social skills research and training. *Ecological Psychology, 1*, 383–405.

Van Dijk, J., Kerkhofs, R., van Rooij, I., & Haselager, P. (2008). Can there be such a thing as embodied embedded cognitive neuroscience? *Theory & Psychology, 18*, 297–316.

Van Ulzen, N. R., Lamoth, C. J. C., Daffertshofer, A., Semin, G. R., & Beek, P. J. (2008). Characteristics of instructed and uninstructed interpersonal coordination while walking side-by-side. *Neuroscience Letters, 432*, 88–93.

Warren, W. H. (1984). Perceiving affordances: Visual guidance of stair climbing. *Journal of Experimental Psychology: Human Perception and Performance, 10*, 683–703.

Warren, W. H. (2006). The dynamics of perception and action. *Psychological Review, 113*, 358–389.

White, R. W. (1959). Motivation reconsidered: The concept of competence. *Psychological Review, 66*, 297–333.

Whyte, W. W. (1980). *The social life of small urban spaces* [Motion picture]. (Available from the Project for Public Spaces, New York.)

Zajonc, R. B. (1965). Social facilitation. *Science, 149* (3681), 269–274.

5

Sociality in Extremis
Removing the Boundaries Between Self and Other

GÜN R. SEMIN

This chapter examines the conditions where an extreme or unusual state of sociality is achieved, namely, when the boundaries between individuals are dissolved and when there is no sense of distance between the self and the other.

This is a state and situation that occurs very infrequently in normal Western experience and may therefore appear somewhat outlandish because of this infrequency. It is a state involving the dissolution of the boundaries between the "self and other." An indication of this means can be evidenced in the case of an audience applauding in unison (e.g., Néda, Ravasz, Brechet, Vicsek, & Barabasi, 2000; Néda, Ravasz, Vicsek, Brechet, & Barabasi, 2000), and when they experience the unusual state of clapping their hands as a synchronized unit. The wave that large crowds display in sports events is another instance of this unusual and infrequent state of sociality. Another illustration is the remarkable phenomenon observed at the opening of the Millennium footbridge in London in 2000. Pedestrians spontaneously synchronized their steps with one another after the number of people on the bridge exceeded a certain point (e.g., Eckhardt, Ott, Strogatz, Abrams, & McRobie, 2007). The synchronization of walking was due in this case to the small vibrations in the material substrate, namely, the supporting frame and the bridge, which in turn connected the individuals as oscillators. What we have in all three examples is a self-organizing system, "one in which some kind of higher-level pattern emerges from the interactions of multiple simple components *without the benefit of a leader, controller, or orchestrator*" (Clark, 1997, p. 73, emphasis added). The focus of this chapter is to examine the conditions of such an interpersonal emergent state and its psychological implications.

By definition, states in which individual identity is suspended require two or more persons for their emergence. Moreover, the emergence of such states requires very specific types of coaction and associated neural conditions that are different from those normally involved in everyday social interaction. The first part of this contribution derives from a dynamic model of social cognition (Semin & Cacioppo, 2008, 2009). With this model, it is possible to specify the necessary neural and behavioral conditions under which self and other boundaries are likely to be dissolved.

The second part is the application of this model to the particular case of social interaction, which is predicted to give rise to the dissolution of self–other boundaries. The distinctive feature of interaction for this state to arise is entrainment or synchronization, namely, spontaneous phase-locked pattern formation of actions.

The concluding section examines how one can come to terms with a synchronized unit that has emerged "without the benefit of a leader, controller, or orchestrator" and thus not driven by any identifiable agent. Such collectively synchronized situations present an interesting epistemic phenomenon since it is difficult to rest the explanation of "unintentionally" entrained behavior on individual causation. Synchronization of actions introduces a *qualitative shift* due to the difficulty of applying an individual-centered explanation of collectively produced coaction. It is therefore likely for the parties to the interaction to search for explanations that are extraordinary or supraindividual. Thus, the final section elaborates upon potential explanatory sources that can be recruited to account for the experienced state in a meaningful manner.

THE SOCIAL COGNITION MODEL AND THE NECESSARY CONDITIONS FOR THE DISSOLUTION OF SELF AND OTHER BOUNDARIES

It may be surprising to note that predictions about the suspension of individual consciousness and the dissolution of self and other boundaries can be derived from a neurophysiologically grounded model of social cognition (SC; Semin & Cacioppo, 2008, 2009). This model derives in part from one of the remarkable discoveries of neuroscience over the last 15 years, namely, the demonstration that observed human bodily movements can be mapped onto our own bodies and that this is a species-specific process (e.g., Buccino et al., 2004). The evidence for such mapping comes primarily (but not only) from neurophysiological work revealing that the neural systems responsible for the execution of an action are coactivated when such action is observed (see Iacoboni, this volume, Chapter 2). This system appears to involve a prereflective, automatic mechanism of mirroring (Rizzolatti & Craighero, 2004), reproducing what is going on in the brain of other people when they are moving. In other words, other human beings constitute a class of stimuli that is distinctive from other animate or inanimate types of stimuli in our environment. Thus, this type of sensory neural representation of the other has an entirely different status from knowledge about the world in general.

The main implication of this "discovery" is that different knowledge bases drive our interactions with our social and nonsocial world. Whereas *social* interaction entails a common representational format for action and perception, all other types of interaction derive from an individual's ability to recognize and perform "action possibilities" that are latent in the environment (e.g., Gibson, 1979). A neural system for mapping others' bodily movements, the mirror neuron system (Puce & Perrett, 2003; Rizzolatti & Craighero, 2004), is important in grounding social interaction since it bridges the epistemic gulf separating single individuals—a gulf that has shaped the way we think about human functioning as well as the methods with which we have examined human functioning. The focus is often, if not always, on the individual. However, human functioning takes place in a social context and not a vacuum. Oddly enough, even the neuroscientific (but also psychological) research that has revealed the social nature of mirroring systems has implicitly treated subjects as passive individual observers (Smith & Semin, 2004) in their examination of, for instance, the mirror neuron strategy (MNS). Such individual-centered vision informs theorizing in this field (Semin & Cacioppo, 2009).

A distinctive, functional feature of the MNS is that it is uninterruptedly available unless it is actively suppressed by inhibition (Iacoboni et al., 1999). This system is likely to facilitate a prereflexive "understanding"[1] of others by simulating some of what is going on in the brain of other people by producing similar activities in the brain areas that are involved in the performance of the observed actions of others. The adaptive function of the MNS, a system that is involved in the continuous monitoring of what others in our social environment are engaged in, includes a mechanism that allows us to simulate getting under the skin of the other person without reasoning explicitly about it. This forward monitoring mechanism sending out impulses similar to those that could actually control movement also facilitates the smooth flow of all aspects of our social interaction whether in a game or a dialogue but without confusing ourselves as the person we observe or respond to. Notably, such a neural system mapping others' bodily movements constitutes an automatic bridge between self and other, inducing a degree of reflexive similarity between self and other.

But predictive monitoring is not enough to engage in social interaction. Take for example a tennis game: I have to monitor my partner to be able to actually respond with a countermove if I want to play the game. Obviously, a system that predictively monitors the other's movements is not sufficient to play a game. I need to execute the countermove (see also Graf, Schütz-Bosbach, & Prinz, this volume, Chapter 3). Thus, we require a system that implements action. Indeed, a system that anatomically overlaps with the MNS but is functionally distinct is one referred to as the motor preparation system (MPS) and is responsible for the implementation of one's goals and intentions to perform an action (e.g., Fogassi et al., 2005). Unfortunately, neuroscientific research has relied on the acts of an individual or the observation of an action, but rarely on an interaction where a person acts and influences the other who then re-acts, and so on (see Tognoli, Lagarde, DeGuzman, & Kelso, 2007, for an exception).

A more detailed analysis of the well-documented finding of neural synchronization between action and action perception by the MNS and the functionally distinct but overlapping MPS suggests that under certain circumstances it will be difficult to distinguish between self and other. The question is, when is this likely to happen. The social cognition model that John Cacioppo and I have advanced (see Semin & Cacioppo, 2008, 2009, for details) furnishes a framework to specify the conditions that are necessary for the dissolution of the self–other boundary.

THE SOCIAL COGNITION MODEL

The SC model we advanced (Semin & Cacioppo 2008, 2009) adopts the notion of *social* to refer to the regulation of social interaction. This by definition entails the processes involved in the adaptive coregulation of interactions. Understanding what social cognition means not only explicating that cognition is *distributed across brains* in a distinctive manner. It also involves understanding the processes by which the regulation of others' behavior and the coregulation of social interaction are achieved. Figure 5.1 captures the model we have developed for this purpose. To represent the model, I shall go through the steps starting with the observation of an action, the higher-order neurophysiological sensorimotor processes that it recruits, and conclude with the execution of an action by the agent.

The observation of an action (Point 1 in Figure 5.1) performed by another person serves as a stimulus. The effects of this stimulus depend on whether it is goal relevant. Irrespective of whether a significant goal is activated, the stimulus activates a *monitoring process* (Point 2a in Figure 5.1). We refer to this monitoring process as *synchronization* and define it as *jointly and simultaneously recruited sensory motor processes* that are evident in a neurophysiological mirroring of the producer by the perceiver. The function of time-locked synchronization processes is to enable organisms to continuously monitor and adaptively respond to their social environment. Such monitoring takes place in recurrent *discrete*, and *short-lived temporal intervals*, which maintain the sensitivity of the organism to changes in the environment. Synchronization processes rely on a discrete system (the mirror neuron system) in the brain, which is critical in allowing the actions of others to be perceived, embodied, and understood by our motor system (see Iacoboni, this volume, Chapter 2). The main components of this system are the inferior parietal sulcus, the premotor cortex, and the superior temporal sulcus (Iacoboni et al., 1999).

Aside from their monitoring function, synchronization processes link two or more human agents, putting them on a similar footing. *Jointly recruited processes* with partially *overlapping* "identities" facilitate prereflexive understanding (co-cogitation) and adaptive coaction (coregulation) between two or more individuals. In other words, such mechanisms facilitate reaching a state of correspondence between the individuals. What counts for the one member may not initially have counted for the other, but through interaction these two become synchronized to approach being on the same page—that is, for what counts for one individual also counting for the other. Such synchronization can occur without the presence of explicit intent or goals. Synchronization promotes partial and not full correspondence between producer and perceiver. If these processes were to induce complete correspondence, then this would result in an endless loop of continuously performing the very same action leading to confusion between self and other (Figure 5.1, Point 2a; however, see concluding section for exceptions).

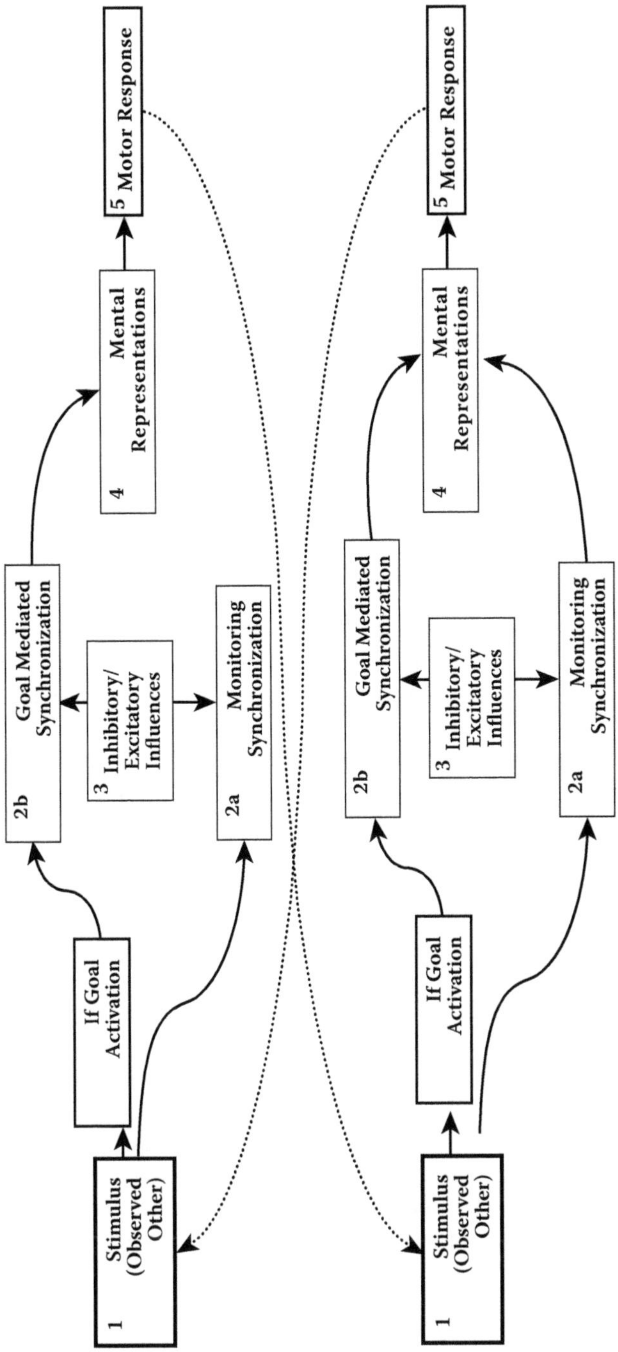

Figure 5.1 The social cognition model.

The adaptive nature of social cognition and the complexity of the social environment necessitate *selective responding to significant features of a dynamic social environment* by setting goals for action. Thus, one has to address how adaptive action is induced in response to "significant" stimuli. For instance, in a tennis game you have to monitor your partner's action, but to win the game you have to take *complementary* action to counter your partner's move. A goal-relevant stimulus (forehand smash by your tennis partner) recruits higher-level cognitive processes that activate a system in the brain that is anatomically overlapping with the *mirror neuron system* but functionally distinct, namely, the *motor preparation system* (e.g., Tognoli, Lagarde, deGuzman, & Kelso, 2007). This system is responsible for the implementation of goal-relevant action. Thus, if the stimulus is goal relevant, then higher-level cognitive processes are recruited, which entail goal-mediated synchronization of neurophysiological activations whose specific form need not mirror the actions that are observed. Although the monitoring process is critical, adaptive action is not merely a product of monitoring processes. Consequently, the identification of significant stimuli recruits goal-driven, higher-level decision processes that can run in addition to continuous monitoring processes (see Figure 5.1, Point 2b).

Although they involve anatomically overlapping systems, the higher-order goal-mediated motor preparation system and adaptive action depicted in Figure 5.1, Point 2b are separable functionally from the mirror neuron system–driven monitoring synchronization depicted in Figure 5.1, Point 2a. One reason for this functional distinction is that the processes depicted in Point 2a are thought to be automatic, whereas those depicted in Point 2b involve automatic and controlled processes. In the tennis example, this means that the forehand smash of the opponent is monitored—a process that is achieved by the nonconscious synchronization of neurophysiological activations corresponding to that motor movement. Synchronization as a continuous monitoring process serves a predictive function by detecting changes in the environment. Yet, the tennis player has to make a decision about how to counter the forehand smash and defend himself or herself. This decision to counter the forehand leads to the requisite neurophysiological activation for the execution of the countermove by engaging the motor preparation system rather than simply the mirror image of the observed action. Although specific aspects of goal-mediated synchronization can be automated, the act as a whole is not.

Both goal-mediated processes and monitoring synchronization recruit neurophysiological activity and jointly contribute to the shape of the representations that are translated into motor action (Point 4 in Figure 5.1). In the absence of goal-mediated synchronization, the neurophysiological activation from monitoring synchronization shapes the representation. However, this does not necessarily mean the automatic execution of the observed action, because other factors can contribute to the representation. Moreover, both excitatory and inhibitory factors (Figure 5.1, Point 3) can modulate the contributions of the processes depicted in Figure 5.1, Points 2a and 2b to the representation. For instance, inhibitory processes can contribute to blocking continuous automatic reproduction of what is observed (Buccino et al., 2004).

The structural features of the environment or of the task shape the type of action coregulation between two or more persons. These features can be socially shaped (e.g., dancing, playing tennis, conversation) or shaped by the physical characteristics of a joint task (e.g., carrying a large and heavy object, etc.). Both present distinctive affordances that contribute to the shape of the coregulation. For any social interaction the behavior of one individual becomes the stimulus for the other when the individuals are actively interacting, with each iteratively producing coaction effects. Consequently, synchronization and adaptive coregulation of behaviors are detectable when the unit of analysis is at the social rather than the individual level.

The important feature of the SC model is that it represents the result of coaction as *emergent social cognition* as represented in Figure 5.1 with direct loops from Point 5 to 1. Thus the model captures situations where the behavior of a member of the dyad provides information pickup for the other member in an iterative process.

CONDITIONS FOR THE DISSOLUTION OF SELF AND OTHER BOUNDARIES

The dissolution of self–other boundaries is likely to be manifested with a specific set of conditions applying in the case of three critical parameters of the SC model: (a) *monitoring synchronization*, (b) *higher-order goal-mediated synchronization*, and (c) *structural features of the environment or task* that provide the social and physical context for social interaction. These conditions can be analyzed with the example in the introduction, the *spontaneous* transition of an applauding audience from disordered clapping to entrained clapping and then back again to disordered clapping only for entrained clapping to reemerge a little later as a synchronized unit (Néda, Ravasz, Brechet, et al., 2000; Néda, Ravasz, Vicsek, et al., 2000).

This remarkable phenomenon is evidenced despite considerable individual differences in clapping tempos. It would appear that the transition to entrained clapping enhances noise intensity and requires less effort, whereby each clapper affects the other both locally and globally. Entrained behavior occurs rhythmically and one way of capturing its regularities is to model its cycles, periods, frequencies, and amplitudes. Depending on the particular behavior and interaction in question, behavioral cycles of entrainment in interpersonal behavior can range from milliseconds to hours. Indeed, entrainment as we refer to it here is a pervasive phenomenon not specific to human social behavior alone (e.g., Strogatz, 2003). Entrainment can be captured in terms of characteristic cycles, periods, frequencies, and amplitudes, and its investigation can focus on the degree to which behavioral cycles of a couple are in phase or not.

One distinctive feature of this particular "phenomenon" is a social environment that creates an unarticulated common goal—in the example, an outstanding performance. The situation constitutes an instance of complete convergence between the higher-order goal-mediated synchronization or motor preparation system and monitoring synchronization or the mirror neuron system. Such a complete correspondence results in a continuous loop of performing the very same action leading to dissolution between self and other and the emergence of an entrained unit. The resulting effect is the materialization of a *supraindividual* behavioral phenomenon, that is, extended behavioral cycles that are phase locked. In the concluding section, the analytical and psychological implications of extended phase-locked behavioral cycles are addressed.

CONCLUSIONS AND IMPLICATIONS

Social interaction involving extended periods of phase-locked behavior cycles do not belong to the routine repertoire of events that are experienced, particularly those involving more than two people. Indeed, the few familiar ones (military parades, religious chanting, etc.) are increasingly out of fashion. However, the question is how one would approach a closer understanding of entrainment, particularly if it is manifested in a group larger than a dyad. Coordination dynamics is one option to investigate the dynamic properties of actual behavior taking place between individuals. This approach is concerned with identifying key coordination variables for complex behavior and deriving patterns from the coupling of such variables during social interaction (Jirsa & Kelso, 2004). A complementary perspective is examining how individuals who find themselves in spontaneously emerging periods of phase-locked behavior cycles account for the situation they find themselves in. I focus on the latter option.

Generally, social events are explained with reference to individual and situational factors that contribute to the emergence of the event. The degree to which the person or the situational constraints shape the nature of the event will vary from situation to situation, from the perspective of the person (actor or observer), or from culture to culture. However, an event that involves prolonged multimodal entrainment that is produced by three or more actors introduces a *qualitative shift* that is difficult to capture with person- or situation-centered accounts. Extended periods of phase-locked behavior cycles produced by three or more people, particularly if they emerge spontaneously, cannot be easily reduced to personal agency. A satisfactory account has to be found in some source that is supraindividual.

A distinctive feature that prolonged entrainment introduces is dissolution of self–other boundaries. Extended entrainment means complete convergence between the higher-order goal-mediated synchronization or motor preparation system and monitoring synchronization or the mirror neuron system. It constitutes a continuous loop of performing the very same action as the other. This conveys a sense of unity that is likely to induce a strong sense of collective identity or synchronized unit with strong positive affective concomitants.

Such situations have an opaque plasticity that is pregnant to interpretational diversity when experienced for the first time. The situated context within which such an experience emerges will channel the type of explanation that will constitute the account for the experience. The combination of an unusual event in search of explanation that cannot be reduced to an individual cause, along with the powerful sense of unity and sense of belongingness, presents the ideal combination for the creation of supraindividual explanations that provide the base for enduring cultural myths. The extreme case of spontaneously induced entrainment is likely to be perceived as an experience that supersedes the immediacy of individually driven causes and interpreted as a "transcendental experience." It constitutes an event that is likely to be inexplicable with the current currency of the primacy of self or other referent individual experience or causation.

ACKNOWLEDGMENTS

I would like to express my thanks to Gerald Echterhoff for his constructive, critical, and most helpful comments on an earlier version of this chapter.

NOTES

1. Note that "understanding" is used in a different way than its standard use in the mirror neuron literature and this use has come to justifiable criticism (e.g., Hickok, 2009; Lingnau, Gesierich, & Caramazza, 2009).

REFERENCES

Buccino, G., Lui, F., Canessa, N., Patteri, I., Lagravinese, G., Benuzzi, F., Porro, C. A., & Rizzolatti, G. (2004). Neural circuits involved in the recognition of actions performed by nonconspecifics: An fMRI study. *Journal of Cognitive Neuroscience, 16*, 114–126.

Clark, A. (1997). *Being there*. Cambridge, MA: MIT Press.

Eckhardt, B., Ott, E., Strogatz, S. H., Abrams, D. M., & McRobie, A. (2007). Modeling walker synchronization on the Millennium Bridge. *Physical Review, E, 75*, 021110.

Fogassi, L., Ferrari, P. F., Gesierich, B., Rozzi, S., Chersi, F., & Rizzolatti, G. (2005). Parietal lobe: From action organization to intention understanding. *Science*, 308, 662–667.

Gibson, J. J. (1979). *The ecological approach to visual perception*. Boston: Houghton Mifflin.

Hickok, G. (2009). Eight problems for the mirror neuron theory of action understanding in monkeys and humans. *Journal of Cognitive Neuroscience, 21*(7), 1229–1243.

Iacoboni, M., Woods, R. P., Brass, M., Bekkering, H., Mazziotta, J. C., & Rizzolatti, G. (1999). Cortical mechanisms of human imitation. *Science*, 286, 2526–2528.

Jirsa, V. K., & Kelso, J. A. S. (2004). *Coordination dynamics: Issues and trends*. New York: Springer.

Lingnau, A., Gesierich, B., & Caramazza, A. (2009). Asymmetric fMRI adaptation reveals no evidence for mirror neurons in humans. *Proceedings of the National Academy of Sciences, 106*(24), 9925–9930.

Néda, Z., Ravasz, E., Brechet, Y., Vicsek, T., & Barabasi, A. L. (2000). The sound of many hands clapping: Tumultuous applause can transform itself into waves of synchronized clapping. *Nature, 403*, 849–850.

Néda, Z., Ravasz, E., Vicsek, T., Brechet, Y., & Barabasi, A. L. (2000). Physics of the rhythmic applause. *Physical Review E, 61*, 6987–6992.

Puce, A. & Perrett, D. (2003). Electrophysiology and brain imaging of biological motion. *Philosophical Transactions of the Royal Society, London B, 358*, 435–445.

Rizzolatti, G. & Craighero, L. (2004). The mirror-neuron system. *Annual Review of Neuroscience, 27*, 169–192.

Semin, G. R. & Cacioppo, J. T. (2008). Grounding social cognition: Synchronization, coordination, and co-regulation. In G. R. Semin & E. R. Smith (Eds.), *Embodied grounding: Social, cognitive, affective, and neuroscientific approaches* (pp. 119–147). New York: Cambridge University Press.

Semin, G. R. & Cacioppo, J. T. (2009). From embodied representation to co-regulation. In J. A. Pineda (Ed.), *Mirror neuron systems: The role of mirroring processes in social cognition* (pp. 107–120). New York: Humana Press.

Smith, E. R. & Semin, G. R. (2004). Socially situated cognition: Cognition in its social context. *Advances in Experimental Social Psychology, 36*, 53–117.

Strogatz, S. (2003). *Rhythms of nature, rhythms of ourselves*. London: Allan Lane.

Tognoli, E., Lagarde, J., DeGuzman, G. C., & Kelso, J. A. S. (2007). The phi complex as a neuromarker of human social coordination. *Proceedings of the National Academy of Sciences, 104*, 8190–8195.

Section *II*

Sociality and Memory

6

On the Virtues of an Unreliable Memory

Its Role in Constructing Sociality

WILLIAM HIRST AND ADAM BROWN

Psychologists recognized long ago that memory is not like a tape recorder, in that its accuracy is almost always suspect. As a result, one might expect that two people who experience the same event may remember it quite differently. Memory errors of both omission and commission are not random, however. There is a pattern, a systematicity to them. As Bartlett (1932) noted, errors of commission, in particular, seem to be a product of reconstruction based not exclusively on decaying stored representations of the past, but also on current attitudes, schemata, and, importantly, the social and physical environment in which the remembering occurs. The different attitudes, schemata, and social and physical environments in which people remember can lead them to recollect the past in ways that differ from one person to the next. In this chapter, we want to explore another, albeit paradoxical, consequence of memory's malleability: that the same attitudes, schemata, and social and physical environments that promote individual differences can also transform initially disparate memories into shared recollections.

The consequences of the development of shared renderings of the past cannot be understated. Halbwachs (1925/1992) referred to them as collective memories. Suffice it to say for the present, collective memories are memories shared by a community that help shape that community's collective identity (see Hirst & Manier, 2008, and Manier & Hirst, 2008, for discussions about the definition of collective memory). From this perspective, they are the collective variant of autobiographical memories, which are individually held memories that help shape personal identity. For Halbwachs, and those that follow in his tradition, collective memories are important for a community because of this identity-constructing function. Regarding the focus of this volume, they are important because they promote sociality. Clearly, they help define and bind together a group. Americans are, to a degree, Americans because they share the same rendering of the past. And Americans differ from Russians, in part, because the two hold different renderings of the same past. For instance, these two nations remember War World II differently. Americans tend to remember D-Day as being the most important battle of the war; Russians remember the most important battle as the Battle of Leningrad (Wertsch, 2002). Their different memories help shape the way Russians and Americans see their place in the world and how they conceive of themselves as a nation.

This chapter is mainly concerned with how individually held memories can become shared by a group. As Bartlett (1932) suggested, shared memories (he disliked the term *collective memories*) are sometimes formed and retained because community members hold similar attitudes and possess similar schemata. Community members are raised together, attend the same school, read the same books, and generally share many of the same experiences. This continuity of social learning and experience will often lead to a common set of beliefs and attitudes, and these in turn will shape the way community members remember their past. A good example of the effect of shared schemata on the formation of collective memory can be found in the classic study of Hastorf and Cantril (1954), which examined the memories Dartmouth and Princeton students held of a critical and brutal football match between the two schools. The Dartmouth and Princeton students held similar attitudes within a student body, but different attitudes across student bodies. As a result, the memories of the Dartmouth students were similar, as were those of the Princeton students, but the two similar memories differed across schools.

This chapter, however, is not concerned with how shared attitudes can lead to shared memories. Rather we are interested in situations in which the initial memories differ across individuals in a community. Even if community members share many attitudes and schemata, they also achieve their individuality in the community, in part, because they also possess other, unshared attitudes and schemata. These individually specific attitudes and schemata can often lead members of the same community to remember the same event quite differently, as Kurosawa's famous film *Rashomon* dramatically illustrated. It is the claim here that these individually distinct memories can become shared over time.

The present chapter seeks to understand the process by which the malleability of memory promotes the formation of shared memories. It rests on the assumption that members of a community interact with one another more often than members from different communities. These social interactions can reshape initially disparate memories into shared renderings, which are more likely to be held within a community than across communities.

In what follows, we will unpack this claim. We will first explore in more detail the concept of collective memory. We will then turn to the specific ways social interactions can promote the formation of collective memory. Here we will focus on conversational interactions. Within a conversation, speakers could reshape their own memories or reshape the memories of listeners. We will be concerned with the conditions under which such "reshaping" can occur and whether it will lead to a shared rendering of the past.

A GENERAL NOTE ON THE CONCEPT OF COLLECTIVE MEMORY

Before exploring the processes by which collective memories are formed, we should make some general comments on the concept of collective memory, in that it has not figured much in most psychological work on memory or identity (for a general overview of the topic of collective memory, see Nünning & Erll, 2008). Since Halbwachs (1925/1992) first introduced the term, most social scientists have treated collective memories as "publicly available symbols maintained by society" (Olick, 1999). As such, they mainly study commemorations, memorials, or, more generally, the memory practices of a society, in that these are means by which society maintains publicly available symbols. In their discussion of commemorations, memorials, and memory practices, students of collective memory are interested in the process by which society constructs these symbols and retains them, and the way subgroups marshal resistance to these efforts (Bodnar, 1992; Wertsch, 2002). They are interested, for instance, in the political conflicts arising over the construction of a museum exhibition, a memorial, or the establishment of a commemoration or a "tradition" (for a review of this approach, see Hirst & Manier, 2008). These political conflicts are often referred to as "memory wars."

This work does not, however, address what is the concern here: How does the malleability of memory lead to shared memories rather than a collection of distinct renderings of the past? For us, as psychologists, it is puzzling that the individual consumers of mnemonic resources, the people who interact with them, rarely figure in the discussions of collective memory. The study of collective memory from a social science perspective appears to be only about establishing and maintaining mnemonic resources. The individuals interacting with and reacting to these resources simply do not appear. There might have been a fierce memory war over design decisions surrounding a Smithsonian museum exhibition on the bombing of Hiroshima, and it is no doubt important to understand the politics surrounding these issues, as several sociologists have done (Nobile, 1995). But, as legitimate as these concerns are, they bear only tangentially on the basic question we wish to address here: Why does the exhibit lead to a shared memory of the bombing rather than distinctively different ones? The issue is not simply about how to undertake appropriate "market researching" on each particular exhibit, memorial, commemoration, and social interaction, following the lead of commercial market research, which often undertakes separate studies of each new product introduced into the market. Rather the issue is to understand more deeply how individual human psychology places constraints and offers efficiencies in the extent to which exhibits, memorials, commemoration, or, more generally, social interactions among people or between people and social artifacts, such as memorials and commemorations, can reshape participants' memories. In doing so, individual human psychology may contribute significantly to an understanding of how the memory practice of a community promotes shared rather than distinctive recollections of the past.

In focusing on the consumer, we are treating collective memories as individual memories widely held across a community rather than simply publicly available symbols. Of course, as noted, collective memories are not simply shared individual memories. Just as autobiographical memories are individual memories bearing on personal identity, so are collective memories shared memories bearing on collective identity (Assmann, 1995). As a result, not all shared memories are collective memories. Spaniards may share a memory of the value of *pi*, but this memory is not a Spanish collective memory because it does not shape Spanish identity. On the other hand, the Madrid bombing of May 11 is a Spanish collective memory because not only is it a widely shared individual memory among Spaniards, it also influences Spanish collective identity.

That being said, our interest here is in the way our understanding of individual human psychology can promote the formation of shared memories. A memory must become shared before it can bear on collective identity. The relation between these shared memories and collective identity is beyond the scope of this chapter. Olick (1999) has differentiated *collective memories* from *collected memory* and argued that the latter term is better suited when the discussion is about widely shared memories. Olick would only want to grant the label *collective* to those memories that society seeks to maintain and hence has a function for society. For Olick, the study of collective memories is distinctly different from the study of collected memories. For us, an understanding of how a memory becomes collected is integral to the study of collective memory—in that one cannot fully appreciate how a memory can come to shape a community's identity if one cannot understand how it became widely shared. From this perspective, the present concern with the role social interaction plays in promoting mnemonic convergence addresses, at least in part, not only the issue of how collected memories are formed, but also the formation of collective memories.

PATHS TO CONVERGENCE THROUGH SOCIAL INTERACTION

As we have stated, our concern here will mainly be with social interactions among people, specifically, conversational interactions. This focus on conversation should not be viewed as limiting the relevance of our discussion. As many scholars have noted, collective memories, even for something as large as a nation, are often formed through conversations (Fentress & Wickham, 1992; Wertsch, 2002). To be sure, collective memories are not formed in a large community though one monstrous conversation, but through a large series of conversations that in the end involve the entire community. In their multiplicity, conversations can serve as important vehicles through which to build a collective memory. Their role is particularly relevant for the formation of what has variously been called informal, vernacular, or counter-memories (Bodnar, 1992; Foucault, 1977; Zerubavel, 1998). For instance, Lithuanians of Lithuanian descent know their nation's history not through the Russian textbook they use in school, but through the many informal conversations they have with acquaintances, friends, and relatives (Schuman, Rieger, & Gaidys, 1994).

As we view the spread of a memory, one person may talk to another, who talks to a third person, who, in turn, has a conversation with the first person. Of course, this network of connections can become much more complex, but this simple example suffices to illustrate how the repeated circulation of a memory through a chain of conversation can lead to convergence onto a shared rendering. Convergence would be straightforward if the fidelity of the transmission were perfect from one person to the next. But, as we have stressed, memories are unreliable and malleable. The fidelity of transmission is rarely, if ever, perfect. A central question for the formation of a collective memory, then, is an understanding of the condition under which convergence will occur. The resulting shared rendering could have little in common with the original memory of the first person in the chain, but that does not mitigate the fact that convergence took place. Rumors are one example of how collective memories are formed through this method of transmittal (DiFonzo & Bordia, 2007).

We are interested here in what might be considered a variant of the situation just described. In the case of rumors, for instance, each member of the chain, at least on the first go-around, is learning for the first time about the rumor. The situation we are interested in is when each member in the chain already has a memory, albeit a different one from all the other members. Consider a simple example of a chain of two people. Both may have heard about Mary's divorce from John, but they have different renderings of the events that led up to this divorce. We will focus on how conversations between these two people about the divorce can lead to a shared memory of the divorce.

Thus, in the present chapter, we focus on the role of conversations in promoting collective memory and reduce our community by and large to groups of two. We take these steps because we believe that if we can appreciate the manner by which a conversation between two people can promote the convergence of initially distinct renderings through memory's mutability, then we have fulfilled what might be thought as the first step in understanding how a network of connected individuals, a community of individuals, if you like, can come to converge upon a shared rendering of the past.

We will chiefly be interested here in how a speaker can shape the memories of listeners. Echterhoff, Higgins, and others have focused on how what speakers say can reshape their own memory in a manner that leads to mnemonic convergence between speaker and listener—what they called shared reality (see in this volume Echterhoff & Higgins, Chapter 7, and Higgins, Chapter 8; see also Hirst & Echterhoff, 2008). We will focus our discussion on how what a speaker says can reshape the listener's memory in a manner that leads to mnemonic convergence between speakers and listeners.

A speaker's recounting may differ from a listener's memory in several ways. We will be interested in instances in which a speaker either (1) offers information about the event unknown to the listener, (2) says something that contradicts what the listener know, or (3) omits information from his recounting that both he and the listener know. We will first address Situations 1 and 2 together, under the label of *social contagion*, and then address (3) separately, under the label of *induced forgetting*.

SOCIAL CONTAGION

The General Phenomenon

The study of social contagion can be traced back to the groundbreaking work of Elizabeth Loftus on eyewitness testimony. In what is now a paradigmatic experiment, Loftus and her colleagues showed individual participants a sequence of slides depicting a traffic accident (for a review, see Loftus, 2005; Echterhoff, Hirst, & Hussy, 2005). An orally presented "postevent" narrative then followed, which introduced new information or information that contradicted what was originally experienced. Finally, a memory test for the content of the original slides ended the experiment. For instance, the slides might show a car slowing at a corner and then turning despite the presence of a stop sign, whereas the postevent narrative would allude to a yield sign rather than a stop sign. Loftus and her colleagues have shown repeatedly that people will often falsely remember the material in the postevent narrative as initially occurring in the slide show.

To ensure that the misleading postevent information effect applies to what occurs in everyday life and not just material constructed for a laboratory experiment, Loftus and other researchers made people believe through the introduction of postevent information that they have gotten lost in a shopping center, knocked over a wedding cake at a relative's wedding, or saw a Hanna-Barbera cartoon character at Disneyland (Loftus, 2005). In each case, the event did not occur (in the case of the cartoon character, could not have occurred). Nevertheless, people not only came to believe that it did, but often went beyond the information given to supply an elaborate narrative about the event.

The social interaction in the standard experiment on postevent misinformation effect is minimal, in that the experimenter supplies the postevent narrative with as minimal interaction with the experimental participant as possible. But it is possible to inject complex social interactions into the paradigm by introducing another participant into the experiment. One participant could serve as the purveyor of the postevent information, that is, be a "speaker," while the other participant could be the receiver of the postevent information, the "listener." In this case, the interest is in whether the social interaction between the speaker and listener will lead the speaker to impose his or her memories onto the listener, that is, whether there is mnemonic contagion from speaker to listener.

In perhaps the best known of these studies, Meade and Roediger (2002) created this situation by asking a participant to study a complex picture, then jointly recall the picture with a confederate, who was instructed to recall information that was not in the original pictures. Finally, Meade and Roediger asked the participant to recall the picture individually. The collaborative recounting with the confederate was tightly controlled, with each individual taking turns recalling one item from the complex picture. The results were clear: The confederate could implant into participants' memories items that were not in the original picture. Such implantations were more likely if the fictional item was something that might be expected in the original picture, but they still occurred for unexpected items.

More recently, the same social contagion has been shown for free-flowing conversations. For instance, Wright, Self, and Justice (2000) showed two individuals slightly different pictures and then asked them to recall the content of the pictures jointly, without any restriction on how this conversational act of remembering would unfold. They also ran a control condition, again, with an individual recollection replacing the joint recounting. They found more false recognitions for the critical item (the items in the pictures that differed across versions) in the experimental than the control condition.

What makes this research relevant to the formation of collective memory is that in each study, "speakers" are imposing their memories onto "listeners," so that in the end, both speakers and listeners share the same memories. Cuc, Ozuru, Manier, and Hirst (2006) specifically tested this possibility, looking at conversations among four rather than two people. The larger group allowed for a great range of conversational interaction and offered a stronger test for mnemonic convergence than one would have with a pair of participants. In one experiment, they asked their four unrelated participants to read a story, recall it individually (pregoup individual recollection), then either recount it as a group or again individually (group recounting or control individual recollection), and then finally once again to recall the story individually (postgroup individual recollection). Cuc et al. compared the size of the overlap of the individual group members' pregroup recollections with the size of the overlap of their postgroup recollections. They found that the overlap was greater among the postgroup recollections than the pregroup recollections. Interestingly, in other experiments, they found that this convergence occurred when the final postgroup memory test involved forced-choice recognition rather than free recall. Here the original stories read by the four participants differed slightly in detail, with each member of the four-person group receiving different details. The final recognition test consisted of the four different versions of a "critical detail" in the story. After the conversation, the chance of recognizing a new item from the conversation increased. These results provide strong evidence that conversations do indeed change the memories of the participants and in doing so promote the formation of a collective memory.

As previously mentioned, if participants were first visually presented with a car at a stop sign but then subsequently listened to a narrative that included a car at a yield sign, participants were more likely to recall having seen the yield sign in the initial presentation. However, by modifying the paradigm, McCloskey and Zaragoza (1985) demonstrated that if participants saw in the slide show a stop sign and heard in the postevent narrative about a yield sign, they were more likely to correctly recognize a stop sign if forced to choose between traffic light and stop sign than between yield sign and stop sign. This finding suggests that the originally studied material is still in memory. At present, the preferred explanation for the misleading postevent information effect and social contagion relies on the known difficulty people have monitoring the source of a memory (Johnson, Hashtroudi, & Lindsay, 1993). People confuse their own memories with the memories introduced by other participants into the conversation. They simply cannot remember whether the memory they have of a yield sign had as its source the original videotape or what was said in the conversation.

Social Contagion and Conversational Dynamics Not all conversations are equal, at least when it comes to the promotion of a collective memory. A conversation will promote the formation of a collective memory when aspects of a memory known only to one conversational participant become known to all others. Social contagion is not possible if new or contradictory memories are never introduced in the conversations. Yet many conversations do not fulfill this simple requirement. As Wittenbaum, Stasser, and their colleagues have shown, people are more likely to recount in a conversation information that they share with all the other participants rather than information known only to themselves (Wittenbaum & Park, 2001; Wittenbaum & Stasser, 1996). In this case, the conversation will only reinforce those memories that are already shared. The reason for a shared-memory bias is purely stochastic: If the probability of mentioning an item in a group recounting is equal across items and participants, then an item shared by all members of the group is simply more likely to be mentioned than an item known only to one member of the group. With a shared-memory bias, conversations should be likely to reinforce what is shared among the group, thereby strengthening the collective memory that existed prior to the conversation rather than transforming already-existing collective memories.

There are, of course, exceptions to this shared-memory bias, exceptions that might lead to the promotion of a new collective memory rather than reinforcement of an already-existing one. Cuc, Koppel, and Hirst (2006) focused on one possible exception, conversations in which one person dominates the discussion, labeled by Hirst and his associates as the *dominant narrator* (Hirst & Manier, 1996; Hirst, Manier, & Apetroaia, 1997). In many conversations, group members participate equally, that is, no dominant narrator is present. But in others, a dominant narrator emerges. Building on the Wittenbaum–Stasser work, Cuc et al. (2006) argued that dominant narrators would have an advantage in introducing their unshared memories, inasmuch as the more a conversational participant speaks, the more likely it is that she will recount one of her uniquely held memories. Inasmuch as these introduced, unshared recollections will, in turn, become implanted into the memories of the other conversational participants, Cuc et al. predicted that when a dominant narrator is present in a group recounting, the formation of a collective memory through conversational interaction would be facilitated (2006). Importantly, they further predicted that the emergent collective memory should be the dominant narrator's pregroup rendering of the past.

Cuc et al. (2006) confirmed these predictions. They used the standard pregroup–group–postgroup paradigm, but, unlike many previous studies, carefully analyzed the conversational remembering that intervened between the two individual recall tests. Their analysis of the conversations allowed them to identify whether a dominant narrator was present in a conversation. As per their predictions, Cuc et al. found that dominant narrators were more likely to introduce their unshared pregroup recollections into the group recounting than were nonnarrators. More important, they revealed that the collective memory emerging in the postgroup recollections was that of the dominant narrator when one could clearly identify his or her presence in the conversation. Recently, Brown, Coman, and Hirst (2009) extended this work on narratorship and showed that the contribution of narratorship to the formation of collective memory could not be attributed to any perceived expertise other members of the group might confer on the dominant narrator. Rather it could be traced, at least in part, to the amount the dominant narrator talked.

When a person dominates a discussion, then, she has the ability to reshape the memories of the group so that the group comes to render the past in a manner similar to her own views. One can only speculate about the various factors that might lead an individual to dominate a discussion, but the influence this individual has on the community's collective memory should be clear.

Resistance and Social Contagion In most of the studies reviewed to date, participants have no reason to suspect that the source of postevent information might be unreliable or purposefully misleading. Indeed, Gricean maxims of conversations indicate that, unless there are good reasons to believe the principles are being violated, listeners should trust what the speaker says (Grice, 1975). But in the real world, there are many good reasons to suspect that Gricean maxims are being violated. People often realize that their memories may be influenced by what others say, come not to trust the source of this information, and consequently, *resist* any possible influence. Such resistance is often viewed as limiting the ability of authorities and sources of power to shape the collective memory of a community. As the community becomes suspicious of authority, they may make every effort to resist the authority's influence. This resistance could lead to a collective memory, not one sought by the authority, but one built around the resistance to authority. Vernacular memories, countermemories, or subaltern memory are typical when a group rather than a lone individual resists (Bodnar, 1992; Foucault, 1977; Stoler & Strassler, 2000).

Experimentalists have sought to make participants resist the influence of others in experiments by explicitly warning participants that the postevent narrative or other participants in the experiment may mislead them (see Echterhoff, Hirst, & Hussy, 2005, for a review). Warnings have been presented either before or after the postevent information is produced. Almost all researchers have found that prewarnings limit social contagion. An effect of postwarnings is more difficult to produce, but can be found, even in conversational settings. Warnings can also take on various forms. They can be explicit or social. An *explicit warning* simply indicates that some of the information supplied in the postevent narrative may be misleading. A *social warning* suggests that another person (and not the text itself) exerts a biasing influence. Echterhoff et al. have shown that social warnings are more effective than explicit warnings.

Prewarnings and postwarnings probably work through different mechanisms. Greene, Flynn, and Loftus (1982) suggest that the effect of prewarnings may arise either because participants decide (1) not to pay attention to what is said to them, or (2) to increase their attention in an attempt to discriminate old from new information. Echterhoff et al. (2005) has argued that the postwarnings decrease the level of false recognitions because, with the warning, people make an effort to monitor for the source of their memories in the final recognition test. Interestingly, the effort at source monitoring comes with a cost. With postwarning, as Echterhoff, Groll, and Hirst (2007) pointed out, as rememberers increase their effort to monitor the source of a memory, they may have an increased tendency to reject old items that appeared in both the original material and the postevent information. Without a pre- or postwarning, rememberers may benefit from the repetition of an item in the postevent narrative, but with a warning, they may actually find themselves falsely rejecting valid recognition probes.

As to prewarnings, if anything, inasmuch as they precede rather than follow the postevent misinformation, one would expect that they should be exceedingly effective. Although the extant literature suggests that they generally are, Muller and Hirst (2010) have shown that a careful consideration of conversational dynamics and individual differences in mnemonic ability reveals some weaknesses.

Consider first the effect of conversational dynamics, specifically, whether a dominant narrator is present in the postevent conversation and serves as the source of misleading information. In this instance, it becomes difficult for other participants to ignore what the dominant narrator says, without also ignoring (not paying attention to) the conversation. On the other hand, when the source of the misleading information is a nonnarrator, it may be much easier for a listener to ignore what nonnarrators say, especially when they make only a minimal contribution to the recounting. As a result, building on Greene et al.'s (1982) suggestion that two strategies guide responses to prewarnings, Muller and Hirst (2010) predicted that, after a prewarning, listeners will pay little attention to the warned-against speaker when she is a nonnarrator in the postevent conversation, but will increase their attention and try to discriminate between old and new when she is a dominant narrator.

This observation leads to specific predications about the effect of prewarnings on false recognitions. The predictions will depend not simply on the conversational role of the speaker, but also on the mnemonic ability of the listener. When the speaker in a nonnarrator, the mnemonic ability of the listener does not matter. The listener should react to the prewarning by not paying attention to what the speaker says, with the result that the rate of false recognitions for the new information introduced in the group recounting should decline dramatically. On the other hand, if the source is a dominant narrator, the mnemonic ability of the listener to discriminate old from new matters, inasmuch as with a dominant narrator, a warning should encourage listeners to try to discriminate between old and new. If the quality of listener's memory for the original material is good, then the increased effort should lead to a decrease in the proportion of false recognitions. On the other hand, if the quality of the listener's memory is poor, then the listener may increase her attention to what the speaker recollects in an effort to distinguish old from new. Although this effort will most likely fail, the effort the listener undertakes to monitor the speaker may increase the likelihood that a lasting trace of the new information is formed. This newly acquired trace could lead to an increase in false recognition, exactly the opposite effect from what a prewarning is thought to accomplish. In other words, to state the predictions in terms of collective memory, when a dominant narrator is present in the group recounting and the listener has a poorly formed memory of the original material, prewarning might have the paradoxical effect of increasing the effect of conversational remembering on the formation of a collective memory.

Muller and Hirst (2006) tested these predictions by employing a modified version of the paradigm used by Cuc et al. They asked four participants to study different versions of the same story, then to recall the story either individually or as a group, and then finally complete a four-item forced-choice recognition test, with the items in the recognition probe consisting of the four versions of the critical items in the originally studied stories. Unlike Cuc et al., (2006), the stories were devised so that without an accompanying picture, they made little sense (see Bransford & Johnson, 1973, for further discussion of such manipulations). Half of the participants in the group read the stories with the picture—and hence had a good memory for the story. The other half read the stories without a picture, ensuring that their memory for the story was poor. Along the same lines, for half of the groups of four they tested, the group recounting was preceded by a warning about the intentions of one of the group members. For the other groups, no warning was given. As in Cuc et al., Muller and Hirst determined who in the story was the dominant narrator and found, as predicted, that when the source of a critical false recognition was a nonnarrator, prewarnings were effective. On the other hand, when the warned-against person was the dominant narrator and the listener possessed a poor memory, the prewarning actually increased the proportion of critical false recognitions.

What these studies of resistance demonstrate is that warnings may not always be effective in limiting the influence of a speaker on the formation of a collective memory. Postwarnings may limit the degree to which conversational remembering promotes the formation of a collective memory, but may also limit the extent to which community members embrace the collective memory held prior to the group recounting. As to prewarnings, although these are usually thought of as extremely effective means of limiting the influence of a speaker on a listener's memory, again, there are troubling restrictions. To frame the results in terms of collective memory, prewarnings can have the paradoxical effect of promoting the formation of collective memory when a suspicious speaker dominates the discussion and the listener has a poor memory for the original material. The intersection of these two conditions occurs in the real world with unfortunate frequency. One often finds a person in authority dominating a discussion about a topic of which those listening have only a tentative grasp. The surprise is that as people become suspicious of this authority, they may become more, rather than less, vulnerable to its influence.

INDUCED FORGETTING

As Marsh (2007) recently noted, "retelling is not recalling." When people recollect an event to another person, their recollection will vary as a function of the speaker's goals, the audience, and the social context more generally. Moreover, when people recount an event as a group, the group dynamics will prevent everything that the group is capable of remembering from emerging in the group recounting (Basden, Basden, Bryner, & Thomas, 1997; Weldon, 2001). To be sure, the group will remember more than an individual might in a pregroup individual recollection, what is referred to as collaborative facilitation. Nevertheless, the group recounting will contain less than the sum of what the group showed they were capable of remembering in a pregroup or control recollection. We have already seen how this principle will lead to reluctance to introduce unshared memories into the group discussion (Wittenbaum & Park, 2001; Wittenbaum & Stasser, 1996). In other words, a conversation is almost always selective in content, either by intention and design or as an unintentional consequence of group dynamics.

One consequence of this selective retelling is that people are often silent about various aspects of the past. They will mention some aspects, but remain "silent" about others. What happens to information that goes unmentioned by a speaker? As we shall see, these silences can induce forgetting in both the speaker and the listener. As a result of a conversation, then, both speaker and listener will end up forgetting similar aspects of the past. In this way, a conversation cannot only promote a collective memory, but also its counterpart, *collective amnesia*.

Within-Individual Retrieval-Induced Forgetting

Clearly, one is less likely to remember information that goes unmentioned in a conversation than mentioned information. The effect of rehearsal, even if it only consists of listening to another person repeat previously studied material, is well established. When we want to explore forgetting as a result of "silences," we are interested in exploring whether selective retrieval will actually induce forgetting.

Retrieval-induced forgetting has been studied mainly in terms of the effect of retrieval on the memory of the individual rememberer, *within-individual retrieval-induced forgetting* (WI-RIF). Perhaps the best known work is that of Anderson and his colleagues (Anderson, 2007; Anderson, Bjork, & Bjork, 1994). They showed that practice at remembering information leads people not only to remember the practiced material better, but, perhaps counterintuitively, to forget *related* information more than they would without the practice. In the standard experimental WI-RIF paradigm, participants first study category–exemplar paired associates (Anderson et al., 1994). Several pairs have the same category cue, with several categories across the list. For instance, participants might study the pairs *Fruit–Apple, Fruit–Orange*, as well as pairs such as *Bird–Robin* and *Bird–Swallow*. The second phase of the study involves retrieval practice, which consists of the completion of pairs such *Fruit–Ap___*. They receive practice on some of the categories and not others. They may receive practice on the paired associates involving *Fruit*, but not those involving *Bird*. Within each of the practiced categories, participants receive practice only on a subset of the relevant paired associates. For instance, they would be asked to complete the pair *Fruit–Ap______*, but not the pair *Fruit–Or______*. In the test phase, participants are supplied with the category labels and asked to list the studied exemplars.

This experimental design creates three conditions: *Rp+* (for Retrieval practice+), in which participants are tested on pairs they have practiced (*Fruit–Apple*); *Rp–*, in which participants are tested on the unpracticed pairs involving a practiced category (*Fruit–Orange*); and *Nrp* (for No retrieval practice), in which participants are tested on unpracticed pairs that involve a category retrieval cue different from any that figured in the practice trials (*Bird–Robin; Bird–Swallow*). WI-RIF occurs if Rp– < Nrp < Rp+. This telltale pattern suggests that retrieval of some information about the past will induce forgetting of unretrieved but related information. Importantly, because Rp– < Nrp, one can conclude that WI-RIF occurs not because of a failure to rehearse information, but because retrieval practice induces forgetting.

WI-RIF is often accounted for in terms of inhibition. According to the inhibition model, the presentation of a retrieval cue activates associated responses. Consequently, a rememberer must isolate from the array of activated material the desired target and does so by inhibiting the nontarget-activated material. The unpracticed but related material thereby becomes harder to remember than either the practiced material or the unpracticed and unrelated material.

Socially Shared Retrieval-Induced Forgetting

Whereas Anderson et al.'s (1994) work focuses on the effect of retrieval on the rememberer/speaker herself, our interest is the influence that a speaker has on a listener, that is, the effect of an act of remembering on someone listening to the remembering. Cuc et al. (2007) began to investigate this situation by placing a second person in the RIF experimental paradigm. This person, the listener, studied the material along with the "speaker," and then listened to the speaker complete stems aloud during the practice phase. The listeners were not instructed explicitly to remember the material in the practice phrase. As in WI-RIF, a final test of memory follows the practice phase, with both listener and speaker individually recalling the original material. In other words, the experiment proceeds in a manner similar to Anderson et al., but now a listener monitors what is being remembered during the practice phase.

Cuc et al. (2007) predicted that the listener should show the same pattern for forgetting as the speaker if he or she concurrently retrieves with the speaker. Here they are not referring to the overt remembering that occurs with the speaker, but covert retrieval—silently remembered, but not overtly articulated. As a result of this covert, concurrent remembering, the listener will selectively remember in the same way as the speaker and consequently should demonstrate the same retrieval-induced forgetting. This similarity in forgetting should facilitate the formation of a collective memory, or more precisely, the formation of a collective amnesia.

Of course, socially shared retrieval-induced forgetting depends on the listener concurrently retrieving, even if covertly. At least in part, concurrent retrieval should depend on the goal listeners have while attending to a speaker, specifically, how they monitor what the speaker says. If the listener is encouraged to monitor for accuracy, then the listener might be expected to concurrently retrieve along with the speaker. If the listener monitors for superficial features, such as the fluidity of the speaker's responses or the entertainment value of what the speaker says, then the listener might not be expected to concurrently retrieve. Both types of monitoring occur in daily life. Jury members might monitor during their deliberations how accurately their fellow jurors recall the testimony presented in the trial, whereas a husband may be more concerned about how entertaining his wife is when recounting a story at a dinner party about their recent vacation rather than how accurately she renders it. Cuc et al. (2007) claimed that these different ways of monitoring a conversation will have a profound effect on the ability of the speaker to induce forgetting in the listener—monitoring for accuracy should produce SS-RIF; monitoring for superficial characteristics of the speaker's speech should not.

Cuc et al. (2007) tested their predications by changing the nature of the practice phase in the Anderson et al. (1994) paradigm. Now during the practice phase, there were two participants. In some instances, one person (the listener) was asked to attend to the other member of the pair (the speaker) as the speaker selectively practices the material one more time. In other instances, the two participants freely recounted the previously studied material jointly. Cuc et al. (2007) found that concurrent retrieval, and hence socially shared retrieval-induced forgetting, varies with conversational goals and the monitoring strategies of the listener. When listeners monitored for the accuracy of what the speaker is selectively recalling, per experimenter instructions, both within-individual retrieval-induced forgetting for the speaker and socially shared retrieval-induced forgetting for the listener was found. On the other hand, when listeners monitored for superficial features, such as the fluidity of the speaker's response, only within-individual retrieval-induced forgetting for the speaker was observed. There was no evidence of socially shared retrieval-induced forgetting in the listeners' final recollection. When participants were asked to jointly recall a previously studied story, now, once again, both within-individual and socially shared retrieval-induced forgetting were observed.

Two observations are in order. First, although the experiment shows that conversations can serve as a site of socially instigated induced forgetting, one should not assume that all conversations will have this function. The goal of the conversation was to jointly recount the story. Presumably, with that goal in mind, a listener will monitor for the accuracy of what the speaker recollects. Other conversational acts of remembering may not induce concurrent retrieval, for instance, ones with the goal of entertainment alone. Under such instance, one might not expect SS-RIF to emerge in the conversation.

Second, SS-RIF is more pronounced when there was a free-flowing conversation than when there was well-controlled paired associate recollection. That is, the proportional impairment [((Nrp) – (Rp–))/(Nrp)] for SS-RIF was .22 when a listener merely attended to what the speaker said, .74 when speaker and listener participated in a free-flowing conversation. Research has shown that WI-RIF is more likely to occur if the practice session does not allow for a deep, time-consuming search (Chan, McDermott, & Roediger, 2006). Free-flowing conversation, especially with quick turn-taking, creates just such constraints. The speaker controls the speed with which one narrative unit follows another, and, if the listener is to be engaged in the conversation, she must keep up with him. The same cannot be said for the studies in which the practice is more deliberate, as in a WI-RIF experiment. Often 10 or 15 seconds pass between practice trials.

SS-RIF for Different Memories

Our emphasis on concurrent remembering as the cause of SS-RIF raises an intriguing possibility. A speaker may say something in a conversation which will remind the listener not of a shared memory, but of something else, a past event unique to the listener. A speaker, for instance, might mention a combat experience, and this recollection might remind the listener of her own combat experience, at least covertly. In both cases, what the speaker says and what the listener remembers (covertly) will probably be only aspects of their respective memory. As a result, what the speaker recollects may induce forgetting in the listener, but now of an event the speaker never experienced.

Induced forgetting along these lines are of interest to students of collective memory because social constraints exist on what people can or cannot say. A soldier remembering his war experiences, for instance, might feel that it is socially inappropriate to talk about how he and his fellow soldiers won the battle, the nitty-gritty of how he killed the enemy, or how his friend was blown up next to him. Conservatives might find themselves failing to report on a personal political experience at a dinner party attended mainly by liberals. And intimate details of a relationship may not be conveyed to others as one works through why the relationship failed. In each instance, the failure of the speaker to mention details about his personal past could lead the listener to forget similar details about her own past, even if the specifics differ between speaker and listener. The result is a collective amnesia not around specifics, but around classes of events: the horrors of war, certain general classes of political events, intimate details about relationships.

Coman, Manier, and Hirst (2009) tested this possibility by asking pairs of individuals to jointly recount the way they spent their day on September 11, 2001, when New York and Washington, DC were attacked by terrorists. All the participants were in or around New York City on September 11. At the beginning of the experiment, the researcher asked participants to individually complete a questionnaire that probed for details about their day. The questions were broken into categories, which were clearly labeled on the questionnaire—categories such as time or location. Examples of questions under the time category are: What time did you wake up? What time did you first learn of the attack? There were between four and six questions for each of eight categories. After a brief distraction phase, two participants were introduced to each other and then asked to talk to each other about the circumstances in which they learned of the event and the attack itself. A final recognition followed, with the recognition probe consisting of an initial presentation of a question from the original questionnaire, followed by either the participant's answer or a distracter. Coman et al. measured response times to the recognition probe, examining in their analysis only correct responses. Thus, to be precise, they did not examine retrieval-induced forgetting, but retrieval-induced inaccessibility.

As in the previous experiment, conversations were transcribed and event items collected from the questionnaire were classified as to which participant was the source and whether the memory was Rp+, Rp–, or Nrp, with one proviso. Coman et al. (2009) assumed that if the speaker mentions an item, what the listener covertly and concurrently retrieves is not the same memory, but a similar one. For instance, if a speaker said in the conversation that he woke up at 8 o'clock, then Coman et al. assumed that the listener retrieved similar, albeit different material, covertly remembering that he woke up around noon. In this case, Coman et al. classified the probe that captured the pairing time–awoke time as Rp+ for both speaker and listener. To reiterate, Coman et al.'s interest was in whether what the speaker said initiates concurrent retrieval of an associated memory, not a shared memory and, as a result, induces forgetting for this associated memory. The results confirmed the predictions: Socially shared retrieval-induced forgetting could be found even when speaker and listener possessed different memories. What mattered is whether what the speaker said elicited concurrent retrieval in the listener.

These experiments on both WI-RIF and SS-RIF illustrate the power that conversations can have on what both speakers and listeners not only remember, but also forget following a conversation. Inasmuch as the conversation exerts its influence in similar ways for both speakers and listeners, they can shape the memories of speakers and listeners. The experiments indicate that they may do so not only by reinforcing certain memories, but also inducing both speaker and listener to forget in similar ways. The resulting shared memories—and shared amnesias—can no doubt foster sociability.

GENERAL DISCUSSION

Let us return to where we began: Is there some benefit in allowing memory to be malleable? If humans could make a memory system that is not easily influenced by outside forces, as a computer memory clearly is, why hasn't evolution accomplished a similar feat? As we have argued here, it is not simply that memory is good enough for human purposes, despite its flaws. Rather the malleability of memory serves to enhance human sociability, by promoting the formation of collective memories. Humans are social creatures and any device that fosters sociability should not be viewed as a flaw, but a virtue. In this chapter, we have illustrated how the malleability of memory leads not simply to individual differences in memory, but to a convergence among interacting individuals onto a shared rendering of the past. This shared rendering can in turn shape a shared identity, and it is through this shared identity that sociability is fostered.

We have concentrated on conversations as the medium of interaction. There were good reasons for doing so: People are constantly talking to one another and much of this talk is about the past. As we have seen, even something as frequent and ordinary as a conversation can radically reshape memories. Speakers alter both their own memories as they talk, as well as the memories of listeners. Moreover, the influence of speakers on themselves and others is not merely a matter of externally driven rehearsal. A speaker can implant memories in a listener and can induce a listener to forget, even memories that people believe they will never forget, such as their memories of the terrorist attack of 9/11. People may experience the same event and walk away with a *Rashomon*-like divergence of memories. Nevertheless, their social interactions will foster a convergence onto a shared rendering of the past. The malleability of human memory ensures that this convergence occurs, that is, if the social interaction occurs.

This latter point is key. Conversations can only reshape memories onto a shared representation of the past if the conversations take place. Ordinarily, people converse mainly with others in their social sphere. Even for large communities, like nations or religions, conversations are ongoing within that community, rarely across communities. Conversations, then, can reinforce already-existing social relations. They can accomplish this task in various ways. We want to emphasize their role in promoting the formation of a collective memory. With this collective memory comes a collective identity, which not only assists in strengthening a sense of community, but also in creating an intimacy among those who share this memory (Wegner, 1986).

Of course, conversations can occur across communities, albeit with less frequency. Such conversations are usually viewed as an exchange of different ideas and opinions, but we would see them also as a vehicle for the construction of a collective memory. As we have noted, the reshaping of memory through conversation can occur in the absence of any intentionality, and in some instances, even resistance might not prevent conversational interaction from promoting the convergence of initially distinct memories onto a shared representation. The old adage that conversation among enemies is good may be true not only because the discussants may come to understand one another's perspectives better, but also because they may come to see the past in similar ways, even if they do not intend to.

What is particularly intriguing about the research we reviewed is that many of the effects of conversation on memory are not intuitively obvious. Why should talking about a topic induce forgetting? Why should resistance to mnemonic change lead in some cases to the mnemonic change a listener wants to avoid? In each instance, people may unexpectedly find themselves more socially connected to an individual in ways that they would not expect because the dynamics of memory have unfolded in unexpected ways. Evolution seems to have made it difficult for us to avoid forming a shared rendering of the past. The research we have described, then, is not simply about memory and the conditions of memory change. Rather it is an attempt to understand, even in unexpected situations, how people can come to feel socially connected with each other through, in many cases, the unintentional construction of a collective memory.

REFERENCES

Anderson, M. (2007). Inhibition: Manifestations in long-term memory. In Y. Dudai, R. Roediger, & S. Fitzpatrick (Eds.), *Science of memory: Concepts* (pp. 295–300). New York: Oxford University Press.

Anderson, M. C., Bjork, R. A., & Bjork, E. L. (1994). Remembering can cause forgetting: Retrieval dynamics in long-term memory. *Journal of Experimental Psychology: Learning, Memory, & Cognition, 20*, 1063–1087.

Assmann, A. (1995). *Errinnerungsräume. Formen und Wandlungen des kulturellen Gedächtnisses*. Munich, Germany: Beck.

Bartlett, F. (1932). *Remembering: A study in experimental and social psychology*. New York: Cambridge University Press.

Basden, B. H., Basden, D. R., Bryner, S., & Thomas, R. L. (1997). A comparison of group and individual remembering: Does collaboration disrupt retrieval strategies? *Journal of Experimental Psychology: Learning, Memory, and Cognition*, 23, 1176–1191.

Bodnar, J. (1992). *Remaking America: Public memory, commemoration, and patriotism in the twentieth century*. Princeton, NJ: Princeton University Press.

Bransford, J. D. & Johnson, M. K. (1973). Considerations of some problems of comprehension. In W. G. Chase (Ed.), *Visual information processing* (pp. 383–462). New York: Academic Press.

Brown, A. D., Coman, A., & Hirst, W. (2009). The role of narratorship and expertise in social remembering. *Social Psychology, 40*, 119–129.

Chan, J. C. K., McDermott, K. B., & Roediger, H. L. III. (2006). Retrieval-induced facilitation: Initially nontested material can benefit from prior testing of related material. *Journal of Experimental Psychology: General, 135*, 553–571.

Coman, A., Manier, D., & Hirst, W. (2009). Forgetting the unforgettable through conversation: Socially shared retrieval-induced forgetting of September 11 memories. *Psychological Science, 20*, 627–633.

Cuc, A., Koppel, J., & Hirst, W. (2007). Silence is not golden: A case for socially-shared retrieval-induced forgetting. *Psychological Science, 18*, 727–733.

Cuc, A., Ozuru, Y., Manier, D. & Hirst, W. (2006). On the formation of collective memories: The role of a dominant narrator. *Memory & Cognition, 34*, 752–762.

DiFonzo, N. & Bordia, P. (2007). *Rumor psychology: Social and organizational approaches*. Washington, DC: American Psychological Association.

Echterhoff, G., Groll, S., & Hirst, W. (2007). Tainted truth: Overcorrection for misinformation influence on eyewitness memory. *Social Cognition, 25*, 367–409.

Echterhoff, G., Hirst, W., & Hussy, W. (2005). How eyewitnesses resist misinformation: Social postwarnings and the monitoring of memory characteristics. *Memory & Cognition, 33*, 770–782.

Fentress, J., & Wickham, C. (1992). *Social memory*. Oxford, UK: Blackwell.

Foucault, M. (1977). *Language, counter-memory, practice*. Ithaca, NY: Cornell University Press.

Greene, E., Flynn, M., & Loftus, E. (1982). Inducing resistance to misleading information. *Journal of Verbal Learning and Verbal Behavior, 21*, 207–219.

Grice, H. P. (1975). Logic and conversation. In P. Cole & J. L. Morgan (Eds.), *Syntax and semantics* (Vol. 3, pp. 225–242). New York: Seminar Press.

Halbwachs, M. (1992). *On collective memory* [L. A. Coser, Trans]. Chicago: University of Chicago Press. (Original work published in 1925)

Hastorf, A. & Cantril, H. (1954). They saw a game: A case study. *Journal of Abnormal and Social Psychology, 49*, 129–134.

Hirst, W. & Echterhoff, G. (2008). Creating shared memories in conversation: Towards a psychology of collective memory. *Social Research, 75*, 183–216.

Hirst, W. & Manier, D. (1996). Social influences on remembering. In D. Rubin (Ed.), *Autobiographical memory* (pp. 271–290). New York: Cambridge University Press.

Hirst, W. & Manier, D. (2008). Towards a psychology of collective memory. *Memory, 16*, 183–200.

Hirst, W., Manier, D., & Apetroaia, I. (1997). The social construction of the remembered self: Family recounting. In J. G. Snodgrass & R. L. Thompson (Eds.), *The self across psychology* (pp. 163–188). New York: The New York Academy of Sciences.

Johnson, M. K., Hashtroudi, S., & Lindsay, D. S. (1993). Source monitoring. *Psychological Bulletin, 114*, 3–28.

Loftus, E. F. (2005). Planting misinformation in the human mind: A 30-year investigation of the malleability of memory. *Learning & Memory, 12*, 361–366.

Manier, D., & Hirst, W. (2008). A cognitive taxonomy of collective memories. In A. Nünning & A. Erll (Eds.), *Cultural memory studies: An international and interdisciplinary handbook* (pp. 253–262). Berlin, Germany: de Gruyter.

Marsh, E. J. (2007). Retelling is not the same as recalling: Implications for memory. *Current Directions in Psychological Science, 16*, 16–20.

Meade, M. L. & Roediger, H. L. (2002). Explorations in the social contagion of memory. *Memory & Cognition, 30*, 995–1009.

McCloskey, M. & Zaragoza, M. (1985). Misleading postevent information and memory for events: Arguments and evidence against memory impairment hypotheses. *Journal of Experimental Psychology: General, 114*, 1–16.

Müller, F. & Hirst, W. (2010). Resistance to the influence of others: Limits to the formation of a collective memory through conversational remembering. *Applied Cognitive Psychology*, 24, 608–625.
Nünning, A. & Erll, A. (Eds.) (2008). *Cultural memory studies: An international and interdisciplinary handbook*. Berlin, Germany: de Gruyter.
Nobile, P. (Ed.). (1995). *Judgment at the Smithsonian*. New York: Marlowe & Co.
Olick, J. K. (1999). Collective memory: The two cultures. *Sociological Theory, 17*, 333–348.
Schuman, H., Rieger, C., & Gaidys, V. (1994). Collective memories in the United States and Lithuania. In N. Schwarz & S. Sudman (Eds.), *Autobiographical memory and the validity of retrospective reports* (pp. 313–333). New York: Springer-Verlag.
Stoler, A. & Strassler, K. (2000). Castings for the colonial: Memory work in "New Order" Java. *Comparative Studies in Society and History, 42*, 4–48.
Weldon, M. S. (2001). Remembering as a social process. In G. H. Bower (Ed.), *The psychology of learning and motivation* (Vol. 10). (pp. 67–120). New York: Academic Press.
Wegner, D. (1986). Transactive memory: A contemporary analysis of the group mind. In B. Mullen & G. Goethals (Eds.), *Theories of group behavior* (pp. 185–208). New York: Springer-Verlag.
Wertsch, J. (2002). *Voices of collective remembering*. New York: Cambridge University Press.
Wittenbaum, G. M. & Park, E. S. (2001). The collective preference for shared information. *Current Directions in Psychological Science, 10*, 70–73.
Wittenbaum, G. M. & Stasser, G. (1996). Management of information in small groups. In J. L. Nye & A. M. Brower (Eds.), *What's social about social cognition?* (pp. 3–38) Thousand Oaks, CA: Sage.
Wright, D. B., Self, G., & Justice, C. (2000). Memory conformity: Exploring misinformation effects when presented by another person. *British Journal of Psychology, 91*, 189–202.
Zerubavel, E. (1998). *Social mindscapes: An invitation to cognitive sociology*. Cambridge, MA: Harvard University Press.

7

How Communication Shapes Memory
Shared Reality and Implications for Culture

GERALD ECHTERHOFF AND E. TORY HIGGINS

Culture is a cornerstone, perhaps even the epitome, of human sociality. Culture has been defined in various ways. In cultural social psychology, it has become common to characterize culture by the knowledge and beliefs distributed within a population or community that are distinct from the knowledge and beliefs held by other populations or communities (e.g., Chiu & Hong, 2006, 2007; Lehman, Chiu, & Schaller, 2004). A key challenge for research is to understand the origin and bases of prevalent cultural knowledge. Where do culturally characteristic knowledge and beliefs come from, and what are the processes by which they are formed and maintained?

One process that has received increasing attention by researchers is communication (Fast, Heath, & Wu, 2009; Lehman, Chiu, & Schaller, 2004; McIntyre, Lyons, Clark, & Kashima, 2004; Schaller, Conway, & Tanchuk, 2002). This approach is based on the notion that people disseminate and receive culturally relevant information through interpersonal exchange and conversation. Indeed, several lines of research suggest that culturally relevant knowledge and beliefs can be produced and reproduced through communication, yielding shared representations of the world (Chiu & Hong, 2006; Kashima & Bratanova, this volume, Chapter 10; Sperber, 1996). For instance, information consistent with culturally shared stereotypes tends to be passed along from person to person in the course of communication (e.g., A. E. Clark & Kashima, 2007; Lyons & Kashima, 2003).

The communicative account of culture has been widely welcomed and has opened important avenues of research. Still, studies in a neighboring area of social psychology, on the processes and effects of interpersonal communication, suggests that important distinctions and qualifications need to be made. This is the general thrust of this chapter. In particular, we argue that research on the "saying-is-believing effect" (Higgins & Rholes, 1978; for reviews, see Higgins, 1992, 1999; McCann & Higgins, 1992) and the creation of shared reality through communication (Echterhoff, Higgins, & Levine, 2009; Hardin & Higgins, 1996) demonstrates that whether cultural knowledge is produced and reproduced through interpersonal communications critically depends on the goal, or motive, underlying a communication.

Specifically, the research we review in this chapter shows that communication shapes memory and knowledge to the extent that it is motivated by *the goal of creating a shared reality* with the communication partner. From this perspective, the verbal communication of information per se is not sufficient for the production or reproduction of cultural knowledge; what is necessary for the transmission and retention of knowledge through communication is the pursuit of an appropriate communication goal. In other words, even if conversations look the same on the surface given that they have the same message content, only those that are undertaken with the goal of sharing reality will create and perpetuate culturally relevant knowledge.

We begin our chapter by outlining the concept of shared reality. We then review empirical research on how shared reality is achieved through communication. In so doing, we focus on how tuning messages to an audience's presumable view (attitudes, judgment) about a message topic shapes the communicators' own cognitive representation or memory of the topic. This focus is important because memory is essential for the transmission and maintenance of culture-specific beliefs and knowledge (e.g., Norenzayan & Atran, 2004). Indeed, effects on memory are necessary for the production and reproduction of cultural knowledge, because for culture to be handed down cultural knowledge has to be retained over time. This view is consistent with the notion that culture is to society what memory is to individuals (Kluckhohn, 1954; see also Chiu & Hong, 2006). After our review of communication effects on memory, we discuss how this conceptualization is distinct from related constructs, such as empathy, perspective taking, common ground, embodied synchrony and mirroring, and socially distributed knowledge. We conclude with implications for the formation and transmission of culture.

SHARED REALITY: SITUATING AND DEFINING THE CONCEPT

People constantly create shared views about the world. For instance, when people meet a new employee at their workplace, they tend to form their impressions of the newcomer jointly with their colleagues, and they feel more confident in their impressions when others agree. People take into account the (inferred) views of others, especially significant others, to construct or verify views about various types of issues. For example, cues as to what others think help or enable us to evaluate other people or groups; to develop a sense of which movies are worthwhile seeing; to decide about a candidate to vote for in an election; or to form general political, moral, or religious convictions. The absence of social sharing can have detrimental consequences not only for people's physical well-being and feelings of connectedness, but also for their sense of reality. When others deny an expected shared reality, such as in the classical conformity studies by Asch (1951), people are left uncertain, uncomfortable, even physically agitated.

Theories and empirical research in social psychology and other social sciences have long emphasized the socially shared basis of psychological processes and representations (e.g., Asch, 1952; Bar-Tal, 1990, 2000; Cooley, 1902/1964; Festinger, 1950; Heider, 1958; Higgins, 1992; Lewin, 1947; Mead, 1934; Moscovici, 1981; Schachter, 1959; Schütz, 1932/1967; Sherif, 1935, 1936; J. C. Turner & Oakes, 1997). Since Hardin and Higgins' (1996) comprehensive review of shared reality approaches in social psychology, interest in the socially shared nature of individuals' evaluations and representations has soared in social psychology (e.g., Echterhoff, Higgins, & Groll, 2005; Frey & Schulz-Hardt, 2001; Higgins & Pittman, 2008; Lau, Chiu, & Lee, 2001; Levine & Higgins, 2001; Levine & Moreland, 2004; Lyons & Kashima, 2003; Pinel, Long, Landau, Alexander, & Pyszczynski, 2006; Postmes, Haslam, & Swaab, 2005; Ruscher, 1998; Semin & Cacioppo, 2008; Sinclair, Huntsinger, Skorinko, & Hardin, 2005; Tindale & Kameda, 2000) and related fields such as memory (Hirst & Manier, 2002; Weldon, 2001), cognition (Barsalou, Niedenthal, Barbey, & Ruppert, 2003; Smith & Semin, 2004), psycholinguistics (Pickering & Garrod, 2004), sociology (Thompson & Fine, 1999), organizational behavior (e.g., Salas & Fiore, 2004), developmental psychology (Meltzoff & Decety, 2003), evolutionary psychology (Caporael, 2007; de Waal, 2008), social neuroscience (e.g., Gallese, Keysers, & Rizzolatti, 2004), biology (e.g., Dunbar & Shultz, 2007), and philosophy (e.g., Thagard, 1997). In recent years, scholars have also examined related phenomena, such as empathy (de Vignemont & Singer, 2006; de Waal, 2008), interactive alignment (Garrod & Pickering, 2004), embodied simulation (Barsalou et al., 2003), and neural mirroring (Gallese et al., 2004; Iacoboni, 2008), thereby enriching and challenging traditional approaches in social psychology (see Semin, 2007).

What is clear is that researchers have recognized the importance of social sharing and related phenomena and have begun paying more attention to them. But what is *shared reality*, and how can it be defined? The term *shared* generally means "to have in common." However, a closer examination of the term reveals different meanings of *shared* (see Thompson & Fine, 1999). At least four meanings can be distinguished that come increasingly close to our conceptualization of sharing—a conceptualization that emphasizes the experience of having common inner states, that is thoughts, views, and attitudes, regarding a target referent (see Echterhoff, Higgins, & Levine, 2009).

The first possible meaning of *shared* is "communicated or disclosed to others." This meaning focuses on the process whereby speakers make their internal personal reactions, for instance about a new colleague at work, known to others. In this sense, the fact that something is shared implies that the audience becomes aware of what another individual believes or feels, but it does not require that the audience has something in common with the speaker or that the audience agrees with what the speaker communicates. Thus, the first possibility is mute as to whether the inner state of the audience about some aspect of the world is the same as the inner state of the speaker about this aspect of the world. What this meaning of *shared* does highlight, however, is the important role of interpersonal communication in allowing some information to be shared with another person.

According to a second meaning, *shared* means "divided up into portions," such as when we say that a task is shared among different people. This meaning refers to the division of (cognitive) labor or of responsibilities for different subdomains of a task. In this sense, the term implies that there is a joint task or project, and that each of the participating individuals is responsible for her or his specialized part in the task. This meaning of *shared* emphasizes the collaborative nature of information being shared between persons. Note, however, that this meaning highlights the differences between the individuals concerned with a common task. As in the first case, it is not required that the individuals have the same inner state about a target referent or have something in common (other than working on the same task or project).

In contrast, a correspondence or commonality between inner states about the world is implied in a third sense of the term: "partaking in a consensus," such as when we say that "people share an opinion." This possibility designates a state in which the views of at least two individuals are consensual or in common. Note that this meaning refers principally to an objective condition of "sharedness" that can be identified by an outside observer, rather than to the feeling of sharedness experienced by the individuals holding the same view. Thus, in this third sense, people may hold similar or identical views without being aware of each other's views or subjectively experiencing a commonality of views.

There is also a fourth possible meaning of *shared*: "held and experienced in common." In this case, the individuals involved do perceive their inner states as being in agreement (also see Bar-Tal, 2000). When we say, for instance, that "A shares B's enjoyment of foreign cuisine when traveling," we imply that Person A experiences a commonality between the inner state of Person B and her or his own inner state about a target referent. This fourth meaning of *shared* comes closest to our concept of sharing. According to this concept, developed in more detail later, sharing captures people's experience that their inner state about some referent target or entity (such as their beliefs or feelings about a third person, a movie, a political party, or a moral issue) converges with the inner state of one or more others regarding that target.

Subjective experience is not only critical for understanding sharedness, but also for understanding the term *reality*. From a psychological perspective, *reality* refers to people's subjective perceptions of something as being real and truthful, not to whether something can be corroborated as real or truthful from an external (scientific) perspective. Thus, what matters is people's experience of what is real (see Brickman, 1978). The motivation to achieve this experience is so strong that people can prefer objectively less accurate over objectively more accurate knowledge if the former produces a stronger subjective sense of knowing or establishing what is real (Higgins, 2010). This greater striving for the subjective experience rather than objectively verifiable knowledge of reality is epitomized by the pervasive power of political and religious ideologies (see also Jost, Ledgerwood, & Hardin, 2007).

Our Concept of Shared Reality

According to a definition we have recently proposed (Echterhoff, Higgins, & Levine, 2009), shared reality is the product of the motivated process of experiencing a commonality of inner states about the world. Our conceptualization presumes that four main conditions underlie shared reality. First, the commonality between individuals that is implied by a shared reality refers to their inner states and not just their overt behaviors. Second, shared reality is "about something"—that is, it implies a target referent about which people create a shared reality. Third, shared reality as a product cannot be divorced from the process through which it is attained—in particular, the underlying motives. Fourth, there is no shared reality unless people experience a successful connection to someone else's inner state. We will now elaborate and justify these conditions, with empirical support only being mentioned in passing. The following section will present the empirical evidence for this conceptualization of shared reality in more detail.

As to the first condition, a shared reality involves a commonality between people's inner states, which include their beliefs, judgments, feelings, or evaluations concerning a target referent. To achieve a shared reality, people cannot simply replicate the observable behavior of others—instead, they need to obtain a sense of others' inner states about the world. For the occurrence of a shared reality, a correspondence between observable states or behaviors is not sufficient—it needs to involve a commonality between inner states (see Brickman, 1978). This claim is supported by the fundamental and well-established role that the perception of others' inner states plays in human development, motivation, and sociality. People know not only that the outcomes for a person (self or other) depend critically on another person's overt responses to that person (e.g., Ostrom, 1984), but also that the other person's responses are mediated by his or her inner states, such as his or her attitudes and beliefs (Higgins, 2005, and this volume, Chapter 8; Nelson, 2005). Indeed, the discovery of the mediating role of others' inner states in how they respond to the world is a significant step in human development (see Higgins & Pittman, 2008). Once this level of social consciousness is reached, others' inner states begin to play a vital role in human self-regulation. Children, for example, cannot rely merely on observing other people's outward behaviors and the external stimulus conditions associated with their behaviors to ensure their well-being, enter the social world, and establish relationships. Rather, they have to learn to infer a caretaker's beliefs, feelings, attitudes, and so on (e.g., that mashed peas taste good, that a certain behavior is dangerous, or that a particular TV program is fun to watch).

Because understanding others' inner states (rather than overt states or behaviors) is an essential ingredient of human social life, we argue that a shared reality involves the experience of common inner states. To be sure, exhibiting the same overt states or behaviors may signal to people that they also share inner states. For instance, two listeners clapping hands at the speech of a political candidate will assume that the other shares his or her favorable attitude toward the candidate. However, for each listener to achieve a shared reality it is critical to not only observe the other clapping but also to infer the other's inner state from the overt behavior—in this case, to infer a favorable attitude toward the candidate. Inferring that someone is simply mimicking one's own behavior may even be detrimental to the experience of a shared reality. Consider, for example, a teenage boy who mimics every gesture and movement of his sister for a while one evening, including mimicking her head nodding as she listens to her favorite song. From this commonality of overt states, the sister would not derive a sense of shared reality but rather a sense of being mocked or teased by her brother.

The achievement of this first condition, the perceived sharing of inner states, requires processes that allow people to pick up or infer someone else's inner state. Psychological research suggests a plethora of mechanisms by which this can be accomplished (see, e.g., Higgins & Pittman, 2008; Malle & Hodges, 2005). People can draw on various aspects of others' nonverbal behavior, such as their facial expressions and gestures, to intuit their feelings, needs, and intentions. They grasp others' mental states, such as others' beliefs, attitudes, and feelings, drawing on mechanisms like conscious reasoning, unconscious simulation, and theory of mind (e.g., Keysers & Gazzola, 2007; Leslie, Friedman, & German, 2004); causal theories and schemata (e.g., Heider, 1958; Idson & Mischel, 2001; Malle, 1999); or projection of their own inner states (e.g., Keysar & Barr, 2002; Nickerson, 2001). Such mechanisms help people to "bridge the divide between self and others" (title of a volume edited by Malle & Hodges, 2005), to experience others' inner states in the first place. This precondition is a building block of the first condition for shared reality—the perceived sharing of inner states and not just overt behaviors.

The previous argument makes implicit reference to the second condition of shared reality—shared reality is about some target referent. For a shared reality to occur it is not sufficient that people simply exhibit corresponding inner states, such as corresponding heart rates or mood states. If corresponding inner states are not about (i.e., not in reference to) some aspect of the world, then one cannot speak of a shared reality. This is because *reality* refers to the objects or referents of knowledge—that is, to phenomena that are experienced by actors as being part of the world in the present, as well as in the past and future (such as future desired end-states; Higgins & Pittman, 2008). Thus, shared reality goes beyond simply replicating another person's inner state in that it requires sharing states that are about some target referent: for example, about a new colleague at work, about a specific TV program, about a particular politician, or about abstract political or religious issues (see Jost et al., 2007).

Like the first condition, this second condition—that shared reality is about some target referent—requires that a critical precondition be met. Specifically, it requires mechanisms that allow people to infer the target referent of their sharing partner's inner state, such as the referent of another person's feeling. Research has identified various mechanisms by which this can be achieved. One basic mechanism is to follow the direction of someone else's eye gaze (e.g., Baron-Cohen, 1995; Call, 2005; Tomasello, 2008; Tomasello, Carpenter, Call, Behne, & Moll, 2005) to identify the referent of that person's sustained interest or emotional response, such as what it is that she or he fears. Eye-gaze following, together with imputing intentionality to the other person, allows the allocation of shared interest in an object (Baron-Cohen, 1995). Other mechanisms include following someone else's pointing movements or manipulations of objects (e.g., H. H. Clark, 2003; Tomasello, 2008) and interpreting verbal utterances as referring to an object (e.g., H. H. Clark, 1996; H. H. Clark & Marshall, 1981). Last but not least, people may infer the referent of a sharing partner's inner state without concurrent perceptual input or verbal directions from the sharing partner by using, for example, their own background knowledge of the sharing partner and the likely referent of his or her inner states in particular situations. For instance, a person may assume that her or his friend's mother is the likely referent of the attitude the friend expresses after finishing a phone conversation. General knowledge of established rules of interaction for different situations can also be used (e.g., H. H. Clark, 1996; Higgins, 1981, 1998; Krauss & Fussell, 1991). These and other mechanisms allow people to infer the referent of a sharing partner's inner state and to infer what that inner state is about, which is a precondition for the second condition for shared reality—that shared reality is about something.

We now turn to the third condition—that shared reality as a product cannot be divorced from the motives that drive the achievement of common inner states. This condition is the focus in the present chapter since it is most relevant to the formation and transmission of cultural knowledge through communication. We believe that it is crucial to take into account the source of a commonality between people's inner states in addition to the fact of a commonality. An analogy would be that democracy concerns not only consensus as an outcome or state of agreement but also the processes by which people reach a consensus (see, e.g., Bohman & Rehg, 1997). How a consensus or agreement is reached and whether the right procedures are observed to arrive at a consensus are, in many cases, more important than the product or outcome itself (Mackie & Skelly, 1994; J. C. Turner & Oakes, 1997). More generally, end states often attain their value from how they were reached and not just from the outcome per se (Higgins, 2006). Similarly, conceptualizing shared reality only as an outcome or end product of inner states held in common would overlook important psychological underpinnings, namely, the processes through which shared reality is achieved, including its underlying motives. The view of the motivational underpinnings is compatible with earlier conceptualizations in phenomenological sociology (Schütz, 1932/1967) and ethnomethodology (Garfinkel, 1967; also see J. H. Turner, 1987). Scholars in these fields understood that social actors "are motivated to create a sense, even an illusory sense, that they share a common universe," so that they might "generate a tacit presumption that there is an external factual order 'out there'" (J. H. Turner, 1987, p. 19).

What, then, are the motives driving the creation of a shared reality? Given the variety of core human motives that have been proposed and are still debated (e.g., Crocker, 2007; Fiske, 2008; Higgins & Pittman, 2008), any attempt to provide an exhaustive or exclusive list at this point would be premature. Instead, to exemplify the processes driving the sharing of inner states, we refer to two motives that have figured prominently in the literature on social motivation in general and on shared reality in particular: epistemic and relational motives (Bar-Tal, 2000; Fiske, 2008; Hardin & Conley, 2001; Hardin & Higgins, 1996; Jost et al., 2007). *Epistemic motives* refer to the effort after meaning (e.g., Bartlett, 1932; Silver & Wortman, 1980), the need to achieve a valid and reliable understanding of the world (Hardin & Higgins, 1996) and to establish what is real (Higgins, 2010).

Improving understanding and knowledge of the world increases the sense of predictability and subjective efficacy in dealing with the environment. The strength of epistemic motives typically increases with uncertainty or ambiguity about a target referent (e.g., Berlyne, 1962; Hogg, 2007; Kruglanski, 2004). Consistent with this notion, Festinger (1950) argued that the more ambiguous and difficult to interpret experiences are, the more people seek a social reality provided by appropriate (i.e., sufficiently trustworthy) others (also see Byrne & Clore, 1967; Deutsch & Gerard, 1955; Festinger, 1954; Sherif, 1936). Given that, as we have argued, shared reality is about a target referent, it follows that the creation of shared reality always serves, at least to some extent, epistemic motives.

Relational motives induce people to affiliate and feel connected to others. Feeling connected to others has several positive consequences, including emotional well-being (e.g., Diener & Seligman, 2002), a sense of security, and self-esteem (e.g., Baumeister & Leary, 1995; Bowlby, 1969). The desire for connectedness is reflected, for example, in the affiliative tendency that people exhibit when they are confronted with potentially anxiety-arousing situations (Schachter, 1959).

The potential satisfaction of core human motives, particularly epistemic and relational motives, is an important force that drives social sharing (Hardin & Conley, 2001; Hardin & Higgins, 1996; see also Kruglanski, Pierro, Mannetti, & De Grada, 2006). Shared realities with others are attractive because they allow individuals to experience a more valid and reliable view of the world and to obtain or maintain a sense of connectedness and belonging. This dual appeal of shared reality can be illustrated by the way in which current members of a group create a shared view about a newcomer (see Levine & Higgins, 2001). Observable information about another person (such as her or his behaviors) is often ambiguous. For example, the talkativeness of the newcomer may signal that she or he is sociable and cordial (positive traits) or boastful and ingratiating (negative traits). The group members can resolve this ambiguity by creating a shared reality about the newcomer, serving their epistemic motives. When the group members share their colleagues' inner states about the newcomer, they will feel more certain about their impressions. But consensus serves more than just this epistemic function. When the group members agree about a newcomer, the social bond between them is strengthened, serving their relational motives. Through sharing their inner states about the newcomer, they feel connected with one another, as they gain or corroborate a sense of sharing the same values and norms, which contributes to identification with others. Supporting the notion that shared reality can satisfy both epistemic and relational motives, research shows that people exchange information consistent with shared stereotypes about others both to confirm their common ground and to connect with members of their community (A. E. Clark & Kashima, 2007).

According to our concept, the motivational process that has led to a commonality of inner states is critical to whether the commonality is a shared reality. Adopting another person's inner state could be driven just by instrumental goals of securing beneficial social responses or maximizing personal outcomes (see Higgins, 1981; Jones & Thibaut, 1958). Social actors pursue such instrumental goals, for instance, when they ingratiate themselves with others (Jones, 1964) or take the perspective of a competitor to prevail in a social conflict (Epley, Caruso, & Bazerman, 2006). In such cases, actors adopt another person's inner state not because they want to achieve a better understanding of a reference target or to establish what is real, but because they hope to attain other, alternative goals. Because such cases of a commonality of inner states are not driven by epistemic motives that are characteristic of shared reality, we posit that they do not involve a shared reality. Later, we describe communication studies (Echterhoff, Higgins, Kopietz, & Groll, 2008) in which a commonality between a communicator and an audience is created in the service of motives other than relational or epistemic motives—what we call non-shared-reality goals—and show that such commonalities do not have the same effects as a commonality based on shared reality motives.

The three conditions for shared reality discussed so far (commonality of inner states, "aboutness," and appropriate motivation underlying the commonality) contribute to a shared reality. However, there is an additional condition that plays a critical role. According to our fourth condition, a shared reality requires that the participating individuals actually experience the sharing—that is, that they experience a commonality with someone else's inner state. Consistent with this view, Bar-Tal (2000) has argued that sharing of beliefs entails more than merely an objective commonality between people that can be identified by an external observer. Instead, sharing must involve the subjective experience or awareness of a commonality. Even if people are motivated to share inner states with others, they may end up not establishing a commonality (e.g., due to a failure in communication). Thus, it is not enough to have taken action to create a commonality with another person's inner state in the service of appropriate (such as relational or epistemic) motives. It is also necessary that one perceives the commonality to have been, in fact, established.

By including the fourth condition that individuals actually experience the sharing, we emphasize the critical role of the subjective sense of sharing. This aspect can be further elaborated in the context of the first and second conditions for shared reality, thus suggesting possible interrelations among the conditions. For the achievement of shared reality, people need to subjectively experience both the commonality of inner states and the referential aboutness of inner states. From this perspective, there can be a shared reality even if both assumptions of sharing are objectively wrong. That is, for Person A to experience a shared reality with Person B, it is not necessary for B to actually have the same inner state as A or for B's inner state to actually refer to the same referent that A has in mind. What is critical is that A believes that B's inner state and the referent of that inner state match A's inner state and referent. Consider, for example, a new member (A) in a research lab who believes that the current members in the lab are arrogant and wants to create a shared reality with another newcomer (B) about these members. For Newcomer A to have a shared reality with B, it is critical that A infers (e.g., by observing that B acts in a tense and uncomfortable manner at a lab meeting) that B has a shared inner state about the current members as referent (i.e., B also believes that they are arrogant). If Newcomer B later makes clear that the current members are her academic idols and that she always feels uncomfortable in encounters with admired people, then A's sense of a shared reality will be eliminated.

Research on egocentric projections of knowledge (e.g., Nickerson, 2001) and false consensus (e.g., Ross, Greene, & House, 1977) demonstrates that people tend to presume inner states in others that match their own inner state. Indeed, the motivation to establish a subjective experience of reality by social sharing is so strong that people often assume that most others agree with them even when this is not the case (also see Higgins, 2010). There is also evidence of the importance of the subjective experience of sharing as compared with objective sharedness alone. Pinel et al. (2006), for instance, found that the subjective sense of sharing inner states had a robust effect on liking of an interaction partner, whereas objective sharedness of characteristics, such as coming from the same hometown, only had an effect when the subjective experience of sharing was also high. Such findings testify to the dissociability of individual experiences of sharing from objective sharedness.

People not only tend to presume inner states in others that match their own inner state, but they also tend to presume shared referents. For instance, research on referential communication has found that listeners assume that a speaker is referring to whichever object they are paying attention to or have in mind (e.g., Keysar, Barr, Balin, & Brauner, 2000; also see Keysar & Barr, 2002). This assumption of a common referent is not always correct, but, fortunately for effective conversation, it is often correct (H. H. Clark, 1996; H. H. Clark & Marshall, 1981).

So far, we have described four conditions for shared reality in order to sharpen the concept. In the next section, we will review evidence from communication studies that supports our definition of shared reality; specifically, the motivational underpinnings. Later, we will discuss how our conceptualization of shared reality differs from such related concepts, such as empathy, perspective taking, theory of mind, common ground, embodied synchrony, and socially shared knowledge.

EMPIRICAL EVIDENCE FOR THE ROLE OF SHARED REALITY GOALS

To summarize the discussion thus far, we argue that shared reality is the result of experiencing a commonality between one's own and others' inner states (thoughts, feelings, evaluations) about the world, a commonality that is driven by appropriate motives (including epistemic and relational motives). In this section, we focus on interpersonal communication as a means of creating a shared reality and on empirical studies of such communication that have employed the saying-is-believing paradigm (Higgins, 1992; Higgins & Rholes, 1978). When people are motivated to create a shared reality with others, they often communicate with these others about a target referent.

The communication studies we present here are based on the hypothesis that communicating about a target referent can affect communicators' cognitive representations of that target. Studies employing the saying-is-believing paradigm have demonstrated such communication effects on subsequent cognition (e.g., Higgins, Echterhoff, Crespillo, & Kopietz, 2007; Higgins & Rholes, 1978; Sedikides, 1990; for reviews see Higgins, 1992, 1999; McCann & Higgins, 1992). In this paradigm, participants are introduced to an ostensible referential communication task (involving a communicator, a target, and an audience) in which they take the role of the communicator. The participants, who are typically students, read an essay about another student (the target person) who supposedly has volunteered to be part of a long-term research project on interpersonal perception. They are told that their task is to describe the target person's behaviors—without mentioning the target's name—to another volunteer (the audience) who knows the target person. On the basis of their message description, the "audience" volunteer would try to identify the target person as the referent of the message from among a set of several possible targets in the alleged research project.

A short essay consisting of several passages provides the input information about the target person. The behaviors described in each passage are evaluatively ambiguous; they can be interpreted as indicating either a positive or a negative trait with approximately equal likelihood (e.g., persistent vs. stubborn or independent vs. aloof). For example, the behavior described in the following sample passage could be labeled as either independent or aloof: "Other than business engagements, Michael's contacts with people are surprisingly limited. He feels he doesn't really need to rely on anyone" (e.g., Echterhoff et al., 2008).

To manipulate the audience's supposed attitude toward the target person, the researchers informed the participants (in an offhand way) that their audience either likes the target (positive audience attitude) or dislikes the target (negative audience attitude). In their subsequent communication, participants typically exhibit audience tuning: They evaluatively tailor, or "tune," their messages to their audience's attitude (i.e., they create evaluatively positive messages for an audience who likes the target and evaluatively negative messages for an audience who dislikes the target).

After a delay (from approximately ten minutes in some studies to several weeks in other studies), researchers tested the participants' memory for the original input information. Participants were asked to recall, as accurately as possible, the original essay about the target person in a free, written format. It is important to note that in demonstrations of the saying-is-believing effect the evaluative tone of the communicators' own recall for the original input information matches the evaluative tone of their previous, audience-tuned message. In other words, communicators' own memory representations of the message topic reflect the audience-tuned view expressed in their message rather than just the original target information. Communicators end up believing and remembering what they said rather than what they originally learned about the target. (The evaluative tone of participants' message and recall protocols is often determined by two coders who rate the overall valence based on positive or negative distortions relative to the original input information, with intercoder reliabilities typically above .85.)

After the initial demonstrations of the saying-is-believing effect, a number of studies using other paradigms have shown that people's mental representations of an experience can be profoundly shaped by how they verbally describe the experience to others (e.g., Adaval & Wyer, 2004; Schooler & Engstler-Schooler, 1990; Tversky & Marsh, 2000; for reviews, see Chiu, Krauss, & Lau, 1998; Marsh, 2007). Thus, the influence of verbal communication on subsequent cognition is well established. Also, the saying-is-believing effect in particular has been replicated with several variations in methodology and extended to new areas. For instance, although the effect was originally demonstrated for tuning to the audience's attitude toward the target (Higgins & Rholes, 1978), it has also been found for tuning to the audience's knowledge about the target (Higgins, McCann, & Fondacaro, 1982). Also, the effect occurs regardless of whether communicators know their audience's view before or after encoding the input information (Kopietz, Hellmann, Higgins, & Echterhoff, 2010). The effect has been extended from situations in which the communication topic is a single individual to situations in which the topic target is a small group (Hausmann, Levine, & Higgins, 2008). Furthermore, the effect occurs not only with verbal stimulus material as input information about a target, but also with complex visual input material, namely, video-filmed behaviors of target persons (Hellmann, 2007; Kopietz, Echterhoff, Niemeier, Hellmann, & Memon, 2009). Using a procedure that greatly differed from the standard saying-is-believing paradigm, Kopietz et al. (2009) found that audience-congruent retellings of a witnessed event can bias eyewitnesses' own event memory, thus extending the evidence to a new domain.

Critical to our current analysis, recent research (e.g., Echterhoff et al., 2005, 2008; Echterhoff, Lang, Krämer, & Higgins, 2009; Higgins et al., 2007; Kopietz et al., 2010) has demonstrated that the saying-is-believing effect occurs to the extent that communicators create a shared reality (characterized by the four conditions outlined earlier) with their audience about the target person. In the studies by Echterhoff, Higgins, and colleagues, communicators' memory representations of the target person (assessed by free recall) were biased by their audience tuning under conditions that support creating a shared reality but not under conditions that undermine creating a shared reality. The creation of a shared reality can fail when any one of the four conditions described earlier fails to be sufficiently satisfied.

In this chapter we focus on the motives underlying interpersonal communication. A discussion of evidence consistent with the other three conditions can be found in Echterhoff, Higgins, and Levine (2009). We note that this article also provides a detailed review and discussion of evidence that rules out alternative explanations for the saying-is-believing effect.

The Motivation Leading to a Shared Reality

Studies using the saying-is-believing paradigm provide evidence consistent with the idea that the motivation behind the creation of commonality with another person's inner state (i.e., the third condition) is a key condition for the achievement of shared reality. The experiments suggest that communicators create a shared reality with their audience only when their production of audience-congruent messages is appropriately motivated. In one set of studies, Echterhoff et al. (2008) manipulated the goals underlying audience tuning. It was assumed that, in the standard saying-is-believing conditions (e.g., Higgins & Rholes, 1978), audience tuning serves epistemic motives that are characteristic of shared reality. Specifically, the ambiguity inherent in the behavioral-input information about the target person should elicit the epistemic motivation to reduce uncertainty. By tuning messages to the audience, communicators construct an audience-congruent representation of the target and, thus, attain a greater sense of certainty about what the target is like.

In the Echterhoff et al. (2008) studies, this standard shared-reality-goal condition was compared with conditions in which audience tuning served non-shared-reality goals. The non-shared-reality goals included obtaining monetary incentives for producing an audience-congruent message and entertaining the audience with an exaggerated, caricature-like description of the target person (Echterhoff et al., 2008, Experiments 2a and 2b). Based on this rationale, it was hypothesized that communicators in the shared-reality goal condition should adopt the audience's inner state during message production to reduce uncertainty about the target person. In contrast, in the non-shared-reality-goal conditions communicators should adopt their audience's inner state primarily to attain goals unrelated to the epistemic motivation that is characteristic of shared reality; they pursue alternative, or "ulterior," goals that are not conducive to a shared reality.

As predicted, it was found that communicators in these alternative, non-shared-reality-goal conditions tuned their messages even more strongly to their audience's attitude than did communicators in the shared-reality-goal condition. However, the audience-tuning memory bias was not found when messages were tuned in the service of these alternative, non-shared-reality goals, whereas it was found as usual in the standard shared-reality-goal condition. Consistent with shared-reality assumptions, additional measures revealed that audience tuning was motivated by external demands to a greater extent in the alternative-goal conditions than it was in the shared-reality-goal condition. Also, communicators' epistemic trust in the audience and their audience-congruent message was significantly higher in the shared-reality-goal condition than in the alternative, non-shared-reality-goal conditions.

Follow-up research by Kopietz et al. (2010, Experiment 1) revealed similar effects of audience tuning (i.e., shared-reality goal vs. non-shared-reality goal), even when communicator participants had already encoded the target input information at the time of the goal manipulation. Furthermore, the researchers assessed the communicators' attainment of epistemic motives by asking them to indicate their certainty about their own view of the target after audience tuning. Communicators in the shared-reality-goal condition exhibited both the usual recall bias and higher certainty (relative to an alternative-goal condition). These effects were statistically mediated by communicators' epistemic trust in the audience's view, lending further support to the critical role of epistemic motives that are assumed to be characteristic of shared reality.

These findings suggest that when people merely want to go along with another person—for instance, to obtain rewards from this person—a shared reality with that person is not produced. Although communicators pursuing such goals generate audience-congruent representations, as reflected in their audience-tuned messages, their motivation does not lead them to experience a shared reality with the audience. Thus, when people generate representations corresponding to another person's inner state without being motivated to create a shared view about a target, they do not achieve a shared reality. What matters is not the fact of a commonality with another person per se, but the motivation that produces that commonality.

In another set of studies, the creation of a shared reality was shown to depend on whether communicators were motivated to share inner states with the particular person who was the audience for their message (Echterhoff et al., 2005, Experiment 2; Echterhoff et al., 2008, Experiment 1; Kopietz et al., 2010). Presumably, communicators do not regard just any person to be an appropriate partner with whom to share inner states. As suggested by research on social comparison (e.g., Suls, Martin, & Wheeler, 2002) and group-anchored knowledge (e.g., Festinger, 1950; Kruglanski et al., 2006), individuals regard others who possess certain qualities, such as sufficient similarity and trustworthiness, as more appropriate partners with whom to share reality than others who lack these qualities. Among these qualities, membership in a perceiver's in-group (versus out-group) is likely to be particularly important.

Group research suggests that contact with members of one's in-group is rewarding because it fulfills various motives (Yzerbyt, Castano, Leyens, & Paladino, 2000), including fundamental epistemic motives (e.g., Hogg, 2007; Kruglanski et al., 2006) and relational needs (Fiske, 2008; Levine & Kerr, 2007). Thus, people should be less motivated to create a shared reality with out-group members than with in-group members. Nonetheless, in the standard saying-is-believing paradigm, which involves a referential communication task, communicator participants can still be expected to tune their message to an out-group audience. However, compared to tuning messages to an in-group audience, tuning messages to an out-group audience should be motivated more by task fulfillment and politeness demands than by the desire to achieve a shared reality with the audience for epistemic and relational motives. In the standard saying-is-believing paradigm, shared reality motives are typically induced, but when the audience is an out-group member alternative, non-shared-reality motives should take precedence. Thus, if the motivation behind audience tuning is critical, then communicators tuning to an out-group audience should exhibit little if any audience-congruent recall bias.

This is precisely what Echterhoff, Higgins, and colleagues found. Although communicators with an out-group audience tailored their message to their audience's attitude to the same extent as did communicators with an in-group audience, they did not incorporate the audience-tuned message into their own memory of the target. They also exhibited lower epistemic trust in their audience's view than did communicators tuning to an in-group audience (Echterhoff et al., 2005, Experiment 2; Echterhoff et al., 2008, Experiment 1). Furthermore, participants (German students at a German university) who communicated to an audience belonging to a stigmatized out-group (Turks) reported more often that they made an active effort to adapt their messages to their audience's views than did participants communicating to an in-group (German) audience (Echterhoff et al., 2008, Experiment 1). These findings suggest that people producing audience-congruent messages merely to comply with external demands (e.g., behaving in a polite or unprejudiced manner; see Dovidio, Gaertner, Kawakami, & Hodson, 2002; Richeson & Trawalter, 2005) do not create a shared reality.

Researchers have also examined eyewitness retellings toward different audiences and found evidence consistent with this view, thereby extending the scope of findings beyond the standard saying-is-believing paradigm. In a study by Kopietz et al. (2009), student participants tuned their retelling of a witnessed incident to their audience's evaluation of the suspects in the incident. It was found that participants' own memories and judgments regarding the incident were more biased toward their audience when they were more motivated to create a shared view with a particular audience (a student with a similar vs. a dissimilar academic background).

In another study, Kopietz et al. (2010, Experiment 2) directly manipulated the extent to which communicators are motivated by the epistemic benefits afforded by a shared reality. These investigators assumed, as suggested earlier, that audience tuning in the saying-is-believing paradigm reduces uncertainty about the target person arising from the evaluative ambiguity of the original information about the target. To directly examine the role of epistemic uncertainty, the investigators provided communicators at the beginning of the experiment with (bogus) feedback about their performance in a task that required forming judgments of people embedded in social settings. The depicted scenes allowed several different interpretations and were highly ambiguous, like the pictures in the well-known Thematic Apperception Test (Murray, 1943). Communicators who received negative feedback about their performance (presumably the reliability of their judgments about others) were induced to feel more uncertainty about their social judgments than were those who received positive feedback on their performance.

The study found that the high-uncertainty communicators tuned to their audience more than did the low-uncertainty communicators, which is consistent with their stronger epistemic motive to share reality with another person. Furthermore, a saying-is-believing effect (assessed by the association between audience-congruent message and subsequent recall) was found for high-uncertainty communicators but not for low-uncertainty communicators. These findings support the idea that the creation of a shared reality as a function of message tuning depends on the strength of epistemic motives. Additional evidence for greater social sharing under high uncertainty has also been obtained with other paradigms (e.g., Fu et al., 2007; Kruglanski et al., 2006; Lun, Sinclair, Whitchurch, & Glenn, 2007).

As previously outlined, the communicators' motivation to share reality with a given audience can depend on the audience's membership in the communicator's in-group versus out-group. However, although group membership is an important attribute of interaction partners, there may be additional attributes that affect communicators' motivation to share reality. Echterhoff, Lang, et al. (2009) examined the role of other audience characteristics in the saying-is-believing paradigm in the context of personnel assessment in an organization. Student communicators described an employee to either an equal-status audience (a student temp) or a higher-status audience (a company board member). The higher-status audience clearly possessed higher domain-specific expertise, such as professional competence in the assessment of employees. Although audience tuning occurred in both audience-status conditions, the memory bias from audience tuning was found only in the equal-status condition. Apparently, communicators were more willing to share reality with the equal-status audience than with the higher-status audience. An extended measure of trust in the audience, which includes epistemic components (e.g., trust in the audience's judgments in general and about other people in particular) and relational components (e.g., readiness to affiliate and be close), was also higher in the equal-status condition and statistically mediated the audience-status effect on memory bias.

These findings show that an audience's domain-specific expertise or status is not sufficient to motivate communicators to create a shared reality with the audience. Rather, the audience's epistemic and relational trustworthiness is more critical. The feeling of general trust and the readiness to connect and affiliate covered by the extended trust measure in Echterhoff, Lang, et al. (2009) cannot be reduced to mere expertise. What matters is whether communicators want to make an epistemic and relational connection to the audience. Last but not least, finding differences in the memory bias for different types of audiences belonging to the same principal group (i.e., the same company) also suggests that shared reality is not an all-or-nothing affair but instead varies within audiences from the same social in-group.

Regarding the role of epistemic motivation, Echterhoff, Lang, et al. (2009) found that study participants exhibiting stronger epistemic needs, as indicated by higher scores on the Need for Cognitive Closure scale (Kruglanski, Webster, & Klem, 1993), also exhibited a stronger audience-tuning memory bias. When presented with ambiguous input information, people with a greater need for definite and unambiguous representations apparently use audience tuning to a greater extent to create a confident, unambiguous memory representation of the target person.

With the exception of the latter experiment by Echterhoff, Lang, et al. (2009), all other evidence regarding the motives underlying the saying-is-believing effect involves the epistemic dimension. As stated earlier, the desire for connectedness and affiliation with others is another core motive that can drive the creation of shared reality. Further evidence for the role of relational motives in the sharing of inner states has been found in several recent studies. These investigations have employed procedures other than the saying-is-believing paradigm, thus extending the scope of empirical evidence for our concept of shared reality.

In one program of research investigating participants' motives for forming a positive relationship with an interaction partner, Sinclair, Hardin, and colleagues (Sinclair, Huntsinger, et al., 2005; Sinclair, Lowery, Hardin, & Colangelo, 2005) examined how participants' views of a social category (e.g., endorsement of stereotypes of African Americans) or themselves (self-stereotyping) shifted toward the ostensible views of that partner. The relational motive varied as a function of either a situational induction (the partner's manipulated similarity or likeability) or participants' existing affiliative motivation (assessed by personality scales). Results showed that participants' views shifted more toward their interaction partner's ostensible views when the social relationship motive was strong than when the relationship motive was weak. There was also evidence that an independent measure of participants' relational motivation mediated these effects (Sinclair, Lowery, et al., 2005). These authors concluded that participants created a shared reality with their interaction partners to the extent that they were motivated to have a positive relationship with them.

Additional studies by Pinel and her colleagues (2006) provide evidence for the role of relational motives in social sharing of experiences unrelated to stereotypes, such as being amused by a target person's unusual voice, loving a particular band, or exhibiting the same spontaneous responses to word stimuli. The investigators focused on effects of sharing subjective experiences on an important interpersonal variable, namely liking one's interaction partner. Participants' need for connectedness differed as a function of either individual differences (assessed by a personality questionnaire, Pinel et al., 2006, Study 4) or an experimental manipulation (inducing feelings of existential isolation, Pinel et al., 2006, Study 5). Results showed that the effect of sharing inner states on liking their partner was higher when participants' need for connectedness was high.

These two lines of research demonstrate the role of relational motives in the sharing of inner states. The findings supplement the evidence from studies conducted within the saying-is-believing paradigm that has largely emphasized epistemic factors.

SHARED REALITY AND RELATED CONCEPTS

It has long been understood that people's behaviors, thoughts, motivation, and feelings are shaped by exchange and contact with others. As noted earlier, research in recent years has made great strides in the empirical demonstration and investigation of various related phenomena (see Semin, 2007). So what can our notion of shared reality tell us about such interpersonal phenomena that is not yet covered by the rapidly accumulating body of research in this field? What is the distinctive contribution of our concept?

We believe that shared-reality theory addresses issues that are not fully captured by existing accounts and hence provides a new and comprehensive perspective on social-sharing phenomena. In this section, we discuss relations between phenomena described by other, related concepts (empathy, perspective taking, theory of mind, embodied synchrony, common ground, interactive alignment, and socially shared knowledge) and phenomena captured by our notion of shared reality. Despite critical differences revealed by the following analysis, there are potential connections and interfaces between shared reality and these other concepts. Indeed, some of the neighboring phenomena can be regarded as building blocks for shared reality, as they provide preconditions for creating common inner states (corresponding with our first condition) or determining the aboutness of these states (corresponding with our second condition). For instance, empathy, theory of mind, and embodied synchrony involve processes by which perceivers pick up or infer another person's inner state. Thus, these phenomena can contribute to the experience of common inner states (our first condition).

The Interpersonal Matching of Affective States: Empathy and Mood Contagion

Empathy (de Vignemont & Singer, 2006; de Waal, 2008) and emotional or mood contagion (Hatfield, Cacioppo & Rapson, 1994; Neumann & Strack, 2000) are among the most prominent phenomena that involve the sharing of inner states between self and other. In these cases, people try to replicate or simply "catch" another person's affective state, resulting in an interpersonal matching of affective states. From our perspective, these phenomena are similar to shared reality in that they involve a subjectively experienced commonality of inner states. However, the phenomena differ from shared reality because they can occur without the perceiver sharing the other person's view about an object or target referent—that is, without satisfying our condition of aboutness (the second condition for shared reality). For instance, Person A may feel sorrow after hearing that Person B's wife has left him. Person A feels sorrow about the simple fact that Person B is clearly in pain, whereas Person B feels sorrow about his wife leaving him. In this case, the commonality of feeling sorrow does not extend to sharing the referent or target of the sorrow—there is no sharing of what the sorrow is about.

Indeed, according to current definitions (e.g., de Vignemont & Singer, 2006; de Waal, 2008), empathy requires that empathizers share another person's inner state, but it does not require that the sharing extend to a referent target (i.e., what the inner state is about). For instance, among three potential criteria for empathy discussed by de Waal (2008, p. 281) ["the capacity to (a) be affected by and share the emotional state of another, (b) assess the reasons for the other's state, and (c) identify with the other, adopting his or her perspective"], only the first is explicitly identified as necessary: "the term 'empathy' … applies even if only criterion (a) is met" (p. 281). This view is consistent with empirical approaches to empathy that do not entail target referents of emotional states (e.g., Carr, Iacoboni, Dubeau, Mazziotta, & Lenzi, 2003; Schulte-Rüther, Markowitsch, Fink, & Piefke, 2007).

A similar case can be made for commonalities of emotional states that do not involve attempts to empathize. For instance, fear can rapidly spread in a flock of birds just as distress may spread in a room full of newborns without a commensurate awareness of what triggered the initial reaction (de Waal, 2008). Also, the aboutness of inner states is sometimes not clearly established in empirical studies on the interpersonal matching of emotions. For instance, Wicker et al. (2003) measured brain activity while participants viewed short movie clips of actors sniffing the contents of a glass and reacting with a pleased or disgusted facial expression. Participants were then themselves exposed to pleasant or disgusting odorants. It was found that anterior insula, a brain region implicated in the processing of both olfactory and painful stimuli, was activated both by the experience of disgust and the observation of the disgusted facial expressions of others. However, it was not reported whether the observing and observed person actually felt similarly about the object of their experience (i.e., the glass or its content). Thus, it remained unclear whether there was a sharing of inner states about the target of the observed experience. Of course, if it is ascertained that the matching responses in the observer extend to the same target object, our second condition of aboutness for shared reality would be satisfied. However, the motivational processes leading to such a commonality of emotional states (our third condition) would still have to be analyzed for the particular phenomenon.

Regarding another type of affective state, when a perceiver picks up another person's positive or negative mood, that mood is not necessarily in reference to something. For instance, Neumann and Strack (2000) demonstrated that mood states can be transferred interpersonally without the perceiver being aware of its origin or referent object. Thus, it is not necessary that the person catching another person's mood knows the source of the other person's mood state.

Although these cases of matching affective states do not satisfy the aboutness condition of shared reality (our second condition), they still might contribute to a shared reality because they involve processes by which perceivers pick up another person's inner (here, affective) state. Earlier in this chapter, we have argued that such processes are necessary for the achievement of the first condition for shared reality: the sense of a commonality of inner states. In other words, some type of (subjectively experienced) access to another person's inner state is a critical precondition or building block of shared reality. By our view, then, processes involved in empathizing and mood contagion can be regarded as such building blocks and thus might serve as precursor mechanisms in the unfolding of a full-blown shared reality.

Perspective Taking

In contrast to mood matching or the discussed cases of empathy, perspective taking or role-taking requires aboutness or referentiality because it involves views about some aspect of the world (Higgins, 1981; Krauss & Fussell, 1991; Mead, 1934; Piaget & Inhelder, 1956). In perspective taking, a person intuits, as accurately as possible, another person's viewpoint, perceptions, thoughts, knowledge, attitudes, or goals. More generally, perspective taking entails taking the role of someone else (Mead, 1934). Its primary purpose is to see and appreciate a situation, state, or object as others experience it. We suspect that the difference between this notion of perspective taking and our notion of shared reality lies in the extent to which perceivers experience a commonality of inner states. To the extent that perspective taking implies an appreciation of the difference between one's own and another person's view—that is, nonegocentrism (Piaget & Inhelder, 1956)—it does not entail the experience of having common inner states. For instance, when a company executive takes the perspective of a blue-collar employee advocating a strike, the executive recognizes ways in which the employee views the salary negotiations differently. Clearly, taking the employee's perspective does not require that the executive hold the same view or inner state about the negotiations or the strike. Similarly, when a professor takes the perspective of a student regarding the workload in her seminar she may recognize the student's attitude toward the work assignments, but this does not mean that she shares that student's attitude. Perspective taking can produce a change in beliefs or attitudes about a target referent, but this change need not produce a commonality of inner states. Indeed, realizing another party's views, beliefs, or goals through perspective taking may even increase people's resolution to bolster or intensify their own position, especially in the context of diverging interests or social conflict (Epley et al., 2006).

Although perspective taking differs in these respects from shared reality, there are also possible interactions between the two phenomena. Because perspective taking implies an awareness of the object or referent of another person's view, it may involve processes that allow perceivers to recognize or infer the target of others' inner states. Thus, mechanisms implicated in perspective taking may be building blocks or precursor processes for the creation of shared reality. To achieve a sense of shared inner states about a target referent, perceivers first need to identify the target referent of another person's inner state. Processes of perspective taking may allow perceivers to examine whether another person actually has in mind or is attending to the same object that they have in mind.

Theory of Mind

Given that we have emphasized the appreciation of others' inner states in mediating their overt behavior, we also want to address the relation between our notion of shared reality and the concept of theory of mind. Theory of mind is another phenomenon in which people obtain access to others' inner states in relation to some target referent. In comparison with the commonality of affective states that we have analyzed, theory of mind encompasses a wider range of inner states, such as beliefs, intentions, and desires. Historically, there has been a close relation between the concept of perspective taking and the concept of theory of mind, given that they were both offered as explanations for an important developmental shift in young children's understanding of their social world: the recognition that individuals have inner states like thoughts and feelings that influence their behavior. The two concepts differ, however, in the mechanism postulated as underlying the inference about others' inner states.

In their seminal paper, Premack and Woodruff (1978) defined theory of mind as the ability to impute mental (i.e., inner) states such as beliefs or desires to others and to predict behavior on the basis of such states. A theory of mind allows humans to represent propositions about the world (e.g., "The new colleague is nice") at a second-order level by relating them to a person's mental state concerning the world: "Thomas believes that the new colleague is nice." As for perspective taking, the difference between our notion of shared reality and the concept of theory of mind is clear with respect to our first (and fourth) condition for shared reality—experiencing a successfully created commonality of inner states. You know that Thomas believes the new colleague is nice, but that does not mean that you share this belief about the new colleague. To the extent that theory of mind underlies people's ability to influence others, it implies an initial discrepancy of inner states rather than a commonality. Social influence situations involve attempts at managing others' inner states (Higgins & Pittman, 2008) precisely because, by applying your theory of mind, you have discovered that their inner state (e.g., their belief, attitude, or feeling about something) is different from your own on some matter. Given this, you try to change the other's inner state to bring it closer to your own.

There is a further implication of this difference. As described by Leslie (1987), the result of the mentalizing involved in theory of mind is that the primary proposition (that the new colleague is nice) becomes opaque (Quine, 1961). The proposition is placed in parentheses, stripping it of its referential truth value. When it is said that "Thomas believes that the new colleague is nice," the question of whether the new colleague is actually nice is suspended. In theory of mind, then, the recognition of another person's inner state does not involve assigning objectivity or truth to that inner state (also see Leslie et al., 2004). Inferring that Thomas believes the new colleague is nice does not say anything about whether Thomas's belief is accurate. In contrast, if someone creates a shared reality with Thomas about the new colleague being nice, then that person will experience the shared belief about the new colleague as being the truth.

Embodied Synchrony and Mirroring

How does shared reality relate to the phenomena of embodied social synchrony (c.g., Barsalou et al., 2003; Gallese et al., 2004; Iacoboni, 2008) that have recently commanded much attention and inspired debates about the nature of interpersonal and social processes (see Semin, 2007; Semin & Cacioppo, 2008)? We acknowledge that the mirror metaphor has been criticized, for instance, for failing to account for the complementarity of human actions (see Graf, Schütz-Bosbach, & Prinz, this volume, Chapter 3). Still, we use the term here as it has been used in abundance in recent research and debates.

In embodied synchrony or mirroring, an observer is assumed to simulate the observed person's inner state. In other words, the observation of another person's expression of an inner state creates a matching inner state in the observer—typically patterns of neural or mental activation that underlie the performance of an action or the expression of an emotion (e.g., Carr et al., 2003). Studies on embodied synchronization typically assess the correspondence of inner (neural) states between observing and observed individuals. However, such correspondence does not necessarily mean that the observer shares the observed person's inner state about a target referent (beliefs, attitudes, etc.). First, there are pertinent studies that do not examine or discuss whether the correspondence of inner states extends to corresponding experiences of a target or object (e.g., Carr et al., 2003; Schulte-Rüther et al., 2007; Wicker et al., 2003). Second, some studies have revealed neural simulation for intransitive actions. Intransitive actions, for example, dancing, lack any specific reference object (Calvo-Merino, Glaser, Grèzes, Passingham, & Haggard, 2005; Cross, Hamilton, & Grafton, 2006). Thus, phenomena of embodied synchrony can occur without the aboutness that we have described as one condition of shared reality.

We recognize that many other studies in this field have investigated neural mirroring for actions that are related to a reference object. Indeed, the groundbreaking studies by Rizzolatti, Gallese, and colleagues (see Gallese et al., 2004) demonstrated mirror neuron activity in the brain of monkeys who observed actions directed at an object (e.g., food items). Furthermore, research with human participants indicates that the activity of the mirror neuron system may be sufficiently context-sensitive to allow the distinction of different intentions underlying an action. For instance, Iacoboni et al. (2005) investigated mirror activities when participants saw a video clip of a hand grasping a mug. The authors found that neural activity differed depending on whether the context suggested that the underlying intention was drinking (when the mug was filled with tea and other items on a table, such as cookies, were prepared for consumption) or cleaning up (when the mug was empty and other items, such as cookie crumbs, indicated finished consumption). They concluded that neural mirroring can even facilitate understanding the intentions of others' actions—that is, inner states as they relate to a referent object.

However, such mirroring phenomena cannot be equated with shared reality as conceptualized in this chapter. Context-sensitive mirroring and neural simulation may facilitate understanding others' intentions, but it is important to note that understanding intentions is *not* the same as sharing intentions. The fact that neural responses allow an observer to better understand the intentions of an observed action regarding a target object (e.g., drinking or cleaning up with reference to the state of a mug) by no means requires that the observer has the same intention regarding the object. Understanding an intention is different from having intentions in common.

Although this analysis suggests critical differences between shared reality and embodied synchrony or mirroring, we think it is important to recognize possible ways in which these phenomena may be interrelated. As we have argued, there are preconditions for the creation of a shared reality. For instance, perceivers need to infer others' inner states in order to share reality with them. Embodied synchrony and mirroring are basic processes that may support such inferences: They may allow perceivers to obtain access to others' neural and mental states automatically—that is, with remarkable speed and without the need to allocate conscious effort. However, for a full-blown shared reality, perceivers also need to experience that they and the other person have a common inner state about a target referent.

Common Ground and Interactive Alignment

The creation of a commonality between communicators has figured prominently in research on common ground (H. H. Clark, 1996; H. H. Clark & Marshall, 1981) and interactive alignment in conversation (Garrod & Pickering, 2004). Common ground is the background information that participants in a conversation take for granted as being mutually understood. For instance, when a scientist mentions to a politician the critical role of IRBs in the progress of research, there will be common ground when the politician knows that the scientist refers to institutional review boards (that supervise the observation of ethical standards in research conducted at universities) and not to something like Internet radio broadcasting or intermittent radioactive beams. To use another example, when a speaker asks an addressee to pick "the loafer" from an array of different objects, there is common ground when the addressee knows what object the speaker refers to (Brennan & Clark, 1996).

In what ways does shared reality differ from common ground? Common ground involves shared background knowledge, which permits or at least facilitates conversation. However, common ground, as it is typically used in the literature, does not require that the conversationalists hold the same inner states (views, beliefs, or feelings) about the topic of the conversation. In the previous example, when both speaker and addressee know what IRB or the loafer refer to, they do not have to share the same view, belief, or feeling about the referent. For instance, the scientist may hold a skeptical attitude about the role of IRBs because of rigid formal supervision procedures enforced by some IRBs. In contrast, the politician may hold a positive attitude about IRBs because they can prevent unethical scientific investigations. Two people may agree on the topic of the conversation without having a common inner response to this topic (i.e., without achieving a shared reality as defined in this chapter).

A similar argument can be made for the processes of interactive alignment, which are not assumed to require explicit or conscious negotiation (Garrod & Pickering, 2004). Alignment of linguistic representations and situation models allows successful conversation, but it need not result in conversationalists holding congruent attitudes or feelings about the topic of their conversation. Common ground and alignment denote a shared basis for exchanging information about inner states, but not a commonality of these inner states. Shared reality, thus, goes a step beyond common ground or interactive alignment in that it involves common inner states about the world—shared attitudes, beliefs, or feelings about some target referent.

Again, such differences do not preclude a meaningful interplay between these phenomena and shared reality. The establishment of common ground ensures that conversationalists refer to the same object or topic. Thus, common ground involves processes that allow perceivers to infer or verify the target of others' inner states. Because such an inference is a precondition for the achievement of aboutness, grounding in conversation is conceivably an important building block of a full-blown shared reality (also see Kashima, Klein, & Clark, 2007).

Socially Distributed Knowledge

Research on socially shared or distributed knowledge (e.g., Gaskell & Fraser, 1990; Sperber, 1996) represents another field that is sufficiently close to shared reality to warrant examination. Shared or distributed knowledge can be roughly understood as the body of beliefs and ideas that are spread across communities or societies. This concept involves two of our conditions for shared reality: commonality of inner states (rather than just overt behaviors) and the principle of aboutness (in that they are about a target referent). However, these phenomena differ from shared reality in at least one central respect. For something to count as socially distributed knowledge, it must be, in fact, held in common between or among some set of individuals. This is not a necessary condition for shared reality. For shared reality, it is sufficient that an individual experience an inner state about something that is in common between him or her and some other person—even if, in fact, there is no such inner state in common (see Bar-Tal, 2000).

Moreover, the experience of there being a commonality is critical to whether there is a shared reality. In contrast, there can be socially distributed knowledge among a set of individuals without those individuals experiencing this commonality. Indeed, if anything, this experience of commonality is unlikely among members of larger collectives, such as societies and large-scale communities, which have been highlighted in theories of socially shared or distributed knowledge. It should also be noted that our theoretical analysis of shared reality places greater emphasis on the motivational underpinnings of sharing, especially the role of relational motives, than do approaches to distributed knowledge.

CONCLUSION: IMPLICATIONS FOR THE (RE)PRODUCTION OF CULTURE

What then are the implications of shared reality research for the formation and transmission of culture? The creation of shared reality through communication highlights a potentially important everyday mechanism underlying the construction of culturally shared memories and knowledge—a basic mechanism for constructing social, cultural, and political beliefs (see Hausmann et al., 2008; Jost et al., 2007; Lau et al., 2001). Consider community members who trust one another, want to maintain relationships with one another, and are thus prepared and motivated to create a shared reality. When community member A is aware of community member B's view (presumable or actual) regarding some topic (e.g., his or her beliefs or attitudes about something), audience tuning during interpersonal communication is likely to occur. Given that the audience tuning serves a shared-reality goal, it will shape communicator A's later memories and beliefs about the topic in the direction of the audience. Rather than remembering the topic information as originally received, communicator A will remember this information as represented in her or his tuned message. A similar process may then occur when another community member C, being aware of A's communicatively formed belief, talks about the same topic to member A, and then community member D talks to C, and so on. As a result of continued communication on the topic, the community members will come to hold increasingly shared beliefs.

This process may occur not only for individuals as topic targets but also for groups as topic targets (see Hausmann et al., 2008; Klein, Tindale, & Brauer, 2008; Lyons & Kashima, 2003), and this could be an important factor in the development of community-shared stereotypic beliefs about other groups. Social tuning toward audiences, which is ubiquitous in everyday life, can thus create a shared but biased perspective on the world within a community.

While we have focused in the present chapter on the effects of shared reality–driven communication on the communicators themselves, these effects are likely to apply to the recipients as well. Support for this notion comes from a recent study by Stukas, Bratanova, Kashima, Peters, and Beatson (2010). These authors found that recipients' beliefs about a target group were biased by messages tuned toward their presumable beliefs, whereas in fact they initially did not know the target group and thus did not hold preexisting attitudes. Consistent with shared-reality theory, the effect on recipients was stronger for those recipients who reported a greater willingness and experience of shared reality with the communicator. Thus, communicators' expectations about recipients' attitudes toward a group can initiate a confirmatory process by which both communicators and recipients come to hold the expected attitudes, thus giving rise to a shared reality created without anyone holding an initial view of that "reality"! Importantly, this communicatively fulfilled prophecy apparently depends on the interlocutors' experienced creation of a shared reality with each other.

The shared-reality research we have presented has new and counterintuitive implications regarding the role of the content of communicated information in cultural knowledge formation. Even if the content is exactly the same in two conversations, it does not mean that both have the same effect on cultural knowledge formation. A conversation will shape cultural knowledge and beliefs only when the communicators' message production and recipients' message comprehension are sufficiently motivated by the achievement of a shared reality. Hence, communication that appears similar at the surface might have different consequences for the transmission and retention of culture. Although we acknowledge that language use and communication may have many interesting unintended effects on both communicators and recipients (e.g., Fiedler, 2008; Holtgraves & Kashima, 2008), we believe that the pursuit of an appropriate communication goal, that is, the goal of creating shared reality, is critical for the effective transmission and retention of cultural knowledge through communication.

In sum, we have argued that the goal of creating a shared reality plays a critical role in how communication contributes to the formation and maintenance of cultural knowledge. In addition to the theoretical arguments and related evidence we have mustered, support for this claim can also be found in standard views about the functions and benefits of culture. By a widely endorsed notion, cultural knowledge not only enables people to operate successfully in their environment and to coordinate their actions, but it also allows them to interpret experiences and to construct an understanding of the world they inhabit (e.g., Bruner, 1990; Chiu & Hong, 2006; Lau, Chiu, & Lee, 2001; Shore, 1996)—what we refer to as creating a "shared reality."

ACKNOWLEDGMENTS

The preparation of this chapter was supported by grants from the German Research Foundation (Deutsche Forschungsgemeinschaft, reference numbers EC 317/2 and EC 317/3) to Gerald Echterhoff. We thank Olivier Klein and Gün Semin for providing helpful comments on previous drafts of this chapter.

REFERENCES

Adaval, R. & Wyer, R. S., Jr. (2004). Communicating about a social interaction: Effects on memory for protagonists' statements and nonverbal behaviors. *Journal of Experimental Social Psychology, 40*, 450–465.

Asch, S. E. (1951). Effects of group pressure upon the modification and distortion of judgments. In H. S. Guetzkow (Ed.), *Groups, leadership and men* (pp. 177–190). Pittsburgh, PA: Carnegie Press.

Asch, S .E. (1952). *Social psychology*. Englewood Cliffs, NJ: Prentice Hall.

Baron-Cohen, S. (1995). *Mindblindness: As essay on autism and theory of mind*. Cambridge, MA: MIT Press.

Barsalou, L.W., Niedenthal, P.M., Barbey, A., & Ruppert, J. (2003). Social embodiment. In B. Ross (Ed.), *The psychology of learning and motivation* (Vol. 43, pp. 43–92). San Diego, CA: Academic Press.

Bar-Tal, D. (1990). *Group beliefs: A conception for analyzing group structure, processes, and behavior*. New York: Springer-Verlag.

Bar-Tal, D. (2000). *Shared beliefs in a society: Social psychological analysis*. Thousand Oaks, CA: Sage.

Bartlett, F. C. (1932). *Remembering: A study in experimental and social psychology*. Cambridge, UK: Cambridge University Press.

Baumeister, R. F. & Leary, M. R. (1995). The need to belong: Desire for interpersonal attachments as a fundamental human motivation. *Psychological Bulletin, 117*, 497–529.

Berlyne, D.E. (1962). Uncertainty and epistemic curiosity. *British Journal of Psychology, 53*, 27–34.

Bohman, J. F. & Rehg, W. (Eds.). (1997). *Deliberative democracy*. Cambridge, MA: MIT Press

Bowlby, J. (1969). *Attachment and loss: Vol. 1. Attachment*. New York: Basic Books.

Brennan, S. E. & Clark, H. H. (1996). Conceptual pacts and lexical choice in conversation. *Journal of Experimental Psychology: Learning, Memory, and Cognition, 22*, 1482–1493.

Brickman, P. (1978). Is it real? In J. H. Harvey, W. Ickes, & R. F. Kidd (Eds.), *New directions in attribution research* (Vol. 2, pp. 5–34). Hillsdale, NJ: Erlbaum.

Bruner, J. (1990). *Acts of meaning*. Cambridge, MA: Harvard University Press.

Byrne, D. & Clore, G. L. (1967). Effectance arousal and attraction. *Journal of Personality and Social Psychology, 6*, 1–18.

Call, J. (2005). The self and other: A missing link in comparative social cognition. In H. S. Terrace & J. Metcalfe (Eds.), *The missing link in cognition: Origins of self-reflective consciousness* (pp. 321–341). Oxford, UK: Oxford University Press.

Calvo-Merino, B., Glaser, D. E., Grèzes, J., Passingham, R. E., & Haggard, P. (2005). Action observation and acquired motor skills: An fMRI study with expert dancers. *Cerebral Cortex, 15*, 1243–1249.

Caporael, L. R. (2007). Evolutionary theory for social and cultural psychology. In A. W. Kruglanski & E. T. Higgins (Eds.), *Social psychology: Handbook of basic principles* (2nd ed., pp. 3–18). New York: Guilford.

Carr, L., Iacoboni, M., Dubeau, M.-C., Mazziotta, J. C., & Lenzi, G. L. (2003). Neural mechanisms of empathy in humans: A relay from neural systems for imitation to limbic areas. *Proceedings of the National Academy of Sciences, USA, 100*, 5497–5502.

Chiu, C.Y. & Hong, Y.-Y. (2006). *Social psychology of culture*. New York: Psychology Press.

Chiu, C.Y. & Hong, Y.-Y. (2007). Cultural processes: Basic principles. In A. W. Kruglanski & E. T. Higgins (Eds.), *Social psychology: Handbook of basic principles* (2nd ed., pp. 785–804). New York: Guilford.

Chiu, C. Y., Krauss, R. M., & Lau, I. Y.-M. (1998). Some cognitive consequences of communication. In S. R. Fussell & R. Kreuz (Eds.), *Social and cognitive approaches to interpersonal communication* (pp. 259–278). Hillsdale, NJ: Erlbaum.

Clark, A. E., & Kashima, Y. (2007). Stereotypes help people connect with others in the community: A situated functional analysis of the stereotype consistency bias in communication. *Journal of Personality and Social Psychology, 93*, 1028–1093.

Clark, H. H. (1996). *Using language*. New York: Cambridge University Press.

Clark, H. H. (2003). Pointing and placing. In S. Kita (Ed.), *Pointing: Where language, culture, and cognition meet* (pp. 243–268). Hillsdale, NJ: Erlbaum.

Clark, H. H. & Marshall, C. E. (1981). Definite reference and mutual knowledge. In A.K. Joshi, B. Webber, & I. Sag (Eds.), *Elements of discourse understanding* (pp. 10–63). Cambridge, UK: Cambridge University Press.

Cooley, C. H. (1964). *Human nature and the social order*. New York: Schocken Books. (Original work published 1902)

Crocker, J. (2007). *What are the fundamental human needs? Summary of responses*. E-mail to the spsp-discuss list (spsp-discuss@stolaf.edu), October 8, 2007.

Cross, E. S., Hamilton, A. F., & Grafton, S. T. (2006). Building a motor simulation de novo: Observation of dance by dancers. *NeuroImage, 31*, 1257–1267.

De Vignemont, F. & Singer, T. (2006). The empathic brain: How, when, and why? *Trends in Cognitive Sciences, 10*, 435–441.

De Waal, F. (2008). Putting the altruism back into altruism: The evolution of empathy. *Annual Review of Psychology, 59*, 279–300.
Deutsch, M. & Gerard, H. B. (1955). A study of normative and informational social influences upon individual judgment. *Journal of Abnormal and Social Psychology, 51*, 629–636.
Diener, E. & Seligman, M. E. P. (2002). Very happy people. *Psychological Science, 13*, 81–84.
Dovidio, J. F., Gaertner, S. L., Kawakami, K., & Hodson, G. (2002). Why can't we just get along? Interpersonal biases and interracial distrust. *Cultural Diversity and Ethnic Minority Psychology, 8*, 88–102.
Dunbar, R. I. M. & Shultz, S. (2007). Evolution in the social brain. *Science, 317*, 1344–1347.
Echterhoff, G., Higgins, E. T., & Groll, S. (2005). Audience-tuning effects on memory: The role of shared reality. *Journal of Personality and Social Psychology, 89*, 257–276.
Echterhoff, G., Higgins, E. T., Kopietz, R., & Groll, S. (2008). How communication goals determine when audience tuning biases memory. *Journal of Experimental Psychology: General, 137*, 3–21.
Echterhoff, G., Higgins, E. T., & Levine, J. M. (2009). Shared reality: Experiencing commonality with others' inner states about the world. *Perspectives on Psychological Science, 4*, 496–521.
Echterhoff, G., Lang, S., Krämer, N. & Higgins, E. T. (2009). Audience-tuning effects on communicators' memory: The role of audience status in sharing reality. *Social Psychology, 40*, 150–163.
Epley, N., Caruso, E. M., & Bazerman, M. H. (2006). When perspective taking increases taking: Reactive egoism in social interaction. *Journal of Personality and Social Psychology, 91*, 872–889.
Fast, N. J., Heath, C., & Wu, G. (2009). Common ground and cultural prominence: How conversation reinforces culture. *Psychological Science, 20*, 904–911.
Festinger, L. (1950). Informal social communication. *Psychological Review, 57*, 271–282.
Festinger, L. (1954). A theory of social comparison processes. *Human Relations, 7*, 117–140.
Fiedler, K. (2008). Language: A toolbox for sharing and influencing social reality. *Perspectives on Psychological Science, 3*, 38–47.
Fiske, S. T. (2008). Core social motivations: Views from the couch, consciousness, classroom, computers, and collectives. In W. Gardner & J. Y. Shah (Eds.), *Handbook of motivation science* (pp. 3–22). New York: Guilford.
Frey, D. & Schulz-Hardt, S. (2001). Confirmation bias in group information seeking and its implications for decision making in administration, business, and politics. In F. Butera & G. Mugny (Eds.), *Social influence in social reality: Promoting individual and social change* (pp. 53–73). Seattle, WA: Hogrefe & Huber.
Fu, J. H.-Y., Morris, M. W., Lee, S.-L., Chao, M., Chiu, C.-Y., & Hong, Y.-Y. (2007). Epistemic motives and cultural conformity: Need for closure, culture, and context as determinants of conflict judgments. *Journal of Personality and Social Psychology, 92*, 191–207.
Gallese, V., Keysers, C., & Rizzolatti, G. (2004). A unifying view of the basis of social cognition. *Trends in Cognitive Sciences, 8*, 396–403.
Garfinkel, H. (1967). *Studies in ethnomethodology*. Englewood Cliffs, NJ: Prentice-Hall.
Garrod, S. & Pickering, M. (2004). Why is conversation so easy? *Trends in Cognitive Sciences, 8*, 8–11.
Gaskell, G. & Fraser, C. (1990). The social psychological study of widespread beliefs. In C. Fraser & G. Gaskell (Eds.), *The social psychological study of widespread beliefs* (pp. 3–24). Oxford, UK: Clarendon Press.

Hardin, C. D. & Conley, T. D. (2001). A relational approach to cognition: Shared experience and relationship affirmation in social cognition. In G. B. Moskowitz (Ed.), *Cognitive social psychology: The Princeton Symposium on the legacy and future of social cognition* (pp. 3–17). Mahwah, NJ: Erlbaum.

Hardin, C. D. & Higgins, E. T. (1996). Shared reality: How social verification makes the subjective objective. In R. M. Sorrentino & E. T. Higgins (Eds.), *Handbook of motivation and cognition: The interpersonal context* (Vol. 3, pp. 28–84). New York: Guilford Press.

Hatfield, E., Cacioppo, J. T., & Rapson, R. L. (1994). *Emotional contagion*. Cambridge, UK: Cambridge University Press.

Hausmann, L. R. M., Levine, J. M., & Higgins, E. T. (2008). Communication and group perception: Extending the "saying is believing" effect. *Group Processes and Intergroup Relations, 11*, 539–554.

Heider, F. (1958). *The psychology of interpersonal relations*. New York: John Wiley & Sons.

Hellmann, J. H. (2007). *How event retellings shape eyewitnesses' memory: A saying-is-believing effect for complex visual material*. Unpublished master's thesis, Bielefeld University, Bielefeld, Germany.

Higgins, E. T. (1981). Role taking and social judgment: Alternative developmental perspectives and processes. In J. H. Flavell & L. Ross (Eds.), *Social cognitive development: Frontiers and possible futures* (pp. 119–153). New York: Cambridge University Press.

Higgins, E. T. (1992). Achieving "shared reality" in the communication game: A social action that creates meaning. *Journal of Language and Social Psychology, 11*, 107–131.

Higgins, E. T. (1998). The aboutness principle: A pervasive influence on human inference. *Social Cognition, 16*, 173–198.

Higgins, E. T. (1999). "Saying is believing" effects: When sharing reality about something biases knowledge and evaluations. In L. L. Thompson, J. M. Levine, & D. M. Messick (Eds.), *Shared cognition in organizations: The management of knowledge* (pp. 33–48). Mahwah, NJ: Erlbaum.

Higgins, E. T. (2005). Humans as applied motivation scientists: Self-consciousness from "shared reality" and "becoming." In H. S. Terrace & J. Metcalfe (Eds.), *The missing link in cognition: Origins of self-reflective consciousness* (pp. 157–173). Oxford, UK: Oxford University Press.

Higgins, E. T. (2006). Value from hedonic experience and engagement. *Psychological Review, 113*, 439–460.

Higgins, E. T. (2010). *Beyond pleasure and pain: The new science of motivation*. Manuscript in preparation, Columbia University.

Higgins, E. T., Echterhoff, G., Crespillo, R., & Kopietz, R. (2007). Effects of communication on social knowledge: Sharing reality with individual versus group audiences. *Japanese Psychological Research, 49*, 89–99.

Higgins, E. T., McCann, C. D., & Fondacaro, R. (1982). The "communication game": Goal directed encoding and cognitive consequences. *Social Cognition, 1*, 21–37.

Higgins, E. T., & Pittman, T. S. (2008). Motives of the human animal: Comprehending, managing, and sharing inner states. *Annual Review of Psychology, 59*, 361–385.

Higgins, E. T., & Rholes, W. S. (1978). "Saying is believing": Effects of message modification on memory and liking for the person described. *Journal of Experimental Social Psychology, 14*, 363–378.

Hirst, W. & Manier, D. (2002). The diverse forms of collective memory. In G. Echterhoff & M. Saar (Eds.), *Kontexte und Kulturen des Erinnerns* [*Contexts and cultures of remembering*] (pp. 37–58). Constance, Germany: Universitätsverlag Konstanz GmbH.

Hogg, M. A. (2007). Uncertainty-identity theory. In M. P. Zanna (Ed.), *Advances in experimental social psychology* (Vol. 39, pp. 69–126). San Diego, CA: Academic Press.

Holtgraves, T. M. & Kashima, Y. (2008). Language, meaning, and social cognition. *Personality and Social Psychology Review, 12*, 73–94.

Iacoboni, M. (2008). *Mirroring people: The new science of how we connect with others*. New York: Farrar, Straus, & Giroux.

Iacoboni, M., Molnar-Szakacs, I., Gallese, V., Buccino, G., Mazziotta, J. C., & Rizzolatti, G. (2005). Grasping the intentions of others with one's own mirror neuron system. *Public Library of Science: Biology, 3*, 529–535.

Idson, L. C. & Mischel, W. (2001). The personality of familiar and significant people: The lay perceiver as a social-cognitive theorist. *Journal of Personality and Social Psychology, 80*, 585–596.

Jones, E. E. (1964). *Ingratiation: A social psychological analysis*. New York: Appleton-Century-Crofts.

Jones, E. E. & Thibaut, J. W. (1958). Interaction goals as bases of inference in interpersonal perception. In R. Tagiuri & L. Petrullo (Eds.), *Person perception and interpersonal behavior* (pp. 151–178). Stanford, CA: Stanford University Press.

Jost, J. T., Ledgerwood, A., & Hardin, C. D. (2007). Shared reality, system verification, and the relational basis of ideological beliefs. *Social and Personality Psychology Compass, 2*, 171–186.

Kashima, Y., Klein, O., & Clark, A. E. (2007). Grounding: Sharing information in social interaction. In K. Fiedler (Ed.), *Social communication* (pp. 30–77). New York: Psychology Press.

Keysar, B. & Barr, D. J. (2002). Self anchoring in conversation: Why language users do not do what they "should." In T. Gilovich, D. W. Griffin, & D. Kahneman (Eds.), *Heuristics and biases: The psychology of intuitive judgment* (pp. 150–166). Cambridge, UK: Cambridge University Press.

Keysar, B., Barr, D.J., Balin, J.A., & Brauner, J.S. (2000). Taking perspective in conversation: The role of mutual knowledge in comprehension. *Psychological Science, 11*, 32–38.

Keysers, C. & Gazzola, V. (2007). Integrating simulation and theory of mind: From self to social cognition. *Trends in Cognitive Sciences, 11*, 194–196.

Klein, O., Tindale, S., & Brauer, M. (2008). The consensualization of stereotypes in small groups. In Y. Kashima, K. Fiedler, & P. Freytag (Eds.), *Stereotype dynamics: Language-based approaches to the formation, maintenance, and transformation of stereotypes* (pp. 263–292). New York: Erlbaum.

Kluckhohn, C. (1954). Culture and behavior. In G. Lindzey (Ed.), *Handbook of social psychology* (Vol. 2, pp. 921–976). Cambridge, MA: Addison-Wesley.

Kopietz, R., Echterhoff, G., Niemeier, S., Hellmann, J. H., & Memon, A. (2009). Audience-congruent biases in eyewitness memory and judgment: Influences of a co-witness' liking for a suspect. *Social Psychology, 40*, 138–149.

Kopietz, R., Hellmann, J. H., Higgins, E. T., & Echterhoff, G. (2010). Shared-reality effects on memory: Communicating to fulfill epistemic needs. *Social Cognition, 28*, 353–378.

Krauss, R. M. & Fussell, S. R. (1991). Perspective taking in communication: Representations of others' knowledge in reference. *Social Cognition, 9*, 2–24.

Kruglanski, A. W. (2004). *The psychology of closed mindedness*. New York: Psychology Press.

Kruglanski, A. W., Pierro, A., Mannetti, L., & De Grada, E. (2006). Groups as epistemic providers: Need for closure and the unfolding of group-centrism. *Psychological Review, 113*, 84–100.

Kruglanski, A. W., Webster, D. M., & Klem, A. (1993). Motivated resistance and openness to persuasion in the presence or absence of prior information. *Journal of Personality and Social Psychology, 65*, 861–876.

Lau, I. Y. M., Chiu, C.-Y., & Lee, S. L. (2001). Communication and shared reality: Implications for the psychological foundations of culture. *Social Cognition, 19*, 350–371.

Lehman, D. R., Chiu, C.-Y., & Schaller, M. (2004). Psychology and culture. *Annual Review of Psychology, 55*, 689–714.

Leslie, A. M. (1987). Pretense and representation: The origins of "theory of mind." *Psychological Review, 94*, 412–426.

Leslie, A. M., Friedman, O., & German, T. P. (2004). Core mechanisms in "theory of mind." *Trends in Cognitive Sciences, 8*, 528–533.

Levine, J. M. & Higgins, E. T. (2001). Shared reality and social influence in groups and organizations. In F. Butera & G. Mugny (Eds.), *Social influence in social reality: Promoting individual and social change* (pp. 33–52). Seattle, WA: Hogrefe & Huber.

Levine, J. M. & Kerr, N. L. (2007). Inclusion and exclusion: Implications for group processes. In A. E. Kruglanski & E. T. Higgins (Eds.), *Social psychology: Handbook of basic principles* (2nd ed., pp. 759–784). New York: Guilford.

Levine, J. M. & Moreland, R. L. (2004). Collaboration: The social context of theory development. *Personality and Social Psychology Review, 8*, 164–172.

Lewin, K. (1947). Group decision and social change. In T. M. Newcomb & E. L. Hartley (Eds.), *Readings in social psychology* (pp. 330–344). New York: Holt.

Lun, J., Sinclair, S., Whitchurch, E. R., & Glenn, C. (2007). (Why) do I think what you think? Epistemic social tuning and implicit prejudice. *Journal of Personality and Social Psychology, 93*, 957–972.

Lyons, A. & Kashima, Y. (2003). How are stereotypes maintained through communication? The influence of stereotype sharedness. *Journal of Personality and Social Psychology, 85*, 989–1005.

Mackie, D. M. & Skelly, J. J. (1994). The social cognition analysis of social influence: Contributions to the understanding of persuasion and conformity. In P. Devine, D. Hamilton, & T. Ostrom (Eds.), *Social cognition: Impact on social psychology* (pp. 259–289). New York: Academic Press.

Malle, B. F. (1999). How people explain behavior: A new theoretical framework. *Personality and Social Psychology Review, 3*, 23–43.

Malle, B. F. & Hodges, S. D. (Eds.). (2005). *Other minds: How humans bridge the divide between self and others*. New York: Guilford.

Marsh, E. J. (2007). Retelling is not the same as recalling: Implications for memory. *Current Directions in Psychological Science, 16*, 16–20.

McCann, C. D. & Higgins, E. T. (1992). Personal and contextual factors in communication: A review of the "communication game." In G. R. Semin & K. Fiedler (Eds.), *Language, interaction and social cognition* (pp. 144–171). London: Sage.

McIntyre, A., Lyons, A., Clark, A., & Kashima, Y. (2004). The microgenesis of culture: Serial reproduction as an experimental simulation of cultural dynamics. In M. Schaller & C. Crandall (Eds.), *The psychological foundations of culture* (pp. 227–259). Hillsdale, NJ: Erlbaum.

Mead, G. H. (1934). *Mind, self, and society*. Chicago: University of Chicago Press.

Meltzoff, A. N. & Decety, J. (2003). What imitation tells us about social cognition: A rapprochement between developmental psychology and cognitive neuroscience. *Philosophical Transactions of the Royal Society London, Series B, 358*, 491–500.

Moscovici, S. (1981). On social representations. In J. P. Forgas (Ed.), *Social cognition: Perspectives on everyday understanding* (pp. 181–209). London: Academic Press.

Murray, H. A. (1943). *Thematic Apperception Test*. Cambridge, MA: Harvard University Press.

Nelson, K. (2005). Emerging levels of consciousness in early human development. In H. S. Terrace & J. Metcalfe (Eds.), *The missing link in cognition: Origins of self-reflective consciousness* (pp. 116–141). Oxford, UK: Oxford University Press.

Neumann, R. & Strack, F. (2000). "Mood contagion": The automatic transfer of mood between persons. *Journal of Personality and Social Psychology, 79*, 211–223.

Nickerson, R. S. (2001). The projective way of knowing: A useful heuristic that sometimes misleads. *Current Directions in Psychological Science, 10*, 168–172.

Norenzayan, A. & Atran, S. (2004). Cognitive and emotional process in the cultural transmission of natural and nonnatural beliefs. In M. Schaller & C. Crandall (Eds.), *The psychological foundations of culture* (pp. 149–170). Hillsdale, NJ: Erlbaum.

Ostrom, T. M. (1984). The sovereignty of social cognition. In R. S. Wyer, Jr. & T. K. Srull (Eds.), *Handbook of social cognition* (Vol. 1, pp. 1–38). Hillsdale, NJ: Erlbaum.

Piaget, J. & Inhelder, B. (1956). *The child's conception of space*. New York: Norton.

Pickering, M. J. & Garrod, S. (2004). Toward a mechanistic psychology of dialogue. *Behavioral and Brain Sciences, 27*, 169–225.

Pinel, E. C., Long, A. E., Landau, M. J., Alexander, K., & Pyszczynski, T. (2006). Seeing I to I: A pathway to interpersonal connectedness. *Journal of Personality and Social Psychology, 90*, 243–257.

Postmes, T., Haslam, S. A., & Swaab, R. I. (2005). Social influence in small groups: An interactive model of social identity formation. *European Review of Social Psychology, 16*, 1–42.

Premack, D. & Woodruff, G. (1978). Does the chimpanzee have a theory of mind? *Behavioral and Brain Sciences, 4*, 515–526.

Quine, W. V. (1961). *From a logical point of view*. Cambridge, MA: Harvard University Press.

Richeson, J. A. & Trawalter, S. (2005). Why do interracial interactions impair executive function? A resource depletion account. *Journal of Personality and Social Psychology, 88*, 934–947.

Ross, L., Greene, D., & House, P. (1977). The false consensus effect: An egocentric bias in social perception and attribution processes. *Journal of Experimental Social Psychology, 13*, 279–301.

Ruscher, J. B. (1998). Prejudice and stereotyping in everyday communication. In M. P. Zanna (Ed.), *Advances in experimental social psychology* (Vol. 30, pp. 241–307). San Diego, CA: Academic Press.

Salas, E. & Fiore, S. M. (Eds.). (2004). *Team cognition: Understanding the factors that drive process and performance*. Washington, DC: American Psychological Association.

Schachter, S. (1959). *The psychology of affiliation: Experimental studies of the sources of gregariousness*. Stanford, CA: Stanford University Press.

Schaller, M., Conway, L. G., III, & Tanchuk, T. L. (2002). Selective pressures on the once and future contents of ethnic stereotypes: Effects of the communicability of traits. *Journal of Personality and Social Psychology, 82*, 861–877.

Schooler, J. W. & Engstler-Schooler, T. Y. (1990). Verbal overshadowing of visual memories: Some things are better left unsaid. *Cognitive Psychology, 22*, 36–71.

Schulte-Rüther, M., Markowitsch, H. J., Fink, G. R., & Piefke, M. (2007). Mirror neuron and theory of mind mechanisms involved in face-to-face interactions: A functional magnetic resonance imaging approach to empathy. *Journal of Cognitive Neuroscience, 19*, 1354–1372.

Schütz, A. (1967). *The phenomenology of the social world*. Evanston, IL: Northwestern University Press. (Original work published 1932)

Sedikides, C. (1990). Efforts of fortuitously activated constructs versus activated communication goals on person impressions. *Journal of Personality and Social Psychology, 58*, 397–408.

Semin, G. R. (2007). Grounding communication: Synchrony. In A. W. Kruglanski & E. T. Higgins (Eds.), *Social psychology: Handbook of basic principles* (2nd ed., pp. 630–649). New York: Guilford.

Semin, G. R. & Cacioppo, J. T. (2008). Grounding social cognition: Synchronization, coordination, and co-regulation. In G. R. Semin & E. R. Smith (Eds.), *Embodied grounding: Social, cognitive, affective, and neuroscientific approaches* (pp. 119–147). New York: Cambridge University Press.

Sherif, M. (1935). A study of some social factors in perception. *Archives of Psychology, 27*(Whole No. 187).

Sherif, M. (1936). *The psychology of social norms*. New York: Harper & Brothers.

Shore, B. (1996). *Culture in mind: Cognition, culture, and the problem of meaning*. New York: Oxford University Press.

Silver, R. L. & Wortman, C. B. (1980). Coping with undesirable life events. In J. Garber & M. E. P. Seligman (Eds.), *Human helplessness* (pp. 279–340). New York: Academic Press.

Sinclair, S., Huntsinger, J., Skorinko, J., & Hardin, C. D. (2005). Social tuning of the self: Consequences for the self-evaluations of stereotype targets. *Journal of Personality and Social Psychology, 89*, 160–175.

Sinclair, S., Lowery, B. S., Hardin, C. D., & Colangelo, A. (2005). Social tuning of automatic racial attitudes: The role of affiliative motivation. *Journal of Personality and Social Psychology, 89*, 583–592.

Smith, E. R. & Semin, G. R. (2004). Socially situated cognition: Cognition in its social context. In M. P. Zanna (Ed.), *Advances in experimental social psychology* (Vol. 36, pp. 53–115). San Diego, CA: Academic Press.

Sperber, D. (1996). *Explaining culture*. Oxford, UK: Blackwell.

Stukas, A., Bratanova, B., Kashima, Y., Peters, K., & Beatson, R. (2010). The effect of social tuning and shared reality on recipients' beliefs and impressions. *Social Influence, 5*, 101–117.

Suls, J., Martin, R., & Wheeler, L. (2002). Social comparison: Why, with whom, and with what effect. *Current Directions in Psychological Science, 11*, 159–163.

Thagard, P. (1997). Collaborative knowledge. *Nous, 31*, 242–261.

Thompson, L. & Fine, G. A. (1999). Socially shared cognition, affect, and behavior: A review and integration. *Personality and Social Psychology Review, 3*, 278–302.

Tindale, R. S. & Kameda, T. (2000). "Social sharedness" as a unifying theme for information processing in groups. *Group Processes & Intergroup Relations, 3*, 123–140.

Tomasello, M. (2008). *Origins of human communication*. Cambridge, MA: MIT Press.

Tomasello, M., Carpenter, M., Call, J., Behne, T., & Moll, H. (2005). Understanding and sharing intentions: The origins of cultural cognition. *Behavioral and Brain Sciences, 28*, 675–691.

Turner, J. C. & Oakes P. J. (1997). The socially structured mind. In C. McGarty & S. A. Haslam (Eds.), *The message of social psychology: Perspectives on mind in society* (pp. 355–373). Cambridge, MA: Blackwell.

Turner, J. H. (1987). Toward a sociological theory of motivation. *Annual Sociological Review*, 52, 15–27.

Tversky, B. & Marsh, E. J. (2000). Biased retellings of events yield biased memories. *Cognitive Psychology, 40*, 1–38.

Weldon, M. S. (2001). Remembering as a social process. In D. L. Medin (Ed.), *The psychology of learning and motivation: Advances in research and theory* (Vol. 40, pp. 67–120). San Diego, CA: Academic Press.

Wicker, B., Keysers, C., Plailly, J., Royet, J. P., Gallese, V., & Rizzolatti, G. (2003). Both of us disgusted in my insula: The common neural basis of seeing and feeling disgust. *Neuron, 40*, 655–664.

Yzerbyt, V. Y., Castano, E., Leyens, J.-P., & Paladino, P. (2000). The primacy of the ingroup: The interplay of entitativity and identification. In W. Stroebe & M. Hewstone (Eds.), *European review of social psychology* (Vol. 11, pp. 257–295). Chichester, UK: Wiley.

Section III

Sociality: Underlying Motives, Dialogical Practice, and Culture

8

Sharing Inner States
A Defining Feature of Human *Motivation*

E. TORY HIGGINS

What makes human motivation *human*? How do the motives of humans differ from the motives of other animals? I believe that the best single answer to these questions is that *humans are motivated to share their inner states*. This motive is captured in the urgency of a 1-year-old girl who is trying to grab her father's attention to share with him her feelings about, her thoughts about, the object she is excitedly pointing to. This motive for *joint evaluation*, for *joint understanding*—for *sharing* an *inner* state—is what makes us so different motivationally from other animals.

This chapter is about the uniquely human motive of wanting to share inner states. I begin with a general discussion of how the uniqueness of human motivation has been insufficiently appreciated by psychologists. I postulate four fundamental developments of the human animal that together produced distinct human motives. I describe the motivational significance of *social consciousness* for children. I then discuss in more detail how shared reality—the motive for sharing inner states—influences the development of social consciousness at different stages of child development. I discuss how this development in turn impacts the development of basic motivational systems of self-regulation in their human form. This includes the development of shared inner standards and goals—regulatory self-guides—concerning the type of person we *ideally* want to *become* in the future or believe we *ought* to *become* in the future. I end by discussing the development of shared inner states more generally, including shared perceptions, shared thoughts, shared feelings and attitudes, shared competencies, and shared reference values (goal and standards).

What is the nature of human motivation? Perhaps more than anyone else, Darwin's seminal work in the second half of the 19th century (e.g., Darwin, 1859) had a revolutionary effect on scientists' approach to answering this question. Scientists reasoned that if humans evolved from other animals—if we were descended from them—then it would make sense to use the characteristics of nonhuman animals as clues for discovering the characteristics of the human animal. This is, indeed, one conclusion that could be inspired by Darwin, but it is not the only possibility. In fact, there are two different general conclusions that could be inspired by Darwinian logic, each associated with a different meaning of *evolve* (see *Webster's Ninth New Collegiate Dictionary*, 1989).

One meaning of *evolve* is to derive, which in turn has the meaning of originate in, formed by, and made up of. Thus, as just described, the first general implication of Darwinian evolution is that if humans evolved—*derived*—from other nonhuman animals, then they must share characteristics in common with these other animals. But another meaning of *evolve* is to develop, which in turn has the meaning of growth, elaboration of possibilities, and improvement. And if humans *developed* from other nonhuman animals in a direction of increasing complexity, then they must have some special or greater capacities that make them different from (better than?) other animals.

These two distinct general conclusions drawn from Darwinian logic suggest very different research agendas. The "derived from" conclusion suggests that psychologists should look for evidence of humans having characteristics much like other animals that cause them to function in similar ways. The "developed from" conclusion suggests that psychologists should look for evidence of humans having new characteristics that allow them to function in different and often more elaborate and sophisticated (i.e., less "primitive") ways. Which conclusion, then, was drawn by psychologists? Which directed psychology's research agenda? In fact, both conclusions were drawn and substantially impacted psychological theory and research. What is interesting, however, is that the impact of these two conclusions was not the same across all psychological areas. Instead, to a large extent, psychology chose the "developed from" implication for the domain of *cognition*, but the "derived from" implication for the domain of *motivation*!

When it came to cognition, psychologists (and other disciplines) were inspired by how humans' creation and use of symbol systems and cultural artifacts were so special and advanced compared to the cognitive expressions of other animals (e.g., language, art, music, math, law, religion). But when it came to motivation, psychologists (and, again, other disciplines) were impressed by how humans' needs, drives, and self-regulatory mechanisms were so much like other animals. In one sense, this differential treatment of cognition and motivation is not surprising. It was already highlighted in classic pre-Darwinian formulations, such as Descartes' *Passions of the Soul* (1647/1985), which argued that animal-like motivational inclinations needed to be controlled by human-like thought and reason.

Of course, not everyone took this perspective. There were traditional learning theorists such as Thorndike (e.g., 1935), Hull (e.g., 1943), and Skinner (e.g., 1953) who applied the "derived from" conclusion not only to motivation but also to cognition. And there were some psychodynamic psychologists who applied the "developed from" conclusion not only to cognition but also to motivation. For example, in response to the traditional learning theories, Maslow (1943) early on explicitly counseled psychologists that "motivation theory should be human-centered rather than animal-centered" (p. 370). But, generally speaking, these were the exceptions to what became the general approach in psychology (and other disciplines) for the last half century—treat cognition as "developed from" and treat motivation as "derived from." This general approach has produced, and continues to produce, an image of humans as having *the mind of a god and the motives of a brute*. It is an image that is both wrong and damaging.

In sum, the "derived from" conclusion that was drawn for motivation suggested that a good way to learn what human motivation is really like is to study what motivates other animals. If sex and aggression, hunger and thirst, and other instincts or drives are basic to animal motivation, then they are likely to be basic to human motivation as well. If the pleasure principle of approaching pleasure and avoiding pain is the central motivational principle for explaining animal behavior, then it should also be the central motivational principle for explaining human behavior. The Darwinian lesson was that by understanding the basic motives of our animal ancestors, psychologists would learn what was basic to human motivation. The approach to studying human motivation was as follows: *discover the motivational consequences of humans being animals*.

In a recent *Annual Review* chapter, Thane Pittman and I (Higgins & Pittman, 2008) have argued that for both cognition and motivation there are useful lessons from both general conclusions of the Darwinian logic, but what currently is most in need of correction is the failure to appreciate sufficiently the "developed from" conclusion for the area of motivation. Recognizing that any development has both costs and benefits and human motivation is no exception, we emphasize that there was a motivational development—a fundamental growth that resulted in human motives that are distinct from, and advanced in comparison to, other animals—and we argue that this development needs to be highlighted and emphasized more. In that chapter, we attempt to correct the balance of attention from the motives of the animal that happens to be human to the motives of the *human* animal. This chapter is a continuation of that attempt, with special attention being paid to the motivational significance of the unique human development of the desire to share inner states.

Which aspects of human development are critical for understanding the distinct nature of human motivation? We proposed (Higgins & Pittman, 2008) that there are four fundamental developments of the human animal that together produce distinct human motives: (1) social consciousness or awareness that the significance of a person's action depends on how another person reacts to it; (2) recognizing that people's inner states can mediate their outward behaviors; (3) relating the present to both the past and the future (mental time travel); and (4) sharing reality with other people.

Historically, the type of consciousness that has received special attention in psychology and other disciplines is the differentiation of self from others that is involved in reflective self-consciousness (e.g., Leary, 2004, 2007; Leary & Buttermore, 2003). But years ago Cooley (1962/1909) argued against the traditional view (e.g., Descartes) that gave primacy and antecedence to self-consciousness as opposed to social consciousness or awareness of society: "In general, then, most of our reflective consciousness, of our wide-awake state of mind, is social consciousness, because a sense of our relation to other persons, or of other persons to one another, can hardly fail to be part of it. Self and society are twin-born, we know one as immediately as we know the other, and the notion of a separate and independent ego is an illusion" (p. 5). In an earlier chapter, I have proposed that social consciousness is, indeed, critical to understanding what is distinctive about human motives (see, for example, Higgins, 2005). Such social consciousness involves an awareness that the outcomes of a person (self or other) are determined by the reactions of others to what that person does. As I will discuss later, I also believe that such social consciousness is itself dependent on the human motive to share reality with significant others.

Social consciousness could remain at the behavioral or action level—an awareness that the significance of an action performed by one person (self or other) depends on another person's reaction to it (Mead, 1934). However, there is another fundamental human development that radically changes the nature of social consciousness—the recognition that *inner states*, such as beliefs, feelings, expectancies, and desires, mediate human reactions to one another. This startling discovery, which human children make between 3 and 6 years of age (for recent reviews, see Higgins, 2005; Nelson, 2005), is described in more detail later. It involves children understanding that the social regulation of them by powerful others, such as their parents, is determined by what these others' want of them and believe about them. To control their reactions effectively and efficiently, you need to know about their inner states and not just their outward behaviors.

It could be that once children know what a significant other desires, prefers, or expects them to be, then they are all set going forward—what is true now about what is needed to satisfy the significant other will always be true. But once again there is another fundamental human development that complicates matters considerably—it is not only what you are now that matters but also what you are becoming (see Allport, 1955; Higgins, 2005). Parents, for example, respond to how their child is growing and developing. Positive responses from parents depend on a child improving and learning over time. Such responses by parents to what a child is becoming and the child's appreciation for the nature of such contingencies depend on another remarkable development—the ability to relate the present self to both the past self and the future self or "mental time travel" (Tulving, 1983). And it is not only the parent–child relationship that involves a concern with "what is becoming" rather than just "what is." It is true of parent–teacher, boss–employee, coach–player, and so on. Groups and nations are also concerned with what they are becoming and not just what they currently are. And, again, this critical human development depends on there being a human motive to share reality with significant others.

The fact that humans are aware that they and others have expectancies and desires, including others' having expectancies and desires for what they will become, has major implications for the nature of human motivation. But just as remarkable about humans is their strong desire to share these expectancies and desires and other kinds of knowledge and feelings (see Hardin & Higgins, 1996)—*the human desire to share inner states*. Other animals will pay attention to what other animals are looking at (Call, 2005), but only humans, including very young children, share their knowledge with one another, including creating joint attention and deliberate teaching (Nelson, 2005; Terrace, 2005). I believe that this need to share reality about inner states is a defining feature of human motivation. This chapter is concerned with the critical role in human motivation of the motive to share reality with others, and, particularly, to share inner states. It underlies the development of social consciousness, the development of "becoming" as a distinct human concern, and the development of shared realities more generally, including the use of imagined future-self states as goals and standards in self-regulation. I will discuss each of these developments in turn.

SHARED REALITY AND THE DEVELOPMENT OF SOCIAL CONSCIOUSNESS

As discussed earlier, social consciousness involves an awareness that the significance of a person's action (self or other) is determined by the reactions of others to that action. When the person is the self, social consciousness goes hand in hand with reflective self-consciousness. I believe that a major factor in humans' developing social (and self) consciousness is the fact that they are highly dependent on conspecifics for survival (see Higgins, 2005). More than any other animal, human children need adults to provide them with nurturance and security for many years to survive. Even as adults, humans as individuals are relatively helpless and survive by working together with other humans. This dependency means that humans must get along with others. To a large extent, personal agency is social agency. To survive, people need to predict and influence what others do. This can be done more effectively by understanding how one fits into one's social world (see also Brewer, 2004; Caporael, 2007). Social consciousness is a necessary ingredient for such understanding. Self-regulation in a social context involves understanding what significant others hope for and expect of you—social consciousness.

The Self Digest

The *self digest* model of self-regulation (see Higgins, 1996a; Higgins & May, 2001) forms the underpinnings of my motivational perspective on social consciousness. Thus, I will begin by briefly reviewing this model. The self digest model assumes that human survival requires adaptation to the surrounding social environment. For children to obtain the nurturance and security they need to survive, they must establish and maintain relationships with caretakers who fulfill these needs (see Bowlby, 1969, 1973), which in turn means that they must learn to regulate their appearance and behaviors to suit the interpersonal contingencies set by their caretakers (cf. Bowlby, 1969, 1973; Cooley, 1902/1964; Mead, 1934; Sullivan, 1953). In brief, children need to acquire a self digest. A digest summarizes a body of information, especially contingency rules and conclusions. A digest serves regulatory functions. The notion of a self digest is meant to capture the idea that self-knowledge summarizes information about oneself as an object in the world, knowledge which serves self-regulatory functions—*a summary of what the world is like in relation to oneself.*

The self digest is a tool for survival. It summarizes a person's relations to the world and the personal consequences of these relations. It is a handy sourcebook for people about their person–environment fit that helps them to fulfill their needs when interacting with their world. The self digest model does not claim that only self-knowledge contains functional information about the world. However, self-knowledge concerns the only object in the world that a person must continually regulate to survive. Thus, self-knowledge has a unique functional status among our stored knowledge of objects in the world. The notion of a self digest is intended to emphasize the self-regulatory nature of self-knowledge rather than the self-descriptive nature of self-knowledge that has been emphasized in the previous literature (e.g., Epstein, 1973; Lecky, 1945; Markus, 1980; McGuire & Padawer-Singer, 1976; Rogers, 1951; Sarbin, 1952; Snygg & Combs, 1949). Self-knowledge as self digest contains quite different kinds of information than self-knowledge as self-description. Self-knowledge as self-description involves representations of decontextualized "facts" about oneself in isolation, whereas self-knowledge as self digest involves representations of oneself in relation to other persons and activities in the world and the consequences of these relations.

The novel proposal of the self digest is that there is not a single actual self involving a descriptive representation of personal attributes but, rather, there are three different actual self-representations serving three distinct self-regulatory functions—an *instrumental self*, a *monitored self*, and an *expectant self*. Each of these self-regulatory functions occurs in a social context and requires taking into account other people's judgments, hopes, and wishes for oneself. It requires developing a shared reality with others, which in turn requires the development of different levels of social consciousness. Let us now consider the nature of this development.

Developmental Stages of Shared Reality and Social Consciousness

A fundamental characteristic of people is that they derive meanings from the events in their lives and then respond to those meanings. This insight into the nature of people was clearly developed at the turn of the 20th century in the work of Weber, Durkheim, Freud, James, Cooley, and others. It is nicely captured in Thomas and Thomas's (1928) statement, "If men define situations as real, they are real in their consequences." In social psychology as well, Asch (1952), Lewin (1935), and Mead (1934) early on emphasized the importance of the psychological situation in determining people's motivations and actions. But where do the meanings assigned to life events come from? Our social interactions are a major source. The ways that others respond to us communicate about the world around us and our place in it—messages about our person–environment fit (Mead, 1934). *By accepting these messages about who we are in the world, we create a shared reality with the people in our lives* (see Hardin & Higgins, 1996; Higgins, 1996b).

Almost a century ago, the eminent social scientist Max Weber (1967, pp. 156–157) stated, "In 'action' is included all human behavior when and in so far as the acting individual attaches a subjective meaning to it. … Action is social in so far as, by virtue of the subjective meaning attached to by the acting individual (or individuals), it takes account of the behavior of others and is thereby oriented in its course."

Thus, action is social when its meaning and orientation take account of other people. Self-regulation develops from social regulation, from children learning to take other people into account. From this perspective, self-regulatory responses are social actions.

Socialization involves individuals adopting the values and beliefs of their group, and when it is effective, people end up wanting to behave as others want and expect them to behave. As Jones and Gerard (1967, p. 77) point out, the "fascination stems from the fact that most of society's codes and values become part of the very fabric of an individual's personality during the process of socialization." This is, indeed, a fascinating issue, and it has been central to the work of Freud, Lewin, Murray, Vygotsky, Mead, and other founders of social-motivational science in psychology.

How does it all begin? To discuss the changes in self-regulation that develop a shared reality with others and increasing self-consciousness, I rely on the classic developmental literature that has described general shifts in children's ability to get along in the social world (e.g., Case, 1985; Damon & Hart, 1986; Fischer, 1980; Selman, 1980; see also Higgins, 1989, 1991).

Six to 12 Months By the end of the first year of life, children can represent the relation between two events, such as the relation between a response that they produce and their mother's response to them (see Case, 1985). Children can produce and interpret communicative signals and anticipate the occurrence of some event, and thus they are capable of the preliminary form of role taking that Mead (1934) described—the ability to anticipate the responses of a significant other with whom one is interacting. During this initial period, children begin to acquire the *instrumental self*. Actual self-knowledge serving an instrumental function represents one's self-attributes in relation to the responses they elicit from other people:

Something about me → How others respond to me

This is the first step in acquiring interpersonal contingencies that will become increasingly complex. This preliminary instrumental function is not unique to humans. Certainly chimpanzees, for example, learn observable behavioral contingencies concerning their behavior and the responses of others to them (see Povinelli, 2000). What is unique to human children during this period is social referencing or "shared attention," in which a child and an interaction partner will point out to each other some interesting object or event in the immediate environment and together pay attention to it (see Tomasello, 1999; Tomasello, Carpenter, Call, Behne, & Moll, 2005).

This joint attentional interaction provides an early example of the distinctive human motive for shared reality. Other animals will behave in ways that get others to do something they want, which includes getting their attention. Such behaviors are in the service of agency. But the joint attentional interaction of human children and their partners is in the service of understanding. It is this *sharing of an understanding* that is unique to humans. It is reflected in the unique way in which human adults actively instruct children about how the world works, which is the basis for cultural evolution (see Tomasello, 1999; Tomasello et al., 2005). It permits a kind of imitative learning that is unique to humans in that the child and adult are both motivated to have a common understanding of how to do something. Rather than just copying or mimicking an observed behavior, it involves collaborating to share an understanding of how the world works and how to get along in it.

Sixteen Months to 2 Years During the second half of children's second year, there is a major shift in children's ability to represent events, which has been traditionally associated with the emergence of symbolic representation (e.g., Bruner, 1964; Case, 1985; Fischer, 1980; Piaget, 1951; Werner & Kaplan, 1963). Children can now represent the bidirectional relationship between themselves and another person as an interrelation between two distinct mental objects, self-as-object and other-as-object (see Bertenthal & Fischer, 1978; Harter, 1983; Lewis & Brooks-Gunn, 1979). Their ability to represent themselves and other persons as distinct objects in the world is reflected in their use of the pronouns "I" and "you." Children can now represent the relation between two relations: (a) the relation between a feature of themselves (e.g., their action, response, physical appearance) and a particular response by another person, and (b) the relation between a particular response by another person and a particular state that they will experience. Children, for example, can represent the relation between their making a mess at mealtime and their mother's frowning, yelling, or leaving, and the relation between their mother's frowning, yelling, or leaving and their experiencing a negative state.

This higher level of perspective taking that appears by 2 years of age is critical for what sociologists call *symbolic interaction*—the ability to anticipate the responses of others to their actions and the personal consequences of these social responses (see Stryker & Statham, 1985). Children's significant others link them to the larger society by providing the shared reality or social meaning of the child's features (i.e., societal responses to the child's features), as well as the importance of the child's features (i.e., the state produced in the child by these societal responses). In this way, children learn the interpersonal significance of their self-features. By representing the *interpersonal significance* of their self-features and using this information to plan their actions, children are better able to delay gratification, to control their momentary impulses, and to free themselves from the demands and forces of the immediate situation (see Miller & Green, 1985; Mischel & Moore, 1980; Mischel & Patterson, 1978).

Three to 6 Years From a cognitive perspective on human development, the development described earlier—symbolic capacity—has special significance, and for many scholars it defines what it means to be human. The 3- to 6-year-old period does involve the classic cognitive shift from egocentric to nonegocentric thought described in Piagetian theory (see Feffer, 1970; Flavell, Botkin, Fry, Wright, & Jarvis, 1968; Piaget, 1965; Selman & Byrne, 1974), but this would not be considered as fundamental as the development of symbolic capacity. From a motivational perspective, however, I believe that the most dramatic shift in human development occurs between 3 to 6 years of age. Notably, this is the same developmental phase described in Freudian theory as the phallic or oedipal period in which people develop a superego or *conscience* or the phase described in Eriksonian theory in which initiative or guilt is emphasized (see Erikson, 1950/1963; Freud, 1905/1953, 1920/1952).

According to Erikson, this 3- to 6-year-old period is especially significant in a couple of respects. The first has to do with locomotion. During this period children are able to move independently and vigorously; they can forget they are *doing* the walking and instead discover what they can *do with* the walking. The implication that Erikson draws from this development is that a new *intrusive mode* dominates much of the behavior of children during this period—a movement away from themselves into ever new facts and activities, reflecting a new curiosity that compels intrusion into the unknown. This intrusive mode is reflected in what Erikson calls initiative—being on the make, attacking a task for the sake of being active and on the move. The second significant aspect of this period is the danger that there will be a sense of guilt over what is being initiated, over the pleasure in attack and conquest. Harking to Freud's (1923/1961) ideas that this period is when the superego and the conscience develops, Erikson states that children gradually develop a sense of moral responsibility during this period, gaining insight into the institutions and roles that permit responsible participation. He points out that a child's superego can be uncompromising and produce overcontrol.

I agree with the emphasis that psychodynamic theory places on the 3- to 6-year-old period regarding its critical role in the development of social consciousness. I believe that the development during this period defines *what it means to be human motivationally*. This is because, as I discuss more fully next, this period involves the development of shared motivational concerns, the development of children wanting to become what significant others want them to become. Both the regulatory focus difference between promotion and prevention concerns and the regulatory mode difference between locomotion and assessment concerns take on their uniquely human character during this period. In the next two sections I will elaborate on these critical developments in more detail.

Developing Shared Motivational Concerns

During the 3- to 6-year-old period, children become capable of coordinating two separate systems of interrelations, such as coordinating observable responses with unobservable responses (see Case, 1985), which underlies the ability to make inferences about the thoughts, expectations, motives, and intentions of others (see Shantz, 1983). Children now understand that other people have different attitudes about different types of responses, that they prefer some types of responses over others. They understand that performing the types of responses preferred by others is related to others' positive responses to them. Thus, they are motivated to learn the types of responses that are preferred by their significant others. In addition to learning about a significant other's preferences from his or her personal reactions to them, children also learn by observing the significant other react to others (i.e., observational learning; see Bandura, 1977, 1986). For example, children can observe how their mother reacts to their sibling's responses and thereby infer which types of responses their mother prefers (see Bandura, 1986; Bandura & Walters, 1963).

The critical development during this period is that children learn that the relation between one of their self-features and another person's response to it depends on the other person's viewpoint or standpoint on this feature. A standpoint on the self is defined as a point of view from which a person can be judged that reflects a set of attitudes, opinions, or values (see Turner, 1956). For example, they can now represent the fact that it is the discrepancy between their behavior and the behavior that their mother prefers that underlies the association between their behavior and their mother's response to it (see Higgins, 1989). That is, children now understand that social regulation of them is mediated by others' standpoints on them.

This is a discovery of shattering importance. Children at this age are still totally dependent on older conspecifics for survival. It is clear to them that these older people are different from them, especially in their possession of essential resources that the children want to be used for them and not against them. Their highest priority is to figure out what determines how these resource-rich persons allocate their resources. Children want to tame these powerful animals called Mommy and Daddy by learning what motivates them.

The social-cognitive literature (in both developmental and social psychology) for decades has emphasized people's motivation to explain the behaviors of others (why questions), such as dispositional versus situational explanations. Although explaining others' actions is important, I believe that the major concern of both children and adults is to figure out what resources a target person has and whether they are likely to be used for or against them. These resources extend well beyond the typical traits that have been studied in the classic literature. They include the observable status and power of a person that is reflected in how family members and visitors treat that person. Rather than causal explanations for others' behaviors, children are trying to understand the who, what, and where of resource allocation. Who makes the final decisions? Whose word is law? Does this vary by activity? For those things I want to happen, such as getting a new toy, who is in charge of what? For things I don't want to happen, such as getting punished, who is in charge of what? For things I enjoy doing, such as playing, who is a good playmate for which activity? For those things I don't enjoy doing, such as going to bed early, who allows me not to do which activity? I need to figure out who has which resources and then figure out what motivates them to use these resources for me rather than against me.

By the age of 6, children are much more masters of their universe than before. They have figured out that other people have wishes, hopes, expectancies, and demands of them. Other people like and dislike different things than they do. By taking others' motivational orientations into account—a new and critical kind of shared reality—children can plan their actions to increase the likelihood that others will use their resources for them and not against them. This increasing ability to take others' motivational orientations into account is also demonstrated in children's increasing ability to cooperate and collaborate with one another in a way that is not found in other animals, including primates (see Povinelli, 2000; Tomasello, 1999).

Developing Shared Promotion Ideals and Prevention Oughts

Promotion-focus concerns with nurturance and growth and prevention-focus concerns with safety and security are both basic to survival (for a discussion of regulatory focus theory, see Higgins, 1996b). Thus, human children before 3 years of age, and other animals as well, can have a promotion or prevention focus in their self-regulation. However, the development that occurs in human children from 3 to 6 years of age creates a shared reality between children and their significant others regarding what is expected and desired for them to be and to become—a shared reality about inner states—that uniquely arises in human children during this period. It transforms the regulatory focus systems of promotion and prevention such that self-regulation is never the same again for children and differs from any other animal. This transformation of the regulatory focus systems plays an important part in the development of human motivation.

By taking into account others' standpoints on them, children develop a new kind of social consciousness and a new kind of actual self-function. These standpoints become standards of self-evaluation—self-guides (see Higgins, 1989, 1991). Children now use self-guides as a basis for self-evaluation by assessing the amount of congruency or discrepancy between their current self-state and the end state that a significant other desires or demands of them (e.g., How am I doing in relation to what Father wants or demands of me?). They can then respond to any perceived discrepancy by taking action to reduce it. They can also plan action by taking potential discrepancies into account, thereby using prospective self-evaluation in the service of self-regulation (see also Bandura, 1986; Carver & Scheier, 1990). Thus, self-guides function both as standards of self-evaluation and as desired end-states to be attained or maintained.

Self-evaluation in relation to self-guides creates a new actual self-function—the monitored self. The monitored self is an actual self-representation that provides self-regulatory information regarding one's current state in relation to some desired end-state, which together provide feedback about how well one is doing in meeting standards and pursuing desired goals:

Something about me → How well am I doing?

For young children, the desired end-state is a shared reality with a significant other about what the child will hopefully accomplish in the future (ideals) or what are the child's duties and responsibilities (oughts). Whether the shared reality between child and significant other involves an emphasis on fulfilling promotion-focus ideals or an emphasis on fulfilling prevention-focus oughts emerges through different kinds of parent–child interactions—socialization episodes in which children learn about what a significant other wants and expects of them (see Higgins, 1991, 1996b). Children develop strong ideal self-guides when their caretakers combine bolstering (when managing success) and love withdrawal (when disciplining failure). (For conveniences, I will from this point refer to caretakers as parents. Parenting can be done by members of the family other than the parents, as well by nonfamily members, and I will refer to all caretakers as parents.) Bolstering occurs, for instance, when parents encourage the child to overcome difficulties, hug and kiss them when they succeed, or set up opportunities for the child to engage in success activities—it creates an experience of the presence of positive outcomes in the child. Love withdrawal occurs, for instance, when parents end a meal when the child throws some food, take away a toy when the child refuses to share it, stop a story when the child is not paying attention—it creates an experience of the absence of positive outcomes in the child. Together, the combination of bolstering and love-withdrawal interactions creates shared promotion-focus concerns with accomplishment and advancement, with ensuring the presence of positive outcomes and ensuring against the absence of positive outcomes.

Children develop strong ought self-guides when their parents combine prudence (when managing success) and punitive/critical interactions (when disciplining failure). Prudence occurs, for instance, when parents childproof the house, train the child to be alert to potential dangers, or teach the child to mind your manners—it creates an experience of the absence of negative outcomes in the child. Punitive/critical interactions occur, for instance, when parents play roughly with the child to get his or her attention, yell at the child when he or she doesn't listen, criticize the child when he or she makes a mistake—it creates an experience of the presence of negative outcomes. Together, the combination of prudent and critical/punitive interactions creates shared prevention-focus concerns with safety and security, with ensuring the absence of negative outcomes and ensuring against the presence of negative outcomes.

Developing Shared Locomotion and Assessment Concerns Self-regulation involves individuals deciding what they want that they don't currently have, figuring out what they need to do to get what they want, and then doing it. This conception captures two key functions in self-regulation. The first is individuals assessing both the different goals to pursue and the different means to pursue them, and the second is individuals locomoting or "moving" from their current state in pursuit of some alternative goal-pursuit state. More generally stated, locomotion constitutes the aspect of self-regulation that is concerned with movement from state to state, and assessment constitutes the aspect of self-regulation that is concerned with making comparisons. Some version of these assessment and locomotion functions is contained in all major models of self-regulation. In classic control theory terms, for example, the purpose of regulation is to minimize the discrepancy between a current state and a desired end-state, and self-regulation involves both moving toward the desired end-state and determining the extent of discrepancy between the current state and the desired end-state. Both locomotion and assessment, therefore, are involved in both promotion self-regulation in relation to ideal end-states and prevention self-regulation in relation to ought end-states.

Like promotion and prevention as two distinct regulatory focus systems, locomotion and assessment as two distinct regulatory mode functions are both basic to survival (for a discussion of regulatory mode theory, see Higgins, Kruglanski, & Pierro, 2003). Indeed, control theory models of self-regulation, as in the everyday conception of self-regulation, assessment, and locomotion, are conceived as working together as parts of the same goal-pursuit orientation. They are integrated tools of goal attainment. As such, they are both critical for effective self-regulation and, therefore, critical to survival. Given this, like promotion and prevention self-regulation, human children before 3 years of age, and other animals as well, can have a locomotion or an assessment mode in their self-regulation. But also like the promotion and prevention foci, I believe that the locomotion and assessment modes are transformed by the unique development that occurs in human children from 3 to 6 years of age, a development that emerges from children's interactions with significant others that creates a shared reality about what is desirable. I believe this development transforms the regulatory mode functions of locomotion and assessment such that self-regulation is never the same again for children and differs from any other animal—a transformation that also plays an important part in the development of human motivation.

To understand what happens during this period, let us reconsider the insights of Erikson (1950/1963) regarding the special significance of the 3- to 6-year period of development. Erikson says that there are two especially significant developments. First, he says that this is a period of initiative—being on the make, attacking a task for the sake of being active and on the move. He himself relates this to locomotion. He uses the example of walking but clearly means something broader when discussing this period's curiosity and intrusion into the unknown. Locomotion for Lewin (1951) as well was not just physical movement but mental movement, which is how regulatory mode theory conceptualizes locomotion (see Higgins et al., 2003). Second, Erikson says that this is a period in which there is the danger that there will be a sense of guilt over what is being initiated, over the pleasure in attack and conquest. This is the period of critical self-evaluation, of conscience and a sense of moral responsibility. Such critical self-evaluation is a defining characteristic of assessment functioning in regulatory mode theory (Higgins et al., 2003; Kruglanski et al., 2000).

It is instructive that Erikson (1950/1963) refers to what is happening during this period as "Initiative *Versus* [emphasis added] Guilt." This highlights the idea that for different individual children there could be more initiative or more guilt; that is, more locomotion or more assessment. How much of a child's self-regulation involves initiative/locomotion and how much it involves guilt/assessment is likely to depend on what is emphasized in the child's interactions with significant others. In contrast to the assumption of control theories, which generally consider the functions of assessment and locomotion to be inseparable parts of the whole of self-regulation and treats them as functionally interdependent, regulatory mode theory proposes that locomotion and assessment can also function as independent orientations that can receive differential emphasis by different people and in different situations (see Higgins et al., 2003). This is consistent with Erikson's "versus" idea—locomotion versus assessment rather than locomotion with assessment. This is not to say that locomotion and assessment cannot work together in a manner suggested by control theory, but only that it is better to treat them as separate functions that can receive differential emphasis. This perspective suggests that children 3 to 6 years of age create a shared reality with their significant others about how much locomotion should be emphasized in self-regulation (with motivational concerns or positions such as "just do it" and "doing anything is better than doing nothing") and how much assessment should be emphasized (with motivational concerns or positions such as "do the right thing" and "it is better to do nothing than to do the wrong thing"). As research on locomotion and assessment orientations has shown (see Higgins et al., 2003; Kruglanski et al., 2000), these different motivational values or concerns have profound effects on human motivation.

I have now discussed one critical development during the 3- to 6-years-of-age period—the development of shared motivational concerns. I have described both the development of shared regulatory focus concerns and shared regulatory mode concerns. In the next section I will discuss the other critical development during this period—the development of children wanting to become the kind of person that their significant others want them to become—a shared reality about "becoming."

Shared Reality About "Becoming"

Imagine the following scenario. A young animal is rewarded for performing a certain behavior. But after a while, the young animal is no longer rewarded for performing that behavior. In classic terms, one would say that the animal now experiences a period of extinction trials for that behavior. When the young animal performs a behavior that takes more effort or greater skill than the earlier behavior, it is that behavior that is now rewarded. But after a while, that new behavior is also no longer rewarded. For most young animals, this would be very confusing. Indeed, it is not clear whether any animal could figure out the reinforcement contingency, with one key exception—human children.

To my knowledge, this kind of improvement or progress reinforcement contingency has not been explicitly investigated with either human children or young animals. Exactly when human children are able to figure out this kind of reinforcement contingency has not been studied. What is clear is that the development of a monitored self described earlier, which occurs between 3 and 6 years of age, typically involves such contingencies. As described earlier, during this period children figure out that parents (and others) have wishes, hopes, expectancies, and demands of them. But often what parents hope and expect of children is that they progressively become something that the parents have in mind for them. The parents want their child to improve, to make progress. The parents respond to children depending on whether they are successful in becoming, over time, what the parents have in mind. Thus, to control parental responses, children need to discover how the becoming contingency works. And, indeed, they do! They demonstrate (show off?) to parents what they can do now that they could not do earlier.

The monitored self provides feedback to children on how well they are doing in meeting the goals and standards (self-guides) for them that they share with their significant others. The discovery of becoming contingencies shared with others creates a new level of social consciousness for the monitored self. Children need to be conscious of where they are now, have been, and plan to be in relation to these inner-state self-guides or desired end-states. They now evaluate themselves in terms of their success or failure in becoming. The positivity of the current self does not depend simply on whether it is congruent or discrepant from a self-guide but also on whether it is an improvement or progress from the past self (see Carver & Scheier, 1990). But if children want in the future to have a current self that is an improvement from their past self, then they have to plan in the present to have a future self that is better than their current self.

Contingencies of becoming, therefore, create motivational demands on children *to interrelate their past, present, and future inner states*. Contrary to what is necessary for most self-regulation, self-regulating improvement or progress requires not simply knowing in the present what your inner states are like now, but also knowing how your inner states were in the past and how you want them to be in the future. To compare the current self with the past self requires having specific memories of what you were like in the past. It is no coincidence, then, that the developmental literature reports that it is during the 3- to 6-years-of-age period described earlier that children develop narrative self-consciousness and episodic memory (see Nelson, 2005; Tulving, 1983, 2005).

Consciousness of becoming is also involved in young children's social modeling. Children at this age are fascinated with other children who are older than them, but not too much older. If children were simply interested in observing advanced skills, they would be as interested or more interested in watching adults than older children. But they are not. Their interest in older children is because they are fascinated with where they are going. They understand that they have improved from the past and watch somewhat older children to predict where they are going in the future.

Like consciousness in general, consciousness of becoming also develops further over time. To appreciate this development, let me briefly describe what happens during the next period of development.

Development From 8 to 10 Years

Between 8 and 10 years of age, children become capable of coordinating values along two distinct dimensions (see Case, 1985; Fischer, 1980; Piaget, 1970). When comparing their performance to that of another child, for example, children can now consider simultaneously the difference in actors' outcomes and the difference in actors' effort, thus making ability inferences possible (see Ruble, 1983). To be good at something now means to be better than others at something that is worthwhile, something that matters, as defined by a represented standard of value that is shared with others. Now the value of a target of comparison, such as performance on some task, depends on its relation to a represented goal or self-guide. Being bad or good at something thus acquires new significance—it relates to a shared reality about character traits and abilities as inner states of people.

The social comparison processes that develop during this period are a new way in which children take into account their own and others' inner states during self-regulation. Through social comparison, children learn what is distinctive about their inner traits, abilities, attitudes, and preferences in relation to the social world around them. They learn what to expect about their own reactions to the world that need not be the same as other people's reactions. When doing certain things, not everyone has the same experience because their abilities or their preferences vary; for instance, some people enjoy vanilla ice cream more than chocolate, whereas the opposite is true for others. By comparing their inner experience of an activity to the inner experience of other children, a child learns how the world relates to their inner states in particular. The *expectant self* represents the relation between inner self-attributes and activity experiences:

Something about me → How I experience the world

Whereas the instrumental actual self answers the question "How does the world respond to me?" the expectant actual self answers the question "How do I respond to the world?" The expectant self includes stable personal preferences as well as personal skills or talents. The expectant self also develops from a shared reality. Significant others, both adults and peers, contribute to the construction of the expectant self by pointing out to children what is special and distinctive about them. Those distinctive self-attributes that are positive, such as talents, are perceived as resources by children's significant others. The significant others support (or pressure) the children to develop their talents further, such as spending hours on some artistic or athletic activity.

The actual self-representations during this period also develop into more global forms of inner states that refer to being a general type of person rather than a particular kind of behavior—being an honest person rather than just behaving honestly, being a dancer rather than just dancing. Children not only can evaluate a particular action they just performed by considering another person's likely response to it; they can also evaluate how the general traits they believe they possess relate to the general traits that significant others desire or expect them to possess. That is, they can now evaluate their success or failure at being the type of person that others desire or expect them to be.

The changes that occur between 8 and 10 years of age also create new ways of becoming. By being capable of coordinating values along two distinct dimensions, children can now compare their becoming with the becoming of another child. "How am I doing?" becomes relative to other peers. "Am I improving on this skill faster or slower than other kids?" This level of consciousness contributes to the expectant self because personal talent (or deficit) is defined less by what you can do than by how quickly you improve relative to others.

In sum, children's use of becoming in their self-regulation provides an additional push to social consciousness. This push involves children becoming conscious of others' wanting them to improve and make progress, a motive about their inner states that they share with these others. This shared reality motivates them not only to interrelate their present inner states with both their past and future inner states but to compare their progress with the progress of others.

THE DEVELOPMENT OF SHARED INNER STATES MORE GENERALLY

Higgins and Pittman (2008) provide a structural framework for considering people's general concerns with comprehending, managing, and sharing the inner states of self and others. Our framework is organized in terms of five broad types of inner states with which people are concerned—perceptions, thoughts, feelings and attitudes, competencies, and reference values (goals and standards). Next, I will briefly consider each of these inner states in turn, with particular emphasis on reference values because of their importance in human self-regulation.

Perceptions

With respect to human motivation, people's concerns with perceptions as an inner state has been mostly studied with respect to others' present perceptions, and, especially, people's inferences and concerns about whether what they see is shared by another person. Bruner (1983) argues that when children learn language in their interactions with caretakers, joint attention is an essential underlying factor. Very young children (6–9 months) try to get their caretaker to attend to what they are looking at by crying, pointing, and so on. It has been stated that such attempts at joint attention, called protodeclarative acts, have been observed only in humans (e.g., Terrace, 2005). More controversial is whether the actions of some nonhuman primates, such as chimpanzees, take into account what is seen by another animal (e.g., Povinelli, 2000). What is clear is that even very young human children do so. Of special significance is how humans, when recognizing that others are not seeing what they see, are motivated to construct a shared perception. The classic example of this phenomenon is Sherif's (1936) study of individuals constructing over time a group norm about what they were seeing when exposed to a stationary light in a dark room (the autokinetic effect). It is also notable that when an individual violates a group norm about what is or is not being seen in a given situation, the deviate individual's perception is stigmatized with labels like delusion or hallucination. This reflects the significance to people of sharing perceptions.

Thoughts

Thoughts refer not only to people's thinking per se but also to the knowledge and beliefs underlying that thinking, as well as to people's reasoning and recollecting. There is a substantial developmental literature on theory of mind, which reports that children by approximately 3 or 4 years of age begin to comprehend that another person's actions can be influenced by his or her thoughts, beliefs, and knowledge (e.g., Wellman, Cross, & Watson, 2001). There is even evidence suggesting that distinct, domain-specific brain regions exist for such comprehension (e.g., Saxe, Carey, & Kanwisher, 2004). A major characteristic of cultural socialization is people managing the development of another person's thoughts (especially a child's thoughts) and trying to ensure that the other person shares their thoughts—the process of *education*. This educational motive of wanting to share with others some knowledge that you possess but they don't (including gossip) is pervasive among humans but absent in other animals. To the extent that individuals (e.g., students) willingly and knowingly expose themselves to such educational input, they are managing in the present what their thoughts will become in the future. More often it is others who have in mind what thoughts an individual will have or should have in the future and try to shape or construct those thoughts. This is done not only by parents and teachers, but also by managers, coaches, religious leaders, reporters, therapists, and so on.

Feelings and Attitudes

Feelings refer not only to affective and emotional experiences, such as experiencing pain or pleasure, but also to motivational experiences such as feeling that it is easy or difficulty to do something and feeling the force of attraction to or repulsion from something. Attitudes and preferences, such as liking or disliking something, evaluating something as good or bad, also involve emotional and motivational experiences. With respect to human motivation, people's concerns with feelings and attitudes as inner states have been studied extensively. Regarding the inner state of attitudes alone, the bulk of psychological research has been concerned with managing the future *attitudes* of others; that is, how people persuade someone to change his or her present attitude to a new (future) attitude that they want that person to share with them (e.g., Crano & Prislin, 2006; Eagly & Chaiken, 1993).

Competencies

Competencies refer not only to people's skills or abilities but also to other underlying personal characteristics that affect their performance and agency in the world, such as their self-confidence, energy, persistence, reliability, responsibility, or independence. Competencies also include social skills, such as knowing how to be helpful, polite, empathic, get along with others, and so on (e.g., social intelligence). How people comprehend the competencies of self and others has received substantial attention in the social psychological literature, beginning with the classic work of Heider (1958). For example, people also use social category membership, such as their own or another person's gender, to infer underlying competencies, an inferential phenomenon extensively studied in the literature on stereotyping (e.g., Schneider, 2004; Stangor, 2000).

People want to share with others the view they have of their own competencies and the view they have of the other's competencies (e.g., Murray, Holmes, & Griffin, 2000; Swann, Bosson, & Pelham, 2002). People also attempt to manage how others perceive their own competencies, as when a person in power (e.g., a parent, teacher, coach, manager, military officer) tries to influence the future performance-related motivation of subordinates (children, pupils, players, workers, soldiers) by shaping their comprehension of their current or future (potential) competencies. This motive of managing others' own comprehension of their competencies is distinctively human. So too is the case of people attempting to manage how others comprehend them, such as a person's use of impression management techniques (Schlenker & Weigold, 1992) to manage others' inferences about his or her competencies.

People work toward a shared reality between themselves and their significant others regarding how their competencies are comprehended, both by managing others' comprehension of them and by managing their own comprehensions of themselves so that it becomes shared (McNulty & Swann, 1994; Murray, Holmes, & Collins, 2006; Murray, Holmes, & Griffin, 2000). There is evidence that to have a satisfying close relationship people need to perceive that their partner, and even the family of their partner (MacDonald & Jessica,

2006), shares their own comprehension of their competencies (Murray et al., 2000, 2006), sometimes even including their comprehension that they possess negative competencies (Swann, Hixon, & De La Ronde, 1992).

Reference Values: Goals and Standards

Goals and standards are reference values that function as desired end-states that both guide action and provide a comparison point for evaluating current states (Boldero & Francis, 2002; Higgins, 1991). These reference values include needs, purposes, objectives, aspirations, ideals, norms, demands, prescriptions, proscriptions, and oughts. With respect to human motivation, people's concerns with reference values as inner states have been studied mostly with respect to self and others' present reference values.

For reference values as inner states, an especially significant concern of people is comprehending and managing whether self or other is currently congruent with the reference value, and whether self or other is in the process of becoming congruent with the reference value (e.g., Carver & Scheier, 1990; Higgins, 1987, 1991). As described earlier with respect to the development of self-regulation in children, this involves both self-regulation and social regulation. Regarding social regulation, a fundamental aspect of human socialization—in the family, at school, at work—involves people (e.g., parents, teachers, managers, relationship partners) trying to manage another person such that he or she learns to share, that is, accept, the goals and standards that they hold for him or her and becomes motivated to attain and meet those reference values (i.e., learns to identify with these goals and standards).

In close relationships (dating, marital), people want their partner to see them as becoming, if not having become already, the kind of person that they would ideally like to be (Murray et al. 2000, 2006; Swann, Bosson, & Pelham, 2002). This requires them managing their partner's comprehension of them, as well as their partner managing their own comprehension of them, to achieve a shared reality about their attaining their ideals. To accomplish this effectively, their partner needs to comprehend what it is they hope or wish to be or become. Although the literature has tended to focus on ideals, it would also be important for their partner to comprehend their oughts and believe that they are meeting them as well.

A distinctive characteristic of humans is that they also share with significant others imagined future-self competencies—shared realities about who they might become, hope to become, dream of becoming, fear of becoming—and then use these future-self competencies as reference values for self-regulation in the present (e.g., Carver, Reynolds, & Scheier, 1994; Higgins, 1987; Markus & Nurius, 1986; Oettingen, 1996; Oyserman & Markus, 1990). Scholars have recognized for a long time that people imagine their future selves—their "potential" self (James, 1890/1948), their "ideal" self (Cooley, 1902/1964; Rogers, 1951), their "ego ideal" (Freud, 1923/1961), and so on. It was not until the late 1980s, however, that the motivational and emotional significance of people's imagined future selves began to receive extensive empirical study. Psychologists began to investigate two important functions of imagined future selves: (1) as goals or incentives (to be approached or avoided) that influence current planning and decisions (Oettingen & Mayer, 2002; Oyserman and Markus, 1990), and (2) as standards or reference points for evaluating and interpreting the current self (Higgins, 1987; Markus & Nurius, 1986).

As mentioned earlier, people's imagined-future-desired selves tend to be shared with significant others—with parents, friends, romantic partners, teachers, bosses, coaches, and so on. Because of this, simply activating a significant other can activate the shared becomings (Higgins, 1987, 1996; Moretti & Higgins, 1999). For example, in a study on transference by Andersen and Chen (2002), one of the participants' parents was activated by learning about a new person who happened to resemble that parent. The participants' actual self was discrepant from either that parents' ideals for them or that parents' oughts for them. When the new person resembled a parent with ideal selves for them, the participants uniquely experienced more dejection-related feelings, whereas when the new person resembled a parent with ought selves for them, they uniquely experienced more agitation-related feelings. In a different study by Shah (2003), half of the participants had father-related words primed while they were working on an anagram task. After they had completed the task, the participants received either success or failure feedback. Earlier, the participants had been asked how much their father would ideally want them to do well on the anagram task, and how much their father would feel they ought to do well. Shah (2003) found that when *father* was primed, participants' father-ideal ratings uniquely predicted their cheerfulness-dejection reaction to the success or failure feedback, and their father-ought ratings uniquely predicted their quiescence-agitation reaction.

Human's use of desired (and undesired) future selves to evaluate the current self is remarkable. Certainly, humans like other animals experience emotions from the actual or expected outcomes of their actions or decisions (with the outcomes typically occurring in a narrow time frame). In contrast, here we are describing human emotions being produced not by an outcome but by a comparison between the perceived present state of self and the imagined future state of self. Thus, the emotional significance of a present-self state does not depend only on the current outcomes from that state but also on the extent to which that self state is *becoming* the imagined future-self state, an imagined future-self state that typically is shared with a significant other. For this reason, individuals with the same present-self states can have different current emotional lives if they are imagining different future selves that function as shared reference values.

CONCLUDING COMMENT

It has been popular in the last decades to explain the wars and conflicts among nations, races, religious and ethnic groups as deriving from the combination of human advancement in cognition, reflected in weapon-related advances, and human nonadvancement in our base animal-like motives. Indeed, at the same time as intellectuals trumpet the angel-like intellectual and artistic achievements of humans they deplore our animal-like ferocity—one of the few animals who kills members of their own species. This chapter takes a different viewpoint. Humans are not like other animals motivationally. Human motivation to share inner states is incomparable to other animals. Indeed, one could argue (see Higgins & Pittman, 2008) that it is this distinctly human motivation that provides a better explanation for human conflict than our supposedly animal-like motives because it is precisely these motives that would produce the intensity of in-group versus out-group misunderstanding and mistrust that create uniquely human conflicts.

I have argued in this chapter for the importance to human motivation of the distinct motivation to share inner states. A point that I have not made explicit is that, to the extent that this is correct, these motives would not have the same strength for everyone. It is a given that motivational states will vary as a function of many variables—situational, personality, developmental, cultural, and so on. In psychology, the variation in the motivation to share inner states has received most attention for the dimension of developmental differences. We know, for example, that this motivation is different for very young children than for adults. Less attention, albeit not totally ignored, has been on how this motivation varies as a personality difference, a historical difference, or a cross-cultural difference. This raises fascinating questions for future research. To what extent are some personality types or conditions a reflection of strength of motivation to share inner states (e.g., autism)? To what extent can cultures be classified in terms of their strength of motivation to share inner states? What conflicts and misunderstandings arise between individuals and between cultures from differences in this motivation?

REFERENCES

Allport, G. W. (1955). *Becoming*. New Haven, CT: Yale University Press.

Andersen, S. M. & Chen, S. (2002). The relational self: An interpersonal social-cognitive theory. *Psychological Review, 109*, 619–645.

Asch, S.E. (1952). *Social psychology*. Englewood Cliffs, NJ: Prentice-Hall.

Bandura, A. (1977). *Social learning theory*. Englewood Cliffs, NJ: Prentice-Hall.

Bandura, A. (1986). *Social foundations of thought and action: A social cognitive theory*. Englewood Cliffs, NJ: Prentice-Hall.

Bandura, A. L. & Walters, R. H. (1963). *Social learning and personality development*. New York: Holt, Rinehart and Winston.

Bertenthal, B. I. & Fischer, K. W. (1978). Development of self-recognition in the infant. *Developmental Psychology, 14*, 44–50.

Boldero, J. & Francis, J. (2002). Goals, standards, and the self: Reference values serving different functions. *Personality and Social Psychology Review, 6*, 232–241.

Bowlby, J. (1969). *Attachment and loss: Vol. 1. Attachment*. New York: Basic Books.

Bowlby, J. (1973). *Attachment and loss: Vol. 2. Separation: Anxiety and anger*. New York: Basic Books.

Brewer, M. B. (2004). Taking the social origins of human nature seriously: Toward a more imperialist social psychology. *Personality and Social Psychology Review, 8*, 107–113.

Bruner, J. S. (1964). The course of cognitive growth. *American Psychologist, 19*, 1–15.

Bruner, J. S. (1983). *Child's talk: Learning to use language*. New York: Norton.

Call, J. (2005). The self and other: A missing link in comparative social cognition. In H. S. Terrace and J. Metcalfe (Eds.), *The missing link in cognition: Origins of self-reflective consciousness* (pp. 321–341). Oxford, UK: Oxford University Press.

Caporael, L. R. (2007). Evolutionary theory for social and cultural psychology. In A. W. Kruglanski and E. T. Higgins (Eds.), *Social psychology: Handbook of basic principles* (2nd ed., pp. 3–18). New York: Guilford.

Carver, C. S., Reynolds, S. L., & Scheier, M. F. (1994). The possible selves of optimists and pessimists. *Journal of Research in Personality, 28*, 133–141.

Carver, C. S. & Scheier, M. F. (1990). Origins and functions of positive and negative affect: A control-process view. *Psychological Review, 97*, 19–35.

Case, R. (1985). *Intellectual development: Birth to adulthood.* New York: Academic Press.

Cooley, C. H. (1962/1909). *Human nature and the social order*. (Revised edition) New York: Charles Scribner's Sons. (Original work published 1902)

Crano, W. D. & Prislin, R. (2006). Attitudes and persuasion. *Annual Review of Psychology, 57*, 345–374.

Damon, W. & Hart, D. (1986). Stability and change in children's self-understanding. *Social Cognition, 4*, 102–118.

Darwin, C. (1859). *Origin of species*. London: John Murray.

Descartes, R. (1985). *The passions of the soul*. In J. Cottingham, R. Stoothoff, & D. Murdoch (Eds.), The philosophical writings of Descartes (Vol. 1). Cambridge, UK: Cambridge University Press. (Original work published 1647)

Eagly, A. H. & Chaiken, S. (1993). *The psychology of attitudes*. New York: Harcourt Brace Jovanovich.

Epstein, S. (1973). The self-concept revisited: Or a theory of a theory. *American Psychologist, 28*, 404–416.

Erikson, E. H. (1963). *Childhood and society* (Rev. ed.) New York: W. W. Norton & Co. (Original work published 1950)

Feffer, M. (1970). Developmental analysis of interpersonal behavior. *Psychological Review, 77*, 197–214.

Fischer, K. W. (1980). A theory of cognitive development: The control and construction of hierarchies of skills. *Psychological Review, 87*, 477–531.

Flavell, J. H., Botkin, P. T., Fry, C. L., Wright, J. W., & Jarvis, P. E. (1968). *The development of role-taking and communication skills in children*. New York: Wiley.

Freud, S. (1952). *A general introduction to psychoanalysis*. New York: Washington Square Press. (Original work published 1920)

Freud, S. (1953). Three essays on the theory of sexuality. *Standard Edition*, Vol. 7. London: Hogarth Press. (Original work published 1905)

Freud, S. (1961). The ego and the id. In J. Strachey (Ed. and Trans.), *The standard edition of the complete psychological works of Sigmund Freud* (Vol. 19, pp. 3–66). London: Hogarth Press. (Original work published 1923)

Hardin, C. & Higgins, E. T. (1996). Shared reality: How social verification makes the subjective objective. In R. M. Sorrentino & E. T. Higgins (Eds.), *Handbook of motivation and cognition: Vol. 3. The interpersonal context* (pp. 28–84). New York: Guilford.

Harter, S. (1983). Developmental perspectives on the self-system. In P. H. Mussen (Ed.), *Handbook of child psychology: Vol. 4. Socialization, personality, and social development* (pp. 275–385). New York: Wiley.

Heider, F. (1958). *The psychology of interpersonal relations*. New York: Wiley.

Higgins, E. T. (1987). Self-discrepancy: A theory relating self and affect. *Psychological Review, 94*, 319–340.

Higgins, E. T. (1989). Continuities and discontinuities in self-regulatory and self-evaluative processes: A developmental theory relating self and affect. *Journal of Personality, 57*, 407–444.

Higgins, E. T. (1991). Development of self-regulatory and self-evaluative processes: Costs, benefits, and tradeoffs. In M. R. Gunnar and L. A. Sroufe (Eds.), *Self processes and development: The Minnesota symposia on child psychology, Volume 23* (pp. 125–165). Hillsdale, NJ: Erlbaum.

Higgins, E. T. (1996a). The "self digest": Self-knowledge serving self-regulatory functions. *Journal of Personality and Social Psychology, 71*, 1062–1083.

Higgins, E. T. (1996b). Shared reality in the self-system: The social nature of self-regulation. *European Review of Social Psychology, 7*, 1–29.

Higgins, E. T. (1997). Beyond pleasure and pain. *American Psychologist, 52*, 1280–1300.

Higgins, E. T. (2005). Humans as applied motivation scientists: Self-consciousness from "shared reality" and "becoming." In H. S. Terrace and J. Metcalfe (Eds.), *The missing link in cognition: Origins of self-reflective consciousness* (pp. 157–173). Oxford, UK: Oxford University Press.

Higgins, E. T., Kruglanski, A. W., & Pierro, A. (2003). Regulatory mode: Locomotion and assessment as distinct orientations. In M. P. Zanna (Ed.), *Advances in experimental social psychology* (Vol. 35, pp. 293–344). San Diego, CA: Academic Press.

Higgins, E. T., & May, D. (2001). Individual self-regulatory functions: It's not "we" regulation, but it's still social. In C. Sedikides & M. B. Brewer (Eds.), *Individual self, relational self, collective self* (pp. 47–67). Philadelphia: Psychology Press.

Higgins, E. T., & Pittman, T. (2008). Motives of the human animal: Comprehending, managing, and sharing inner states. *Annual Review of Psychology, 59*, 361–385.

Hull, C. L. (1943). *Principles of behavior*. New York: Appleton-Century-Crofts.

James, W. (1948). *Psychology*. New York: The World Publishing Company. (Original work published 1890)

Jones, E. E. & Gerard, H. B. (1967). *Foundations of social psychology*. New York: John Wiley & Sons.

Kruglanski, A. W., Thompson, E. P., Higgins, E. T., Atash, M. N., Pierro, A., Shah, J. Y., & Spiegel, S. (2000). To "do the right thing" or to "just do it": Locomotion and assessment as distinct self-regulatory imperatives. *Journal of Personality & Social Psychology, 79*, 793–815.

Leary, M. R. & Buttermore, N. R. (2003). The evolution of the human self-tracing the natural history of self-awareness. *Journal for the Theory of Social Behaviour, 33*, 365–367.

Leary, M. R. (2004). Digging deeper: The fundamental nature of "self-conscious" emotions. *Psychological Inquiry, 15*, 129–131.

Leary, M. R. (2007). Motivational and emotional aspects of the self. *Annual Review of Psychology, 58*, 317–344.

Lecky, P. (1945). *Self-consistency: A theory of personality*. New York: Island Press.

Lewin, K. (1935). *A dynamic theory of personality*. New York: McGraw-Hill.

Lewin, K. (1951). *Field theory in social science*. New York: Harper.

Lewis, M. & Brooks-Gunn, J. (1979). *Social cognition and the acquisition of self*. New York: Plenum.

MacDonald, G. & Jessica, M. (2006). Family approval as a constraint in dependency regulation: Evidence from Australia and Indonesia. *Personal Relationships, 13*, 183–194.

Markus, H. (1980). The self in thought in memory. In D. M. Wegner & R. R. Vallacher (Eds.), *The self in social psychology* (pp. 102–130). New York: Oxford University Press.

Markus, H. & Nurius, P. (1986). Possible selves. *American Psychologist, 41*, 954–969.

Maslow, A. H. (1943). A theory of human motivation. *Psychological Review, 50*, 370–396.

McGuire, W. J. & Padawer-Singer, A. (1976). Trait salience in the spontaneous self-concept. *Journal of Personality and Social Psychology, 33*, 743–754.

McNulty, S. E. & Swann, W. B., Jr. (1994). Identity negotiation in roommate relationships: The self as architect and consequence of social reality. *Journal of Personality and Social Psychology, 67*, 1012–1023.

Mead, G. H. (1934). *Mind, self, and society*. Chicago: University of Chicago Press.

Miller, S. M. & Green, M. L. (1985). Coping with stress and frustration: Origins, nature, and development. In M. Lewis & C. Saarni (Eds.), *The socialization of emotions* (pp. 263–314). New York: Plenum.

Mischel, W. & Moore, B. (1980). The role of ideation in voluntary delay for symbolically presented rewards. *Cognitive Therapy and Research, 4*, 211–221.

Mischel, W. & Patterson, C. J. (1978). Effective plans for self-control in children. In W. A. Collins (Ed.), *Minnesota symposia on child psychology* (Vol. 11, pp. 199–230). Hillsdale, NJ: Lawrence Erlbaum.

Moretti, M. M. & Higgins, E. T. (1990). Relating self-discrepancy to self-esteem: The contribution of discrepancy beyond actual-self ratings. *Journal of Experimental Social Psychology, 26*, 108–123.

Moretti, M. M. & Higgins, E. T. (1999). Own versus other standpoints in self-regulation: Developmental antecedents and functional consequences. *Review of General Psychology, 3*(3), 188–223.

Murray, S. L., Holmes, J. G., & Collins, N. L. (2006). Optimizing assurance: The risk regulation system in relationships. *Psychological Bulletin, 132*(5), 641–666.

Murray, S. L., Holmes, J. G., & Griffin, D. W. (2000). Self-esteem and the quest for felt security: How perceived regard regulates attachment processes. *Journal of Personality and Social Psychology, 78*, 478–498.

Nelson, K. (2005). Emerging levels of consciousness in early human development. In H. S. Terrace & J. Metcalfe (Eds.), *The missing link in cognition: Origins of self-reflective consciousness* (pp. 116–141). Oxford, UK: Oxford University Press.

Oettingen, G. (1996). Positive fantasy and motivation. In P. M. Gollwitzer and J. A. Bargh (Eds.), *The psychology of action: Linking cognition and motivation to behavior* (pp. 236–259). New York: Guilford.

Oettingen, G. & Mayer, D. (2002). The motivating function of thinking about the future: Expectations versus fantasies. *Journal of Personality and Social Psychology, 83*, 1198–1212.

Oyserman, D. & Markus, H. R. (1990). Possible selves and delinquency. *Journal of Personality and Social Psychology, 59*, 112–125.

Piaget, J. (1951). *Play, dreams and imitation in childhood*. New York: Norton.

Piaget, J. (1965). *The moral judgment of the child*. New York: Free Press. (Original translation published 1932)

Piaget, J. (1970). Piaget's theory. In P. H. Mussen (Ed.), *Carmichael's manual of child psychology* (Vol. 1, 3rd ed., pp. 703–732). New York: Wiley.

Povinelli, D. J. (2000). *Folk physics for apes: The chimpanzee's theory of how the world works*. Oxford, UK: Oxford University Press.

Rogers, C. R. (1951). *Client-centered therapy: Its current practice, implications, and theory*. Boston: Houghton Mifflin.

Ruble, D. N. (1983). The development of social comparison processes and their role in achievement-related self-socialization. In E. T. Higgins, D. N. Ruble, & W. W. Hartup (Eds.), *Social cognition and social development: A sociocultural perspective* (pp. 134–157). New York: Cambridge University Press.

Sarbin, T. R. (1952). A preface to a psychological analysis of the self. *Psychological Review, 59*, 11–22.

Saxe, R., Carey, S., & Kanwisher, N. (2004). Understanding other minds: Linking developmental psychology and functional neuroimaging. *Annual Review of Psychology, 55*, 87–124.

Schlenker, B. R. & Weigold, M. F. (1992). Interpersonal processes involving impression regulation and management. *Annual Review of Psychology, 43*, 133–168.
Schneider, D. J. (2004). *The psychology of stereotyping*. New York: Guilford.
Selman, R. L. (1980). *The growth of interpersonal understanding: Developmental and clinical analyses*. New York: Academic Press.
Selman, R. L. & Byrne, D. F. (1974). A structural-developmental analysis of levels of role taking in middle childhood. *Child Development, 45*, 803–806.
Shah, J. (2003). The motivational looking glass: How significant others implicitly affect goal appraisals. *Journal of Personality and Social Psychology, 85*, 424–439.
Shantz, C. U. (1983). Social cognition. In J. H. Flavell & E. M. Markman (Eds.), *Cognitive development, Vol. 3* in P. H. Mussen (Ed.), *Carmichael's manual of child psychology* (4th ed., pp. 495–555). New York: Wiley.
Sherif, M. (1936). *The psychology of social norms*. New York: Harper Collins.
Skinner, B. F. (1953). *Science and human behavior*. New York: Macmillan.
Snygg, D. & Combs, A. W. (1949). *Individual behavior*. New York: Harper and Row.
Stangor, C. (Ed.). (2000). *Stereotypes and prejudice: Key readings in social psychology*. Philadelphia, PA: Psychology Press.
Stryker, S. & Statham, A. (1985). Symbolic interaction and role theory. In G. Lindzey & E. Aronson (Eds.), *Handbook of social psychology* (Vol. 1, pp. 311–378). New York: Random House.
Sullivan, H. S. (1953). *The collected works of Harry Stack Sullivan: Vol. 1. The interpersonal theory of psychiatry* (H. S. Perry & M. L. Gawel, Eds.). New York: Norton.
Swann, W. B., Bosson, J. K., & Pelham, B. W. (2002). Different partners, different selves: Strategic verification of circumscribed identities. *Personality and Social Psychology Bulletin, 28*, 1215–1228.
Swann, W. B., Hixon, J. G., De La Ronde, C. (1992). Embracing the bitter "truth": Negative self-concepts and marital commitment. *Psychological Science, 3*, 118–121.
Terrace, H. S. (2005). Metacognition and the evolution of language. In H. S. Terrace & J. Metcalfe (Eds.), *The missing link in cognition: Origins of self-reflective consciousness* (pp. 84–115). Oxford, UK: Oxford University Press.
Thomas, W. I., & Thomas, D. S. (1928). *The child in America*. New York: Knopf.
Thorndike, E. L. (1935). *The psychology of wants, interests, and attitudes*. New York: Appleton-Century-Crofts.
Tomasello, M. (1999). *The cultural origins of human cognition*. Cambridge, MA: Harvard University Press.
Tomasello, M., Carpenter, M., Call, J., Behne, T., & Moll, H. (2005). Understanding and sharing intentions: The origins of cultural cognition. *Behavioral and Brain Sciences, 28*, 675–735.
Tulving, E. (1983). *Elements of episodic memory*. New York: Oxford University Press.
Tulving, E. (2005). Episodic memory and autonoesis. Uniquely human? In H. S. Terrace and J. Metcalfe (Eds.), *The missing link in cognition: Origins of self-reflective consciousness* (pp. 3–56). Oxford, UK: Oxford University Press.
Turner, R. H. (1956). Role-taking, role standpoint, and reference-group behavior. *American Journal of Sociology, 61*, 316–328.
Weber, M. (1967). Subjective meaning in the social situation. In G. B. Levitas (Ed.), *Culture and consciousness: Perspectives in the social sciences* (pp. 156–169). New York: Braziller.
Webster's Ninth New Collegiate Dictionary. (1989). Springfield, MA: Merriam-Webster.
Wellman, H. M., Cross, D., Watson, J. (2001). Meta-analysis of theory-of-mind development: The truth about false belief. *Child Development, 72*, 655–684.
Werner, H. & Kaplan, B. (1963). *Symbol formation*. New York: Wiley.

9

The Use of Prediction to Drive Alignment in Dialogue

MARTIN J. PICKERING AND SIMON GARROD

ABSTRACT

Dialogue (or conversation) is extremely complex, yet people generally have little problem with it. To explain this, we have argued that interlocutors construct equivalent representations during production and comprehension at many different linguistic levels (Pickering & Garrod, 2004). This results from an apparently automatic process of interactive alignment. In addition, there is good evidence that comprehenders make predictions during comprehension by using the language production system (Pickering & Garrod, 2007). We argue that such predictions are particularly useful in dialogue, both to construct aligned representations "ahead of time" and to allow management of aspects of the dialogue such as turn-taking. Moreover, the regular switching between production and comprehension in dialogue specifically emphasizes production-based prediction. We interpret this account in terms of emulation and argue that it provides an example of how prediction supports social interaction.

For the great majority of intellectual history, attempts to understand mental life have focused on the individual. Cognitive psychology constitutes an excellent recent example of this tradition, in that it has concerned itself almost entirely with the study of the representations and processes used in autonomous activities. For example, researchers study how individuals perceive, remember, reason, or act in isolation. The question of how individuals use such representations and processes to take each other into account in performing joint actions has not been addressed in detail. If we are able to do so, we may start to explain the mental foundations of human sociality.

In this chapter, we consider this broad question by considering the specific activity of dialogue (or conversation)—the use of language in social interaction. Language is a particularly relevant domain because its primary use is in communication, and therefore necessarily implies interaction between individuals. It is used internally (to aid thought), and it is also used to communicate with displaced addressees (for example, when writing for posterity), but its evolutionary and developmental origins are in interaction. However, the great majority of work on language processing, development, and impairment has focused on isolated individuals, as is clear from both traditional and recent textbooks on psycholinguistics (e.g., Fodor, Bever, & Garrett, 1974; Harley, 2007). Here, we propose an alternative approach to psycholinguistics in which we seek to understand the representations and processes underlying communication among individuals.

We first address the nature of dialogue and ask why people appear to find it so easy. We propose that interlocutors use representations that are common to production and comprehension, and align on those representations with each other during the conversation. We then argue that they use a production-based *emulator* (Grush, 2004) to predict aspects of what their interlocutors are going to say. Such predictions can be used to facilitate dialogue. We then suggest how different forms of dialogue (narrative, free conversation, interviews, etc.) are likely to differ in the amount of prediction that occurs and hence the flow of the dialogue. Finally, we consider the extent to which the principles of prediction apply to other forms of coordinated activity, and conclude that they are most important for tightly coupled activities and ones that involve communication.

CONVERSATION AND THE ALIGNMENT OF REPRESENTATIONS

Conversation involves an extremely complicated set of processes in which the interlocutors have to interweave their activities with precise timing, and yet it is a skill that all speakers seem very good at (Garrod & Pickering, 2004). To understand how remarkable this is, consider this transcript of a dinner-party conversation (Tannen, 1989), with brackets indicating overlapping speech and numbers indicating noticeable pauses in seconds:

1 *A:* I shook hands with Rubenstein once? [and his hand
2 *B:* [Yeah we did together
3 *A:* That's right. we were together. wasn't it incredible?
4 *B:* (*laughing*) oh it was like a cushion.
5 *C:* What's this?
6 *A:* [I (*0.5*) we shook] hands with Rubenstein.
7 *B:* [Rubenstein's hands.]
8 *D:* and he had —?
9 *A:* his hands —
10 *D:* short stubby hands?
11 *A:* they were like (*0.5*) [jelly. they were like — (*1.0*)
12 *B:* [a famous concert pianist

A: they were like (*0.5*) putty. (*0.5*)
D: [really?
A: [just completely soft and [limp
B: [mush
A: just mush. it was as though there was [no bone
B: [and warm.
D: and short stubby fingers?
A: short stubby fingers but just (0.5) totally covered with—
B: fat.
A: fat

This conversation differs greatly from formal prose (such as the rest of this chapter). In particular, the interlocutors regularly produce elliptical and fragmentary utterances that would make little sense on their own (e.g., Lines 7, 10, 12, 16, 17, 20). It is jointly constructed by all four interlocutors, and involves a great deal of interruption, overlapping speech, and disfluency. However, the interlocutors appear to be satisfied with the conversation. They seem to understand what everyone produces, as do nonparticipants such as ourselves. How can this be?

The more we think about conversations such as this, the more remarkable they appear. The interlocutors cannot be sure what contributions their partners are going to make, so they cannot securely plan far in advance. They have to construct their utterances so that they are appropriate for their addressee at that particular point, and therefore must pay constant attention to any feedback (e.g., whether a particular term is understood). For example, *B*'s interruption at (Line 2) causes *A* to abandon the current utterance (Line 1) and produce the appropriate response (Line 3) on the fly. They have to decide whether to contribute to a conversation and if so precisely when they should do so, and they may have to decide whom to address. In addition, they have to constantly switch between production and comprehension, even though such task switching is often difficult. None of this is necessary in monologue. Yet everyone can hold a conversation, but producing a speech (or even listening to one) is a complex skill that requires considerable training.

A few years ago, we wrote an article asking why people find conversation (or dialogue) so easy, in comparison to monologue (Garrod & Pickering, 2004). In that article, we argued that conversation is easy because interlocutors tend to become aligned at different levels of linguistic representation and therefore find it easier to perform joint activity. We explain the process of alignment in more detail in terms of their interactive-alignment model. According to this account, dialogue is successful to the extent that interlocutors come to understand the relevant aspects of the world in the same way as each other. More specifically, interlocutors construct mental models of the situation under discussion, and successful dialogue occurs when these models become aligned. In accord with the text-comprehension literature, we assume that situation models include information about people, time, space, causality, and intentionality (e.g., Zwaan & Radvansky, 1998). Such alignment largely occurs as a result of the tendency for interlocutors to repeat each other's choices at many different linguistic levels, such as words and grammar (e.g., Branigan, Pickering, & Cleland, 2000; Brennan & Clark, 1996; Garrod &

Anderson, 1987). Essentially, interlocutors prime each other to speak about things in the same way, and people who speak about things in the same way are more likely to think about them in the same way as well.

A critical aspect of this model is what we term *representational parity*—the same representations are constructed during production and comprehension. It amounts to a claim that language involves use of a common code for representing your own actions and your partner's actions. It explains why linguistic repetition occurred in experiments such as Branigan et al. (2000), who had participants take turns to describe and match picture cards, and found that they tended to use the form of utterance just used by their interlocutor. For example, they tended to use a prepositional object form such as "the pirate giving the book to the swimmer" following another prepositional object sentence but a "double object" form such as "the pirate giving the swimmer the book" following another double object sentence (though both sentences have essentially the same meaning). In such cases, the same grammatical representation is activated during production and comprehension. Though the common-coding assumption may appear to follow from the reasonable claim that language users do not involve different knowledge of language when speaking and comprehending, it is important to realize that traditional psycholinguistic theories of production and comprehension have largely developed in isolation from each other (see again Fodor et al., 1974; Harley, 2007).

However, parity may not be enough to make dialogue easy by itself. Just because production and comprehension draw on the same representations does not in itself mean that switching between them should be straightforward. One way to make things easier would be to activate production mechanisms during comprehension in readiness for their use in production. Essentially, if comprehension involves activating production mechanisms as well as comprehension mechanisms associated with what is being comprehended, then this should facilitate subsequent production of language that is related to what is being comprehended. In the following, we argue that such covert production does take place, and that it is used during comprehension to make predictions about what is likely to be heard. We then show that it also facilitates actual production in dialogue.

PREDICTION AND EMULATION IN LANGUAGE

Evidence for Prediction in Language Comprehension

A lot of data are consistent with prediction during spoken and written language comprehension, although until recently much of it was not interpreted in this way. First, it has been known for a long time that people find it easier to process upcoming words when the linguistic context is sufficiently constraining and hence makes the words predictable (so-called high-cloze contexts), as is demonstrated by experiments using word naming, eye-tracking, and event-related potentials. For example, people are faster at making a lexical decision about a more likely word, such as "the tired mother gave her dirty child a *bath*," than a less likely one, such as "the tired mother gave her dirty child a *shower*," even when the words are equally plausible (Schwanenflugel & Shoben, 1985). Likewise, very predictable words are read particularly quickly and are often skipped during reading (Ehrlich & Rayner, 1981). They also lead to reduced N400 event-related potential (ERP) effects, which are indicative of degree of anomaly (Kutas & Hillyard, 1984).

These early results are compatible with two different accounts. It could be that people find it easier to integrate likely words into the prior linguistic context. But it is also possible that people predict the words that are likely to occur next, and when the predicted words do occur, comprehension is facilitated. More recent evidence supports this latter account.

Thus, Van Berkum, Brown, Zwitserlood, Kooijman, and Hagoort (2005) had participants listen to or read high-cloze texts in Dutch such as the following:

1. *De inbreker had geen enkele moeite de geheime familiekluis te vinden.* [The burglar had no trouble locating the secret family safe.]

Deze bevond zich natuurlijk achter een groot$_{\text{neuter}}$ *maar onopvallend schilderij*$_{\text{neuter}}$. [Of course, it was situated behind a big$_{\text{neuter}}$ but unobtrusive painting$_{\text{neuter}}$.] (Predictable)
Deze bevond zich natuurlijk achter een grote$_{\text{common}}$ *maar onopvallende boekenkast*$_{\text{common}}$. [Of course, it was situated behind a big$_{\text{common}}$ but unobtrusive bookcase$_{\text{common}}$.] (Not predictable)

The adjective *groot* agrees in gender with the predictable noun *schilderij*, whereas the adjective *grote* does not. If participants predict the upcoming noun (including its gender), they should be disrupted when the adjective is incongruent. Such a finding would be hard to reconcile with the integration account. In accord with this prediction, Van Berkum et al. found that participants were disrupted when they encountered *grote* in comparison to *groot*, for spoken language comprehension (using event-related potentials) and written language comprehension (using self-paced reading).

Comparable results occur with article gender in Spanish (Wicha, Moreno, & Kutas, 2004), and together suggest that people's predictions include the syntactic properties of words. However, another study suggested that they predict aspects of their phonology as well. DeLong, Urbach, and Kutas (2005) measured event-related potentials while participants read contexts such as:

2a. The day was breezy so the boy went outside to fly a kite.
2b. The day was breezy so the boy went outside to fly an airplane.

As expected, the unpredictable *airplane* in (2b) led to a larger N400 effect than the predictable *kite*. The interesting finding was that this effect also occurred on the preceding article, indicating that readers were surprised to encounter *an* and therefore had predicted *kite* and in particular that it began with a consonant. Finally, Vissers, Chwilla, and Kolk (2006) found that a misspelled word that sounds identical to a highly predictable word (e.g., *boekun* for *boeken* [books]) elicited a P600 ERP effect. This effect appears to reflect reanalysis and presumably results from a clash between it and the predicted form (*boeken* [books]).

Perhaps not surprisingly, all of these studies are about predicting words. But language is richly structured, and can be described in terms of sound, grammar, and meaning. Contexts can be very constraining at these levels. Because it is very likely that an adjective will be followed by a noun, a comprehender can predict a noun after encountering an adjective. In many cases, predictability is greater at these levels than at the lexical level (e.g., articles are almost always followed by either nouns or adjectives). There is much psycholinguistic evidence from both production and comprehension that people compute different representations (e.g., Harley, 2007) and thus they could make predictions at any of these levels.

Just as with words, there is evidence for prediction of grammatical categories and aspects of meaning. Again, the early evidence was consistent with integration. Thus, many studies show that people are faster at naming words when they are syntactically compatible with prior context, even when they bear no semantic relationship to the context (e.g., Deutsch & Bentin, 1994; Wright & Garrett, 1994). At a semantic level, Peterson, Burgess, Dell, and Eberhard (2001) found that unexpected abstract words were processed faster following a context that predicted an idiomatic continuation, and concrete words were processed faster following a context that predicted a literal continuation. This is compatible with the prediction of whether an upcoming word is likely to be concrete or abstract. However, these results could again reflect ease of integration rather than prediction.

Two recent studies provide better support for prediction. First, Lau, Stroud, Plesch, and Phillips (2006) found that early syntactic anomaly effects in the ERP record were affected by whether the linguistic context predicted one particular syntactic category for the upcoming word or was compatible with different syntactic categories. Specifically, a preposition led to a stronger early anomaly effect if the context clearly predicted that a noun would occur than if it predicted more than one syntactic category apart from a preposition. Another study showed reading "or the subway" was faster following "the team took either the train …" than following "the team took the train" (Staub & Clifton, 2006). The presence of *either* makes the upcoming syntax more predictable by ruling out a misanalysis in which *or* starts a new clause, and thus facilitates comprehension.

There is also good evidence that people predict meanings when interpreting sentences about scenes, as measured by the comprehenders' eye movements to potential entities or events in the scenes. Altmann and Kamide (1999) found that participants tended to start looking at edible objects more than inedible objects when hearing "the man ate the" (but did not do so when *ate* was replaced by *moved*). This suggests that people predict entities by combining linguistic and nonlinguistic context, though it is possible that the predictions may not extend to syntax or phonology. Knoeferle, Crocker, Scheepers, and Pickering (2005) found that when participants listened to "the princess washes apparently the pirate" (in German) while viewing a picture of a princess washing a pirate and a fencer painting the princess they tended to look at the pirate before hearing *pirate*, thereby indicating that they predicted the event (i.e., the princess washing the pirate). Further studies have shown that predictive eye movements depend on the meaning of the whole context, not just the meaning (or lexical associates) of the verb (Kamide, Altmann, & Haywood, 2003). Moreover, visual information is integrated with prosody (Weber, Grice, & Crocker, 2006), grammatical case-marking (Kamide, Scheepers, & Altmann, 2003), and discourse context (Kaiser & Trueswell, 2004) to drive predictive eye movements.

Evidence That Such Prediction Involves Production

What system might be responsible for such predictions? One possibility is that there is a special-purpose system for making linguistic predictions. But a more parsimonious alternative would be to use aspects of the production system to make predictions. When speakers produce language, they need to generate representations of the meanings, grammatical forms, and sounds that make up the planned utterance (e.g., Levelt, 1989). It is easy to see how parts of this system could be utilized during comprehension. While encountering "The tired mother gave her dirty child a …," the reader could use the production system to construct representations of the meaning of *bath*, its grammatical category (noun), and its sounds. These representations can then be matched against the analysis of the input, so that comprehension is facilitated if *bath* actually occurs.

So what is the evidence that such prediction does use production mechanisms? First, there is direct evidence for involvement of articulation in speech comprehension, with listeners activating appropriate muscles in the tongue and lips while listening to speech but not during nonspeech (Fadiga, Craighero, Buccino, & Rizzolatti, 2002; Watkins, Strafella, & Paus, 2003). Additionally, increased muscle activity in the lips is associated with increased activity (i.e., blood flow) in Broca's area, suggesting that this area mediates between the comprehension and production systems during speech perception (Watkins & Paus, 2004). Other fMRI studies have also demonstrated a large overlap between the cortical areas active during speech production and those active during passive listening (Pulvermüller et al., 2006; Wilson, Saygin, Sereno, & Iacobini, 2004). Thus, comprehension activates the production system and leads to covert imitation. (Notice that the motor activation is likely to follow from the activation of the production system rather than itself be the cause of imitation.) There is also evidence for the activation of brain areas associated with production during aspects of comprehension from phonology (Heim et al., 2003) to narrative structure (Mar, 2004). Some of this evidence is used to provide support for the motor theory of speech perception, according to which speech comprehension involves the direct perception of motor gestures (Galantucci, Fowler, & Turvey, 2006).

Another reason to suspect that comprehension uses the production system comes from the evidence of the pervasiveness of spontaneous (overt) imitation at many linguistic levels, which implies that people construct imitative plans at the relevant stages in the production process. Much of this evidence comes from studies of dialogue and has already been noted (e.g., Branigan et al., 2000; Brennan & Clark, 1996; Garrod & Anderson, 1987), but there is also evidence for linguistic imitation in the absence of an interlocutor (e.g., Bock, Dell, Chang, & Onishi, 2007). For imitation to be used by the comprehension system, it must occur very quickly and result from automatic processes rather than conscious decisions. In fact, there is clear evidence that phonological or acoustic imitation is extremely rapid (Fowler, Brown, Sabadini, & Weihing, 2003) and the faster the imitation, the more faithful it is (Goldinger, 1998). Furthermore, interlocutors are almost entirely unaware that they imitate each other's grammar or choice of words (see Pickering & Garrod, 2004).

The Mechanisms of Emulation

We now outline the emulation framework (Pickering & Garrod, 2007) and show how it allows people to make predictions during comprehension. An emulator is a kind of forward model of an external system that runs simulations of that system in real time. For example, it has been argued that people rapidly construct models of actual movements before making those movements and use those models as guides for corrections. Thus before moving your arm, you model the path it should take, and if it deviates from that path, you correct accordingly. Such a forward model can be used much more rapidly than real-world feedback, and additionally provides information about where your arm is likely to be, in the absence of accurate sensory feedback (see Desmurget & Grafton, 2000; Wolpert & Flanagan, 2001).

Pickering and Garrod (2007) proposed that the production system acts as an emulator during language comprehension (see Figure 9.1). At each step the emulator uses the production system to predict the next input unit in the speech stream. The emulator is controlled by feedback from a Kalman filter, which weights predictions from production against analysis of the input at each step (see Grush, 2004). If the prediction is strong (e.g., for a high-cloze word) and the input noisy (e.g., you are at a lively cocktail party), there is low Kalman gain (strong top-down influence on interpretation); if the prediction is poor and the input clear, there is

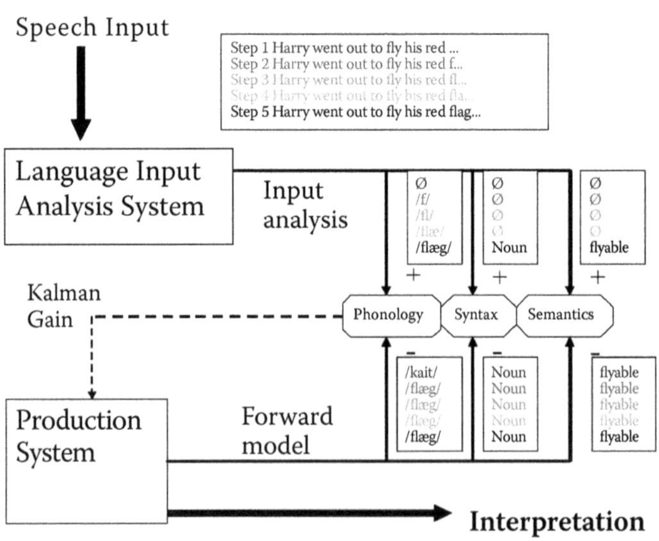

Figure 9.1 Schematic representation of a production-based language emulator.

high Kalman gain (strong bottom-up influence). Figure 9.1 illustrates five steps in comprehending the end of the sentence "Harry went out to fly his red flag." At each step the input analysis and the forward prediction are shown in the same color for three levels of prediction (phonology, syntax, and semantics).

It is possible that the emulator simply makes one prediction at each level. However, we (2007) proposed that it specifies a range of options with associated probabilities, and is compatible with both motor-control theory (see Wolpert & Flanagan, 2001) and experimental evidence (DeLong et al., 2005). What this means is that it can benefit from whatever completion actually occurs, and also (as we shall see) facilitates completion of an interlocutor's utterance in dialogue. These predictions depend on how constraining the context is at a given linguistic level, just as in other forms of emulation. Furthermore, because the emulator is controlled by a Kalman filter, which weights the prediction against the current input and feeds the result back to influence the emulator's next prediction, it is particularly effective at dealing with noisy input.

THE USE OF PRODUCTION-BASED EMULATION IN DIALOGUE

Although some of the evidence for production-based emulation comes from dialogue, we have so far concentrated on how it may occur during the comprehension of monologue. But it may be particularly important in dialogue in two senses. On the one hand, the nature of dialogue leads to particularly strong activation of the production system. On the other hand, emulation may be especially useful for achieving the goals of conversational success (as opposed to monologue comprehension). These two factors are of course related, as we now discuss.

First, dialogue involves regular switching between comprehension and production. When the speaker's turn finishes, the addressee is likely to take the floor. In some forms of dialogue, speaker and addressee constantly change roles. In addition, the addressee may provide "backchannel" feedback during the speaker's turn, such as assertions (*yes; go on*) or queries (*eh?*; *who?*). Even during narrative comprehension, the addressee provides feedback to the speaker (and such feedback enhances the narrative; Bavelas, Coates, & Johnson, 2000). Such turn-taking and feedback does not occur in monologue (by definition). Thus, the production system is constantly activated during dialogue, and hence it may be more active during comprehension of dialogue than comprehension of monologue.

From a slightly different perspective, we can see that an addressee must be constantly prepared to respond. In some conversational settings, a response is normatively required (otherwise the addressee is flouting the rules of turn-taking; see Sacks, Schegloff, & Jefferson, 1974). The simplest example of this is a question directed solely (and nonrhetorically) at the addressee, which requires some response. In monologue, the addressee knows that his only job is to comprehend what he is hearing. He may use production mechanisms to facilitate that comprehension but he does not have to make overt responses.

Indeed, an addressee contrasts with other individuals who may be present in the dialogue setting (e.g., Clark, 1996). Researchers distinguish different roles, typically speaker, addressee, side participant, and nonparticipants (licensed overhearers and eavesdroppers). Importantly the speaker addresses the addressee or addressees (e.g., asking him a question). The side participant is not required to respond but is permitted to contribute during the conversation. Thus we might expect the addressee to predictively process to a greater extent than side participants or overhearers. In accord with this, Branigan et al. (2007) had speakers describe cards to addressees using prepositional object or double object forms (as in Branigan et al., 2000) in the presence of a side participant. They found that addressees were more likely to repeat the grammatical form used by the speaker than were side participants. This suggests that addressees predicted the grammatical form used by the speaker to prepare a response to a greater degree than side participants. In contrast, the tendency to repeat was unaffected by whether the previous addressee or the previous side participant then spoke to the previous speaker or to someone else. This decision is not related to the degree of prediction required during comprehension.

This account also provides an interesting explanation of why addressees understand dialogues better than overhearers (Schober & Clark, 1989): The addressee is constantly preparing potential responses, and is therefore activating his or her production system, thus increasing deep processing and hence understanding. (It contrasts with the authors' explanation, namely, that speaker and addressee jointly construct a common ground, which is not fully accessible to the overhearer; however, both explanations may have some truth.)

A related point is simply that covert imitation leads to overt imitation, and that overt imitation supports conversational success. This is central to the interactive alignment model of dialogue (Pickering & Garrod, 2004), as discussed earlier. The model assumes that alignment at one level of representation leads to alignment at other levels, including the level of the situation model. For example, interlocutors prime each other to use the same words to describe a situation, and thus they each take on board the implications of those words and therefore interpret the situation in similar ways to each other (see Markman & Makin, 1998).

In monologue, the comprehender performs covert imitation using the production system, and so alignment occurs during monologue comprehension. But in dialogue, the interlocutor often performs overt imitation as well as covert imitation. Overt imitation is likely to lead to much stronger activation of representations than covert imitation, perhaps because overt imitation involves "complete" production, whereas covert imitation involves some but not all of the processes involved in production, or perhaps because interlocutors extensively monitor their own speech (Levelt, 1989). Hence, emulation may be more likely to enhance understanding in dialogue than monologue.

Second, emulation can assist with aspects of dialogue that have no equivalent in monologue. In particular, comprehenders can use their emulation of the production system to assist in coordination (i.e., the smooth flow of the joint activity of dialogue). Most dialogue is internally managed, so that interlocutors themselves have to decide when it is appropriate to speak. They are remarkably good at this, because interturn intervals are extremely close to zero milliseconds in most exchanges. This means that the addressee knows precisely when it is appropriate to start speaking.

To do this, the addressee can use the emulator to determine (in effect) how long an utterance the addressee would produce at that point and assumes that the speaker will behave similarly. In accord with this, de Ruiter, Mitterer, and Enfield (2006) found that experimental participants were very accurate at predicting the end of speakers' utterances. Interestingly, their predictions remained accurate when the intonation was removed and the words were left but not vice versa. This follows from our account because the phonological, syntactic, and semantic predictions are largely driven by the words rather than by the intonational contour.

One potential problem is that interlocutors may speak at different rates, in which case the addressee's emulations would not accurately predict the speaker's actual productions. However, the interactive-alignment account predicts that interlocutors align their speech rate, and Giles, Coupland, and Coupland (1992) provide experimental evidence for such alignment. More recently, ten Bosch, Oostdijk, and de Ruiter (2004) found a very strong correlation between interturn intervals before one interlocutor's turns and the other interlocutor's turns in a substantial corpus of both telephone and face-to-face conversations. In addition, Wilson and Wilson (2005) argued that interlocutors align their rate of syllable production and rapidly come into counterphase so that one interlocutor is ready to speak when the other is inhibited. This explains why an addressee rarely starts to speak at the same time as the original speaker and why two addressees can start to speak at the same time. Emulation can bring this about and can thus be used to facilitate turn-taking.

In addition, the processor may emphasize emulation in dialogue rather than monologue because dialogue is in general more predictable than monologue. It tends to be much more repetitive, as we (Pickering & Garrod, 2004) informally noted by comparing the amount of repetition in a stretch of "maze game" dialogue (Garrod & Anderson, 1987) with an equivalent paragraph from their paper (see also Tannen, 1989). Clearly, the more repetitive a text, the more the advantage of emphasizing prediction over bottom-up analysis. Such repetitiveness occurs at many different linguistic levels, not just words. An efficient processor will therefore give relatively more weighting to the forward model versus the analysis of the input. Formally, this is the Kalman gain, and the suggestion is that this should be lower in dialogue than monologue. This leads to a kind of circular effect, whereby the emulation present in dialogue leads to overt imitation, and the occurrence of such imitation in turn leads the processor to set the Kalman gain low.

To illustrate the potential effectiveness of prediction in dialogue, consider the fact that interlocutors regularly finish each other's utterances. In the dinner-party conversation from earlier (Tannen, 1989), *A* described Rubenstein's hands as "Just completely soft and limp," and *B* uttered "mush" simultaneously with "limp" (Lines 15 and 16). It appears that *B* predicted the meaning of what *A* was about to say (but not the exact word). In terms of our proposal, *B* used the emulator to produce a semantic representation of a property of Rubenstein's hands, and was therefore able to complete the process of articulating "mush" without delay. Thus *A* and *B* were aligned in terms of the semantic aspects of their productions, but did not align lexically. In contrast, when *A* later said, "short stubby fingers but just totally covered with," *B* completes with "fat" (Lines 20 and 21). In this case, *A* repeated

B's completion (22), and so it may be that both *A* and *B* were lexically aligned (i.e., with similar patterns of activation for particular lexical items) at the point when *B* spoke (though it is also possible that *A* had not accessed "fat" until after *B* spoke). In such a case, *A*'s behavior is complementary to *B*'s, rather than imitative.

Note that *B*'s behavior was complementary rather than imitative (*B* completed what *A* had begun, rather than repeat what *A* said). To do this, we assume that B has covertly imitated A, predicted what *A* would say next, and then uttered that prediction. An important question is why addressees sometimes overtly imitate (repeating what they have heard or something related to it) and sometimes produce complementary behavior (producing what the speaker might say next; see Pickering & Garrod, 2009). It is also possible that an addressee can sometimes directly emulate the speaker's predicted next utterance, without covertly imitating what the speaker is currently uttering. This account might lead to more rapid prediction, but would require an explanation of when speakers perform imitative emulation and when they go straight to complementary emulation. For a similar discussion in relation to action, see Graf, Schütz-Bosbach, and Prinz, this volume, Chapter 3.

Although our emphasis throughout this discussion is on the use of production-based emulation by the addressee, it is also possible that the speaker uses such emulation to predict potential responses, either to questions or to other utterances that invite a response. For example, a parent might ask a child, "Have you tidied your room?" and use the production system to predict the response "no." The parent might even use this to prepare a further utterance ("Well, do so then"). In this case, the child's response is highly predictable; it does not matter that the parent's prediction derives from an utterance by the parent rather than an utterance of the child. This analysis is compatible with interpretations of contributions to dialogue that emphasize their anticipatory quality (e.g., Linell, 1998).

EMULATION AND THE DIALOGIC CONTINUUM

At this point we can conclude that emulation should occur in both dialogue and monologue but is likely to be greater in dialogue. However, dialogue comes in many forms. Whereas Tannen's (1989) example constitutes a particularly interactive example of dialogue, other forms of dialogue occur with more limited interaction. We might predict that dialogues like Tannen's would involve particularly high degrees of emulation (therefore allowing such completions as noted on Lines 15 and 16 and Lines 20 to 22). But what characteristics of dialogue are going to be important?

As Pickering and Garrod (2004) noted, interactive activities vary according to the degree of coupling between the interacting agents. A tightly coupled activity such as ballroom dancing requires continuous coordination between partners, but a loosely coupled activity such as golf only requires intermittent coordination (one may have to wait until one's partner has struck the ball, quality of play may be affected by how close the scores are, etc.). The same is true of conversation. Whereas holding a one-to-one intimate conversation may require precise and continuous coordination (e.g., interruptions, joint construction of utterances, clarification requests), a diagnostic consultation between doctor and patient might involve long contributions by the patient (e.g., descriptions of symptoms) interrupted by extensive recommendations by the doctor (e.g., recommendations about treatment). In general, we predict that the more highly coupled the dialogue, the lower the Kalman gain, and hence the greater the degree of emulation. But what characteristics might lead to a high degree of coupling? Here we sketch out some suggestions.

Timing. Conversation becomes difficult when interlocutors do not hear each other's contributions immediately as they are uttered (e.g., Krauss, Garlock, Bricker, & McMahon, 1977). Here, the problem is not that the conversation is (necessarily) less predictable than undelayed interaction, but rather that the emulator is out of sync. In other words, the emulator makes predictions that lead to the addressee wishing to contribute (with a full contribution or a backchannel), but the delay prevents the addressee from speaking at that point.

External management. In casual conversation, interlocutors are free to contribute whenever they want, subject to the normal rules of conversation such as not interrupting and not responding to questions addressed to someone else (Sacks, Schegloff, & Jefferson, 1974). But this is not always the case. In a job interview, each member of the appointment panel may take a turn in asking a question of the applicant; it may not be acceptable to speak out of turn. In fact, the order of speaking may be decided before the interview begins. Thus, emulation by members of the panel is largely irrelevant to their actual contributions (though of course emulation by the addressee can be relevant). Moreover, an interlocutor is less likely to speak or to build on any previous speaker's utterance; and in addition, such a dialogue is presumably less repetitive than free conversation. Thus the Kalman gain is likely to be higher.

"Boundaries" of content. Whereas casual conversation between friends is comparatively unrestricted in domain, many interactions are much more restricted. In dialogues between a shopkeeper and a customer, the topics are highly constrained. The shopkeeper is limited to questions such as "Can I help you?" and the customer is in turn largely limited to asking whether the shop sells a particular product, where it is on the shelves, or how much it costs. The shopkeeper then provides little more than answers to these questions or requests for further information (e.g., which brand the customer prefers). Both the content of the utterances and their potential forms are much more restricted in such interactions than casual conversation. This means that that they should admit more emulation, and so in this respect at least the Kalman gain should be low. More ritualized interchanges (e.g., wedding ceremonies) or those admitting very little variation (e.g., military commands) should lead to even higher degrees of emulation.

Group size. There is some evidence that speakers in large groups tend to broadcast to the group as a whole, whereas speakers in small groups behave much more like dyads, responding to the previous speaker (Fay, Garrod, & Carletta, 2000). In accord with this, speakers in large groups tend to align their opinions with those of the dominant speaker, whereas those in small groups tend to align with the previous speaker. Pickering & Garrod (2004) suggested that speakers in large groups behave much more like speakers in monologues than speakers in small groups. Again, the prediction is that emulation should be greater in small group interactions.

It should be clear from these examples that the reasons why emulation is affected by the nature of the dialogue tend to have a nonlinguistic explanation. In some cases, the explanation may be technological, relating to the restrictions on the communicative medium (Krauss et al., 1977). In the case of group size, the appropriate explanation may be in terms of communicative ease or it might be social (e.g., in terms of how comfortable people feel in speaking spontaneously). In other cases, however, the explanation seems to result from institutional practices. For example, the formal structure of interviews (long contributions, no interrupting, etc.) might occur so that the contribution of the candidate can be precisely analyzed afterward or so that all candidates are treated the same way. In the case of the shopkeeper, the explanation may relate to the need to have an efficient means of performing a transaction and the need to avoid the difficulty of raising most topics with a stranger.

When there is a social explanation, the conversation is only likely to work if the parties all realize the rules of the interchange (and realize that each other realize it). They do not necessarily need to realize why these rules exist (they could just be socialized into accepting them) but in the long run the rules are more likely to break down if they cannot be justified. If the interlocutors differ in the extent to which they appreciate the social rules underlying the interchange, they may be less likely to emulate appropriately. Moreover, they will have different beliefs about the probability of a particular conversational move. They therefore either tend to fail to align or learn the rules of the interchange.

So different types of conversation will differ in how predictable they are at levels relating to word choice, grammatical form, content, or structure of turn-taking. It is therefore important to categorize types or dimensions of conversation with respect to their predictability. More generally, psycholinguists should not assume that data derived from one form of language use (such as monologue or cooperative task-oriented dialogue) should necessarily be informative about uses of language elsewhere on the dialogic continuum.

CONCLUSIONS: ALIGNMENT AND CONVERSATIONAL SUCCESS

Conversational interactions are remarkably successful given their enormous complexity. Our explanation of how this can be has two parts. In previous publications, we proposed that such success occurred because interlocutors align their linguistic representations (words, grammar, meaning, etc.) and that such alignment leads to alignment of their situation models in a largely automatic manner (Garrod & Pickering, 2004; Pickering & Garrod, 2004). But in addition, there is good evidence that language comprehension involves extensive prediction at different linguistic levels, and that such prediction makes use of the language production system (Pickering & Garrod, 2007). Most of the evidence for such prediction comes from studies of monologue, but in this chapter, we argue that it plays a particularly important role in dialogue. On the one hand, the constant switching between production and comprehension in dialogue is likely to keep the production system active during periods of comprehension. On the other hand, any such prediction is likely to enhance alignment in dialogue, because the process of emulation involves covert imitation. Such emulation is likely to be affected by specific characteristics of the dialogue. Thus, the study of types of dialogue (with respect to their degree of coupling) should affect how the mechanisms of language production and comprehension are used. Most generally, we argue that dialogue provides a clear example of a way in which prediction facilitates social interaction. It therefore shows how it is possible to develop an approach to an aspect of cognition that provides a basis for interaction, and thus helps begin to break down the rigid division between the individual and the social.

REFERENCES

Altmann, G. T. M., & Kamide, Y. (1999). Incremental interpretation at verbs: Restricting the domain of subsequent reference. *Cognition, 73*, 247–264.

Bock, K., Dell, G. S., Chang, F., & Onishi, K. (2007). Structural persistence from language comprehension to language production. *Cognition, 104*, 437–458.

Bavelas, J.B., Coates, L., & Johnson, T. (2000). Listeners as co-narrators. *Journal of Personality and Social Psychology, 79*, 941–952.

Branigan, H. P., Pickering, M. J., & Cleland, A. A. (2000). Syntactic coordination in dialogue. *Cognition, 75*, B13–B25.

Branigan, H. P., Pickering, M. J., McLean, J. F., & Cleland, A. A. (2007). Syntactic alignment and participant role in dialogue. *Cognition, 104*, 163–197.

Brennan, S. E. & Clark, H. H. (1996). Conceptual pacts and lexical choice in conversation. *Journal of Experimental Psychology: Learning, Memory, and Cognition, 22*, 1482–1493.

Clark, H. H. (1996) *Using language*. Cambridge, Cambridge University Press.

De Long, K. A., Urbach, T. P., & Kutas, M. (2005). Probabilistic word pre-activation during comprehension inferred from electrical brain activity. *Nature Neuroscience, 8*, 1117–1121.

De Ruiter, J. P., Mitterer, H., & Enfield, N. J. (2006). Projecting the end of a speaker's turn: A cognitive cornerstone of conversation. *Language, 82*, 515–535.

Desmurget, M. & Grafton, S. (2000). Forward modelling allows feedback control for fast reaching movements. *Trends in Cognitive Sciences, 4*, 423–431.

Deutsch, A. & Bentin, S. (1994). Attention mechanisms mediate the syntactic priming effect in auditory word identification. *Journal of Experimental Psychology: Learning, Memory, and Cognition, 20*, 595–607.

Ehrlich, S. & Rayner, K. (1981). Contextual effects on word perception and eye movements during reading. *Journal of Verbal Learning and Verbal Behavior, 20*, 641–655.

Fadiga, L., Craighero, L., Buccino, G., & Rizzolatti, G. (2002). Speech listening specifically modulates the excitability of tongue muscles: A TMS study. *European Journal of Neuroscience, 15*, 399–402.

Fay, N., Garrod, S. & Carletta, J. (2000). Group discussion as interactive dialogue or as serial monologue: The influence of group size. *Psychological Science*, 11:481–86.

Fodor, J. A., Bever, T. G., & Garrett, M. (1974). *The psychology of language*. New York: McGraw Hill.

Fowler, C. A., Brown, J., Sabadini, L., & Weihing, J. (2003). Rapid access to speech gestures in perception: Evidence from choice and simple response time tasks. *Journal of Memory and Language, 49*, 296–314.

Galantucci, B., Fowler, C. A., & Turvey, M. T. (2006). The motor theory of speech perception reviewed. *Psychonomic Bulletin & Review, 13*, 361–377.

Garrod, S. & Anderson, A. (1987). Saying what you mean in dialogue: A study in conceptual and semantic co-ordination. *Cognition, 27*, 181–218.

Garrod, S. & Pickering, M. J. (2004). Why is conversation so easy? *Trends in Cognitive Sciences, 8*, 8–11.

Giles, H., Coupland, N., & Coupland, J. (1992). Accommodation theory: Communication, context and consequences. In H. Giles, J. Coupland, & N. Coupland (Eds.), *Contexts of accommodation* (pp. 1–68). Cambridge, UK: Cambridge University Press.

Goldinger, S. D. (1998). Echoes of echoes? An episodic theory of lexical access. *Psychological Review, 105*, 251–279.

Grush, R. (2004). The emulation theory of representation: Motor control, imagery, and perception. *Behavioral and Brain Sciences 27*, 377–442.

Harley, T. (2007). *The psychology of language: From data to theory* (3rd ed.). New York: Psychology Press.

Kaiser, E. & Trueswell, J. C. (2004). The role of discourse context in the processing of a flexible word-order language, *Cognition 94*, 113–147.

Kamide, Y., Altmann, G. T. M., & Haywood, S. L. (2003). Prediction and thematic information in incremental sentence processing: Evidence from anticipatory eye movements. *Journal of Memory and Language, 49*, 133–156.

Kamide, Y., Scheepers, C., & Altmann, G. T. M. (2003). Integration of syntactic and semantic information in predictive processing: Cross-linguistic evidence from German and English. *Journal of Psycholinguistic Research, 32*, 37–55.

Knoeferle, P., Crocker, M. W., Scheepers, C., & Pickering, M. J. (2005). The influence of the immediate visual context on incremental thematic role-assignment: Evidence from eye-movements in depicted events. *Cognition, 95*, 95–127.

Krauss, R. M., Garlock, C. M., Bricker, P. D., & McMahon, L. E. (1977). The role of audible and visible back-channel responses in interpersonal communication *Journal of Personality and Social Psychology, 35*, 523–529.

Kutas, M. & Hillyard, S. A. (1984). Brain potentials during reading reflect word expectancy and semantic association. *Nature, 307*, 161–163.

Lau, E., Stroud, C., Plesch, S., & Phillips, C. (2006). The role of structural prediction in rapid syntactic analysis. *Brain and Language, 98*, 74–88.

Levelt, W. J. M. (1989). *Speaking: From intention to articulation*. Cambridge, MA: MIT Press.

Linnell, P. (1998). *Approaching dialogue: Talk, interaction, and contexts in a dialogical perspective*. Benjamins.

Mar, R. A. (2004). The neuropsychology of narrative: Story comprehension, story production and their interrelation. *Neuropsychologia, 42*, 1414–34.

Markman, A. B., & Makin, V. S. (1998). Referential communication and category acquisition. *Journal of Experimental Psychology: General, 127*, 331–354.

Peterson, R. R., Burgess, C., Dell, G. S., & Eberhard, K. A. (2001). Dissociation between syntactic and semantic processing during idiom comprehension. *Journal of Experimental Psychology: Learning, Memory, and Cognition, 27*, 1223–1237.

Pickering, M. J. & Garrod, S. (2004). Toward a mechanistic psychology of dialogue. *Behavioral and Brain Sciences, 27*, 169–225.

Pickering, M. J. & Garrod, S. (2007). Do people use language production to make predictions during comprehension? *Trends in Cognitive Sciences,* 11, 105–110.

Pickering, M. J. & Garrod, S. (2009). Prediction and embodiment in dialogue. *European Journal of Social Psychology, 39*, 1162–1168.

Pulvermüller, F., Huss, M., Kherif, F., Moscoso del Prado Martin, F., Hauk, O., & Shtyrov, Y. (2006). Motor cortex maps articulatory features of speech sounds. *Proceedings of the National Academy of Sciences, 103*, 7865–7870.

Sacks, H., Schegloff, E.A., & Jerrerson, G. (1974). A Simplest systematics for the organization of turn-taking for conversation. *Language, 50*, 696–735.
Schober, M. F. & Clark, H. H. (1989). Understanding by addressees and overhearers. *Cognitive Psychology, 21*, 211–232.
Schwanenflugel, P. J. & Shoben, E. J. (1985). The influence of sentence constraint on the scope of facilitation for upcoming words. *Journal of Memory and Language, 24*, 232–252.
Staub, A. & Clifton, C., Jr (2006). Syntactic prediction in language comprehension: Evidence from *either …or. Journal of Experimental Psychology: Learning Memory and Cognition. 32*, 425–436.
Tannen, D. (1989). C., *Talking voices: Repetition, dialogue, and imagery in conversational discourse*. Cambridge, UK: Cambridge University Press.
ten Bosch, L., Oostdijk, N., & de Ruiter, J. P. (2004). Durational aspects of turn-taking in spontaneous face-to-face and telephone dialogues. In P. Sojka, I. Kopeček, & K. Pala (Eds.), *Text, speech, and dialogue* (Vol. 3206/2004, pp. 563–570). Berlin: Springer-Verlag.
Van Berkum, J. J. A., Brown, C. M., Zwitserlood, P., Kooijman, V., & Hagoort, P. (2005). Anticipating upcoming words in discourse: Evidence from ERPs and reading times. *Journal of Experimental Psychology: Learning, Memory, and Cognition, 31*, 443–467.
Vissers, C. T., Chwilla, D. J., & Kolk, H. H. (2006). Monitoring in language perception: The effect of misspellings of words in highly constrained sentences. *Brain Research, 1106*, 150–163.
Watkins, K. & Paus, T. (2004). Modulation of motor excitability during speech perception: The role of Broca's area. *Journal of Cognitive Neuroscience, 16*, 978–987.
Watkins, K., Strafella, A. P., & Paus, T. (2003). Seeing and hearing speech excites the motor system involved in speech production. *Neuropsychologia, 41*, 989–994.
Weber, A., Grice, M., & Crocker, M. W. (2006). The role of prosody in the interpretation of structural ambiguities: A study of anticipatory eye movements. *Cognition, 99*, B63–B72.
Wicha, N. Y. Y., Moreno, E. M., & Kutas, M. (2004). Anticipating words and their gender: An event-related brain potential study of semantic integration, gender expectancy and gender agreement in Spanish sentence reading. *Journal of Cognitive Neuroscience, 16*, 1272–1288.
Wilson, S. M., Saygin, A.P., Sereno, M.I., & Iacoboni, M. (2004). Listening to speech activates motor areas involved in speech production. *Nature Neuroscience*, 7, 701–702.
Wilson, M. & Wilson, T. P. (2005). An oscillator model of the timing of turn-taking. *Psychological Bulletin & Review, 12*, 957–968.
Wolpert, D. M. & Flanagan, J. R. (2001). Motor prediction, *Current Biology*, 11, 729–732.
Wright, B. & Garrett, M. F. (1984). Lexical decision in sentences: Effects of syntactic structure. *Memory & Cognition, 12*, 31–45.
Zwaan, R. A. & Radvansky, G. A. (1998). Situation models in language comprehension and memory. *Psychological Bulletin, 123*, 162–185.

10

Situated Sociality and Cultural Dynamics
A Puzzle of Necessary Dependency and Perceived Dissociation

YOSHIHISA KASHIMA AND BOYKA BRATANOVA

Humans are unique among primates in their ability to form, maintain, and transform a large-scale collective. We are capable of living generally peacefully in a very large collective that consists not only of tens and hundreds, but of thousands and millions of individuals who do not, and cannot, have face-to-face direct interaction with each other. What enables us to have this uniquely human sociality? If Dunbar's (1996) conjecture is right and the human neocortex has evolved to sustain groups of the size around 150, it is an evolutionary puzzle and feat that humans are capable of sustaining much larger groups. It is all the more remarkable because we appear to do so without constant reminders to maintain the fabric of such large-scale collectives. To be sure, large-scale collectives such as nation states typically enshrine institutionalized reminders in symbolic forms like national flags, national ceremonies, and commemorations of the war dead (e.g., Connerton, 1989; Wertsch, 2002). These subtle and mundane forms of nationalism may help to form and maintain the citizens' social identification with their countries (e.g., Billig, 1995). Yet, people's perceptions about their societies appear to be highly dissociated from the experiences of their everyday circumstances and routinized activities, as we will discuss later. Even in the absence of our conscious efforts to maintain our large-scale society and even in the face of our psychological detachment from it, our mundane social activities appear to be able to sustain the large-scale collective. How is this possible?

Part of an answer to this question lies in the human capacity to possess a dynamically evolving culture. No consideration of the interface between the individual and the social in humans can afford to overlook the significance of the cultural and its role in the macro-level social dynamics. Although culture is often understood in psychology as an explanatory mechanism for group differences (e.g., Americans and Japanese are different from each other because their cultures are different), culture can be regarded as a collection of socially transmitted and distributed information (e.g., Chiu & Hong, 2006; Kashima, 2000a). As such, cultural information is contrasted to genetic information, and its production and reproduction can be construed as dynamic processes (e.g., Kashima, 2000a). We will draw on this line of thinking to shed light on the twin questions that we alluded to in the first paragraph: (1) why people cognitively dissociate their situated sociality and their large-scale society, and (2) how people are able to maintain a large-scale society despite the cognitive dissociation of the micro-level situated sociality and the macro-level sociocultural dynamics.

First, we will discuss the cognitive dissociation between the micro- and macro-level sociality among people. In particular, we will build on the phenomena of pluralistic ignorance (e.g., Miller & McFarland, 1987) and impersonal impact (e.g., Tyler & Cook, 1984) to argue that people often perceive their large-scale collectives as something remote and separate from the spheres of their routinized mundane activities that involve themselves and their close others. Second, we will introduce a broad metatheory of culture called *neo-diffusionism* and discuss its variants, which regard the transmission of cultural information as a critical mechanism in cultural dynamics. Third, we will describe the *grounding model of cultural transmission* as a special instance of neo-diffusionist theorizing. This model characterizes cultural transmission as *situated joint activities* characterized by coordinated actions among concrete actors in concrete contexts. Finally, we will elaborate on this model's theoretical implications. In particular, we will show how the grounding model points to one possible explanation of the cognitive micro–macro dissociation (the first question) and to one mechanism of macro-level social integration (the second question).

MICRO-SITUATED SOCIALITY AND MACRO CULTURAL DYNAMICS: NECESSARY DEPENDENCY AND PERCEIVED DISSOCIATION

Any macro-level state of affairs in a large-scale collective must emerge from micro-level situated social interactions among its members (Figure 10.1). Macro cultural dynamics is no exception. By macro cultural dynamics, we mean the formation, maintenance, and transformation of culture over time. This includes the distribution of cultural information—broadly including any cultural ideas and practices—in a population and its change over time. Cultural dynamics emerge out of micro situated sociality. It involves concrete individuals and their everyday interactions as part of their routinized mundane activities in their concrete circumstances—people like yourself and others whom you know well, and your interactions with your family at home, your colleagues at work, and even the shop owner from whom you buy your newspaper every day. It is one's local social world with which one is familiar and the kind of social reality that gives one a sense of solidity about one's world and continuity. Obviously, in modern

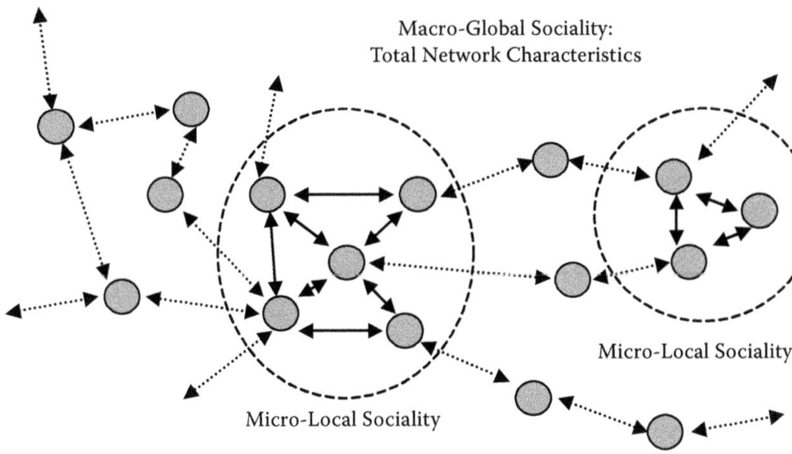

Figure 10.1 Social network representations of micro-sociality and macro-sociality.

society, its political, legal, and economic institutions are at work, and these institutions contribute to the macro-level social phenomena. Yet, they too are carried out by individuals in interaction with others in the society. Thus, the global macro-level cultural dynamics within a large-scale collective is necessarily dependent on the local micro-level situated sociality (e.g., Giddens, 1984; see Kashima, 2000a).

Nonetheless, it is impossible for individual human cognition to grasp the vast totality of the large-scale collective and the intricate complexity of its global dynamics. In fact, there is evidence to suggest that an individual's cognition about a large-scale collective is highly dissociated from his or her own personal circumstances. *Pluralistic ignorance* is an instance of the cognitive micro–macro dissociation. People's perceptions of their group's typical or majority opinions about an issue often diverge from their own opinion or close others' opinions about the same issue (Miller & McFarland, 1987; for a review, see Miller, Monin, & Prentice, 2000). For instance, Prentice and Miller (1993) reported that Princeton undergraduates thought that the average student was fairly comfortable about alcohol use, but expressed slight personal discomfort. Despite most students' personal concerns about drinking on campus, they thought the large-scale collective to which they belonged had a norm of heavy drinking.

One may imagine that mass media could reduce the micro–macro dissociation by providing accurate information about the macro-level distribution of the opinions and behaviors. However, mass media appear to reinforce the cognitive dissociation between micro and macro sociality. For instance, mass media reports affect people's perceptions of risk at the macro-collective level, but not at the personal level. Tyler and Cook (1984) called it mass media's *impersonal impact*. In one of their experiments, these researchers gave mass media reports about alcohol-related social problems (e.g., drunk driving) to some, but not to others, and examined their perceived risk at the societal and personal levels. They found a significant increase in societal risk perception, but not in personal risk perception among those who were exposed to the mass media release. In the meantime, no change was observed in those who were not exposed to the mass media release. In other words, mass media information about the macro-level societal process affects people's views about the macro-level sociality but may not impact on their perceptions about their own local sociality.

These phenomena suggest that people form separate cognitive representations about micro-sociality and macro-sociality. That is, their cognitive representations of their large-scale collective's circumstances including the distribution of opinions and behaviors are distinguished and separated from their cognitive representations about their local circumstances including their own and their close others' behaviors and opinions. The robustness and pervasiveness of pluralistic ignorance suggest that people tend to regard their micro-sociality as unique and different from the macro-sociality such as the norm of their large-scale group. People tend to be ignorant of the typicality of their own circumstances. Then why do they develop such a micro–macro cognitive dissociation despite the obvious dependency of the macro-sociality on the micro-sociality? We suggest that there is a view of culture that can shed light on this puzzle.

NEO-DIFFUSIONIST METATHEORY

Neo-diffusionism (Kashima, Peters, & Whelan, 2008) is a contemporary reincarnation of diffusionism as a culture theory which enjoyed a brief period of popularity in early 20th century anthropology. It viewed culture as consisting of socially transmitted, nongenetic information, broadly construed as a collection of ideas and concepts, beliefs and knowledge, skills and practices, intricate artifacts and complex rituals. Perhaps one of the clearest, if zealous, declaration was made by G. Elliot Smith, a distinguished physical anthropologist of his day:

> Diffusion of culture is the fundamental process of all human activities. All that every individual knows has been derived from the society in which he [sic] lives, or rather from his own reaction to the influences around him. He acquires knowledge from others: but what particular information he accepts and assimilates and how he transforms and uses it is his own affair. The fundamental fact is that in virtue of his distinctively human type of brain, learning from his fellows is the essential factor in his behaviour. (Smith, 1932, pp. 11–12)

His version of diffusionism was quickly discredited because of his extreme stance that there was only one cultural center, namely, the Valley of the Nile, from which all human cultural information originated (Kuklick, 1991). While repudiating Smith's overenthusiasm, Lowie (1937) favorably described a somewhat different version of diffusionism by German ethnologists, Graebner and Schmidt, according to which cultural information originated not in a single place, but in multiple cultural centers, and spread to other peoples as configurations of cultural artifacts and practices.

Neo-diffusionism takes as a starting point the central tenet of the original diffusionism: Cultural information is socially transmitted, and the investigation of cultural transmission process is critical to an understanding of culture. However, it differs significantly from the original diffusionism in its specification of the *process* of cultural transmission.

Generally, it can be characterized by the following set of common assumptions:

1. There exists a unit of cultural meaning (we will use the term cultural meaning unit, or CMU, in the following).
2. A CMU is instantiated in a material form that can be communicated from a sender to a receiver.
3. The receiver learns (or relearns if the receiver has already learned it before) a CMU via a communicated form.
4. The distribution of a CMU within a population results in this population's group characteristics.

CMUs can be any socially transmitted, nongenetic information. Various neo-diffusionist theorists have regarded as CMUs anything from instructions to construct an origami boat (Dawkins, 1999) and various versions of *Little Red Riding Hood* (Sperber, 1996) to the behavioral practice to compete or cooperate (e.g., Boyd & Richerson, 2005) and the idea of God (Dawkins, 1976).

There are several variants of neo-diffusionist theories, which differ in terms of the processes assumed for cultural information transmission. One class of neo-diffusionist theories may be called *Universal Darwinism*, which assumes Darwinian processes of cultural transmission (e.g., Boyd & Richerson, 1985; Campbell, 1975; Cavalli-Sforza & Feldman, 1981; Dawkins, 1976, 1999). According to this view, cultural dynamics follow the same basic processes as genetic dynamics. There exists some variation in CMUs in population, and selective pressures operate, so that some CMUs become more or less prevalent in a population. In other words, it is the processes of random variation, natural selection, and selective retention operating on CMUs that are responsible for the trajectories of macro-level cultural dynamics.

However, within the Universal Darwinian camp, theorists differ in terms of the unit on which natural selection operates. Dawkins's (1976) meme theory assumes that a CMU is a unit of natural selection. He calls a CMU a meme, a cultural analogue of a gene, which is a set of instructions to make certain cultural information manifest in behavior or artifacts. For instance, instructions or procedural knowledge to construct an origami junk boat is a meme, though any particular junk boat is not a meme itself, but a phenotype of the meme. In this theory, a meme is a replicator (a la selfish genes), and selective pressures operate on this CMU. Just as genes that fail to replicate will disappear from a gene pool (a set of genes carried by a population of organisms), CMUs that fail to replicate, or fail to be communicated and learned, will disappear from a meme pool.

In contrast, according to Boyd and Richerson (2005), it is groups carrying the CMUs, but not CMUs per se, that are under selective pressure. They argue that CMUs are too labile to be replicators, but groups may be sufficiently distinct and enduring for natural selection to operate. Following Campbell (1975), they argued that group selection occurs when (1) there are cultural differences among groups, (2) these differences affect the persistence or proliferation of groups, and (3) these differences are transmitted through time. Population genetics has all but ruled out group selection as a basis of biological evolution. This is because for a group-benefiting gene to increase its prevalence within a group, the group benefit must outweigh the individual cost by a very large magnitude—the magnitude so large that it is unlikely to occur in the natural environment. However, Boyd and Richerson (2005) argued that cultural evolution may occur on the basis of group selection for several reasons. First, any CMU can be maintained within a group by punishing those who perform an action that is contrary to the CMU. If people in a group are willing to dispense punishment voluntarily to those who violate a CMU despite some cost to themselves, this can sustain the prevalence of the CMU that benefits the group. Second, people may behave by conformity in accordance with a CMU that is prevalent in a group. There is a well-known general tendency for people to conform to a prevalent norm. Third, intergroup competition may operate so that groups with group-harming CMUs go extinct, but group-benefiting CMUs survive and prosper in the long run. Fourth, groups may acquire by imitation group-benefiting CMUs from neighboring groups. All in all, these intragroup and intergroup processes could ensure the maintenance of group-benefiting CMUs.

To summarize briefly, the Universal Darwinian school of neo-diffusionism regards CMUs as produced and reproduced through random variation, natural selection, and social transmission. Meme theory suggests those CMUs that fail to be remembered and communicated for whatever reason go extinct. In this view, the memorability and communicability of CMUs become a critical determinant of their cultural prevalence and persistence. To put it simply, any CMUs that are easy to remember and to communicate are likely to become prevalent. By contrast, group selection theory suggests that CMUs that benefit groups may be reproduced more and become more prevalent. In this view, CMUs that help groups maintain themselves and adapt to their environment are likely to become more prevalent. Either way, it is the process of adaptation that determines the prevalence of CMUs in a population. In this sense, the Universal Darwinism is a combination of diffusionism and adaptationism in the modern discourse of culture theory.

In contrast, a second class of neo-diffusionist theories takes cultural evolutionary processes to be non-Darwinian. Sperber (1996) likens cultural transmission to epidemiological processes of contagion. Just as germs spread by contagion, CMUs spread by communication. He regards this process not so much as replication like meme theory, but as *transformation*. When a CMU is transmitted from a sender to a receiver, it is more likely modified and transformed than replicated; a resultant CMU may resemble the original, but not an exact copy. In this regard, Sperber and Boyd and Richerson are in broad agreement in their opposition to meme theory. However, Sperber sees the trajectory of successive CMU transformations as not necessarily characterized by the process of selection. According to him, the transmission of a CMU does not result in all or none adoption or rejection of a CMU, but potentially involves a change and innovation by the individual receiver, and eventually tending toward attractors in a conceptual space. Therefore, in Sperber's framework, cultural transmission may vary from exact replication to complete innovation.

Clearly, there are a number of theoretical ambiguities about the neo-diffusionist metatheoretical framework. To begin, it has often been criticized that it lacks a clear definition of a CMU. To this criticism, however, the following defense may be possible. Darwin's evolutionary theory was developed without a clear definition and knowledge of what was transmitted. It was not until Mendelian genetics and Darwinian natural selection were integrated to formulate the modern synthesis (Huxley, 1942/1963) that the contemporary evolutionary biology came into being. Likewise, a Darwinian theory of cultural evolution may be constructed, which regards cultural evolution as resulting from random variation and natural selection of CMUs without a clear definition of what constitutes a CMU.

Also unclear is what constitutes a population, or a group of individuals, who carry the CMUs. Cultural information travels quite freely across what have conventionally been regarded as cultural borders especially in the contemporary world of globalization (e.g., Hermans & Kempen, 1998). In this perspective, it becomes difficult to speak about a group's culture. Any given group of people is likely to carry both indigenous and exogenous cultural information—information that originated in the group in the past and was transmitted across generations and information that this group has acquired and adopted from other groups over time. How many generations does a CMU need to be transmitted in the group for it to be called part of the group's culture? Where should one draw a boundary?

CULTURAL TRANSMISSION AS SITUATED JOINT ACTIVITY

Neo-diffusionism as it stands is best construed as a way of thinking, a framework, or an approach, rather than a grand theory of cultural evolution as envisaged by the 19th-century cultural evolutionists like Spencer and others. What this perspective does is to highlight the importance of the process of *cultural transmission* in cultural dynamics. That is, cultural information must be socially transmitted between people in order for cultural formation, maintenance, and transformation to occur. Then, a critical question is how senders transmit (intentionally or unintentionally as an unintended consequence of other intentional actions) cultural information to receivers and how receivers respond to it.

One perspective in cultural psychology highlights situated social interaction as a central locus of cultural transmission. According to a Vygotsky-inspired observation, cultural transmission typically occurs as part of a *joint activity* in a concrete situation (e.g., Cole, 1996; Rogoff, 2003). By joint activity, we mean a fuzzy category of goal-defined (i.e., participants have a shared understanding of what they are trying to achieve), temporally and spatially bounded events (having a starting point and an end point, and happening at a particular physical location) that involve certain types of objects and settings, and two or more participants. Conferences, dinner parties, and lectures are all examples of joint activities. The basic insight here is that cultural information is transmitted as part of people's everyday social activities—as they interact with each other for their routinized daily events, they end up transmitting various cultural information to each other. Although this perspective is usually linked to children's cultural learning from parents and other adults, or what Cavalli-Sforza and Feldman (1981) called vertical and oblique cultural transmission, it is generalizable to horizontal cultural transmission as well, where cultural information is transmitted among individuals of the same generation (e.g., Wertsch, 1991).

According to this view, cultural transmission is often *incidental* and *instance-based*. Namely, people are not explicitly taught how to behave, but rather cultural information is acquired through participation in their joint activities as an incidental side effect of their participation. In addition, people are not given a general rule about how to behave, but experience and observe behavioral instances, and a cultural practice needs to be acquired as a generalization from those numerous instances.

A concrete example may help to illustrate these points. Imagine that you are in a country where English is spoken, but its culture is different from yours. You have no idea about how social power and status differences are handled in this culture, although attitudes to power and status hierarchy are one of the most critical dimensions on which cultures vary (e.g., Hofstede, 2001). Suppose that you and Mr. B enter Mr. A's room to have a conversation. This joint activity may begin with a simple joint activity to sit together for a conversation. Imagine the following exchange:

1. A: Sit down. [to you and Mr. B with a wave of his hand to chairs]
   B: Yes, sir. [B then sits down in a chair]

This is a particular episode of social interaction among concrete individuals in a concrete situation. Based on this, a cultural practice about power and status differences may be learned. That is, you learn that a person of higher status (A) has a much greater authority than a person of lower status (B) in this country than what you are used to.

It is important to note that much of the utterances in this interaction can be construed as speech acts (Austin, 1962). According to a general theory of speech act, the meaning of an utterance like A's can be understood as A's intention. This interpretation has become widely accepted after Grice's (1957) analysis, although it was initially somewhat contentious. More formally following Schiffer (1972) and Strawson (1964), A's intention can be analyzed as follows:

To mean something by an utterance, x, A must intend:

a. A's utterance of x to produce a certain response r in a certain audience B.
b. B to recognize A's intention (a).
c. B's recognition of A's intention (a) to function as at least part of A's reason for A's response r, where r is B's action of sitting down.

In the interaction illustrated by Exchange 1, B may infer A's intention to *order* B to sit down, and carry out the action, r, of sitting down.[1] As an observer and participant in this joint activity, you may also infer A's intention just like B did, and sit down in another chair, or perhaps simultaneously infer A's intention with the help of B's action and *imitate* B's action. Either way, you would probably infer that A's intention was to order you and B to sit down. You would then infer that B's intention was to *obey* the order. In this joint activity, a particular instance (or a token) of cultural information about social hierarchy was transmitted to you through your inference about the interactants' intentions, and you would have stored in memory an episode of this joint activity.

It is easy to see that A's utterance is critical in your acquisition of cultural information about social hierarchy in this example. However, the critical role of B's utterance may be easily overlooked. It is in fact both A's and B's actions and therefore their joint activity that help you disambiguate the cultural information about social hierarchy. To see this, imagine three other situations similar to Exchange 1 earlier, where A's utterance and nonverbal behavior are identical, but in response to A, B makes three different utterances:

2. Okay.
3. Thanks.
4. Oh, that's a good idea!

In the case of "Okay" as in Exchange 2, you may infer that A's intention is not to *order*, but to *request* B and you to sit down. This is because you may think B, as a well-functioning adult in this culture, would be able to infer A's intention correctly. In other words, you infer A's intention on the basis of B's utterance in response to A's utterance. Similarly, in Exchange 3, you may infer A's intention to *offer* you and B seats, and in Exchange 4, to *advise* you and B to sit down. It is also possible that A may have no clear intention at all as to whether he is ordering, requesting, offering, or advising. But, B's response may have signaled a certain construal of A's intention. In the absence of A's further response or A's backchannel behavior to indicate B's acceptance of A's construal, you and B may infer A's intention as B presented in his response.

In any case, in Searle's (1976) classification of speech acts, to order, to request, to offer, or to advise, are all *directives* in which A attempts to get you and B to do something. But, they imply different degrees of force and A's power distance from you and B. The cultural information about power distance transmitted to you depends on B's uptake of A's utterance; Exchange 1 is probably most distant, and Exchange 3 or 4 is the least distant. In the absence of B's response, A's utterance alone is insufficient to disambiguate the cultural meaning of A's and B's joint activity.

So far, we have used rather sterile and scripted episodes of social interaction to illustrate the properties of cultural transmission. However, it should be obvious that actual episodes of social interaction are likely to be far messier and fraught with mistakes and ambiguities. The interactants within social interaction episodes often coordinate their actions so as to collaboratively disambiguate each other's intention. To illustrate this, imagine the following sequel to Exchange 1:

5. A: Sit down.
   B: Yes, sir.
   A: Well, no, I don't mean that! *Please* have a seat here.

In this instance, A's speech act may be said to have *misfired* (Austin, 1962). B has misunderstood A's intention, and B's uptake is corrected by A, and A makes another utterance that is designed to communicate A's intention to request, rather than to order, you and B to sit down.

One interpretation of this exchange is the following. A took B's utterance to be evidence that B mistook A's intention, and thus made another utterance to present his preferred intended meaning. This is an instance of other-initiated self-repair (Schegloff, Jefferson, & Sacks, 1977). In everyday conversations, this and other types of repairs are prevalent. Alternatively, it can be interpreted slightly differently. B may have thought A's action signaled too great a power distance, and designed his utterance so as to signal his thought that A's action placed himself too far above B in the social hierarchy. A then may have inferred B's intention in this way, and designed a repairing utterance, so as to provide evidence that A has understood B's intention. Here, A is not merely a passive user of information, but an active provider of it. Note that the reason why A's utterance misfired in this instance is different from the previous case. It misfired because an appropriate social institutional basis was absent (i.e., A indeed occupies a status higher than B's within their social institution, or its felicity condition is not satisfied) or because B believes that an appropriate social institutional basis is absent, A's utterance may not have the intended effect.

These analyses of Exchange 5 highlight a highly coordinated, collaborative, and often negotiated nature of inferences about interactants' intentions and therefore instances of cultural transmission. H. H. Clark (1996) called this kind of collaborative establishment of a shared understanding of speakers' intentions *grounding*.

According to Clark, to ground an utterance is to establish its mutual understanding as part of *common ground* well enough for current purposes (H. H. Clark, 1996, p. 221), where common ground is understood as below:

> Proposition p is common ground for members of a group if and only if:
> (i) the members of the group have information that p and that i.

For the present purpose, it suffices to say that common ground can be understood as a set of information that is common knowledge among a set of individuals (e.g., A, B, and you) although there is a complex discussion about its philosophical and formal adequacy.[1] Grounding is the interactants' *joint activity to align their individual representations about the joint activity in which they are engaged* to tacitly establish a shared understanding of the activity and add this shared understanding to the common ground. Thus, as joint activities continue, shared understandings are grounded to common ground.

According to Clark's analysis of common ground, the social interaction episodes like Exchanges 1 to 5 ground at least two kinds of information: (a) the proposition p that was grounded, and (b) the group for which the proposition p was grounded. In the case of (5), p is A's intention to request you and B to do things, and the group is a collection of individuals—A, B, and you. In addition, Pickering and Garrod (2004) suggested that less explicit, potentially nonpropositional information such as choice of words, grammatical rules, and the like (possibly nonverbal behavioral patterns) may also be implicitly grounded. Thus, as a consequence of the coordinated grounding such as Exchange 5, you as a cultural learner learn a particular instance of explicit and implicit cultural practice of status differentiation that applies to the group that consists of A, B, and yourself. This group may be said to be *indexically defined* in that it is defined by those who are present then and there at the time of the grounding of the cultural information. Common ground is in a way a theoretical fiction. Although we may say that the individuals involved in the grounding activity "share" the common ground, their individual representations of the common ground are most likely different from each other. The individuals' representations are similar to the extent sufficient for the current purpose.

Grounding produces psychological effects in the sender and receiver of cultural information. To begin, the receiver acquires an instance of the cultural information. In addition, the sender too may gain some verification of their cultural competence. Higgins and Rholes's (1978) classical research on saying is believing (SIB) speaks to this. In the SIB paradigm, a sender is given ambiguous information about a target person, which may be positively or negatively interpreted (e.g., shooting the Colorado rapids—adventurous or reckless). The sender's task then is to describe the target to a receiver, so that the receiver can identify the target accurately among a number of possible candidates. The receiver is said to like the target in one condition and to dislike the target in the other condition. The sender typically tunes his or her description to the receiver's attitude—positively for the receiver who likes and negatively for the receiver who dislikes the target, and the sender's later recall of the original information is biased in the direction of the communication. When the sender feels he or she has established a mutual understanding with the receiver about the target, it strengthens his or her views about the target (e.g., Echterhoff, Higgins, & Groll, 2005).

In summary, cultural learning is instance based and often incidental to a joint activity between the sender of the cultural information and its receiver/learner. It is a clear example of socially situated cognition (E. R. Smith & Semin, 2004). The encoding of cultural information requires some concept of intentional agency—the idea that the sender is a goal-directed agent with the capacity to hold an intention, so that the learner can construe the sender's intention. However, the sender's intention is not just inferred, but clarified and grounded through coordinated actions to establish a shared understanding of the sender's intention. Furthermore, for the speech act to have an intended social psychological effect, there needs to be an appropriate social institutional basis (or at least a belief in the appropriate social institutional basis). Thus grounded, the particular instance of cultural practice is in the common ground for this particular interaction episode.

However, it is important to recognize some of the inevitable consequences of this type of cultural transmission process. One consequence is that cultural transmission can never be perfect. Even if a shared understanding is obtained and grounded to the interactants' common ground, one interactant's encoding of this common ground is necessarily different from others'. Although the interactants are likely to have encoded some shared aspect of interaction episode, each is likely to have a unique understanding of the interaction episode because they are bound to have had different personal experience, knowledge, and skills. In this sense, this type of cultural transmission process necessarily produces *distributed cognition* (Hutchins, 1995), that is, different people have different types of cultural information, and perhaps little cultural information is completely shared among all people in a cultural group.

The other consequence is that cultural information transmitted this way contains cultural information about only one particular episode and is known to be applicable only for the indexically defined group of people (i.e., those who are then and there in that particular episode of cultural transmission). They need to generalize this particular instance of cultural information to construct a general cultural representation that is seen to be applicable to other relevant contexts. According to Kashima, Woolcock, and Kashima (2000), such generalization can occur as a natural consequence of parallel-distributed information processing mechanisms. They showed that the process of group impression formation, the process by which an individual forms an impression of a group based on concrete instances of social interaction episodes involving members of the group, can be conceptualized as instance-based acquisition of context-general representations. The acquisition of context-general cultural information, which is applicable to a cultural group as a whole, is akin to instance-based group impression formation. It is somewhat different in that, in a typical impression formation situation, the individual cognizer is construed as a passive observer and not a member of the target group, whereas the cultural learner is an active participant-observer in cultural learning and also typically a member of the cultural group. Clearly, the active involvement of the cultural learner's self is a significant issue, which requires careful consideration about embodiment and imitative learning. Nonetheless, the memory mechanism specified in Kashima et al. (2000) can handle instance-based generalization about the cultural learner's own large-scale in-group as well.

More specifically, generalization of a particular episode must occur along three dimensions—temporal, spatial, and social—to construct a generalized cultural representation (Kashima, Klein, & Clark, 2007). First, the individual cultural learner must learn that the instance of cultural information is relevant for the same set of people (i.e., indexically defined set) in the same place at a different point in time (temporal generalization). It involves only a repetition of the same instance and may be regarded simply as evidence of learning. Second, the individual cultural learner must learn that the instance is relevant for the same set of people in a different place at a different point in time (spatial generalization). When temporal and spatial generalization is attained, this cultural information becomes part of the cultural learner's representation of the personal common ground (H. H. Clark, 1996) of this set of people involved in the cultural transmission. Finally, the cultural learner must learn that the instance of cultural information is relevant for not only the same set of people, but also for others like them, in a different place at a different point in time (social generalization). Cultural information that is temporally, spatially, and socially generalized is the cultural learner's representation of Clark's (1996) communal common ground.

Thus, after participating in a large number of social interaction episodes, cultural learners can acquire generalized cultural representations without receiving explicit teaching, but as an incidental side effect of participation in those joint activities. Obviously, this is not the only way cultural information is transmitted and acquired. It is also possible that some cultural learning may be teaching based, that is, designed to intentionally teach a generalized cultural rule. Norbert Elias's (2000) characterization of the history and evolution of etiquette in Europe points to the importance of such processes, and it would be an intriguing empirical question how instance-based and teaching-based cultural learning interact to effect cultural dynamics.

From Context-Specific to Generalized Common Ground

So far, we have sketched out the kind of properties that are needed for a model about how an individual may acquire context-specific cultural information from concrete instances of social interaction and develop more context-general cultural representations. In this section, we consider the trajectory of transmission of generalized cultural representations from the individual. Two types of cultural transmission seem possible: one in which cultural information is transmitted from one person to multiple others, and the other in which it is transmitted from one person to another, who in turn transmits it to another (see Figure 10.2). Bartlett (1932) called experimental designs that simulate these patterns the methods of repeated reproduction and serial reproduction, respectively. We will outline these pathways of cultural transmission in turn.

Parallel Reproduction

This is a situation in which a sender is transmitting cultural information that the sender holds to many others. One of the psychological functions of this activity is, knowingly or unknowingly, to test the generalizability of the cultural information with those others he or she is interacting with. The present perspective suggests that the sender transmits the cultural information that he or she learned in one context to other receivers in other contexts to the extent that the sender socially generalizes the cultural information. If the cultural information is believed to be generalizable, and therefore relevant not only in the specific context where it was acquired, but also in other contexts that involve other people, then it should be transmitted in those other contexts as well. As people engage in further cultural transmission, and unless the cultural information is conclusively falsified for the sender, it is likely to continue to be transmitted.

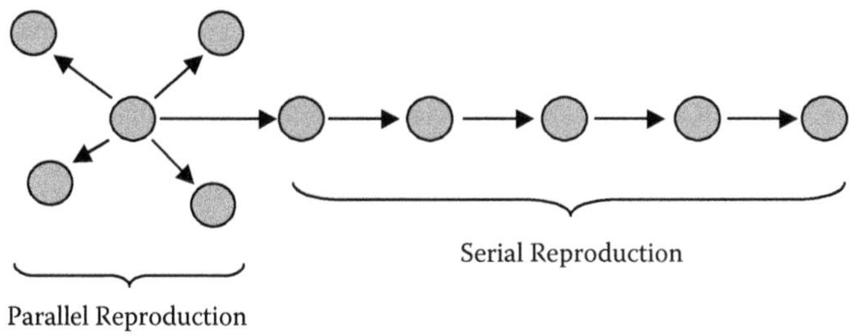

Figure 10.2 Social network representations of repeated and serial reproduction methods.

Bartlett's (1932) method of repeated reproduction can be modified to examine this process. Typically in his experimental paradigm, some complex information is given to a person, who is asked to reproduce it multiple times to the experimenter. In a recent work, Bratanova (2008) modified this paradigm slightly and combined it with Higgins and Rholes's (1978) SIB paradigm (i.e., the sender's grounding of information with a receiver biases his or her memory in the direction of the grounded information) to examine stereotype formation as a cultural transmission process. Like Hausmann, Levine, and Higgins (2008), Bratanova found the SIB effect for a group target; the sender's memory of information about a group was biased in accordance with his or her grounded communication with the first receiver. Furthermore, the bias was stronger when the sender more strongly trusted the receiver as a source of information about the social reality (epistemic trust). The presence of the SIB bias was taken as evidence of stereotype formation. That is, the sender's perception about the target group was believed to have been grounded with the first receiver, and therefore the stereotype as cultural information was formed.

In Bratanova's studies, after the establishment of the SIB effect with the first receiver, the sender was asked to transmit his or her group impression to other receivers who belonged to the same in-group. She found that the sender tended to generalize from the first receiver and to transmit the same stereotype to a second and third receiver, suggesting that the sender was socially generalizing the cultural information about the shared stereotype to others. If this involved the sender's generalization of his or her cultural information from the experience with the first receiver to other receivers, this tendency should be stronger to the extent that the sender believes the same stereotype is shared within the group to which these receivers belong. Consistent with this reasoning, the tendency to repeatedly reproduce the stereotype to second and third receivers was stronger when the sender believed that the group members shared the same stereotype than when the sender did not.

Consistent with the current perspective, Bratanova's findings suggest that the establishment of common ground with specific others in a particular context (i.e., context-specific common ground) is quite different from generalizing it to a large-scale collective when the holder of cultural information does not have direct interaction experience and ground the cultural information with all of its members (i.e., generalized common ground or communal common ground). This finding is consistent with Garrod and Doherty's (1994) finding about differences between dyadic (specific) and group-based (generalized) communication. When two individuals engaged in a joint activity that required verbal communication to coordinate their actions, their communication styles converged to each other. However, when the same people continued to perform the same task (dyadic specific), their communication styles changed over time. In contrast, when two individuals who engaged in the task were drawn from a larger pool of people (group-based generalized), one common style emerged as a group norm and did not change over time.

Also corresponding with the distinction between context-specific and generalized common ground, research on social self has identified relational and collective self (e.g., Brewer & Gardner, 1996; Kashima et al., 1995). Relational self is that aspect of self-concept whose definition is primarily based on one's particular relationships with others (context specific), whereas collective self is the aspect of self-concept defined by one's social category membership (generalized). It may be the case that relational self reflects the self-relevant aspect of the context-specific social interaction episodes, and collective self, the generalization based on the interaction episodes as a member of a large-scale collective. It would be a useful program of research to further examine the coevolution of people's relational self-concept and their perceptions of specific others, as well as their collective self-concepts and their conceptions of large-scale collectives.

Serial Reproduction

The other trajectory of cultural transmission is the diffusion of cultural information from one sender to a receiver, who in turn transmits it to another receiver, and so on in a communication chain. Bartlett's (1932) method of serial reproduction simulates this process. Thompson, Judd, and Park (2000) used this method to examine the diffusion of cultural information. In this experiment, a first generation of three people received some information about a group, with more information consistent with a certain personality characteristic (e.g., sociable) than information contrary to the characteristic (e.g., shy). Each of the three people then wrote three notes to communicate their impressions of the group to others who knew nothing about it. This second generation of three then received the three notes from the first generation of three and formed their impressions; they then transmitted their impressions to a third generation in the same manner. Thompson et al. found that the communicators' impressions of the group became more extreme and more homogeneous as the information was passed on from one generation to next. This process appears to produce a shared stereotype about the group.

Once cultural information like group stereotypes spreads to a large enough number of people, this may establish generalized common ground. People are likely not only to share the cultural information, but also to believe that they do. After all, they receive similar cultural information from a number of disparate sources, and thus socially generalize their context-specific common ground to a large-scale collective as a whole.

What happens when new cultural information is transmitted against some existing common ground? The semiotic relationship between the new cultural information and the existing common ground plays a significant role in the spread of the new information. Again, the method of serial reproduction has been used to examine this process. In one of the first uses of this experimental paradigm, Bartlett had Cambridge students read an Amerindian story, *War of the Ghosts*, and reproduce it from memory and transmit its reproductions in communication chains. He found that an unfamiliar element (e.g., canoe) was modified through the communications to take on a more culturally expected form (e.g., boat). Allport and Postman (1947) found an analogous trend in their research on rumor transmission. They found that information was transformed from an original form, which was neutral or contrary to the prejudice shared among the participants (e.g., a White person assaulting a Black), to something that was more in line with the shared prejudice (e.g., a Black assaulting a White). More recently, Kashima (2000b) showed that information consistent with culturally shared stereotypes (stereotype consistent; SC) is more likely communicated in serial reproduction chains than information inconsistent with them (stereotype inconsistent; SI). This has been called a stereotype consistency bias in serial reproductions.

Note that for the conventionalization to take place, shared ideations (i.e., conventions) need to exist in generalized common ground. Consistent with this, Lyons and Kashima (2003) showed that the stereotypes need to be part of the generalized common ground of the communicators in order for the stereotype consistency bias to emerge in serial reproduction chains. They showed that when the communicators involved in a communication chain did not share the same stereotypes, their reproductions did not show a stereotype consistency bias. Furthermore, it was when the communicators believed most people endorsed and agreed that the stereotypes were true that they showed a stereotype consistency bias in serial reproductions. In other words, the actual sharing of the stereotypes and the perceived sharing and endorsement of the stereotypes were necessary for a conventionalization to occur.

Intriguingly, however, these studies suggest that for SI information to be transmitted, the SI information does not have to be identical with what is already believed to be shared, but can be only consistent with it. Thus, people can extend and cumulate information around the initial shared information, which is actually and also believed to be shared within the community. Once cultural information is widely distributed in a collective and believed to be so, its thematic extension is likely to cumulate over time. This is a version of Tomasello's (1999) ratchet effect. Tomasello noted that different individuals' activities cumulatively add more elements and greater complexities in some cultural traditions. For instance, when a cultural artifact such as a tool is produced and shared within a community, it may be improved upon and made more complex as different individuals add innovations to it. Eventually, the accumulation of such minute modifications may add up to a cultural change in a certain direction—further improvement and greater complexity. Cultural evolution can be cumulative and directional. Like a ratchet that permits the movement of a gear only in one direction, but prevents its reversal, the transmission of culturally consistent information could effect a directional cultural evolution, although it is debatable whether it can always constitute an "improvement" in the case of such culturally shared information as stereotypes.

Why do serial reproduction chains conventionalize transmitted information? Bartlett's (1932) original theory was purely cognitive; schema-consistent information is more memorable. Recently, A. E. Clark and Kashima (2007) proposed a situated-functional model to complement the cognitive account. This model was developed for explaining communication about cultural stereotypes. It suggests that SC information is seen to serve a social connective function (to form and maintain social relationships), and SI information, an informational function (to provide novel information). When communicative context calls for the formation and maintenance of social relationships, people tend to communicate information consistent with the shared cultural stereotypes to those who are seen to share the same culture. However, when context calls for informativeness, they are able and willing to deviate from the shared cultural representation. Consistent with this account, communicators rated SC information in a story as more socially connective but less informative than SI information. When communicating with unknown others who share communal common ground in serial reproduction chains, perceived social connectivity of information predicted the actual communication of the information: Information perceived to be more socially connective survived longer in the serial reproduction chain. Nonetheless, also consistent with the model prediction, when information senders were led to believe that their in-group does not endorse the stereotypes (i.e., does not believe them), SC information was perceived to be less socially connective and therefore less communicated.

In contrast to serial reproductions by unknown in-group members sharing only communal common ground, cultural transmission in a close social circle among close friends, relatives, and others with whom people have personal common ground may operate somewhat differently. The situated-functional model suggests that, when senders are transmitting information to their close others, this may reduce the need to be socially connective—they are already connected—and it may reduce the SC bias in communication. Indeed, there is evidence to suggest that this may be the case (Ruscher, Santuzzi, & Hammer, 2003). Furthermore, the model predicts that when information senders already believe that the receivers have good knowledge of the shared cultural information, they should be more inclined to communicate SI information. This is because strong belief in the sharedness of the cultural information highlights the need to be informative—the receivers already have the cultural information, and so communicating SC information, though socially connecting, may not be sufficiently relevant. Lyons and Kashima (2003) found evidence consistent with this prediction.

The possibility that people who belong in a close social circle can be contrary to each other does not mean that social connectivity is irrelevant. For instance, Lyons and Kashima (2003) found that even if senders knew their audiences shared the exact same knowledge about the stereotypes, they communicated SC information nonetheless, presumably due to its socially connective function. Furthermore, much of the nonconscious aspect of social interaction within a close social circle can become highly coordinated due to both verbal and nonverbal synchronization of behavior. As is well known, people in social interaction automatically mimic each other's nonverbal behavior (e.g., Chartrand & Bargh, 1999; Chartrand, Maddux, & Lakin, 2005, for a review). As Pickering and Garrod (2004, 2007) argued, much of verbal behavior can become coordinated between people engaged in joint activities possibly without their awareness. It is intriguing to speculate that the automatic coordination of verbal and nonverbal behavior may further benefit the exchange of culturally inconsistent, but novel, information within a close social circle by freeing up the cognitive resources that are presumably necessary for the processing of novel information.

Micro–Macro Linkage in Cultural Transmission and Cognitive Micro–Macro Dissociation

The foregoing discussion about cultural information diffusion and the situated-functional model of cultural transmission brings an intriguing insight to some questions about the micro–macro relationship in social psychology of cultural dynamics. We posited at the beginning the following two questions: (1) why people cognitively dissociate their situated sociality and their large-scale society despite the obvious link between them, and (2) how people are able to maintain a large-scale society despite the cognitive dissociation of the micro-level situated sociality and the macro-level sociocultural dynamics. The puzzling issue is this. We seem to psychologically dissociate the macro cultural dynamics in our large-scale collective from our local-micro situated sociality that we partake in our daily routines, but we seem to be able to maintain the large-scale society from which we psychologically dissociate our micro-sociality. How is this possible?

The situated-functional model suggests that people are likely to have two tiers of cultural information flow: one for the micro-local sociality and the other that interfaces with the macro-level society. On the one hand, people are more likely to engage in the transmission of information that is consistent with culturally shared information, or cliché, through their interaction with nonintimate others who belong to a large-scale collective, but outside their local social network. On the other hand, through close others with strong interpersonal ties, they are more likely engaged in the transmission of unique, unusual, or culturally unshared information. It seems that people's close personal social circle provides a basis for cultural innovation, whereas the circulation of cultural information within the public sphere of a large-collective may be characterized by cultural maintenance.

As Lyons, Clark, Kashima, and Kurz (2008) noted, the two-tiered flow of cultural information may result in pluralistic ignorance (e.g., Miller & McFarland, 1987), the phenomena we discussed at the beginning, in which most people believe they differ from the majority of their broader ingroup, an instance of the perceived dissociation between micro- and macro-level sociality. More specifically, in relation to stereotypes, Bowen and Bourgeois (2001) found that student participants perceived the average college student's attitudes toward lesbian, gay, and bisexual students to be more negative compared to their own attitudes and those of their friends. Such a self-congratulatory view of the social world where we believe only we and our friends know better may in part reflect the reality of cultural information transmission.

Nonetheless, the constant flow of culturally shared information in the public sphere when people are interacting with nonintimate others may serve a social connective and social integration function, that is, to socially connect with those nonintimate others and to integrate the large-scale community to which they all belong. In small talks that we engage in with a large number of people in our daily lives, we may indeed be confirming our shared reality of the taken-for-granted social world (e.g., Hardin & Higgins, 1996) and in so doing we may be maintaining and tending the social fabric woven through our vast social networks that span our large-scale collective. Consistent with this line of thinking, Castelli, Pavan, Ferrari, and Kashima (2009) have shown that people who communicate stereotype-consistent information tend to be nonverbally mimicked more than those who communicate stereotype-inconsistent information. If nonverbal mimicry is a social glue that socially connects interactants (Lakin, Jefferis, Cheng, & Chartrand, 2003), stereotype communication—and communication of culturally shared information more generally—precipitates greater social integration in that local milieu, even with those who are of passing significance in our lives.

Concluding Remarks

All in all, the combination of the macro-level collective connectivity and micro-level personal informativeness gives rise to a possibility of an adaptive blend of social integration at a macro-collective level and innovation at a micro-personal level. On the one hand, humans seem to be able to make use of cultural information we believe is shared in our large-scale collective to connect with each other. Just like Dunbar (1996) speculated about the social integrative function of gossip, social sharing of cultural information may help us sustain a large-scale collective, which is believed to share a culture. On the other hand, humans may innovate and spread new information when interacting with their close allies. While using shared information to socially connect with them and automatically coordinating their behavior, they may still be able to produce new information and to transmit it to close others without jeopardizing the integration of the large-scale collective.

Nonetheless, the speed of cultural transformation and the extent to which the close circle of sociality and the wider collective is dissociated may depend on the emphasis placed on innovation and newness relative to what is common and given. Urban (2001) suggests that there are cultural differences in the value of newness in cultural information transmission: Exact replication is valued in traditional societies where technology of information replication is costly (e.g., memorizing in oral traditions or writing in largely illiterate society), whereas innovation is valued in modern societies where technology of information replication is easily available (e.g., recorders, copiers, computer memory chips). Presumably, the greater the emphasis placed on innovation, the faster the likely transformation of cultural information. If indeed cultural innovation is more likely in a close circle of micro-sociality, this close circle is even more likely to be seen to diverge from the wider sociocultural sphere. In the current theorizing of cultural transmission, then, a declining cost of information replication may precipitate a greater amount of perceived micro–macro dissociation. It is ironic that this mechanism may in part sustain sometimes-harmful cultural stereotypes at a great cost to the target of the negative prejudice in today's world of information technology, or rather especially because of it.

NOTE

1. The concept of common knowledge has generated much debate and controversy as to its conceptual soundness. It is well known that there is the problem that, under some understanding of this concept, in order for A and B to have common knowledge, p, A knows that p, A knows that B knows that p, A knows that B knows that A knows that p, and so forth, as well as B knows that p, B knows that A knows that p, B knows that A knows that B knows that p, and so forth ad infinitum (e.g., Clark & Marshall, 1981; Sperber & Wilson, 1995). There are two problems that this criticism presents. First is the problem of "knowledge" as too strong a requirement. Various researchers went around this problem by suggesting that they do not mean "knowledge" in the strong

sense, but mean something much weaker. For instance, H. H. Clark (1996) argues that it should be read as a much weaker cognitive state such as to *perceive, believe, assume, take for granted, or have information* about those things. Similarly, Sperber and Wilson (1995) argued that it should be understood as a weaker cognitive state of *mutual manifestation*. The second problem is the infinite regress. However, Clark (1996, pp. 94–96) argued that the following definition of common ground avoids this problem:

Common ground (shared basis)

p is common ground for members of community C if and only if:

1. every member of C has information that basis *b* holds;
2. *b* indicates to every member of C that every member of C has information that *b* holds;
3. *b* indicates to members of C that *p*.

Basis *b* in Common Ground (shared basis) gives a basis for inferring a speaker's intention. Requirement 2 seems to me to be equivalent to Sperber and Wilson's (1995) mutual manifestness. Further, Clark argued that CG-shared basis can be rewritten as in Common Ground (reflexive) as described in text, which defines common ground as a self-referential representation. Whereas this self-referentiality may present some puzzles for some, Clark argued that it does not present a logical problem, citing Barwise and Etchemendy's (1987) work on logic that permits self-referentiality. We are satisfied for now to proceed with this definition.

REFERENCES

Allport, G. W. & Postman, L. F. (1947). *The psychology of rumor*. New York: H. Holt.

Austin, J. L. (1962). *How to do things with words*. Cambridge, MA: Harvard University Press.

Bartlett, F. C. (1932). *Remembering: A study in experimental and social psychology*. Cambridge, UK: Cambridge University Press.

Barwise, J., & Etchemendy, J. (1987). *The liar*. New York: Oxford University Press.

Billig, M. (1995). *Banal nationalism*. Thousand Oaks, CA: Sage.

Bowen, A. M. & Bourgeois, M. J. (2001). Attitudes toward lesbian, gay, and bisexual college students: The contribution of pluralistic ignorance, dynamic social impact, and contact theories. *Journal of American College Health, 50*, 91–96.

Boyd, R. & Richerson, P. J. (1985). *Culture and the evolutionary process*. Chicago: University of Chicago Press.

Boyd, R. & Richerson, P. J. (2005). *The origin and evolution of cultures*. New York: Oxford University Press.

Bratanova, B. A. (2008). *The formation of collective representations: The role of audience tuning and shared reality in memory and communication*. PhD thesis, University of Melbourne, Australia.

Brewer, M. & Gardner, W. (1996). Who is this "we"? Levels of collective identity and self representations. *Journal of Personality and Social Psychology, 71*, 83–93.

Campbell, D. T. (1975). On the conflicts between biological and social evolution and between psychology and moral tradition. *American Psychologist, 30*, 1103–1126.

Castelli, L., Pavan, G., Ferrari, E., & Kashima, Y. (2009). The stereotyper and the chameleon: The effects of stereotype use on perceivers' mimicry. *Journal of Experimental Social Psychology, 45*, 835–839.

Cavalli-Sforza, L. L. & Feldman, M. W. (1981). *Cultural transmission and evolution*. Princeton, NJ: Princeton University Press.

Chartrand, T. & Bargh, J. (1999). The chameleon effect: The perception-behavior link and social interaction. *Journal of Personality and Social Psychology, 76*, 893–910.

Chartrand, T. L., Maddux, W. W., & Lakin, J. L. (2005). Beyond the perception-behavior link: The ubiquitous utility and motivational moderators of nonconscious mimicry. In R. R. Hassin, J. S. Uleman, & J. A. Bargh, *The new unconscious* (pp. 334–361). New York: Oxford University Press.

Chiu, C.-Y. & Hong, Y.-Y. (2006). *Social psychology of culture*. New York: Psychology Press.

Clark, A. E. & Kashima, Y. (2007). Stereotypes help people connect with others in the community: A situated functional analysis of the stereotype consistency bias in communication. *Journal of Personality and Social Psychology, 93*, 1028–1039.

Clark, H. H. & Marshall, C. R. (1981). Definite reference and mutual knowledge. In A. K. Joshi, B. L. Webber, & I. A. Sag (Eds.), *Elements of discourse understanding* (pp. 10–63). Cambridge, UK: Cambridge University Press.

Clark, H. H. (1996). *Using language*. New York: Cambridge University Press.

Cole, M. (1996). *Cultural psychology: A once and future discipline*. Cambridge, MA: Harvard University Press.

Connerton, P. (1989). *How societies remember*. Cambridge, UK: Cambridge University Press.

Dawkins, R. (1976). *The selfish gene*. Oxford, UK: Oxford University Press.

Dawkins, R. (1999). Foreword. In S. Blackmore, *The meme machine* (pp. vii–xvii). Oxford, UK: Oxford University Press.

Dunbar, R. (1996). *Grooming, gossip, and the evolution of language*. Cambridge, MA: Harvard University Press.

Echterhoff, G., Higgins, E. T., & Groll, S. (2005). Audience-tuning effects on memory: The role of shared reality. *Journal of Personality and Social Psychology, 89*, 257–276.

Elias, N. (2000). *The civilizing process* (E. Jephcott, Trans., & E. Dunning, J. Goudsblom, and S. Mennell, Eds.). Oxford, UK: Blackwell.

Garrod, S. & Doherty, G. (1994). Conversation, co-ordination and convention: An empirical investigation of how groups establish linguistic conventions. *Cognition, 53*, 181–215.

Giddens, A. (1984). *The constitution of society*. Cambridge, UK: Polity Press.

Grice, H. P. (1957). Meaning. *Philosophical Review, 66*, 377–388. Reprinted in D. D. Steinberg & L. A. Jakobovits (Eds.), *Semantics: An interdisciplinary reader in philosophy, linguistics, and psychology* (pp. 53–59). Cambridge, UK: Cambridge University Press.

Hardin, C. & Higgins, E. T. (1996). Shared reality: How social verification makes the subjective objective. In R. M. Sorrentino & E. T. Higgins (Eds.), *Handbook of motivation and cognition, Vol. 3: The interpersonal context* (pp. 28–84). New York: Guilford Press.

Hausmann, L. R. M., Levine, J. M., & Higgins, E. T. (2008). Communication and group perception: Extending the "saying is believing" effect. *Group Processes and Intergroup Relations, 11*, 539–554.

Hermans, H. J. M. & Kempen, H. J. G. (1998). Moving cultures: The perilous problems of cultural dichotomies in a globalizing society. *American Psychologist, 53*, 1111–1120.

Higgins, E. T. & Rholes, W. S. (1978). "Saying is believing": Effects of message modification on memory and liking for the person described. *Journal of Experimental Social Psychology, 14*, 363–378.

Hofstede, G. (2001). *Culture's consequences* (2nd ed.). Thousand Oaks, CA: Sage.

Hutchins, E. (1995). *Cognition in the wild*. Cambridge, MA: MIT Press.

Huxley, J. (1963). *Evolution: The modern synthesis*. London: Allen and Unwin. (Original work published 1942)

Kashima, Y. (2000a). Conceptions of culture and person for psychology. *Journal of Cross-Cultural Psychology, 31*, 14–32.

Kashima, Y. (2000b). Maintaining cultural stereotypes in the serial reproduction of narratives. *Personality and Social Psychology Bulletin, 26*, 594–604.

Kashima, Y., Klein, O., & Clark, A. E. (2007). Grounding: Sharing information in social interaction. In K. Fiedler (Ed.), *Social communication* (pp. 27–77). New York: Psychology Press.

Kashima, Y., Peters, K., & Whelan, J. (2008). Culture, narrative, and human agency. In R. Sorrentino & S. Yamaguchi (Eds.), *Handbook of motivation and cognition across cultures* (pp. 393–421). San Diego, CA: Academic Press.

Kashima, Y., Woolcock, J., & Kashima, E. (2000). Group impressions as dynamic configurations: The tensor product model of group impression formation and change. *Psychological Review, 107*, 914–942.

Kashima, Y., Yamaguchi, S., Kim, U., Choi, S.-C., Gelfand, M. J., & Yuki, M. (1995). Culture, gender, and self: A perspective from individualism-collectivism research. *Journal of Personality and Social Psychology, 69*, 925–937.

Kuklick, H. (1991). *The savage within: The social history of British anthropology, 1885–1945*. Cambridge, UK: Cambridge University Press.

Lakin, J. L., Jefferis, V. E., Cheng, C. M., & Chartrand, T. L. (2003). The chameleon effect as social glue: Evidence for the evolutionary significance of nonconscious mimicry. *Journal of Nonverbal Behavior, 27*, 145–162.

Lowie, R. (1937). *The history of ethnological theory*. New York: Farrar and Rinehart.

Lyons, A., Clark, A., Kashima, Y., & Kurz, T. (2008). Cultural dynamics of stereotyping: Social network processes and the perpetuation of stereotypes. In Y. Kashima, K. Fiedler, & P. Freytag (Eds.), *Stereotype dynamics* (pp. 59–92). Mahwah, NJ: Erlbaum.

Lyons, A. & Kashima, Y. (2003). How are stereotypes maintained through communication? The influence of stereotype sharedness. *Journal of Personality and Social Psychology, 85*, 989–1005.

Miller, D. T. & McFarland, C. (1987). Pluralistic ignorance: When similarity is interpreted as dissimilarity. *Journal of Personality and Social Psychology, 53*, 298–305.

Miller, D. T., Monin, B., & Prentice, D. A. (2000). Pluralistic ignorance and inconsistency between private attitudes and public behaviors. In D. J. Terry & M. A. Hogg (Eds.), *Attitudes, behavior, and social context* (pp. 95–113). Mahwah, NJ: Lawrence Erlbaum.

Pickering, M. J. & Garrod, S. (2004). Toward a mechanistic psychology of dialogue. *Behavioral and Brain Sciences, 27*, 169–225.

Pickering, M. J. & Garrod, S. (2007). Do people use language production to make predictions during comprehension? *Trends in Cognitive Sciences, 11*, 105–110.

Prentice, D. A. & Miller, D. T. (1993). Pluralistic ignorance and alcohol use on campus: Some consequences of misperceiving the social norm. *Journal of Personality and Social Psychology, 64*, 243–256.

Rogoff, B. (2003). *The cultural nature of human development*. New York: Oxford University Press.

Ruscher, J. B., Santuzzi, A. M., & Hammer, E. Y. (2003). Shared impression formation in the cognitively interdependent dyad. *British Journal of Social Psychology, 42*, 411–425.

Schegloff, E. A., Jefferson, G., & Sacks, H. (1977). The preference for self-correction in the organization of repair in conversation. *Language, 53*, 361–382.

Schiffer, S. R. (1972). *Meaning*. Oxford, UK: Clarendon Press.

Searle, J. R. (1976). A classification of illocutionary acts. *Language in Society, 5*, 1–24.

Smith, E. R. & Semin, G. R. (2004). Socially situated cognition: Cognition in its social context. *Advances in Experimental Social Psychology, 36*, 53–117.

Smith, G. E. (1932). *In the beginning: The origin of civilization*. London: Watts & Co.

Sperber, D. (1996). *Explaining culture*. Oxford, UK: Blackwell.
Sperber, D. & Wilson, D. (1995). *Relevance: Communication and cognition* (2nd ed.). Oxford, UK: Blackwell.
Strawson, P. (1964). Intention and convention in speech acts. *Philosophical Review, 73*, 439–460.
Thompson, M. S., Judd, C., M., and Park, B. (2000). The consequences of communicating social stereotypes. *Journal of Experimental Social Psychology, 36*, 567–599.
Tomasello, M. (1999). *The cultural origins of human cognition*. Cambridge, MA: Harvard University Press.
Tyler, T. R. & Cook, F. L. (1984). The mass media and judgments of risk: Distinguishing impact on personal and societal level judgments. *Journal of Personality and Social Psychology, 47*, 693–708.
Urban, G. (2001). *Metaculture*. Minneapolis, MN: University of Minnesota Press.
Wertsch, J. V. (1991). *Voices of the mind*. London: Harvester Weatsheaf.
Wertsch, J. V. (2002). *Voices of collective remembering*. Cambridge, UK: Cambridge University Press.

Section IV

Evolutionary Perspectives on Sociality

11

Too Much Monkey Business

LOUISE BARRETT

Too much monkey business for me to get involved in!

—Chuck Berry

INTRODUCTION

By virtue of their close relationship to humans, we often look to our fellow primates, the monkeys and apes, for clues about the origins and evolutionary significance of many of our own social behaviors and the cognitive mechanisms that underpin them. On the face of it, this is perfectly sensible. Darwin himself suggested that a close study of baboons "would do more for metaphysics than Locke." When considering the results of these efforts, however, it becomes apparent that such comparisons represent an uncritical acceptance of a particular philosophical perspective and often have very little to do with evolution at all. As a result, they do an injustice to both sides, failing to recognize the distinctive nature of nonhuman cognition, on the one hand, and promoting a somewhat misleading view of our own cognitive abilities on the other. In what follows, I want to illustrate how a different philosophical outlook may allow us to ground our own sociality (in the sense of tracing its evolutionary roots) in a way that remains true to Darwin's vision of continuity, without merely constructing other primates in our own image.

DARWIN AND THE APES

It seems that not a day goes by without some amazing feat of human-like social cognition being demonstrated in an ape or a monkey. Orangutans communicate as if they were playing charades (Cartmill & Byrne, 2007), while chimpanzee and bonobo gestures show language-like properties (Pollick & de Waal, 2007). Baboons parse sequences of vocalizations into dramatic narratives (Cheney & Seyfarth,

2005; Jolly, 2007) and hierarchically structure their social world by kinship and rank (Bergman et al., 2003). Capuchin monkeys reject unfair pay (Brosnan & de Waal, 2003). Cotton-top tamarins, rhesus macaques, and chimpanzees can perceive rational, goal-directed action (Wood et al., 2007). In all these cases, it is argued that the human-like nature of the cognitive response shown implies that these animals are smarter than we previously thought. Of course, an equally valid inference to draw is that, as the animals are able to achieve success on these apparently complex tasks with significantly smaller brains, then perhaps these tasks aren't so complex after all.

Our tendency to raise monkeys and apes up toward what we clearly consider to be our own exalted level of ability, rather than reconsider the nature of human social cognition in light of these findings, is an issue worthy of study in its own right. Here, however, the point is simply that most comparative studies of this kind are essentially anthropocentric in nature (and sometimes explicitly so; e.g., de Waal, 2001), where other species are judged against a human standard. As Keeley (2004) suggests, this probably reflects the historical precedent set by Morgan's canon, and its advice that we should not interpret an animal's actions as "the outcome of the exercise of a higher psychical faculty, if it can be interpreted as the outcome of the exercise of one which stands lower in the psychological scale."[1] The anchoring of cognitive ability in these hierarchical terms means that, when we demonstrate facility in an area deemed to require higher faculties (i.e., human cognitive skills), we are drawn to assuming that the animal is more like us, and we do not consider whether, in fact, we may be more like them and that our cognitive mechanisms may perhaps be simpler than we assume.

In addition, for all its apparent scientific rigor, Morgan's canon implicitly assumes a *scala naturae* in terms of the expected distribution of cognitive endowments across the animal kingdom and is, therefore, incompatible with a truly evolutionary approach. The assumption of a ladder-like process of steady improvement in cognitive abilities from lower to higher faculties represents an outmoded view of how evolutionary processes work. Assuming that, for example, chimpanzees will show many of the precursors to human cognition because they are our closest living relatives assumes that, following the split with our common ancestor, chimpanzees stopped evolving leaving only the hominin line to progress. We moved up the ladder and left the chimpanzee stuck on a lower rung. In fact, both lineages have been subject to natural selection following the split from our common ancestor, so that chimpanzees must possess their own unique suite of adaptations, cognitive and otherwise. Although we can expect some similarities between us, one cannot assume that the capacities and abilities that chimpanzees display are accurate reflections of what we were once like, nor should we assume that these abilities are merely some less complex variant of our own.

Such assumptions do, however, pervade comparative studies. The possibility that these creatures may possess some unique skills of their own is rarely, if ever, entertained; a rare exception is the study of chimpanzee working memory by Inoue and Matsuzawa (2007), where chimpanzees outperformed humans by some margin.[2] This in turn helps to reinforce the views we hold regarding the nature of our own sociocognitive skills; when we find the "precursors" of our presumed human skills in our closest relatives, it reinforces the assumptions we hold about the nature of our own sociocognitive skills. If, however, we are mistaken about the essential means by which one human understands another, then all the comparative enterprise achieves is the bedding down of this mistaken view of human social cognition and an ever more distorted view of the cognition of other animals.

THEORY OF MIND OR THEORETICAL MISTAKE?

As I and other authors have argued, the mistake about our own social cognition stems from our assumption that, in order to understand others, we rely on a suite of metarepresentational skills, generally referred to as *theory of mind*, which allow us to infer the nature of others' private, invisible mental states (Antaki, 2004; Costall and Leudar, 2004; Leudar and Costall, 2004; Reddy and Morris, 2004; Barrett and Henzi ,2005; Barrett et al., 2007). This, in turn, reflects some deeper philosophical assumptions about the relation of the individual to the social. That is, the theory of mind approach is an essentially Cartesian view, where as thinking subjects we are detached from the social world (indeed the world in general) and the questions we seek to answer concern how we, and other thinking things, gain knowledge of the world, how we relate to it, and how we gain knowledge and relate to the worlds of others.

Consequently, we take for granted that we use our metarepresentational theory of mind in our dealings with others, but this does not, in fact, provide a very good description for what goes on when people normally act. Although there is no doubt that humans possess a metarepresentational capacity that has no precedent in the animal kingdom, the question of whether we use this capacity at all times and in all situations to predict, and make inferences about, the behavior of others is moot. In many real-world, real-time situations, we infer mental states immediately through tone of voice, eye gaze, body language, and other nonverbal behaviors, without the need for overt thought or reflection. Indeed, we do not feel as though we're making inferences at all. Instead, they seem to be given to us—we perceive them directly—in the same way that we immediately see the color of the postbox on our front door (McArthur and Baron, 1983; Zebrowitz and Collins, 1997; Lieberman et al., 2002; Gallagher, 2005). Lieberman et al. (2002) have suggested this occurs because social engagement triggers our so-called X-system, which they conceive as a distributed connectionist network sensitive to recognizing socially relevant patterns in our everyday behavior. This system enables us, in Heidegger's terminology, to engage in *transparent coping* with others, in just the same way as we do when making effective use of a material object. A hammer is invisible to us as long as all goes smoothly: We do not think of ourselves as an individual that is using a hammer, we are merely hammering. Should the head of the hammer fly off, however, we immediately become aware of the hammer as an object to which we can direct our attention.

The same can be said for our social engagement. As Bruner (1990) neatly summarizes: "When everything is as it should be, the narratives of psychology are unnecessary" (p. 40). Instead of it being our default state, our metarepresentational understanding of others only seems to show up when something goes wrong or at least does not go as smoothly as it should; when others do not behave as we expected or predicted, and we have to explain what happened, and not just predict what others will do. It is only at these moments of breakdown that we become the particular kind of intentional beings that Descartes describes, and we are consciously aware of our inferences regarding others' mental states. The same is true when we consider a person in their absence (Will Dave feel awkward if I invite Bob to dinner along with Sally?) and it is important to note that I am not trying to present an antimentalist, antirepresentational argument here, but merely arguing against our metarepresentational capacity as being the standard, default mechanism by which we negotiate our social worlds. When our engagement with the world and others is going well, a more embodied, situated, pattern-recognition ability seems to do just fine (see also Povinelli et al., 2000).

The idea that we engage actively with the world (and others), rather than struggle to gain knowledge of it (and them), does not, however, seem to have penetrated very far within primate comparative psychology, nor indeed philosophy of mind. This is despite the fact that much of the empirical evidence from human social psychology suggests that we use much simpler mechanisms than metarepresentational inferences to predict others' behavior, such as trait attribution (someone who lets a door slam in another person's face is a rude person) and inductive generalization (we assume that people will generally do what they did on previous occasions; e.g., Lieberman et al., 2002; Hutto, 2004; and especially Andrews, 2005). A lot of comparative work also remains untouched by recent criticisms of the theory of mind framework noted earlier, failing to recognize that what gets learned over the course of development is not the nature of our individualized and occluded Cartesian mental states (Leudar et al., 2004), which, as Sharrock and Coulter (2004) argue, would be impossible to learn. Instead, we learn a language to express ourselves in which behavior is an essential component of mind, and not simply evidence of hidden mental states (Sharrock & Coulter, 2004, Leudar et al., 2004; see also Antaki, 2004; Costall & Leudar, 2004; Leudar & Costall, 2004; Reddy & Morris, 2004). Even those theorists who argue against the need to represent theory of mind processes as conceptually driven statements, instead suggesting that humans possess a modular theory of mind mechanism (ToMM) that forms part of our social instinct, nevertheless argue that human infants and children have mechanisms that "promote attention to mental states" (Leslie et al., 2004, pp. 528–533), and that children respond to these "invisible, intangible, abstract states" directly. The idea that behavior and social engagement may at least partly constitute these mental states is not considered. Whichever developmental framework is considered—"Theory Theory" or modular ToMM—the essentially Cartesian nature of the mind promoted by these studies is taken on board without question by those working on other creatures.

Finally, the idea that embodiment may contribute greatly to action and social interaction is also one that, to date, has received almost no attention in the comparative literature (see, e.g., Brooks, 1999; Clark, 1997; Gallagher, 2005; Pfeifer & Bongard, 2007). In the latter case, this much is evident in studies claiming that, for example, the knowledge of nonhuman primates is propositional or that they show the precursors of intentional understanding (Bergman et al., 2003; Cheney

& Seyfarth, 2005; Wood et al., 2007). So, a mistaken assumption about our own social cognition is used to inform studies about social cognition in other species, thereby acting both to reinforce and compound the initial error. Finally, it is also worth pointing out this Cartesian perception of the disembodied thinking subject is a particularly Western viewpoint (see, e.g., Varela et al., 1991 for a review), and it is not a feature of the folk psychology of all human societies (Lillard, 1998). It is therefore very interesting to note that, of all the studies to date, nonhuman primates show elements of exactly the same European–American theory of mind possessed by the researchers who study them.

SECOND-PARTY PARTICIPATION

One reason, perhaps, why the pull of theory of mind and its precursors is so strong is because of the very nature of scientific study on the one hand, and, ironically, our inability to fully enter the world of the nonhuman primates that we study on the other hand. As, among others, Reddy (1996, 2007) has pointed out, with respect to studies of children's sociocognitive development, although our everyday interactions with other individuals are mainly second-person in nature, experimental studies invariably adopt a third-person perspective. That is, the child is asked to attribute mental states to one individual with respect to his or her social interaction with a second individual. The classic Sally-Anne and Maxi false-belief tasks, for example, explicitly require children to look on as outsiders, rather than engage as participants. As Reddy (1996) notes, children below the age of 4 fail such tests with stunning regularity, yet they have no problem understanding or engaging with the experimenter in mindful ways during the task. In addition, children of this age, and younger, are perfectly capable of displaying deceptive behavior, and other evidence for theory of mind in more naturalistic contexts. This is because, as Reddy and Morris (2004) argue, we primarily engage with other humans in terms of an I–thou relationship, and do not place any distance between our self and the other. A third-person perspective, in contrast, distances us from others, so that we see them as objects—an "it" to be reflected on. In this way, we come to mischaracterize the nature of our own social cognition, as one in which we are observers only, and not active participants in social then used to reconfigure our everyday experience so that this fits with theory rather than vic e versa (Reddy & Morris, 2004).

This same, unacknowledged problem of a third-person perspective pervades many studies of social cognition in nonhuman primates. By definition, as human observers we are forced to look on as outsiders when viewing the social interactions of nonhuman primates. We do not participate in any way, both by choice, because we do not want our behavior to influence the animals, and by necessity, because we simply cannot enter into a true second-person interaction with them: They can only do this with each other. In scientific studies, monkeys and apes must (can only) be objects to be reflected on and not subjects with whom we engage. They become in Heidegger's terminology *present-at-hand*, which is the unique stance that humans are able to take with respect to the world when engaging in scientific pursuits. What seems to happen, then, is that a third-person perspective, which we are forced to use to try to predict and explain the behavior of the animals for our own ends, becomes projected directly onto the animal's themselves, as though they too will use this third-person perspective to predict and influence their response to others. In this way, ape and monkey knowledge becomes a Cartesian, propositional, third-party knowledge, because it is, in fact, our own knowledge reflected back at us.

This projection is sometimes explicit as, for example, in acoustic playback designs, where the response is recorded of one individual to a staged sequence of vocalizations from two or more other animals. We use our own introspective assessment of our own folk psychology to rationalize the behavior of the animals, so that a simple looking-time response becomes an indication of complex cognitive mechanisms (Cheney & Seyfarth, 2005). More often, the projection is implicit in the reasoning used to account for the behavioral response of the animal. So, when a more dominant animal approaches two subordinate animals that are grooming, and the lower ranking of the two cedes her position to the dominant, or when an animal under attack attempts to solicit help from an animal that ranks higher than its attacker, we take this as evidence that the animals are computing the relative ranks of each individual in a nonegocentric fashion, because we see the ranks in this way from our outsider perspective and because the behavior of the animals is consistent with this perspective. As Brooks (1999) and Simons (1996) have pointed out, however, it remains possible that the only cognition present is a mote in our own eye. We see the decision as one based on the computing of relative ranks, but for the animals themselves, all these interactions take place in a subjective, engaged manner: The animal does not stand outside its situation in the way that we are forced to, and the basis on which it solicits support or avoids a dominant may actually reflect a simpler, more embodied process of intentional attunement (e.g., Gallese, 2001, 2003, 2005, 2007), where individuals respond dynamically to the bodily movements, postures, and facial expressions of relevant others (who are themselves responding to these same aspects in others), and in which there is actually no call for a nonegocentric, third-party stance (Barrett et al., 2007; see next section for a fleshed-out example of how individuals could coordinate their behavior in this way). This does not, of course, mean that monkeys could not, and do not, have an understanding of third-party relationships. It is a suggestion that, if we wish to claim they do, our experiments and data need to be a whole lot stronger than they are at present, and we need to keep our own sociocognitive biases in mind at all times, while recognizing that some of these are beyond our conscious control. We need look no further than Heider and Simmel's (1944) famous demonstrations of perceptual animacy, for example, for a salutary reminder of how easily we can be fooled.

A CARTESIAN CONSTRUCTION

Here, then, is the problem. When we try to ground our own sociality from a scientific, evolutionary perspective, the current approach is to decide what kinds of capacities nonhuman primates are likely to have, based on our own contestable assumptions about ourselves and the nature of our own theory of mind, and then design our scientific studies in a way that cannot do anything other than validate this view of who we think we are (Barrett et al., 2007). At present, there seems to be a real danger that other primates, and the great apes in particular, will become nothing more than social constructions (Hacking, 1999) whose ultimate purpose is to allow us to flatter them with human skills in order to flatter ourselves. The devotion with which the popular press and general public subscribe to the notion of bonobos as the "hippie chimp" is very telling in this respect. Here, as a recent article in the *New Yorker* laid out very clearly, scientific research, media attention, and a public appetite for viewing apes as cuter, hairier versions of humans have fed on each other to produce a view of these animals that has become increasingly divorced from ecological reality and where dissenting voices are treated as killjoys (Parker, 2007). Not surprisingly, perhaps, this article was itself derided as a piece of killjoy reporting, with Parker attempting to "deflate the buoyant, mystical aura of the bonobo" (Block, 2007). No one, it seems, has much of an appetite for a "non-human" nonhuman primate.

This is also made clear in a recent issue of *Science* in which an editorial on a study by Wood et al. (2007) appeared under the headline "Nonhuman primates demonstrate humanlike reasoning ability," on the basis of evidence that was, at best, suggestive and, at worst, could be considered as wishful thinking. In the study, cotton-top tamarins, rhesus macaques, and chimpanzees were all shown to differentiate between a human performing a rational goal-directed action (grasping a food container) and a random action (flopping his hand on top of the container). This was interpreted as demonstrating that these primates "spontaneously make inferences about a human experimenter's goal." The results showed that tamarins contacted the targeted container 75% of the time following the rational action and 57% after the random action. The equivalent figures for rhesus macaques and chimpanzees were 85% and 55%, and 80% and 48%, respectively. Although these data show that each species performed better than chance, there are two points that that need to be considered here. First, as Derek Penn points out in the editorial article, these data cannot speak to whether the animals were "representing or reasoning about the [tester's] unobservable psychological states" (p. 1308) because there is nothing intrinsic to the task that can unambiguously reveal whether the animals are responding to mental states rather than behavior (behavior being a criterion for rational action). Rather, as with the playback paradigm, this conclusion is based on an application of human folk psychology to rationalize the animal's action (if they can detect a person's goals, then they will). This brings in the second point, which was made by the comparative psychologist Sara Shettleworth at a symposium on animal cognition at the 2007 International Ethological Congress. Namely, that applying our own folk psychology rigorously to the results of these kinds of studies (although the Wood et al. study was not specifically referred to here) and not just their design reveals a significant flaw: In all cases, the criterion used is that the animal should perform better than chance. As Shettleworth noted, however, if the animals really had the capacities claimed for them, we should surely expect them to perform accurately 100% of the time. The tasks are straightforward and not excessively demanding of memory or other capacities, so why are we apparently satisfied that merely doing better than chance constitutes strong evidence? The obvious counter to this is that even animals that do understand the task may well make mistakes some of the time, just as humans ar e likely to make similar mistakes. Nevertheless, the fact that, across all three species, animals in the Wood et al. (2007) study chose the random container 44% to 52% of the time suggests that performance is not as reliable as one would hope for if the animals were truly proficient at making these kinds of spontaneous inferences. Finally, even if we decide to be generous, and accept that these results are both reliable and demonstrate what is claimed for them, the fact remains that they were reported as evidence for humanlike reasoning, when it is equally true, and perhaps evolutionarily more valid, to argue that humans share this capacity with other members of the primate order: The results show that we are more mundane than we suppose, not that other primates are as "special" as we are.

So, what to do? How can we avoid the pitfalls of anthropomorphic projection and wishful thinking? Our answer has been to suggest that we turn all our preconceptions on their head and draw inspiration from studies of artificial life, robotics, self-organization, individual-based modeling, connectionism, and ecological psychology. The hope here is that we will be able to reconfigure our views of the primates in a way that does not place humans at the comparative center (Barrett et al., 2007). The first thing to do, however, is to rid ourselves of the pervasive Cartesian viewpoint that still dogs much of cognitive science and comparative psychology (Wheeler, 2005). Although we long ago rejected the notion that there is some incorporeal mind stuff distinct from our physical body stuff, we still cling to the idea that it is the brain that does all the cognitive work, sending out instructions to an essentially lifeless body via the message cables of the nervous system (Churchland, 1986). A dualism therefore remains, even among those who describe themselves as materialists and believe they are done with Descartes.

Evolutionarily, such a position is untenable. As, inter alia, Gibson (1979), Reed (1996), Clark (1997), Brooks (1999), Rockwell (2005), and Wheeler (2005) point out, brains evolved in the first place to help an animal move around and regulate its encounters with the environment in a more efficient and productive manner. Brains, then, are there to help animals act in the world, not reflect on it. As we have known since Von Uexküll (1957) and his notion of the *umwelt*, how an animal represents the world, if indeed it represents it at all, depends crucially on how its perception-action mechanisms engage with it. These mechanisms, in turn, reflect the kind of body it has and the kind of niche it occupies. One cannot study higher cognition in an abstract, disembodied way because, outside of a computer interface, there is no such thing as abstract, disembodied cognition. Natural cognition must be grounded ultimately in physical skills and bodily experiences, and, evolutionarily, these will constrain the forms that higher cognitive processes can take.

Another way to put this is to recognize that our singular focus on brains is misplaced because natural selection has elaborated on the nervous system as a whole. The nervous system that lies outside the brain is not merely a network of message cables that relay the commands of the brain back and forth, but an integrated, functional system that includes the brain, but is not superseded by it, and which influences, and is influenced by, both the endocrine and immune systems (Pert, 1997; Gershon, 1999). The enteric nervous system, for example, is a complex neural network that is wrapped around our gut. It can continue operating, with digestion unimpeded, even if the vagus nerve, which connects the stomach to the brain, is severed. It is sensitive to both pressure and chemicals, much like our senses of taste and smell. It shows simple learning properties and produces 95% of all the serotonin, an important neurotransmitter, in our body. Most intriguingly, it is vulnerable to the same lesions that occur in Parkinson's and Alzheimer's disease (Gershon 1999). If our gut works, we work. If it fails, all the brain in the world won't help because it is almost impossible to concentrate on any other task if our digestive system is in uproar.

The second aspect of a Cartesian view that we have to reject is the notion that we are detached observers of the world. In the first instance, this amounts to nothing more than a false dichotomy between organism and environment. As Dewey (1929) and James (1890) both suggested, "mental facts cannot properly be studied apart from the physical environment of which they take cognizance" (James 1900: 3). Similarly, Heidegger (1926/1978) argues that we are always in the world, always a part of it, and therefore inseparable from it. The questions of interest, then, are not those that consider the relation of the detached individual to the social, but those that ask how a private, individual self comes to emerge from a "public, amorphous mass" (Dreyfus, 1991). This position is not one that currently informs comparative primate cognition. Instead of viewing behavior as constitutive of mental states and intentionality, most comparative studies fall into the same trap as many developmental studies and view behavior only as an "arbitrary 'clue'... to a hidden mind" (Leudar & Costall, 2004), which we can only know by inference. This is completely understandable in the context of a view that sees cognition as a wholly internal, purely brain-based enterprise, but it is one that ultimately limits studies of animal social cognition to those that can provide the kind of controlled environment needed to see this "pure brain" in action, and infer the structure of this "hidden mind." Greater recognition is needed of the fact that evolution is uninterested in pure brain and is instead focused on the kinds of emergent mind that brains, bodies, and environments can achieve in concert.

As my colleagues and I have argued in detail elsewhere (Barrett & Henzi, 2005; Barrett et al., 2007), the adoption of an embodied and distributed approach to cognition removes at a stroke these two false dichotomies of brain and body, body and world. As an added bonus, it immediately reduces any anthropocentric tendencies by forcing us to acknowledge and incorporate the physical means by which animals engage with the world. Previously, we have emphasized the role of mirror neurons, and the ways in which they offer us a neurobiological mechanism for the establishment of a meaningful, embodied understanding of others without any need for overt mental state understanding or conscious simulation (Gallese, 2001, 2003, 2005, 2007). Here, I elaborate a little more on how one can use these insights to help ground sociality in terms of the ethological study of primates and how these can be used to inform cognitive studies and, echoing Johnson (2001), can perhaps be considered as studies of cognition in their own right.

PUTTING ECOLOGY INTO PSYCHOLOGY

To do so, we need to draw more specifically on an approach that has long recognized that cognition depends on the interaction of an animal with its world. James J. Gibson's (1979) theory of direct perception, or ecological psychology, has generally received rather bad press, being seen as an approach that is firmly antimentalist and antirepresentational. There have been, however, several efforts to argue for a more Gibsonian approach to human social cognition, and our suggestions here echo many of these earlier proposals (McArthur & Baron, 1983; Zebrowitz & Collins, 1997; Chartrand & Bargh, 1999; Proffitt, 2006a, 2006b).

Although one could argue that some of Gibson's writings do suggest that he held such a stance, the presentation of ecological psychology as antirepresentational is only a crude caricature of a more nuanced position, which argues that representational systems are not mental phenomena alone, but also ways of behaving and regulating actions in the world. Even we humans do not internalize ideas in our heads in a way that is completely divorced from reality (although formal schooling often makes it seem that way); rather, we use these ideas to help regulate and control our encounters with our environment (Reed, 1996). Much more important, however, is the false separation of organism and environment that is denied by ecological psychologists, rather than the existence of mental representations per se. In this, it becomes clear how ecological psychology both embraces the earlier views of James (1900), Dewey (1929), and Heidegger (1926/1978), and anticipates many of the insights that would come from work in embodied robotics/artificial life and distributed cognition (Clark, 1997; Brooks, 1999; Wheeler, 2005; Pfeifer & Bongard, 2007).

The most crucial and important aspect of an ecological approach is the idea that organisms regulate their behavior with respect to the affordances of the environment. Affordances are the opportunities and possibilities for action that particular objects and resources offer to an animal (Gibson, 1979; Reed, 1996). In this way, perception is "written in the language of action" (Michaels & Carello, 1981) so that, for example, we do not see chairs as such, but places to sit; a chimpanzee doesn't see a tree but a place to climb. Canonical neurons in the primate brain, which fire when an object is acted on by an individual and also when an object is merely observed, provide neurobiological support for a theory of affordances, since our perceptual representations of objects therefore contain motor as well as sensory components, and hence blur the distinction between perception and conceptual knowledge. Our perception of a cup, for example, cannot be divorced from its function, from what we can do with it, because such possibilities for action are built directly into our perceptions. When we consider mirror neurons from this perspective, we can easily see how our perceptions of other individuals will generate similar affordances. McArthur and Baron (1983) give a number of examples of how the affordances that other individuals offer can explain the accuracy of our perceptions of others at "zero acquaintance."

Most crucially, the theory of affordances provides a natural means of grounding this knowledge in the world because it recognizes the essentially "loopy" nature of behavior, something that Dewey (1896) made clear in his classic paper refuting the notion of the reflex arc. That is, behavior is not the result of one-way link that goes from stimulus to response, as the behaviorists assumed, but is best characterized as a continuous loop where action generates perceptual feedback that, in turn, generates further action, and so on (Hurley, 1998). Nothing remains internal to the animal because action *in* the world is always an integral part of its conception *of* the world. This is something that is also revealed clearly by studies showing how subjects' perceptions can be influenced by their previous actions in the world, as when subjects who have been treadmill walking perceive that more effort will be required to walk a specified distance subsequently. This reflects the adaptation of the visual-motor system to forward movement effort while remaining stationary (Proffitt, 2006a, 2006b).

OUT OF THEIR HEADS?

The manner in which baboons engage in certain forms of social interaction suggests that a stronger, more ethological focus on the affordances that other individuals offer will pay real dividends in understanding how they regulate their social relations. When a female baboon becomes a mother, for example, the presence of her new infant generates intense interest in other females who will try to approach and handle the infant. They will not always do this gently and sometimes might make off with the infant altogether, putting it at risk of dehydration and, in extreme cases, death. Mothers, not surprisingly, display agitation and avoidance when others approach and attempt to handle their offspring. Grooming the mother, however, apparently increases her tolerance for this kind of interaction, with the level of grooming dependent on the number of infants present in the group. This presumably reflects the degree of stress a mother is experiencing: A single infant in a troop means a high level of social attention, and consequently females may require more grooming before its effects (in terms of endorphin release) are felt (Henzi & Barrett, 2002; Barrett & Henzi, 2006).

This grooming in exchange for handling has, however, been described in terms of a more cognitive process, where it represents potentially deceptive behavior on the part of handlers, who approach and groom in order to disguise their true intention and lull the mother into a feeling of false security (given as example #88 in Byrne & Whiten, 1990). Careful analysis of videotaped interactions of this nature (Barrett & Henzi, unpublished data) indicate that most handling events follow a specific sequence that speaks more to intentional attunement of the kind Gallese (2001, 2003, 2005, 2007) espouses, rather than any form of "intentional" or "functional" deception.

Typically, a female will approach a mother and, particularly if lower ranking, will sit at a distance of 2 to 3 m: a distance that places a female sufficiently out of reach of any form of aggressive attack. Once in this position, potential handlers monitor the mother closely, following her head orientation and gaze. Mothers, for their part, will often turn their back as the handler approaches, forcing the handler to begin circling around the mother in order to keep the mother's face, and the infant, in view. If mothers cannot keep the handler out of their own field of view in this way, then they simply do not glance or gaze in the handler's direction. As long as this situation persists, handlers appear paralyzed and unable to act: They will circle around the edge of the apparent zone of tolerance, but do not approach any closer. Occasionally, they may emit contact grunts of a characteristic kind, used only in the presence of infants. Eventually, a potential handler will drift away from the mother if she remains motionless and does not gaze in the handler's direction. If, on the other hand, she does gaze toward the handler, or even orient her head in that direction, this apparently affords the handler the opportunity to approach. Handlers may not always do so, of course, but approaches only occur if mothers afford the opportunity to do so in this way.

Once the handler is in proximity, mothers may again turn away from the handler. This is especially likely to be the case if the mother's glance in the handler's direction was inadvertent; for example, the mother oriented in that direction in response to a call from another animal or because the mother apparently failed to notice the initial approach of a handler. Once in proximity, and with the mother turned away, showing her back, handlers more often than not begin to groom. Seen in the context of the interaction as a whole, this does not seem to be a ploy to deceive the mother, but occurs because the handler is in an aroused state, is socially motivated, and is afforded the opportunity to groom (presenting the shoulder or back to another animal is a standard signal that precedes grooming among primates). As grooming continues, mothers relax their bodies and often orient more directly toward the potential hander, affording the opportunity to interact with the infant an opportunity that handlers may or may not take. It is not uncommon for potential handlers to become so engrossed in grooming that they push the infant out of the way so that they can continue to groom the mother unimpeded.

Infant handling, then, is about two individuals bringing their behavior into coordination in a real-time dynamic fashion (Johnson, 2001), and not about the execution of preformed goals and intentions that exist in one or a other of the animal's heads: Both grooming and handling emerge from the interaction, rather than representing the goal of it. This, as Johnson (2001) argues further, is at the heart of a distributed approach to cognition, and it is quintessentially ecological, since the psychological phenomena are a function of animal–environment relations, rather than of individual animals alone.

From a practical perspective, adopting a distributed, less representational approach also means that we are able to move away from using terms like *intend* and *understand* (which refer to invisible mental states that can only be inferred) to descriptors like *anticipate* and *notice* (which are both observable and definable). Anticipation can be measured by an increased readiness to respond or a decrease in the onset times of a behavior, whereas noticing can be defined by direction of gaze or the relative timing of signaling behaviors (Johnson, 2001).

Strum et al. (1997) have similarly used an analysis of consort-takeovers by male baboons to illustrate how much of the behavior that is often held up as an example of Machiavellian intelligence (i.e., as sophisticated cognitive strategizing to achieve a specific goal) may actually be the result of how particular animals are either constrained or afforded certain courses of action by the environment. Male baboons socially and sexually monopolize adult females during their fertile periods, remaining in close proximity to them at all times. These close spatial relationships (consortships) can last from a few hours to a week, depending on the specific population of baboons. Among East African populations, these consortships are often disrupted by aggression from other males, who then take over the consort male's position. There are various social tactics that males can employ to either avoid or facilitate a takeover. Strum et al. (1997) focus on one they call "sleeping near the enemy." This designation was based on the observation that, although older males were able to resist consort takeover attempts by younger, more aggressive males during the day, they were less able to do so at sleeping sites, whereas younger males were able to displace them and leave with the female in the morning. Strum et al. (1997) demonstrated that a change in topography from the plains, where the animals foraged during the day, to the cliffs, where they slept at night, was the key factor leading to this difference.

Older, socially experienced males could resist takeover on the plains by using social tactics to divert aggression, such as grabbing a younger animal and using it as a buffer against attack by the male. Such tactics require a high degree of visual contact with others, a significant amount of behavioral coordination, and, therefore, sufficient experience with other animals to deploy them successfully. On the sleeping cliffs, however, these tactics were constrained by topography. The height and narrowness of the cliffs resulted in changes in the mobility of males, their proximity to other animals, and a reduction in overall visibility. All of these factors served to reduce older males' ability to manipulate the situation socially, while at the same time favoring the more direct, aggressive tactics of younger males. Males were, therefore, employing those behaviors in their repertoire that were afforded by the environment, rather than varying their tactics in a Machiavellian fashion to thwart and outwit their rivals. This example illustrates that, in addition to the social affordances offered by other individuals, the affordances of the physical environment can also bring individuals' behavior into coordination—or prevent this from happening—so that similar situations play out in entirely different ways depending on how the environment serves to structure the nature of the event.

AFFECT INDUCTION

The behavioral coordination that animals display in their social interactions also gives us further clues regarding the grounding of sociality, and how social interactions can be manipulated and understood in a more embodied, less representational manner. One particularly conspicuous use of behavioral coordination in several animal groups occurs during coalition formation (where two or more animals jointly direct aggression against a third). In both monkeys and dolphins, this behavior is characterized by close bodily synchrony and coordination between partners. Among baboons, for example, female coalitions (which are rather rare occurrences) involve the participants standing shoulder-to-shoulder and advancing on the target of their aggression in tight formation (Henzi & Barrett, 2007). Capuchin monkeys also show this kind of close bodily contact, but they orient themselves vertically, one on top of the other, so as to present a column of threatening faces toward their target. In somewhat similar fashion, dolphin males surface together and swim together in an equally coordinated fashion during aggressive coalitions (Connor et al., 2007). Such tight behavioral coordination serves to signal solidarity among the coalition partners, and is no doubt a more intense and threatening stimulus to the target. It is, as Owren and Rendall (2001) argue, a form of affect induction, where actions are designed to influence directly a target's nervous/physiological systems, rather than as a means of communicating information about the likelihood of attack or the nature of the relationship that exists between coalition partners. As important, such behavioral coordination can be seen as a form of affect induction for the participants: Close bodily contact during an aggressive encounter may well serve to keep coalition partners' stress at lower levels despite high arousal and the stressful nature of the situation. In doing so, it may reduce the costs of such aggression for participants, especially relative to those of the target, who lacks any such form of contact comfort.

As Owren and Rendall (2001; Owren et al., 2003) have argued in the context of vocal communication, if the aim of such social interactions is to manage and influence the bodily response and behavior of other individuals, and not to change their mental states per se, then there is no need to argue that such visual or vocal signals have meaning in the standard representational sense. Instead, as Owren and Rendall (2001) suggest, signals that act at these low levels of neural organization may play an important role in shaping behavior both directly, in the case of signals that have an unconditioned impact on the perceiver's nervous system (the acoustic startle response is a prime example), or indirectly, where vocalizations or visual signals are linked with affectively significant outcomes experienced by the perceiver via conditioning processes. For example, dominant animals can pair their threat vocalizations with actual aggression, so that subordinates learn the contingency between the two, with the result that, eventually, threat vocalizations alone can produce an avoidance response in subordinates (thus sparing the dominant the cost of actual aggression). Such tactics can also work affiliatively, as when individuals grunt softly upon approach, prior to grooming or attempting infant handling. By learning to associate such grunts with a positive outcome (or at least, in the case of infant handling, a neutral, if not wholly positive, one), animals can bring their behavior into coordination more rapidly and will do so more readily. An affect-induction account can also work to the advantage of "socially impotent" animals as well. The harsh, noisy screams that baboons produce when under attack, for example, are highly aversive stimuli, suggesting that subordinate animals are attempting to make themselves less appealing as objects of aggression via the negative affect such calls produce (Owren et al. 2003).

Animals can also regulate their own affect through the use of vocalizations or specific behaviors; the loud wa-hoo calls of male baboons, for example, are produced in a wide variety of contexts, ranging from aggression within the troop, to the sighting of another troop in the distance, to a rock falling from a cliff. Under such circumstances, calling may serve to regulate the animal's own state of affect, by resolving internal tension, as much as it regulates the behavior of others. Similarly, the lost calls that baboons make when separated from the rest of the troop are perhaps better characterized as distress calls that reflect an animal's stress at being alone and unable to see familiar conspecifics. The fact that such lost calls are most frequently answered by the animal itself, as opposed to individuals within the body of the troop, argues for a primarily self-regulatory, rather than directly communicative, function (see Rendall et al., 1999 for more information).

Affect induction is, by definition, an embodied perspective on how animals regulate their own behavior and that of others: It focuses on physical actions and engagement with the world, and considers physiological responses produced in the body as part and parcel of an animal's cognitive response. As such, it provides us with a way out of the anthropocentric bind in which comparative primate studies are currently situated. An understanding of manner in which the perception of others, and an animal's own actions, afford a particular kind of interaction and induce a particular kind of affect, and how this influences the subsequent sequencing and patterning of behavior (in both the short and long term) provides us with a true grounding for sociality, where individuals are linked together as a brain, body, and world loops. In combination with the distributed perspective advocated by Johnson (2001) and Strum et al. (1997), it also enables us to account for the flexibility and novelty seen in primate social behavior, where the interaction between the affordances of the physical environment and those of the social environment can lead similar kinds of interactions to be played out in fundamentally different ways.

CONCLUSION

Of course, the adoption of a more embodied, more ecological, more embedded perspective does not allow us to escape fully from our anthropocentric bind. We are, after all, trapped in our own umwelt and cannot see the world in anything other than human terms. Nevertheless, an awareness of our own being in the world and a rejection of ourselves as detached observers forces us to approach the issues at stake from a less egocentric perspective, and to appreciate that other bodies will ground concepts in other ways. That is, identifying and investigating how cognitive processes have their basis in bodily, situated engagement with the world allows us to abandon Descartes and get back to Darwin. If we attempt to understand baboons on their own terms, as embedded, embodied subjects with their own unique cognitive skills, then ironically, we may be able to make a more interesting metaphysical contribution regarding the nature of our own cognition.

ACKNOWLEDGMENTS

Thanks to Gün Semin and Gerald Echterhoff for inviting me to contribute to this volume, and for their helpful comments on a previous draft. Thanks also to Peter Henzi and Drew Rendall for their comments and helpful discussion. My work is supported by a Discovery grant from the Natural Science and Engineering Research Council of Canada.

NOTES

1. This denial of higher psychical faculties to other animals was, however, qualified by Morgan, who stated that this should only be done in the absence of any independent evidence to the contrary, so it is important to note that Morgan was not denying categorically that other species might possess higher faculties.
2. Even here, however, the findings were interpreted in anthropocentric terms. One scientist commenting on the findings for BBC news noted, "They are our closest living relatives and thus are in a unique position to inform us about our evolutionary heritage. … These studies tell us that elaborate short-term memory skills may have

had a much more salient function in early humans than is present in modern humans, perhaps due to our increasing reliance on language-based memory skills." The idea that these abilities might be a unique skill that chimpanzees have gained over the course of their own evolutionary history, rather than one that modern humans have lost, is not even raised as a possibility. See http://news.bbc.co.uk/1/hi/7124156.stm

REFERENCES

Andrews, K. 2005. Chimpanzee theory of mind: Looking in all the wrong places? *Mind & Language* 20: 521–536.

Antaki, C. 2004. Reading minds or dealing with interactional implications? *Theory and Psychology* 14: 667–683.

Barrett, L. & Henzi, S. P. 2005.The social nature of primate cognition. *Proceedings of the Royal Society*, 272: 1865–1875.

Barrett, L., Henzi, S. P., & Rendall, D. 2007. Social brains, simple minds: Does social complexity really require cognitive complexity? *Philosophical Transactions of the Royal Society, Series B* 362: 561–575.

Bergman, T. J., Beehner, J. C., Cheney, D. L., & Seyfarth, R. M. 2003. Hierarchical classification by rank and kinship in baboons. *Science* 302: 1234–1236.

Block, S. 2007. The *new war on love-loving chimps: Bonobo bashing in the New Yorker*. Retrieved from http://www.counterpunch.org/block07252007.html

Brooks, R. 1999. *Cambrian intelligence: The early history of the new AI.* Cambridge, MA: MIT Press.

Brosnan, S. F. & de Waal, F. B. M. 2003. Monkeys reject unequal pay. *Nature* 425: 297–299.

Bruner, J. 1990. *Acts of meaning*. Cambridge, MA: Harvard University Press.

Byrne, R. W. & Whiten, A. 1990. Tactical deception in primates: The 1990 database. *Primate Report* 27: 1–101.

Cartmill, E. & Byrne, R. W. 2007. Orangutans modify their gestural signaling according to their audience's comprehension. *Current Biology* 17: 1345–1348.

Chartrand, T. L. & Bargh, J. A. 1999. The chameleon effect: The perception-behaviour link and social interaction. *Journal of Personality and Social Psychology* 76: 893–910.

Cheney, D. L. & Seyfarth, R. M. 2005. Constraints and preadaptations in the earliest stages of language evolution. *Linguistic Review* 22: 135–159.

Churchland, P. 1986. *Neurophilosophy*. Cambridge, MA: MIT Press.

Clark, A. 1997. *Being there: Putting brain, body and world together again*. Cambridge, MA: MIT Press.

Connor, R. C., Smolker, R., & Bejder, L. 2006. Synchrony, social behaviour and alliance affiliation in Indian Ocean bottlenose dolphins, *Tursiops aduncus. Animal Behaviour* 72: 1371–1378.

Costall, A. & Leudar, I. 2004. Where is the "theory" in theory of mind? *Theory and Psychology* 14: 623–646.

De Waal, F. B. M. (2001). *The ape and the sushi master: Cultural reflections of a primatologist*. New York: Basic Books.

Dewey, J. 1896. The reflex arc in psychology. *Psychological Review* 3: 357–370.

Dewey, J. 1929. *Experience and nature*. New York: Dover.

Dreyfus, H. (1991). Husserl, Heidegger and modem existentialism. In: *The great philosophers* (B. Magee, Ed.) (pp. 252–277). Oxford: Oxford University Press.

Gallagher, S. 2005. *How the body shapes the mind*. Oxford, UK: Oxford University Press.

Gallese, V. 2001. The "shared manifold" hypothesis: From mirror neurons to empathy. *Journal of Consciousness Studies* 8: 33–50.

Gallese, V. 2003. The roots of empathy: The shared manifold hypothesis and the neural basis of intersubjectivity. *Psychopathology* 36: 171–180.
Gallese, V. 2005. Embodied simulation: From neurons to phenomenal experience. *Phenomenology and the Cognitive Sciences* 4: 22–48.
Gallese, V. 2007. Before and below "theory of mind": Embodied simulation and the neural correlates of social cognition. *Philosophical Transactions of the Royal Society, Series B* 362: 659–669.
Gershon, M. 1998. *The second brain*. New York: Harper Collins.
Gibson, J. J. 1979. *The ecological approach to visual perception*. Hillsdale, NJ: Lawrence Erlbaum Associates.
Hacking, I. 1999. *The social construction of what?* Cambridge, MA: Harvard University Press.
Heidegger, M. 1978. *Being and time*. Malden, MA: Blackwell. (Original work published 1926)
Heider, F. & Simmel, M. 1944. An experimental study of apparent behavior. *American Journal of Psychology* 57: 243–259.
Henzi, S. P. & Barrett, L. (2002). Commodity in a baboon market. *Animal Behaviour* 63, 915–921.
Henzi, S. P. & Barrett, L. 2007. Coexistence in female-bonded primate. *Advances in the Study of Behavior* 37: 43–81.
Hurley, S. 1998. *Consciousness in action*. Cambridge, MA: Harvard University Press.
Hutto, D. D. 2004. The limits of spectatorial folk psychology. *Mind & Language* 19: 548–573.
Inoue, S. & Matsuzawa, T. 2007. Working memory of numerals in chimpanzees. *Current Biology* 17: R1004–1005.
James, W. 1890. *Principles of psychology*. New York: Dover.
Johnson, C. 2001. Distributed primate cognition: A review. *Animal Cognition* 4: 167–183.
Jolly, A. 2007. The social origin of mind. *Science* 317: 1326–1327.
Keeley, B. L. 2004. Anthropomorphism, primatomorphism, mammalomorphism: Understanding cross-species comparisons. *Biology and Philosophy* 19: 521–540.
Leslie, A. M., Friedman, O., & German, T. P. 2004. Core mechanisms in "theory of mind." *Trends in Cognitive Sciences* 8: 528–533.
Leudar, I. & Costall, A. 2004. On the persistence of the "problem of other minds" in psychology: Chomsky, Grice and theory of mind. *Theory and Psychology* 14: 601–621.
Leudar, I., Costall, A., & Francis, D. 2004. Theory of mind: A critical assessment. *Theory and Psychology* 14: 571–578.
Lieberman, M. D., Gaunt, R., Gilbert, D. T., and Trope, Y. 2002. Reflection and reflexion: A social cognitive neuroscience approach to attributional inference. *Advances in Experimental Social Psychology* 34: 199–249.
Lillard, A. 1998. Ethnopsychologies: Cultural variations in theory of mind. *Psychological Bulletin* 123: 3–32.
McArthur, L. Z. & Baron, R. M. 1983. Toward an ecological theory of social perception. *Psychological Review* 90: 215–238.
Michaels, C. F. & Carello, C. 1981. *Direct perception*. Englewood Cliffs, NJ: Prentice Hall.
Owren, M. J. & Rendall, D. 2001. Sound on the rebound: Bringing form and function back to the forefront in understanding nonhuman primate vocal signaling. *Evolutionary Anthropology* 10: 58–71.
Owren, M. J., Rendall, D., & Bachorowski, J. 2003. Nonlinguistic vocal communication. In D. Maestripieri (Ed.), *Primate psychology* (pp. 359–394). Cambridge, MA: Harvard University Press.
Parker, I. 2007. Swingers. *New Yorker*, July 30.
Pennisi, E. (2007). News of the week: Non-human primates demonstrate human-like reasoning. *Science*, 317: 1308.
Pert, C. B. 1997. *Molecules of emotion*. New York: Scribner.

Pfeifer, R. & Bongard, J. 2007. *How the body shapes the way we think*. Cambridge, MA: MIT Press.

Pollick, A. S. & de Waal, F. B. M. 2007. Ape gestures and language evolution. *Proceedings of the National Academy of Sciences USA* 104: 8184–8189.

Povinelli, D., Bering, J., & Giambrone, S. 2000. Toward a science of other minds: Escaping the argument by analogy. *Cognitive Science* 24: 509–541.

Proffitt, D. R. 2006a. Distance perception. *Current Directions in Psychological Science* 15: 131–135.

Proffitt, D. R. 2006b. Embodied perception and the economy of action. *Perspectives on Psychological Science* 1: 110–122.

Reddy, V. 1996. Omitting the second person in social understanding. *Behavioral and Brain Sciences* 19: 140–141.

Reddy, V. 2007. Getting back to the rough ground: deception and "social living." *Philosophical Transactions of the Royal Society B*, 362: 621–637.

Reddy, V. & Morris, P. 2004. Participants don't need theories. *Theory and Psychology* 14: 647–665.

Reed, E. 1996. *Encountering the world: Toward an ecological psychology*. Oxford, UK: Oxford University Press.

Rendall, D., Seyfarth, R. M., Cheney, D. L., & Owren, M. J. 1999. The meaning and function of grunt variants in baboons. *Animal Behaviour* 57: 583–592.

Rockwell, W. T. 2005. *Neither brain nor ghost: A nondualist alternative to the mind–brain identity theory*. Cambridge, MA: MIT Press.

Sharrock, W. & Coulter, J. 2004. ToM: A critical commentary. *Theory and Psychology* 14: 579–600.

Simons, H. A. (1996). *The Sciences of the artificial*. (3rd ed.). Cambridge, MA: MIT Press.

Strum, S. C., Forster, D., & Hutchins, E. 1997. Why Machiavellian intelligence may not be Machiavellian. In A. Whiten and R. W. Byrne (Eds.), *Machiavellian intelligence II: Extensions and evaluations (pp. 50–85)*. Cambridge, UK: Cambridge University Press,.

Varela, F. J., Thompson, E., & Rosch, E. 1991. *The embodied mind: cognitive science and human experience*. Cambridge, MA: MIT Press.

Von Uexküll, J. 1957. A stroll through the worlds of animals and men. In C. H. Schiller & K. S. Lashley (Eds.), *Instinctive behaviour: The development of a modern concept* (pp. 5–82). New York: International Universities Press. (Original work published in 1934)

Wheeler, M. 2005. *Reconstructing the cognitive world: The next step*. Cambridge, MA: MIT Press.

Wood, J. N., Glynn, D. D., Phillips, B. C., & Hauser, M. D. 2007. The perception of rational, goal-directed action in nonhuman primates. *Science* 317: 1402–1405.

Zebrowitz, L. & Collins, M. A. 1997. Accurate social perception at zero aquaintance. The affordances of a Gibsonian approach. *Personality and Social Psychology Review* 1: 204–223.

12

Revolutionary Darwinism
Sociality Is *the Ground*

LINNDA R. CAPORAEL

My goal for this paper is to ground sociality in two ways. The first is to theoretically ground human sociality in an expanded evolutionary-developmental perspective, or *evo-devo*. The second is to claim that the very form of the evolved human body makes sociality essential, not just possible. Let me discuss these two assertions.

Neo-Darwinism, variously known as genic selectionism, selfish gene theory, or the gene's eye view of evolution, has little to say about sociality. The modern synthesis, between Darwinism and population genetics, was fundamentally about gene transmission (Amundson, 2005; Sansom & Brandon, 2007). Traditional Neo-Darwinism defines evolution as changes in gene frequencies in a population over generations as a result of natural selection and other evolutionary processes.[1] Organisms were viewed largely as the expression of the hereditary information in the genes. While lip service was given to environment and development, the form and formation of organisms belonged to other parts of biology, such as ecology and cell biology. Likewise, paleontology, the science of fossils from the ancient past, and embryology, the study of the development of morphology or form, were peripheral to the "synthesis," although that has been changing (Callebaut, Müller, & Newman, 2007; Eldredge, 1985). By itself, transmission genetics cannot explain why species look and behave differently nor the development of different forms of bodies even though that was the basic material for Darwin's discovery of natural selection. In the modern synthesis, the body is just a "dead end," at best a vehicle for transporting genes across generations (Dawkins, 1982; Griesemer, 2006).

Another reason Neo-Darwinism has little to say about sociality is a lingering argument against "group selection," which traditional evolutionists explained as behavior "for the good of the group." From the "gene's eye" point of view (Dawkins, 1976; Williams, 1966), "altruistic" genes that caused an organism to genetically benefit unrelated others would disappear from the population. "Selfish genes," whether they were a result of migration or mutations in a group of altruists, would eventually replace altruists. Seemingly altruistic social behavior could be understood as kin selection, reciprocal altruism, or as Machiavellian social intelligence benefiting the individual's genes (Byrne & Whiten, 1988). Aggregates of individuals overcame the disadvantages of group living by engaging in deception, exploitation, and other types of interpersonal manipulation, including "soft altruism," the seemingly altruistic behavior that ultimately serves the gene's selfish ends (Wilson, 1978).

The case against group selection and the reification of individualism had led to an odd way of grounding sociality. One must explain why humans are *still* social (Dunbar, 1989, p. 701, emphasis in original). What characteristics make sociality *possible*? The background assumptions to such questions are that group living is costly to individuals, and humans will revert to a primitive state of solitary existence without some positive advantage to grouping. The usual way of satisfying the requirement is to posit intergroup warfare, even while admitting at the same time that evidence is lacking (Alexander, 1989). Yet, one merely needs to look at the human body to see that sociality is *essential*. Humans are unable to reproduce and survive to reproductive age without a group.

Sociality is inscribed on the body. However, as psychologists (with Cartesian license to separate mind and body, see Barrett, this volume, Chapter 11), we talk about the brain and what it does, while the body might as well simmer in a vat. When we discuss "human nature," we locate it in the mind, or for the squeamish, the mind/brain. Evolutionary psychologists are strangers to the body as well. The causal sequence proposed for understanding human psychology goes from "Evolution → Psychological Mechanism → Behavior" (Cosmides & Tooby, 1987, p. 281). But natural selection does not "see" psychological mechanisms; it sees (that is, selection results from) interactions between whole bodies and their environments.

Similarly, humans do not have Stone Age minds in a modern skull, as is frequently claimed; they have modern minds in a Stone Age body. We know from cross-cultural and historical research that such minds are enormously creative and capable of constructing many types of novel material and social realities. So as scientists we wind up with some curious problems. One is that Neo-Darwinism, despite being a theory changes about in gene frequencies, labors in two domains, social and scientific, linked by vivid metaphors such as altruism and self-interest.[2] The problem with Neo-Darwinism in the human domain is that it is easy to tell a story to explain or justify familiar behavior, but hard to test its evolutionary impact on differential reproduction in a population. Another problem is the overlap between theory and folk knowledge on subjects from kinship to rape. Calling on evolutionary theory to justify various folk psychologies would probably serve just as well to reinforce them, much as many origin stories reinforce the social realities that give rise to them. Nonetheless, Darwinism does have the potential to be revolutionary, to provide theoretical frameworks that can help us, as scientists, gain an inch or two of perspective, which might be the best for which we can hope being human ourselves, since we are trapped in our time and place.

Here is a plan to help the reader through this unfamiliar territory to ground sociality: In the following section, I introduce an expanded evolutionary perspective, taking shape under the umbrella of evolutionary-developmental biology, shortened to *evo-devo*. In the narrowest sense, evo-devo is the molecular biology of embryological development. In its broadest sense, evo-devo refers to a variety of perspectives, some reinforcing each other, others competing with each other, but sharing some opposition to traditional Neo-Darwinism and genetic determinism (Callebaut, Müller, & Newman, 2007). This section also suggests a vocabulary, called *repeated assembly*, which recognizes the inheritance of multiple resources. Its heuristic virtue is sidestepping nature–nurture dualism and unsupportable claims about genetic causes.

The second section grounds sociality in "corporeal matters of fact" (Sheets-Johnstone, 1992): the evolved, but overlooked, body. The possibilities inherent in the body in turn ground a more refined perspective on human sociality in the structure and dynamics of face-to-face groups. The vehicle for this discussion is a minimalist scenario of hunter-gatherer groups and the core group configurations for achieving some key tasks. The overarching hypothesis is that, if the model is valid, we should expect correspondences between certain face-to-face group structures and mental systems. Where the individual, material body is the organizing principle in this second section, the third dissolves the material individual body into different levels of psychological "group selves" (See Semin, Chapter 5). The emphasis in this section is on how group structures might function in a complex, modern world where people are epistemically interdependent and have multiple identities in cross-cutting groups. One of the consequences of this exercise is a potentially better understanding of the problem of the relationship between individual and society.

EVO-DEVO AND THE REPEATED ASSEMBLY OF MULTIPLE RESOURCES

An expanded evolutionary theory is necessary for grounding sociality. Neo-Darwinism tells us little about human, bird, or shrimp phenotypes in the absence of what we already know—or think we know—about them. The result is an evolutionary psychology that rationalizes current understanding of mind, but offers few novel conceptual or research directions (Smith, 2000). Lacking theoretical direction and constraints, scientific and popular appeals to Darwinism can be indistinguishable (Landau, 1984; Maynard Smith, 1987; Moser, 1998). In contrast, from the evo-devo perspective, the phenotype results from the constructive interactions of events at different levels of organization as well as activity of the organism itself. While the (material) genes are necessary, they are not a sufficient resource in the self-organization and construction of an organism (Jablonka & Lamb, 2005). Evo-devo has "revealed that evolution can and does repeat itself at the levels of structures and patterns as well as individual genes" (Carroll, 2005, p. 289). The repetition of structure and patterns is discussed next starting from a biological position and reformulated as a vocabulary of "repeated assembly."

Levels of Organization and Self-Organization

The history of life is the history of several major transitions in the physical organization of biological phenomena (Maynard Smith & Szathmáry, 1995). DNA molecules, chromosomes, and multicellular organisms are examples of the products of such reorganizations. The main characteristic of these major reorganizations is that entities capable of self-replication *before* reorganization are replicated as part of a larger entity *after* reorganization. For example, the mitochondria, tiny organs that are involved in the energy production of cells in our bodies, are descended from cells that were free-living billions of years ago (Margulis, 1981). Multicellular organisms are another example of evolutionary innovation, one where some cells "gave up" reproductive autonomy to become body cells as others eventually became reproducing gametes (Buss, 1987). Archaic cells caused the propagation of both their own cell lineage and the organism of which they were part. These variants were more successful than variants that propagated their own cell lineage at the expense of the individual. Cancer is a modern example of cell lineages propagating at the expense of the individual.

Thus, from the evo-devo perspective, the organism embodies multiple different levels of selection. Macromolecules, cells, cell lineages, organisms, and groups are at different levels of the biological hierarchy and the result of major transitions in the evolution of life. Evolution and development result from the outcome of conflicts and synergisms at different levels of organization. Note that individuals and groups constitute two levels of biological organization and development for humans. This is a far richer perspective than the gene's eye view, in which the phenotype is taken for granted.

Evo-devo provides a warrant for grounding an evolutionary vocabulary suitable for the human sciences because the process of selection is *situated, relational,* and *embodied* at different levels of organization (Eldredge & Grene, 1992; Endler, 1986). Individuals provide the embodied *material overlap* between genes and culture for the iterative processes of human reproduction and development (Griesemer, 2002, 2006; personal communication, May 2008). Traditionally, psychologists and others interested in human nature have looked to genes for explaining recurrence (universals) across cultures as well as recurrence (resemblance) from generation to generation. From the evo-devo perspective, the phenotype results from the constructive interactions of events at different levels as well as the activity of the organism itself.

Genes are only part of the phenotype, which is the product of the joint action of genetic and epigenetic components. (Epigenetic components are cellular, environmental, temporal, and spatial factors—in short, everything that is not genes but nevertheless participates in the construction of an organism.) Genes are not a "program" for organizing or using epigenetic components; epigenetic factors organize genetic activity, too. Like genes, they must be reliably present for the formation of an organism. The life span of organisms results from the reciprocal action or ongoing dialectic among genes and successive levels of environment. In other words, organisms are "repeated assemblies" of multiple, heterogeneous resources.

Repeated Assembly

A vocabulary of *repeated assembly* (Caporael, 2003) offers a phenotypic view of evolution. Its primary advantage is that it allows psychologists to develop and participate in a human evolutionary science that is consistent with biology. At the same time, the vocabulary does not require commitments to levels of analysis that are not directly relevant to our research questions.

For example, an animal zygote begins with the repeated assembly of two sources of DNA, centrosomes from the sperm, and other components, all of which, if in the right place, at the right time, automatically result in a zygote. There is no "genetic program" that directs or controls the assembly of the zygote. Instead, the analogy is to a chemical reaction, where, given a set of constituents, against a background of enabling conditions, an explosion, a precipitate, or a vapor results—or repeatedly assembles. The continued development of the embryo is place-dependent (i.e., epigenetic). Cells adhere to each other, lose adhesion, and migrate. Each cell has the same DNA as the original zygote. The difference that makes a difference—that causes the differentiation of cells, tissues, and structures—is time and spatial position and the consequent shifting cellular relationships, which influence genetic activity.

At the level of the organism, genes are always among the multiple, heterogeneous resources of a repeated assembly (the organism), but they require epigenetic components at their own and other levels. Genetic action is dependent on the reliable recurrence of appropriate contexts, from cellular machinery to social events to features of the ecosystem such as atmosphere (Griffiths & Gray, 1994). Some resources will themselves be repeated assemblies, from the biological machinery that generates individual immune systems to the practices, artifacts, and world views that are culturally reproduced (Wimsatt & Griesemer, 2007). Resources may change within lifetimes (e.g., a specific cultural item), indicating low reliability of recurrence, but little about causal pathways.

Language is a paradigmatic example of the familiar nature–nurture dichotomy, and long predates Darwinism, yet this antique conception remains unchanged. The capacity for language is viewed as innate and the specific language one speaks is viewed as learned. Yet, this intuitively obvious distinction throws away crucial information. A natal language is just as much inherited as the "capacity for language." What differs is that specific languages appear and disappear over shorter periods of time than does speech itself. The constructive interactions that produce human attributes are not just from genetic activity, but also from resources that have their own scales and cycles of time (Figure 12.1). Some components, such as the DNA code, have been parts of repeated assemblies since the beginning of life. Other components, such as a cultural environment, have a temporal scale measured in historical terms. Still others recur on the scale of a lifetime. A vocabulary of repeated assembly does not require us to make commitments about genes in the absence of evidence, and it is consistent with a Darwinian model of selection, variation, and retention.

As a vocabulary, repeated assembly enables us to describe and decompose recurrence from the perspective of one's particular research question, which

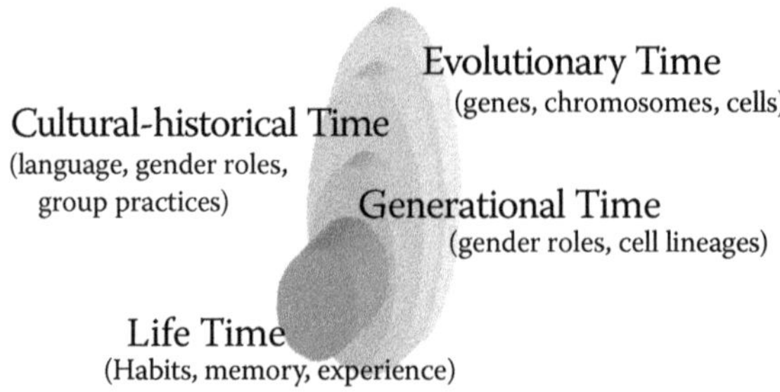

Figure 12.1 The repeated assembly of phenotypic resources.

inevitably picks out an entity and its relevant environment(s). Just as the situated environment for genes is the cellular interactions between DNA and its products, the situated environment for humans is the face-to-face social group, through which they are able to interact with the environment. Some repeated assemblies (e.g., language) are presumed to have an evolutionary history; they repeatedly assemble in human development, in daily life, and plausibly, over evolutionary history (Hendriks-Jansen, 1996).

GROUNDING SOCIALITY: CORE GROUP CONFIGURATIONS

Neo-Darwinists, famous for opposing group selection, often write as if organisms calculate genetic costs and benefits in order to make individual choices about whether to group. Nonetheless, most animals are group living (Pulliam & Caraco, 1984), even if for no other reason than the failure of kin groups to disperse for some part of their life history. In this section, I focus on how the human body grounds sociality in an essential way, and thus provides the point of departure for theory and research on human face-to-face groups as the "natural environment" for the evolution of truly social cognition (Caporael & Baron, 1997).

Corporeal Matters

Primates have lived in social groups for more than 40 million years, and paleoanthropologists concur that humanity evolved over the last few million years in face-to-face foraging groups (Foley, 1996; Klein, 1999; Tattersall, 1999). Humans are a fundamentally social species. They are unable to reproduce and survive to reproductive age without a group. They lack natural defenses such as slashing canines, bodily armor, or fleetness of foot; they have an extended infancy followed by years of further development before they reach reproductive maturity. Many of the evolved characteristics that have permitted humans to adapt to a wide range of physical environments, such as omnivory and tool making, create dependence on collective knowledge and cooperative information sharing among individuals and between generations. As a consequence, human beings are characterized by *obligatory interdependence*, and our evolutionary history is a story of coevolution of genetic endowment, social structure, and culture (Boyd & Richerson, 1985; Caporael, 2001; Fiske, 2000; Janicki, 1998; Li, 2003). Even in the current world of technologies that sever the binding ties of time and space, humans are unable to survive and reproduce without a group.

These signs of interdependence are "corporeal matters of fact" (Sheets-Johnstone, 1992) that anyone can observe; facts that, curiously, are typically overlooked in evolutionary theorizing and usually are reduced to matters of anatomy. Modeling the evolution of human behavior typically appeals to primate evidence, indigenous peoples, fossil interpretations, and traditional neo-Darwinian theory (Andrews, Gangestad, & Matthews, 2002; Schmitt & Pilcher, 2004; Tooby & DeVore, 1987), but rarely (with the exception of fossil material, always incomplete) attends to the most observable and available evidence of that past, the evolved body. Our Darwinian bodies are "not just shaped in morphological ways by evolution but shaped semantically—which means kinetically, gesturally, spatially, behaviorally. Because we are all natural bodies in this sense, we ourselves have a history. Our fundamental human habits and beliefs have an evolutionary past: burying our dead has an evolutionary past; so also does drawing, counting and language. And so also does our intercorporeal semantics" (Sheets-Johnstone, 1992, p. 40). Thus, the visible, observable form of the human body grounds sociality.

Consider how even the most minimalist scenario of human evolution, based on bodily constraints, grounds human sociality. Given their morphology and ecology, the ancestors of evolving hominins must have survived as groups rather than as individuals. Finding food, defense from predation, moving across a landscape—these matters of coping with the physical habitat—would have been largely group processes that began among the earliest arboreal primates, possibly as a result of changing patterns of dispersal in response to climatic and ecological changes. Over time, if exploiting a habitat is more successful as a collective group process than as an aggregate group or individual process, then not only would more coordinated groups persist, but also would individuals better adapted to group living. Because local ecologies limit group size, the number of "niches" in a group is also limited, resulting in a feedforward ratchet and group fission when groups become too large to exist on the local ecology. If individual humans cannot survive outside of groups, then the structural requirements for sustaining groups create systematic constraints on individual biological and psychological adaptations. Humans are certainly capable of self-interest, but the opportunities for self-interest are constrained; just as on other levels of the biological hierarchy, there are mechanisms that prevent runaway replications (e.g., programmed cell death in the development of separated fingers and toes, which can fail, resulting in the fusion of the digits).

Core Configurations

The minimalist scenario can be expanded. A model of *core group configurations* within face-to-face groups draws on considerations of body, group size, and task for the evolution of coordination (Caporael, 1995, 2007). Table 12.1 summarizes an idealized model of four configurations—dyad, task group (work/family group),

TABLE 12.1 Core Configurations

Core Configuration[a]	Group Size	Modal Tasks	Proper Function
Dyad	2	Sex, infant interaction with older children and adults	Microcoordination
Task group	5	Foraging, hunting, gathering, direct interface with habitat	Distributed cognition
Deme (Band)	30	Movement from place to place, general processing and maintenance, work group coordination	Shared construction of reality (includes indigenous psychologies), identity
Macrodeme (Macroband)	300	Seasonal gathering, exchange of individuals, resources, and information	Stabilizing and standardizing language

[a] Core configurations are a function of both size and task. Except for dyads, these numbers should be considered as modal estimates.

band, and macroband—organized as a nested hierarchy. The tasks listed are generally characteristic of hunter-gatherers, but have analogues in the activity patterns of modern peoples. Groups (then and now) are not just an aggregate of individuals, but have recurrent structural properties, called a *demic structure* (Hull, 1988). The recurrence results from the persistent dynamic relations among bodily form, modal tasks, group size, and ecological constraints generations through generations.

If uniquely human sociocognitive processes evolved (or earlier building blocks were reorganized) for dynamic coordination in core configurations, then traces of the mind's natural environment and the processes that evolved in that context should persist despite substantial differences in large-scale social organization (Caporael & Baron, 1997). Core configurations and associated processes are hypothesized to recur ontogenetically as a developmental system, in day-to-day life, and presumably in human evolutionary history. There are, of course, other types of human groupings, but they are not necessarily "core." Also, we would expect that a variety of different mechanisms—not just single mechanisms—would evolve because any configuration is suitable for a variety of recurrent tasks.

Phylogenetically, *dyads* are the most ancient core configuration. At minimum, they are a necessary configuration for internal fertilization, even for those animals that otherwise live in solitary conditions. Dyadic interaction is also the initial—and crucial—relationship for infant survival among humans. Dyads afford the evolution and development of finely coordinated bodily movement such as facial imitation in a mother–infant dyad (Meltzoff & Moore, 1977) and the automatic adjustment of gait that occurs when two people walk together. Among humans (and perhaps primates more generally), dyads are probably evolutionarily significant not so much because new capacities appear, but because this configuration functions in the initial social organization and entrainment of biological clocks, interpersonal rhythmicity, and temporal patterning. Processes such as perception, memory, and attention are based on the synchronization of nested rhythmic patterns in the physical world with the endogenous rhythmic processes of the organism over different levels of organization (Semin & Cacioppo, 2008). Dyadic microcoordination also functions in learning and using precision artifacts; modern examples include learning motor skills in tennis or blowing a pipette in a chemistry lab.

In addition to dyads, there are task groups, demes, and macrodemes. *Task group* configurations afford the evolution of cognitive processes to be distributed over group members. Cognitive tasks such as perception, classification, inference, and contextually cued responses can be distributed over a group, particularly in the face of ambiguous or anomalous data from the habitat. In the hunter-gatherer group, a task group might be a hunting party interpreting signs of animal movements over a landscape. A modern example would be control tower personnel at airports interpreting signs of possible danger from ambiguous signs on a radar screen. The *deme* (in anthropology, the band) affords a shared construction of reality or "common knowledge," as well as skills, practices, and rituals. (The term *deme*, from the Greek *demos*, is used in its original sense of a neighborhood unit rather than the biological sense of breeding population.) The deme or band is the basic economic unit, the first configuration that can be self-sustaining for survival and child rearing (but not reproduction). The deme is the staging ground for domestic life, including task group coordination, and for cooperative alliances, which are the basis for fissioning when the community exceeds resources or is fractured by conflict.

In human evolution, the *macrodeme* afforded the exchange of genes, and information and resources beyond the immediate face-to-face interacting group, including the stabilization and standardization of language. The ethnohistory of some hunter-gatherer groups indicates that related demes met in seasonal gatherings and exchanged marriage partners, gifts, information, performed rituals affirming group identity, and played competitive games (Lee & DeVore, 1968). Today, similar patterns can be seen. Scientific conferences are often seasonal meetings where information and young people are exchanged, and where the standardization and stabilization of distinctive terminology and the reaffirmation of group identity occurs. The macrodeme is important for two reasons. First, seasonal macrodemes demonstrate the persistent collective identity of groups beyond day-to-day engagement. Individual group members may change, but the group as a unit interacting with other groups persists, sometimes across several generations. Macrodemes are the prototypes for modern ethnic groups—geographically extended groups of people who do not necessarily have face-to-face relationships, but define themselves as having a common origin and share interaction norms, socialization experiences, and rituals of group identity (Taylor, 2002). Second, the huge advantage at group and individual levels is to know of distant events, people, and places (Jarvenpa & Brumbach, 1988). Such knowledge at a distance undoubtedly played (and continues to play) an important role in the cultural evolution of language and also of problem solving. In a critical sense, prehistoric macrodemes freed human beings from the limits of face-to-face interaction. Along the way, this newfound freedom would be expected to exert downward causal selection processes on language and social organization itself (Lakoff & Johnson, 1980; see Table 12.1).

Qualifications and Implications

There are a few general points to be made about the core configuration model. First, "what evolve" are unlikely to be high-level complex "modules" dictating preferences, evolved knowledge, or choices. Instead, we should expect to identify low-level activity patterns that initially operate in the early stages of human development and are elaborated through ontogeny (Hendriks-Jansen, 1996). Walking is one such example (Thelen & Smith, 1994). Activity patterns involving a recurrent activity with a recurrent aspect of the environment that evolve in core configurations would repeatedly assemble, presumably from prehistory through the present, in ontogeny and in daily life. Second, core configurations differ in how deeply they are entrenched (Wimsatt, 2001). Dyads are deeply entrenched; a change in critical resources (whether genetic or environmental in origin) for their recurrence should predict poor developmental outcomes. In contrast, macrodemes are shallowly entrenched and are relatively easy to modify. Third, the activity patterns that we identify as having evolved and developed in core configurations clearly must be capable of being extended, combined, and used in new domains. For example, a heart surgery team combines finely tuned microcoordination and distributed cognition—functions rooted in two different configurations. Technology can also provide bridges between the functions of configurations. A group of 500 people given an order to march on a football field are likely to clump and straggle, but if a rousing marching song is broadcast, they can hardly avoid keeping time. Moreover, as the previous example illustrates, artifacts not only coordinate cognition and behavior (Hutchins, 1995) but also shape action, knowledge, and shared values (Bargh & Ferguson, 2000; Hardin & Higgins, 1996).

SOCIETY: REPEATED ASSEMBLIES OF CORE CONFIGURATIONS

Our bodies are Stone Age but our minds are modern. No other creature has constructed social and material worlds so radically different from the conditions in which it evolved. From an expanded evolutionary perspective, a large set of questions concerns the mechanisms, processes, and structures at the source of this generativity. In this section, I suggest that, to some extent, core configurations mediate between individual and society epistemically and through social identity.

Human Ways of Knowing

The previous section implies that different kinds of core configurations can be associated with different epistemologies. Dyads are involved in nonverbal interaction with other people, animals, and things (which are frequently anthropomorphized). Task groups interface between groups and habitats in the discovery and creation of knowledge. They are "on the ground" makers and collectors of knowledge, be it about a mushroom, a chart, or a graph. Task groups produce what Bruner (1986) calls paradigmatic or logico-scientific modes of thought. Only recently, with the invention of slide projectors and PowerPoint, have large numbers of people been able to see the details of mushroom gills held in someone's hand. And even then, the image is to tell already crafted stories about the gills, not to puzzle out their role in, say, spore distribution.

Among other things, demes (or "vehicles of knowledge," see Campbell, 1997) integrate and extend task group knowledge, news that can then spread through macrodemes. Macrodemes seem to exploit narrative modes of thought (Bruner, 1986). A well-formed argument and a well-formed narrative have different operating principles. According to Bruner (1986), the former is evaluated in terms of rules of logic, science, and mathematics; the latter is evaluated in terms of its ability to make sense and reflect on human or humanlike intentions and experience. Paradigmatic modes are expected to lead to factual understanding; narrative modes are expected to be lifelike and to provide different views of subjectivity. Perhaps most notably, causality is understood differently. In paradigmatic modes of thought, the search is for the specific factors or the elimination of competing alternatives in an "x causes y" argument. In the narrative, causality lies in the connection between events. The particular causes in a story are chosen precisely because they make sense of the ending. Of course, there can be confusion between these two, and human evolutionary theory itself is an illustration of the problems (Caporael, 2008; Maynard Smith, 1987). Bruner (1986) does not suggest that argument and narrative are related to group size, but to the extent that argument implies engagement with one or more others, there are constraints that are more readily apparent than in the telling of a story. In modern societies, knowledge, practice, norms, and the rituals that preserve them can spread narratively through overlapping macrodemes. The psychological "gearshifts" through different configurations are hypothesized to be transitions in self and social identity (Caporael, 2001).

The connection between individuals and societies has been a thorny problem in the social and psychological sciences. From one extreme (methodological individualism), society is the aggregate of individual decisions and behavior. From another extreme (methodological collectivism), the individual is the repository of institutional and societal beliefs. Most visions of society appear as a "smooth-textured" aggregate, at best subdivided as nonmutually exclusive categories sharing one or a small number of traits, for example, South Americans, dog fanciers, scientists. Recently, social psychologists have started to integrate these two stances, as in research on individual and collective memory (Hirst & Manier, 2008; see Hirst & Brown, this volume, Chapter 6) and on social cognition and social identity (Abrams & Hogg, 1999; Deaux, Reid, Mizrahi, & Cotting, 1999). The core configuration model is compatible with these efforts and provides an evolutionary framework where further connections may be made.

Turner et al. (1987, p. 208) wrote, "society is in the individual as much as individuals are in society" (see Hogg, 1992). The usual way to understand a statement like this is that society is an aggregate of individuals who absorb and incorporate into their self-identities bits and pieces of society from various sources such as family, school, and community. Increasingly social identity is proposed as a pivotal fulcrum for human action (Brewer & Caporael, 2006; Brewer & Gardner, 1996). Clancey

(1997) argues that the trick to knowing what to do next is "a complex choreography of role, involving a sense of place, and a social identity that *conceptually regulates* behavior" (p. 24, emphasis in original).

The view from evo-devo suggests there might be multiple perspectives. From the individual perspective, the "skin-bounded" human entity (which we commonly take in psychology) is the unique product of, and interactant in, multiple kinds of situated activities or environments. From the social identity perspective, the skin-bounded organism is "dissolved" into other coordinated units of group-level action: Individuals become component parts of more or less coordinated groups, or wholes. Psychologically, these are two perspectives of the same dynamic processes, activity-identity loops, similar to the way that light can be described as waves or packets depending on one's perspective sociality can be perceived as micro-local or global-macro (Kashima, 2000; Kashima & Bratanova, Chapter 10, this volume). Personal identity, as the locus of conscious awareness of goals, plans, and beliefs, is an emergent product of multiple interacting and dynamic selves.

Core Configurations and Transitions in Self and Identity

Figure 12.2 is about the coordinated relationship between individual and society in the core configuration framework. Because that relation is multilayered and complex, there are multiple readings of the figure depending on the focal perspective. In a future world, Figure 12.2 would be an animated image on a digital page. In the current world, the best that can be done is to lead the reader

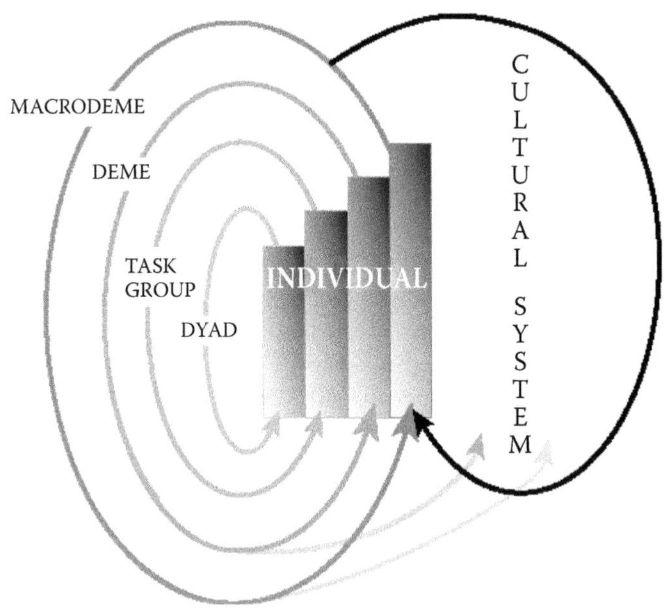

Figure 12.2 Part/whole relationships between individuals and society (read from multiple perspectives as described in text).

through the various interpretations it represents. There are four ways in which the structures and processes in Figure 12.2 are representative. In order, these are (1) the "skin-bounded" individual we typically take as a given, (2) the situated activity of people as they participate as parts of a group or are "dissolved" in a group activity or identity, (3) the development of offspring in an expanding world or other levels of organization, and (4) an evolutionary view.

If we take the Turner et al. (1987) description of the individual in society and society in the individual, we might map it to the central set of bars, representing personalized identity of the skin-bounded individual. The left side of the figure shows core configuration identities, which contribute (the arrows) to the formation of personal identity and self-concept. Activity in core configurations is framed and understood by the actors in terms of the background context of the larger cultural system of artifacts, symbols, stereotypes, and so forth, which is shown on the right, from behind the demic structure of face-to-face groups. At the same time, the skin-bounded individual is also part of various core configurations. As a member of a deme or macrodeme (which are overlooked in familiar accounts of the individual vs. society), the individual may have some impact on a larger cultural system.

The cultural system(s) on the right also provide raw materials for collective identities, in the form of shared reality, institutions, perceptions, and knowledge based on categorizations. These identities include gender, race, ethnicity, and disability, for example, but exclude features that are common but not usually a basis for identity (e.g., height). Of course, there are interesting asymmetries of self-categorizations. Lefties are a discriminated minority in a world tooled by and for right-handers. Righties barely notice one another's or lefties' handedness. Through such complexes of situated activity, society gets realized in the (whole) individual, who is able to coordinate behavior with others.

From a second perspective, the perspective of situated activity, the individual is a part and face-to-face groups are wholes. The idealized core configurations are on the left side of Figure 12.2. Notice that from the perspective of the individual described earlier, configurations were conceived psychologically as group selves (Caporael, 2001). Here they are materially conceived as forms of interaction—as situated activity. As part of a deme or macrodeme, the individual may influence change in a relevant cultural system, as suggested by the light arrows from the demic structure to the cultural system. Haraway's (1989) description of the primatology community and its impact provides a useful source for illustrating the complex interaction of people in groups as well as how ideas and practices across groups may be shared, leading to coordinating beliefs and behavior.

Primatologists, no matter how intense their conflicts and disagreements, are linked as a macrodeme or "invisible college." The specialty areas or schools at the University of California at Berkeley or the Gombe field station are themselves scientific demes. These demes are hierarchically organized and composed of student–mentor relationships (dyads), and active research groups (task group configurations). The scientific demes (Hull, 1988) come together at annual conventions where they compete (e.g., for honors, credit) and exchange new PhDs on the job market. The primatology macrodeme, through its scientific work, both reflects tacit assumptions in cultural systems and alters assumptions on topics such as gender, race, aggression, and culture. The effects of the macrodeme on the cultural system is through popular works for laypeople appearing in print and film media, through influences on other macrodemes (e.g., the National Science Foundation), and through effects on individual writers or artists who also create for a public audience (see Barrett, this volume, Chapter 11). In general, coordinated macrodemes, for example, specific corporate or industry lobbyists, have more impact on cultural systems (which could be American society or the industrialized world) than do smaller configurations. Individuals (e.g., Jane Goodall) and face-to-face groups (the editorial board at *National Geographic*) can have considerable impact on global systems, but that event is probably rare.

A third way of interpreting Figure 12.2 is developmental, which brings identity and core configurations together. This developmental sequence is alluded to by the stepped *Individual* in the figure. The steps represent expanding participation in core configurations; they also represent changes in social identity. (However, the changes are not discontinuous, as steps would imply, but rather blended and overlapping.) If Figure 12.2 were drawn to represent a 3-month-old infant (instead of an adult), the *Individual* would be represented by the dyad configuration and the shortest center bar; the rest of the figure would be shadowy background (or from yet another perspective, future potential). Psychologically, we would not expect differentiation of self-concept at this early age. We can easily observe that very young infants interact with a single caregiver at a time; as they get older and they achieve better control over their bodies, they interact with families and small playgroups.

A huge amount of important knowledge between generations is enacted, and lays foundations for selecting contemporary and future information for action. For example, American parents may tell a young child puttering in the kitchen "mixing stuff" that he is "practicing chemistry" if the child is male or "practicing cooking" if the child is female. The children's actual behavior may be identical, but the description of the activity is based on gender stereotypes and contributes powerfully to personal identity and future expectations. The classroom is typically an even larger group, about the size of a deme, and by high school and the beginning of work life, students easily recognize themselves as part of larger group contexts, say, of the Washington High School student body macrodeme, which is itself part of a school district, in a town, in a region, and in a country. Thus, although we tend to think of infants as becoming increasingly independent as they grow older, it is also the case that they become increasingly *inter*dependent as they engage in more complex core configurations. Their widening scope of interaction increases demands for reciprocity, skills, memory, social judgment, and so on.

The adult individual emerges through interaction with multiple configurations. In the modern world, that emergence also occurs within cross-cutting and overlapping groups (Deaux et al., 1999). Individuals may be members of choirs, businesses, and volleyball teams with no overlapping memberships at all. In such instances, the individual may be alienated. Individuals in modern societies also identify with large-scale categorical groups—actually, aggregates more than groups—such as regions or nation states.

Finally, if we were to take an evolutionary perspective on Figure 12.2, now seeing it as representing Paleolithic hunter-gathers 40,000 years ago, the systemic properties of culture as a background for various subgroups would be quite different—unimaginably different—from what we can imagine as members of literate, globalizing, warlike cultures with high residential density, technological development, division of labor, and inequality. Nevertheless, a common bodily and perceptual-motor system guarantees an extensive repertoire of situated activity that connects modern people *bodily*, not just genetically, through thousands of generations to ancestral humans. Likewise, it is possible that ancient humans did not possess a conscious awareness that we would recognize (although we might share an emotional resonance).

Beyond Core Configurations

However, then is not now. How can we account for coordination at higher levels of organization? Considerable levels of trust are required, for example, in the exchange of labor for pieces of paper that represent value, but in and of themselves are inedible, too small to be used as shelter or clothing, and provide no direct defense against predation or disease. Modern society is less an aggregate of self-interested individuals than it is a mosaic of multiple overlapping, sometimes nested, usually cross-cutting, demic structures and parts of structures, ceaselessly under negotiation across various group boundaries, and yet somehow still coherent enough to merit the term *society*. Society must operate with social cognitive processes evolved for face-to-face core configurations, and the relevant processes must be of a scale and flexibility to be reweaveable for higher-level coordination. Granovetter's (1983) work on the strength of weak ties, for example, parallels the macrodeme in recognizing the value of information from distant "places."

Although specific skills and practices that enable survival and reproduction are concretely situated in face-to-face groups, the psychological correlates of grouping, most especially social identity from the demic and macrodemic levels, may be extended to unsituated, superordinate groups: people connected abstractly by category membership and allegiance to multiple social identities. The capacity for ingroup loyalty that evolved in the context of demes may be evoked, for example, by an evening television broadcast, and extended, with swelling heart and deep pride, to our boys fighting in the war. The collective memory and shaping of identity that occurred (and occurs) in demes and macrodemes can extend to the collective memory of events, such as D-Day, John Kennedy's assassination, or 9/11, which characterize collective memory on a national scale (Pennebaker & Banasik, 1997). However, face-to-face alignment of memory, such as conversations occurring in small groups, must be a crucial mechanism for creating collective memories (Hirst & Echterhoff, 2008).

Obviously, in modern society, not all groups are "core." People might pack themselves into a concert hall or a football stadium. These have no analog in prehistory. There are a variety of different sorts of groups. One surprisingly stable group may be the *sympathy group* (Dunbar, 2008), which looks like a common grouping for combat units, sports teams, juries, steering committees, boards, and other policy groups ranging from 7 to 20 individuals. The sympathy group is highly gendered: Males affiliate with males and females with females (the same is true for the 4- to 7-person "team"). The sympathy group was derived from the number of adults that individuals report contacting in a month (Dunbar & Spoors, 1995) or, originally, questionnaire responses about the number of people toward which sympathy can be extended, which was defined as the circle of friends within which one would find a death upsetting (Buys & Larson, 1979). Dunbar (2008) proposes that the sympathy group evolved from cognitive limitations on group size and functions as "an alliance to buffer one against the stresses of group living" (p. 13).

Sympathy groups may be quite common, but in the evo-devo framework, they would not be a core configuration. Sympathy groups are not embodied, in the sense that a novel group-level function is apparent. They also are not grounded in the sense of there being an ontogeny or group-level function for operating with the habitat or maintaining the group as a more or less cohesive whole. It might be plausible that sympathy groups are the gender division in a deme. Also, while sympathy groups may be friendship alliances, that characterization alone seems to be missing something of importance that we recognize when we think of teams, juries, and combat units.

The sympathy group might be a noncore group with a long cultural history. One just-so story for sympathy groups is that they are products of macrodeme interactions. If each deme in a macrodeme had a representative, the group size would be consistent with the sympathy group. We can also imagine multiple functions for such representative groups: policy making, negotiation among groups, competitive games, and ritual practices. Another just-so story, not mutually exclusive with the first, is that the sympathy group is a relatively new cultural invention, with a function to maintain gender boundaries by teaching and enforcing gender-role performance, particularly for males.

This proposal turns on a distinction between "simple societies" and more complex arrangements of "middle range societies" (e.g., tribes or chiefdoms). Simple societies are organized around kinship. Absent are various institutions such as government, laws, or marketplaces. They are most notable for "extreme" egalitarianism between the sexes and among the males (Knauft, 1990). Violence occurs as part of a consensually approved status leveling, and often ends in homicide. Prestate or middle-range societies are characterized as more complex, with incipient political institutions, pastoralism, status differences, and property ownership. In these societies, violence is a valued dimension of masculinity, takes the form of collective intergroup warfare, and is linked to fraternal interest groups and feuding. Kelly (2000) argues that the origins of war are likely to be in these types of societies.

We started with a fairly general claim that evidence for configurations and for their corresponding functions would be evident in the modern world, despite its high technology and large-scale structure. The fit would be loose, but not totally arbitrary. Table 12.2 is a starter list for possible core and noncore configurations, relabeled now to reflect modern tasks and affordances. The "lower-level" dyads and teams are posited have been repeatedly assembled over a longer period of

TABLE 12.2 Some Contemporary Core and Noncore Group Configurations

Configuration	Size	Modal Tasks	Affords/Enables
Dyad[a]	2	Sex, infant interaction with older children and adults	Microcoordination
Team (task group)	5	Resolving ambiguous data; paradigmatic modes of thought	Distributed cognition
Sympathy group	12	Variable tasks-teams, juries, policy groups	Gender socialization
Community (deme)	30	Work group coordination; special interests; mediating face-to-face and collective plus groups, narrative modes of thought	Shared construction of reality (includes indigenous psychologies), symbolic social identity
Collective group (macrodeme)	500	Occasional gathering, exchange of individuals, resources, information; firms	Stabilizing and standardizing specialized language, norms, civil discourses, etiquette
Categorical	>1000	Communication; mobilization	Shared imaginaries; high residential living with nonfood producing groups (Campbell's ultrasociality), collective divisions of labor (guilds, priestly castes, professional societies), nationalism
Digital	>???	"Breaking" time and space; asynchrony	Disembodied selves, homogenization and homophily, ultra-large-scale anonymous cooperation; small-scale, high-impact defection

[a]Note:

(pre)historical time. They are deeply entrenched (Wimsatt & Griesemer, 2007), and more highly structured by bodily constraints. For example, only one person can hold a baby at a time, and that is likely to have been the case 500,000 years ago, too. Communities and groups, in contrast, would be expected to be more flexible, partly because of their mediating functions with habitat resources that would include other identity groups and networks.

The sympathy group is inserted in the table, even though it is not a core configuration, but arguably has an ancient provenance and appears to be recurrent and persistent. The macrodeme is identified as a collective group, with its stabilizing and standardizing functions extended, acting as an occasional nodal point for regenerating weak ties and servicing cross-cutting group memberships. The "categorical group," a society with high residential living, would have no early precedents, but would be the somewhat hierarchically structured concatenation of different identity groups, with broadly relevant normative expectations, often carried in symbolic artifacts (e.g., flags, banners, crosses) as well as practical skills.

I have added digital groups to Table 12.2 because of their curious possibilities for identities and grouping, and for learning more about thinking and feeling without bodies (or with the substitute bodies of digital avatars; Meadows, 2008). With some exceptions, they currently represent the interesting case of imaginaries without the threads of multiple generations (Boellstorff, 2008).

CONCLUSION

Human evolutionary theory has a history of rejection and reprise. Its undeniable impact on Western thought and policy has been mediated far more by social Darwinism, spread through engrossing narratives about human nature and apemen in the past, than it has been by rigorous theory, scientific practice, and empirical research. The main appeal of the gene's eye view is that it dovetails with a widely shared folk psychology (and an enduring social psychological view; see Allport, 1924) that questions the existence of groups and reifies individualism: People more or less rationally pursue their own outcomes without regard for the outcomes of others. To adopt an evolutionary perspective, one needs simply to ask: "If you were a gene, what would facilitate your survival and reproduction?" (Buss, 1999, p. 13). A severe obstacle to using Darwinism to shed light on human psychology is that as scientists we are both agents and subjects of our own theories and investigation, vulnerable to the charms of a good story and common heuristics and biases.

In this chapter, I have proposed that psychologists join in forging a more sophisticated human evolutionary science, warranted under the umbrella of evo-devo. Without attempting to "think like a gene," I have urged: Just look at the human body. Obviously, humans have no choice but to live in groups. Their interdependence is as obvious as their soft flesh and their tiny, even teeth surrounding dainty canines. Nevertheless, there is still little in the way of readily available vocabularies to express the obvious or the sublime in either evolutionary or embodied perspectives. Embracing embodiment implies the rejection of Cartesian dualism and taking the "naturalistic turn" (Callebaut, 1993, p. 329; see also Barrett, this volume, Chapter 11). One consequence of clearing the view will be the expansion of the range of methodological approaches to understand processes such as synchrony and coordination over multiple levels of organization (Semin, this volume, Chapter 5). Ironically, the once-disdained body will probably be a powerful intellectual tool for illuminating psychology, especially after a century of machines occupied the place of mind and organic bodies: Cinema film, telephone assemblies, holograms, and, most recently, computers (and their hardware and software) have all had their day as models of the human mind or some important part of it.

Core configurations are structures of face-to-face groups that are posited to recur in daily life, ontogeny, and, presumably, prehistory. This scope results from the repeatedly assembled processes of interacting with the habitat such as skilled motor performances in making a handcrafted tool, problem solving such as deciding the edibility of a mushroom, or group maintenance such as the telling of origin stories and proverbs that curtail selfishness and channel sexuality. The empirical claim is that an evolutionary history of face-to-face group living is expected to have shaped human bodies and minds, and that the repeated assembly of such group structures scaffolds human development, cognition, and culture (Wimsatt & Griesemer, 2007). Modern humans are parts of many kinds of groups, some of which could be macrodemes; others, fragments of macrodemes; and still others, group structures that do not fit the kind of categorization suggested here, such as sympathy groups. Nor are the cognitive capacities I discussed the only ones afforded by core configurations and the individual. No doubt, group structures that are constrained by bodies in action afford the evolution of all sorts of capacities.

The essential point is that people do dwell within collectively shared landscapes. Some of these are self-organizing demic structures of unrelated people where face-to-face socialization into the community is still required for acquiring the skills and values of the community (e.g., science, dog fancier clubs, professional communities). Unlike hunter-gatherer bands or even villages, where the constraints of time and space hold a community together, modern humans can belong to overlapping communities that may require no more than sharing some trait (e.g., gender, ethnic identity, or even a disease), where various shared narratives socially construct the rationale for identity, or even communities of physically disembodied, virtually embodied, actors. The superordinate groups of modern humans are hardly smooth-textured aggregates of individuals or exchanging dyads that the thin description of society supposes. Instead, fractal-like structures calling on the same activity patterns of previous generations form lumpy social networks, some held together by the loose ties of shared traits, and others by the generative functions of demic structure. All are connected by a variety of practices, from technoscientific work and its resulting artifacts to the telling and retelling of shared narratives that order intentions, goals, experiences, beliefs, and social relations. Such uniquely human processes have an evolutionary history that is grounded in repeatedly assembled—and observable—instantiations of bodies, tasks, group size, and coordination.

NOTES

1. Whether evo-devo should be viewed as an expansion of Neo-Darwinism or as a replacement program is still debated. See Amundson (2005), Carroll (2005), and Newman (2002).
2. Richard Dawkins, the eminent sociobiologist and progenitor of the "selfish gene," described the entire organism as a "survival machine." Psychologically,

> To a survival machine, another survival machine … is part of its environment, like a rock or a river or a lump of food. It is something that gets in the way, or something that can be exploited. It differs from a rock or a river in one important respect: it is inclined to hit back. This is because it too is a survival machine which holds its immortal genes in trust for the future. Natural selection favours genes which control their survival machines. (1976, p. 71)

Humans are a bit different because of culture, and Dawkins urges them to "rebel against the tyranny of the selfish replicators [genes]" (p. 215). It is not clear how an organism would do that given that they are the products of the selfish replicators.

REFERENCES

Abrams, D. & Hogg, M. A. (Eds.). (1999). *Social identity and social cognition*. Malden, MA: Blackwell.

Alexander, R. D. (1989). Evolution of the human psyche. In P. Mellars & C. Stringer (Eds.), *The human revolution* (pp. 455–513). Princeton, NJ: Princeton University Press.

Allport, F. H. (1924). *Social psychology*. Boston: Houghton Mifflin.

Amundson, R. (2005). *The changing role of the embryo in evolutionary thought*. New York: Cambridge University Press.

Andrews, P. W., Gangestad, S. W., & Matthews, D. (2002). Adaptationism—how to carry out an exaptationist program. *Behavavioral and Brain Sciences, 25*, 489–553.

Bargh, J. A. & Ferguson, M. J. (2000). Beyond behaviorism: On the automaticity of higher mental processes. *Psychological Bulletin, 126*, 925–945.

Boellstorff, T. (2008). *Coming of age in second life*. Princeton, NJ: Princeton University Press.

Boyd, R. & Richerson, P. J. (1985). *Culture and the evolutionary process*. Chicago: University of Chicago Press.

Brewer, M. B. & Caporael, L. R. (2006). An evolutionary perspective on social identity: Revisiting groups. In J. A. Simpson, M. Schaller, & D. T. Kenrick (Eds.), *Evolution and social psychology* (pp. 143–161). New York: Psychology Press.

Brewer, M. B. & Gardner, W. (1996). Who is this "we"? Levels of collective identity and self representation. *Journal of Personality and Social Psychology, 71*, 83–93.

Bruner, J. (1986). *Actual minds, possible worlds*. Cambridge, MA: Harvard University Press.

Buss, D. M. (1999). *Evolutionary psychology*. Boston: Allyn and Bacon.

Buss, L. W. (1987). *The evolution of individuality*. Princeton, NJ: Princeton University Press.

Buys, C. J. & Larson, K. L. (1979). Human sympathy groups. *Psychological Reports, 45*, 547–553.

Byrne, R. W. & Whiten, A. (Eds.). (1988). *Machiavellian intelligence*. Oxford, UK: Clarendon Press.

Callebaut, W. (1993). *Taking the naturalistic turn, or, how real philosophy of science is done*. Chicago: Chicago University Press.

Callebaut, W., Müller, G. B., & Newman, S. A. (2007). The organismic systems approach: Streamlining of the naturalistic agenda. In R. Sansom & R. N. Brandon (Eds.), *Integrating evolution and development: From theory to practice* (pp. 25–92). Cambridge, MA: MIT Press.

Campbell, D. T. (1997). From evolutionary epistemology via selection theory to a sociology of scientific validity. *Evolution and Cognition, 3*, 5–38.

Caporael, L. R. (1995). Sociality: Coordinating bodies, minds and groups. *Psycoloquy [on-line serial], 6*(1), http://www.cogsci.soton.ac.uk/cgi/psyc/newpsy?6.01.

Caporael, L. R. (2001). Parts and wholes: The evolutionary importance of groups. In C. Sedikides & M. B. Brewer (Eds.), *Individual self, relational self, collective self* (pp. 241–258). Philadelphia: Psychology Press.

Caporael, L. R. (2003). Repeated assembly. In S. Scher & F. Rauscher (Eds.), *Evolutionary psychology: Alternative approaches* (pp. 71–89). Boston: Kluwer.

Caporael, L. R. (2007). Evolutionary theory for social and cultural psychology. In A. W. Kruglanski & E. T. Higgins (Eds.), *Social psychology: Handbook of basic principles* (2nd ed., pp. 3–18). New York: Guilford.

Caporael, L. R. (2008). Groups and the evolution of good stories and good choices. In J. I. Krueger (Ed.), *Rationality and social responsibility: Essays in honor of Robyn Mason Dawes* (pp. 275–319). New York: Psychology Press.

Caporael, L. R. & Baron, R. M. (1997). Groups as the mind's natural environment. In J. Simpson & D. Kenrick (Eds.), *Evolutionary social psychology* (pp. 317–343). Hillsdale: NJ: Lawrence Erlbaum.

Carroll, S. B. (2005). *Endless forms most beautiful*. New York: Norton.

Clancey, W. J. (1997). *Situated cognition*. Cambridge, UK: Cambridge University Press.

Cosmides, L. & Tooby, J. (1987). From evolution to behavior: Evolutionary psychology as the missing link. In J. Dupré (Ed.), *The latest on the best: Essays on evolution and optimality* (pp. 277–306). Cambridge, MA: MIT Press.

Dawkins, R. (1976). *The selfish gene*. New York: Oxford University Press.

Dawkins, R. (1982). *The extended phenotype: The long reach of the gene*. New York: Oxford University Press.

Deaux, K., Reid, A., Mizrahi, K., & Cotting, D. (1999). Connecting the person to the social: The functions of social identification. In T. R. Tyler, R. M. Kramer, & O. P. John (Eds.), *The psychology of the social self* (pp. 91–113). Mahwah, NJ: Erlbaum.

Dunbar, R. I. M. (1989). Selfishness reexamined. *Behavavioral and Brain Sciences, 12*, 700–702.

Dunbar, R. I. M. (2008). Cognitive constraints on the structure and dynamics of social networks. *Group Dynamics: Theory, Research and Practice, 12*, 7–16.

Dunbar, R. I. M., & Spoors, M. (1995). Social networks, support cliques, and kinship. *Human Nature, 6*, 273–290.

Eldredge, N. (1985). *Unfinished synthesis: Biological hierarchies and modern evolutionary thought*. New York: Oxford University Press.

Eldredge, N., & Grene, M. (1992). *Interactions: The biological context of social systems*. New York: Columbia University Press.

Endler, J. (1986). *Natural selection in the wild*. Princeton, NJ: Princeton University Press.

Foley, R. A. (1996). An evolutionary and chronological framework for human social behaviour. *Proceedings of the British Academy, 88*, 95–117.

Granovetter, M. (1983). The strength of weak ties: A network theory revisited. *Sociological Theory, 1*, 201–233.

Griesemer, J. (2002). What is "epi" about epigenetics? *Annals New York Academy of Sciences, 981*, 97–110.

Griesemer, J. (2006). Genetics from an evolutionary process perspective. In E. M. Neumann-Held & C. Rehmann-Sutter (Eds.), *Genes in development* (pp. 199–237). Durham, NC: Duke University Press.

Griffiths, P. E. & Gray, R. D. (1994). Developmental systems and evolutionary explanation. *Journal of Philosophy, 91*, 277–304.

Haraway, D. (1989). *Primate visions*. New York: Routledge.

Hardin, C. D. & Higgins, E. T. (1996). Shared reality: How social verification makes the subjective objective. In R. M. Sorrentino & E. T. Higgins (Eds.), *Handbook of motivation and cognition. Vol. 3. The interpersonal context* (pp. 28–84). New York: Guilford Press.

Hendriks-Jansen, H. (1996). *Catching ourselves in the act*. Cambridge, MA: MIT Press.

Hirst, W. & Echterhoff, G. (2008). Creating shared memories in conversation: Toward a psychology of collective memory. *Social Research, 75*, 183–216.

Hirst, W. & Manier, D. (2008). Towards a psychology of collective memory. *Memory, 16*, 183–200.

Hogg, M. A. (1992). *The social psychology of group cohesiveness*. New York: Harvester Wheatsheaf.

Hull, D. L. (1988). *Science as a process*. Chicago: University of Chicago Press.

Hutchins, E. (1995). *Cognition in the wild*. Cambridge, MA: MIT Press.

Jablonka, E. & Lamb, M. J. (2005). *Evolution in four dimensions*. Cambridge, MA: MIT Press.

Janicki, M. G. (1998). Evolutionary approaches to culture. In C. Crawford & D. L. Krebs (Eds.), *Handbook of evolutionary psychology* (pp. 163–207). Mawah, NJ: Erlbaum.

Jarvenpa, R. & Brumbach, H. (1988). Socio-spatial organization and decision-making processes: Observations from the Chipewyan. *American Anthropologist 90*, 598–618.

Kashima, Y. (2000). Conceptions of culture and person for psychology. *Journal of Cross-cultural Psychology, 31*, 14–32.

Kelly, R. C. (2000). *Warless societies and the origin of war*. Ann Arbor, MI: University of Michigan Press.

Klein, R. G. (1999). *The human career: Human biological and cultural origins*. Chicago: University of Chicago Press.

Knauft, B. M. (1990). Culture and cooperation in human evolution. In L. Sponsel & T. Gregor (Eds.), *The anthropology of peace and non-violence* (pp. 37–67). Boulder, CO: Lynne Rienner.

Lakoff, G. & Johnson, M. (1980). *Metaphors we live by*. Chicago: University of Chicago Press.

Landau, M. (1984). Human evolution as narrative. *American Scientist, 72*, 262–268.

Lee, R. B. & DeVore, I. (Eds.). (1968). *Man the hunter*. Chicago: Aldine.

Li, S. C,. (2003). Biocultural orchestration of developmental plasticity across levels: The interplay of biology and culture in shaping the mind and behavior across the life span. *Psychological Bulletin, 129*, 171–194.

Margulis, L. (1981). *Symbiosis in cell evolution*. New York: W. H. Freeman.

Maynard Smith, J. (1987). Science and myth. In N. Eldredge (Ed.), *The Natural History reader in evolution* (pp. 222–229). New York City: Columbia University Press (Original work published 1984.)

Maynard Smith, J. & Szathmáry, E. (1995). *The major transitions in evolution*. New York: W. H. Freeman.

Meadows, M. S. (2008). *I, Avatar: The culture and consequences of having a second life*. Berkeley, CA: New Riders.

Meltzoff, A. N. & Moore, M. K. (1977). Imitation of facial and manual gestures by human neonates. *Science, 198*, 75–78.

Moser, S. (1998). *Ancestral images: The iconography of human origins*. Ithaca, NY: Cornell University Press.

Newman, S. A. (2002). Developmental mechanisms: Putting genes in their place. *Journal of Biosciences, 27*, 97–104.

Pennebaker, J. W. & Banasik, B. L. (1997). On the creation and maintenance of collective memories: History as social psychology. In J. W. Pennebaker, D. Paez & B. Rimé (Eds.), *Collective memory of political events* (pp. 3–19). Mahwah, NJ: Erlbaum.

Pulliam, H. R. & Caraco, T. (1984). Living in groups: Is there an optimal group size? In J. R. Krebs & N. B. Davies (Eds.), *Behavioural ecology* (pp. 122–147). London: Blackwell.

Sansom, R. & Brandon, R. (Eds.). (2007). *Integrating evolution and development*. Cambridge, MA: MIT Press.

Schmitt, D. P. & Pilcher, J. J. (2004). Evaluating evidence of psychological adaptation: How do we know one when we see one? *Psychological Science, 15*, 643–649.

Semin, G. R. & Cacioppo, J. T. (2008). Grounding social cognition: Synchronization, coordination, and co-regulation. In G. R. Semin & E. R. Smith (Eds.), *Embodied grounding* (pp. 119–147). New York: Cambridge University Press.

Sheets-Johnstone, M. (1992). Corporeal archetypes and power: Preliminary clarifications and considerations of sex. *Hypatia, 7*(3), 39–76.

Smith, B. H. (2000). Sewing up the mind: The claims of evolutionary psychology. In H. Rose & S. Rose (Eds.), *Alas, poor Darwin: Arguments against evolutionary psychology* (pp. 155–172). New York: Random House.

Tattersall, I. (1999). *Becoming human: Evolution and human uniqueness*. New York: Harvest Books.

Taylor, C. (2002). Modern social imaginaries. *Public Culture, 14*, 91–124.

Thelen, E. & Smith, L. B. (1994). *A dynamic systems approach to the development of cognition and action*. Cambridge, MA: MIT Press.

Tooby, J. & DeVore, I. (1987). The reconstruction of hominid behavioral evolution through strategic modeling. In W. G. Kinzey (Ed.), *The evolution of human behavior: Primate models* (pp. 183–237). Albany, NY: State University of New York Press.

Turner, J. C., Hogg, M., Oakes, P., Reicher, S., & Wetherell, M. (1987). *Rediscovering the social group: A self-categorization theory.* Oxford: Basil Blackwell.

Williams, G. C. (1966). *Adaptation and natural selection*. Princeton, NJ: Princeton University Press.

Wilson, E. O. (1978). *On human nature*. Cambridge, MA: Harvard University Press.

Wimsatt, W. C. (2001). Generative entrenchment and the developmental systems approach to evolutionary processes. In S. Oyama, R. Gray, & P. Griffiths (Eds.), *Cycles of contingency: Developmental systems and evolution* (pp. 219–237). Cambridge, MA: MIT Press.

Wimsatt, W. C. & Griesemer, J. R. (2007). Reproducing entrenchments to scaffold culture: The central role of development in cultural evolution. In R. Sansom & R. N. Brandon (Eds.), *Integrating evolution and development: From theory to practice* (pp. 227–323). Cambridge, MA: MIT Press.

Author Index

A

B

K

L

M

N

O

P

Q

R

S

Subject Index

D

T

For Product Safety Concerns and Information please contact our EU representative GPSR@taylorandfrancis.com
Taylor & Francis Verlag GmbH, Kaufingerstraße 24, 80331 München, Germany

www.ingramcontent.com/pod-product-compliance
Ingram Content Group UK Ltd.
Pitfield, Milton Keynes, MK11 3LW, UK
UKHW022002180926
475701UK00003B/158
* 9 7 8 1 1 3 8 9 9 2 0 7 8 *